ARCHITECTURE AND ARTIFICIAL INTELLIGENCE

ARCHITECTURE AND ARTIFICIAL INTELLIGENCE

Amanda Chapman
Stephanie Webb

Kruger Brentt
Publishers

2024

Kruger Brentt Publishers UK. LTD.
Company Number 9728962

Regd. Office: 68 St Margarets Road, Edgware, Middlesex HA8 9UU

ISBN: 978-1-78715-116-1

For information on all our publications visit our website at http://krugerbrentt.com/

PREFACE

Artificial intelligence (AI) has had a profound impact on many industries, and architecture is no exception. AI technology is now being used in architectural design and construction to help architects create more efficient, sustainable, and innovative buildings. In this book, we will explore the relationship between architecture and artificial intelligence and how AI is changing the face of architecture. One of the primary ways in which AI is being used in architecture is through generative design. This is a process where architects use AI algorithms to create and evaluate design options automatically. These algorithms can take into account factors such as site conditions, building codes, and client preferences to generate a range of design options that meet the project's requirements. This allows architects to explore more design possibilities than they could do manually and enables them to create more efficient and innovative buildings. AI is also being used to improve energy efficiency in buildings.

Energy simulation software, powered by AI algorithms, can analyze a building's energy usage and suggest ways to reduce energy consumption. This includes things like optimizing building orientation, selecting the right building materials, and incorporating energy-efficient systems such as solar panels and geothermal heating. In addition to design and energy efficiency, AI is also being used to improve the construction process. Construction projects often face delays and cost overruns due to unforeseen problems and issues that arise during the building process. AI-powered construction software can help identify potential issues before they occur, allowing builders to make adjustments and prevent delays. This includes things like identifying areas of the building where there may be conflicts or scheduling issues and optimizing the use of materials and equipment. Another way in which AI is changing architecture is through the use of smart buildings. Smart buildings are buildings that are equipped with sensors and other technology that allows them to monitor and optimize their energy usage, lighting, and other systems. AI algorithms can analyze this data and suggest ways to improve efficiency and reduce waste. This includes things like adjusting lighting and temperature settings based on occupancy patterns and weather conditions.

The present book explains how different manifestations of AI will impact the discipline and profession of architecture. It shows how AI is already being used as a powerful design tool, and how AI-driven information systems will soon transform the design of buildings and cities. It offers a framework for discussion of theoretical foundations of AI, AI applications in the design, AI-based research and information systems. This book is a must-read for all architects and designers – including students of architecture and all design professionals interested in keeping their practice at the cutting edge of technology.

We are grateful to all those persons as well as various books, manuals, periodicals, magazines, journals etc. that helped in the preparation of this book. In spite of the best efforts, it is possible that some errors may have occurred into the compilation and editing of the book. Further queries, constructive suggestions and criticisms for the improvement of the book are always welcomed and shall be thankfully acknowledged.

Amanda Chapman

Stephanie Webb

CONTENTS

CHAPTER 1
INTRODUCTION

Innovations in computing technologies became a large part of fulfilling everyday needs. Artificial intelligence machines are advancing beyond machine-like abilities, which is allowing them to process, analyze, respond, and create just like a human. Nowadays AI machines are majoring in many professional fields that require intelligence, creativity and critical thinking such as architecture. The idea of automated architects taking over the jobs of real architects rises many discussions about the future of architectural practice. Architecture and its practitioners are involved in the rising world of artificial intelligence, and the future upon that is to be investigated.

The development of digital tools throughout the last century and the emergence of highly technological advancements such as Artificial Intelligence (AI), Machine Learning (ML), Internet of Things (IoT), and digital twins have made significant changes and improvements to the way we work and interact with each other. These advancements have enabled the consumption and analysis of large amounts of data in a shorter time than any human ever would be able to do. Suppose computing technologies and the intellectual skills of technologies, such as AI, progress at a similar rate as we have seen for the past 50 years. In that case, people that live today will see the evolution of such technologies surpassing the logic and information of humankind and likely have a personality that is indistinguishable from humans.

This can raise questions regarding what place AI will have in the future of our world. As people are concerned with being replaced by non-intelligent machines today, you could guess that there would be greater concern when intelligent machines such as AI start to outperform humans at work in many aspects. It becomes apparent that humans and AI will have to coexist and so the question of who will make decisions for companies will be of great concern. Which decisions will the AI take, which decisions should humans take, and Even if there is a long way until we can experience an AI with characteristics like those of humans, the AI we have today needs to be addressed in how it will be developed for the future as it can be expected to have a great impact on our society. In the meantime, we can look at how implementation of AI affects human traits such as creativity, which this chapter will explore with an architectural viewpoint. Creativity being a very complex human trait with many factors at play, and that plays a big role in design thinking, the effects AI has on this trait becomes interesting. Digital platforms and tools have since their introduction in the early 60s been seen as supporting design thinking with simulation, and modelling of design options.

They are also viewed as enablers to enhance cognitive strategies and skills, such as creativity. As the development of drawing tools have gotten more and more advanced since the introduction of digital tools like CAD and CAAD in the early 1960s, there is a need for exploration into how the future technologies such as AI will affect the creative design process. Not only because it is a relatively new technology, but because the technology itself challenges the more complex human traits such as creativity. Which decisions would be made in collaboration?

Artificial Intelligence (AI) is already very much part of our everyday lives, even though we might not realize it. For example, spam messages are filtered by AI in our internet accounts, friends on Facebook are identified by it, and our Instagram images are sorted by it, while most navigation, streaming, and ride-sharing apps are based on it. Yet there are many different attitudes to AI. For some it is a necessary part of "the future" - an indispensible aid that is sure to make life easier, while for others - from the late Stephen Hawking to Elon Musk - it poses an existential threat to human being.

After all, if AI already has the capacity to surpass the intelligence of human beings at games of first Chess and now Go, does it not promise huge potential for the future, both positive and negative? However, we wish to debunk some of the more outlandish myths surrounding AI, and try to ascertain its true potential in the field of design. We need to get beyond the "hype" that surrounds the term, and understand AI for what it actually is.

Firstly, AI should be distinguished from the intelligence of human beings, and described as the "intelligence" of machines. Here we must sound our first note of warning: Although the same term "intelligence" is used for both human beings and machines, we must be careful not to equate the two. To begin with, AI merely mimics or simulates human intelligence. Moreover, there are many manifestations of "intelligence," but the meaning of the term, as well as the level of intelligence, changes according to its respective context.

Secondly, we need to distinguish between "Artificial General Intelligence" - also known as "Super intelligence" and "General AI" - and "Narrow AI." At present Artificial General Intelligence is well beyond the range of our technical capabilities, and only appears in the world of the entertainment industry. An example would be Skynet in the Terminator franchise, a pure fiction though. In fact we are still limited to a relatively modest realm of what is known as Narrow AI, which, as its name implies, is narrow and circumscribed in its potential, even though the general public tends to fetishize it and make it out to be more than it is. Nonetheless, it has been predicted by Ray Kurzweil, author of The Singularity is Near, that by 2029 we will have achieved a level of Artificial General Intelligence that will match the intelligence of human beings.

Thirdly, within Narrow AI, we should perhaps distinguish between the broader category of AI itself, "Machine Learning," and "Deep Learning." These three can be seen to be nested within each other - somewhat like a series of Russian dolls, or layers in an onion - in that Deep Learning is part of Machine Learning that is itself part of AI. Early versions of Narrow AI dealt with machines that had to be programmed to deal with a set of data in a somewhat mechanistic way. The important point here is that the machine could only do what it is programmed to do, and could not learn for itself.

By contrast, Machine Learning goes one step further, and uses large data sets in order to train itself. However, the Machine Learning still requires a code to be written for it to classify what it is expected to do. Deep Learning, however, refers to a more recent development whereby the machine is not programmed in any way, and bypasses the classification step. Instead, it teaches itself about a particular subject based on a form of "neural network" that mimics the human brain, and draws upon an even vaster quantity of data.

For example, Google's AlphaGo, which "learnt" to play Go to a level that it could beat the best human experts, effectively taught itself. It did not receive any instruction about any particular move. Equally Google Translate uses Deep Learning through its Neural Machine Translation system that has improved vastly the quality of online translation.

This vision of the future architect was imagined by engineer and inventor Douglas Engelbart during his research into emerging computer systems at Stanford in 1962. At the dawn of personal computing he imagined the creative mind overlapping symbiotically with the intelligent machine to co-create designs. This dual mode of production, he envisaged, would hold the potential to generate new realities which could not be realized by either entity operating alone. Today, self-learning systems, otherwise known as artificial intelligence or 'AI', are changing the way architecture is practiced, as they do our daily lives, whether or not we realize it. If you are reading this on a laptop or tablet, then you are directly engaging with a number of integrated AI systems, now so embedded in our the way we use technology, they often go unnoticed.

As an industry, AI is growing at an exponential rate, now understood to be on track to be worth $70bn globally by 2020. This is in part due to constant innovation in the speed of microprocessors, which in turn increases the volume of data that can be gathered and stored. But don't panic—the artificial architect with enhanced Revit proficiency is not coming to steal your job. The human vs. robot debate, while compelling, is not so much the focus here but instead how AI is augmenting design and how architects are responding to and working with these technological developments. What kind of innovation is artificial intelligence generating in the construction industry?

Assuming you read this as a non-expert, it is likely that much of the AI you have encountered to this point has been 'weak AI', otherwise known as ANI (Artificial Narrow Intelligence). ANI follows pre-programmed rules so that it appears intelligent but is in effect a simulation of a human-like thought process. With recent innovations such as that of Nvidia's microchip in April 2016, a shift is now being seen towards what we might understand as 'deep learning', where a system can, in effect, train and adapt itself. The interest for designers is that AI is, therefore, starting to apply itself to more creative tasks, such as writing books, making art, web design, or self-generating design solutions, due to its increased proficiency in recognizing speech and images.

Significant 'AI winters', or periods where funding has been hard to source for the industry, have occurred over the last twenty years, but commentators such as philosopher Nick Bostrom now suggest we are on the cusp of an explosion in AI, and this will not only shape but drive the design industry in the next century. AI, therefore, has the potential to influence the architectural design process at a series of different construction stages, from site research to the realization and operation of the building.

HISTORY OF ARTIFICIAL INTELLIGENCE

The birth of AI can be traced to as early as the 1940s, where firstly encountered in a short science fiction story by Isaac Asimov. The story depicts a robot created by two engineers, where the plot revolves around the Three Laws of Robotics:

- A robot may not injure a human being or, through inaction, allow a human being to come to harm;
- A robot must obey the orders given to it by human beings except where such orders would conflict with the First Law; and
- A robot must protect its own existence as long as such protection does not conflict with the First or Second Laws.

For generations, the story inspired scientists in robotics, AI, and computer science. However, The Bombe, which was built to break the German Enigma code, is considered to be the first computer and was created by the English mathematician Alan Turing, who brought the ideas of computing intelligent machines to life.

In 1950, Alan Turing published the article "*Computing Machinery and Intelligence*" which to this day is still considered the benchmark for identifying the intelligence of an artificial system.

The word Artificial Intelligence was later coined in 1956 during a summer research project at Dartmouth College in New Hampshire, hosted by Marvin Minsky and John McCarthy (a cognitive scientist and a computer scientist). The field of AI has since had its ups and downs; following the years from its founding, the area flourished. One of the earliest programs was the famous ELIZA computer program, a language processing tool that was able to simulate conversations with a human. Later in the 1970s, there was a critique of the possibilities of AI; a British mathematician stated that the computer programmes would only be able to reach amateur levels of intelligence and that common-sense reasoning would always be beyond the programmes reach. Following this, both the British and the U.S governments cut funding for AI research but later increased research in the 1980s when Japan started to invest heavily in AI.

Since then, AI has found its way into many sectors, evolving from beating world champion chess players to being able to identify human faces, distinguish between pictures of cats and dogs, and much more. It has found its way into the AEC industry, where its possibilities are endless but not yet fully exploited, as the industry is still learning about this relatively new technology. AI is part of the concept of Digital Construction, which can describe the integrated approach of new technologies in the AEC industry that are meant to make construction safer and more productive.

However, the development of AI has been met with concerns regarding robots and machines taking over jobs and the more fictional situation of machines becoming sentient and dominant over humans. Despite the concerns, AI has a great potential to revolutionise the industry in many ways and has done so over the past few years. In construction, AI can, for example, enhance design output, draw buildings within constraints such as building codes, cost, time, and size constraints, and at the same time do clash control with other drawings, do risk scenarios and suggest solutions to mitigate them. Other options for designing a building are for the AI to design with concern for movement patterns of human beings or vehicles, altering the design in relation to noise exposure, or design from a perspective of heat radiation or light input. This can move the design to optimise energy usage in a way we might never have seen before, making some buildings look very futuristic and advanced as they are shaped by the environment they are in.

In architecture and engineering, AI and ML can be found in what is called generative design. The generative design technique consists of generating the best design options, with a strong focus on the best design solution. Contrary to regular design simulation, where you work with a lot of data and with data that is result-based, where each simulation takes place in different test environments, and the result is based on what you ask for, the generative design process takes simulation to the next level. Instead of giving answers to the question, you ask, like; Does this work? What if we change this? How does it work? The generative design will provide the solution to the problem faced by working in an iterative process that learns in each iteration within the given parameters and rules; it provides something that works and lets the designer stop asking questions and start asking for solutions. Generative design tools are, seen by researchers in design thinking, as supporting creativity as you are allowed to generate and explore many design alternatives in early design processes, leaving space for creative potential in divergent thinking, which is seen as an essential trait of creative people.

On the manufacturing part, AI is working through robots, manufacturing, assembling predrawn designs, and suggesting possible manufacturing improvements. AI is also incorporated with heavy machinery when excavating, tunnelling, mining, etc. With the help of sensor technology and AI, autonomous vehicles can carry out this type of work, navigating tunnels and avoiding obstacles without putting human lives at risk.

CREATIVITY

Creativity comes in many forms and definitions; how to define it has been a discussion for many years, and there still seems to be some disagreement or incompletion on the definition of what can be considered one of the most fundamental human capacities (Kim, 2020). The most simple and elemental definition of creativity comes from the Oxford Advanced Learner's Dictionary (no date) and states that creativity is:

"The use of skill and imagination to produce something new or to produce art."

The Oxford definition is relatively straight-forward and could be seen as a simple definition of the word creativity. Still, due to its complex aspects, the oxford definition is insufficient in this study, and a demand for a more precise definition of what creativity is is highly sought after. A reason for the very different approaches to creativity is the interdisciplinary nature of creativity. How the word is defined is subject to which creative context action is performed; in a business context, creativity can be completely different from an art context or a psychological context. This is one of the areas in which researchers agree that creativity is created in a specific environment, and those surroundings play a crucial part in creativity creation. Amabile defined creativity as: "behaviour resulting from particular constellations of personal characteristics, cognitive abilities, and social environments."

Amabile's definition says nothing about producing something but describes how one is creative in their persona. She does characterise creativity as something novel and useful but leaves it out of the definition. A third definition of the word is:

"Creativity is the interaction among aptitude, process, and environment by which an individual or group produces a perceptible product that is both novel and useful as defined within a social context."

AI AND STYLE

This raises the question as to what impacts AI might have on design in the fields of architecture, landscape architecture, and urbanism. Given the general level of confusion that surrounds the term, it is quite possible that this confusion might extend to the field of design. For example, some might imagine that AI will be responsible for a new "style" of design, much in the way that Patrik Schumacher has claimed, somewhat controversially, that "parametricism" is a new global style for architecture that emerges as a result of the introduction of certain digital tools into the design arena.

Let us start by stating clearly that AI itself is unlikely to introduce a new style into design. This is in part for the same reason that digital tools are unlikely to be responsible - in and of themselves - for introducing parametricism as a new global style. No tool forces a designer to design according to a particular style. After all, tools do not "control" our actions. They have no "agency." To understand the impact of tools, we have to see them in terms of their "affordances" - what operations we can or cannot perform with them. We can attempt to bang in a nail with a screw driver, for example, but it would be easier to do so with a hammer.

The capacity of being used to bang in nails could therefore be said to be an affordance of the hammer. By extension, certain computational tools allow us to describe curves more easily than, say, in the days of parallel motion drawing boards. But these tools do not force us to draw curves. In themselves, computational tools are not responsible for the curvilinear forms that we associate with Schumacher's discourse of "Parametricism." Of course, in the context of AI, certain specific operations become easier, and a form of hegemonic expression might begin to emerge as a result of the affordances of the new tool. For example, AI is used in some structural optimization softwares, and we might expect to see a greater incidence of structurally efficient forms, such as parabolas, as a result of increased use of these softwares.

But AI - in and of itself - is unlikely to have any significant impact on the final design itself, although it is likely to have a significant impact on the process of generating that design or outcome.

Indeed, if we look at the question of Big Data, for example, the impact on the design process is likely to be more a question of making the process of design more efficient, rather than producing a new style, despite what Mario Carpo might claim in his The Second Digital Turn: Design Beyond Intelligence. One of the most effective uses of Big Data, after all, has been the introduction of transport network companies, such as Uber. But if we look at Uber cars themselves, we will see that they look identical to ordinary cars, which is precisely because they are the same as ordinary cars. They just operate differently. Thus, Big Data does not promote any particular aesthetic. It simply allows us to operate in a more effective manner performing certain operations.

There is, however, a second reason why AI is unlikely to introduce a new style of design. Broadly speaking, AI deals mainly with questions of "cognition" and "interpretation." This is perhaps the most important issue to be addressed when considering the impact of AI. For example, AI is able to scan visual and acoustic material, and relate it to a much larger data set. Hence it is able to "recognize" faces on Facebook and to categorize images on Instagram or identify music. In this it could be said to "mimic" or "simulate" human cognition, as noted above. Yet these operations belong largely to the realm of the interpretation of forms rather than the generation of forms. Of course, AI can generate forms, but this is based largely on recognition of existing patterns and extrapolation of new forms based on those patterns.

AI MEETS DESIGN

We can talk about the impact of AI on design in terms of both direct and indirect influences. Clearly AI has already played a substantial indirect role in design. After all, how many projects are there being produced these days that do not involve the use of the internet, Facebook, Instagram, or devices such as the cellphone, all of which use AI? In some senses, then, there is nothing that we design these days that is not affected or influenced indirectly by AI.

Moreover, designers are beginning to incorporate AI technology directly into their designs. One example is Behnaz Farahi, an interactive designer trained as an architect who has used an AI-based facial tracking device in Caress of the Gaze, an interactive outfit that responds to the gaze of the onlooker. The device is embedded in the outfit and is capable of detecting the age and gender of the person looking and the direction of his / her gaze. This information is then processed and used to trigger a response in the outfit causing it to ripple where the gaze of the onlooker is directed, employing a mechanism based on Shape Memory Alloys (SMAs) or Nitinol. Farahi has also employed an AI-based facial expression detecting device in another interactive outfit, Opale, which is able to recognize the mood of the onlooker, whether it is sadness, happiness, surprise or anger.

DESIGN DECISION-MAKING

Now that we have located live-updating intelligence for our site, it is time to harness AI to develop a design proposal. Rather than a program, this technology is better understood as an interconnected, self-designing system that can upgrade itself. It is possible to harness a huge amount of computing power and experience by working with these tools, even as an individual. "Now a one-man designer, a graduate designer, can get access to the same amount of computing power as these big multinational companies". The architect must input project parameters, in effect an edited 'design brief', and the computer system will then suggest a range of solutions which fulfill these criteria. This innovation has the potential to revolutionize how architecture is not only imagined but how it is fundamentally expressed for designers who choose to adopt these new methods.

While their work was initially aimed at the automotive and industrial design industries, Dreamcatcher now is beginning to filter into architecture projects. It was used recently to develop The Living's generative design for Autodesk's new office in Toronto and MX3D's steel bridge in Amsterdam. The basic concept is that CAD models of the surrounding site and other data, such as client databases and environmental information, are fed into the processor. Moments later, the system outputs a series of optimized 3D design solutions ready to render. These processes effectively rely on cloud computing to create a multitude of options based on self-learning algorithmic parameters. Lattice-like and fluid forms are often the aesthetic result, perhaps unsurprisingly, as the software imitates structural rules found in nature.

Fig. 1. Computational Architecture Digital Grotesque Project

The Dreamcatcher software has been designed to optimize parametric design and link into and extend existing software designed by Autodesk, such as Revit and Dynamo. Interestingly, Dreamcatcher can make use of a wide and increasing spectrum of design input data - such as formulas, engineering requirements, CAD geometry, and sensor information - and the research team is now experimenting with Dreamcatcher's ability to recognize sketches and text as input data. Bergin suggests he imagines the future of design tools as "systems that accept any type of input that a designer can produce [to enable] a collaboration with the computer to iteratively target a high-performing design that meets all the varied needs of the design team".

This would mean future architects would be less in the business of drawing and more into specifying requirements of the problem, making them more in sync with their machine counterparts in a project. Bergin suggests architects who adopt AI tools would have the ability to "synthesize a broad set of high-level requirements from the design stakeholders, including clients and engineers, and produce design documentation as output", in line with Engelbart's vision of AI augmenting the skills of designers.

AI is also being used directly in software such as Space Syntax's 'depthmapX', designed at The Bartlett in London, to analyze the spatial network of a city with an aim to understand and utilize social interactions and in the design process. Another tool, Unity 3D, is built from software developed for game engines to enable designers to analyze their plans, such as the shortest distances to fire exits. This information would then allow the architect to re-arrange or generate spaces in plan, or even to organize entire future buildings. Examples of architects who are adopting these methods include Zaha Hadid with the Beijing Tower project (designed antemortem) and MAD Architects in China, among others.

CLIENT AND USER ENGAGEMENT

As so much of the technology built into AI has been developed from the gaming industry, its ability to produce forms of 'augmented reality' have interesting potential to change the perception and engagement with architecture designs for both the architects and non-architects involved in a project. Through the use of additional hardware, augmented reality has the ability to capture and enhance real-world experience.

It would enable people to engage with a design prior to construction, for example, to select the most appealing proposal from their experiences within its simulation. It is possible that many architecture projects will also remain in this unbuilt zone, in a parallel digital reality, which the majority of future world citizens will simultaneously inhabit.

Augmented reality would, therefore, allow a client to move through and sense different design proposals before they are built. Lights, sounds, even the smells of a building can be simulated, which could reorder the emphasis architects currently give to specific elements of their design. Such a change in representational method has the potential to shift what is possible within the field of architecture, as CAD drafting did at the beginning of this century.

Additionally, the feedback generated by augmented reality can feed directly back into the design, allowing models to directly interact and adapt to future users. Smart design tools such as Materiable by Tangible Media are beginning to experiment with how AI can begin to engage with and learn from human behavior.

REALIZING DESIGNS AND RISE OF ROBOT CRAFTSMEN

AI systems are already being integrated into the construction industry—innovative practices such as Computational Architecture are working with 'robotic craftsmen' to explore AI in construction technology and fabrication. Michael Hansmeyer and Benjamin Dillenburger, founders of Computational Architecture, are investigating the new aesthetic language these developments are starting to generate. "Architecture stands at an inflection point," researcher suggests on their website, "the confluence of advances in both computation and fabrication technologies lets us create an architecture of hitherto unimaginable forms, with an unseen level of detail, producing entirely new spatial sensations."

3D printing technology developed from AI software has the potential to offer twenty-first-century architects a significantly different aesthetic language, perhaps catalyzing a resurgence of detail and ornamentation, now rare due to the decline in traditional crafts. Hansmeyer and Dillenburger's Grotto Prototype for the Super Material exhibition, London, was a complex architectural grotto 3D-printed from sandstone. The form of the sand grains was arranged by a series of algorithms custom designed by the practice.

The technique allowed forms to be developed which were significantly different to that of traditional stonemasonry. The aim of the project was to show that it is now possible to print building-scale rooms from sandstone and that 3D printing can also be used for heritage applications, such as repairs to statues.

Robotics are also becoming more common on construction job sites, mostly dealing with human resources and logistics. According to AEM, their applications will soon expand to bricklaying, concrete dispensing, welding, and demolition.

Another example of their future use could include working with BIM to identify missing elements in the snagging process and update the AI in real-time. Large scale projects, for example, government-lead infrastructure initiatives, might be the first to apply this technology, followed by mid-scale projects in the private sector, such as cultural buildings.

The challenges of the construction site will bring AI robotics out of the indoor, sanitized environment of the lab into a less scripted reality. Robert Saunders, a researcher into AI and fabrication at the University of Sydney, "robots are great at repetitive tasks and working with materials that react reliably...what we're interested in doing is trying to develop robots that are capable of learning how to work with materials that work in non-linear ways... like working with hot wax or expanding foam or, more practically, with low-grade building materials like low-grade timber."

Fig. 2. Ori System

Saunders foresees robot stonemasons and other 'craftsbots' working in yet unforeseen ways, such as developing the architect's 'skeleton plans', in effect, spontaneously generating a building on-site from a sketch.

Integrating AI systems

This innovation involves either integrating developing artificial technologies with existing infrastructure or designing architecture around AI systems. There is a lot of excitement in this field, influenced in part by Mark Zuckerberg's personal project to develop networked AI systems within his home, wish is to develop simple AI systems to run his home and help with his day-to-day work. This technology would have the ability to recognize the voices of members of the household and respond to their requests.

Designers are taking on the challenge of designing home-integrated systems, such as the Ori System of responsive furniture, or gadgets such as Eliq for energy monitoring. Other innovations, such as driver-less cars that run on an integrated system of self-learning AI, have the potential to shape how our cities are laid out and planned—in the most basic sense, limiting our need for more roads and parking areas. Behnaz Farahi is a young architect who is employing her research into AI and adaptive surfaces to develop interactive designs, such as in her Aurora and Breathing Wall projects. She creates immersive and engaging indoor environments which adapt to and learn from their occupants. Her approach is one of many—different practices with different goals will adapt AI at different stages of their process, creating a multitude of architectural languages.

Researchers and designers working in the field of AI are attempting to understand the potential of computational intelligence to improve or even upgrade parts of the design process with an aim to create a more functional and user-optimized built environment. It has always been the architect's task to make decisions based on complex, interwoven and sometimes contradictory sets of information. As AI gradually improves in making useful judgments in real-world situations, it is not hard to imagine these processes overlapping and engaging with each other. While these developments have the potential to raise questions in terms of ownership, agency and, of course, privacy in data gathering and use, the upsurge in self-learning technologies is already altering the power and scope of architects in design and construction.

As architect and design theorist Christopher Alexander said back in 1964, "We must face the fact that we are on the brink of times when man may be able to magnify his intellectual and inventive capacity, just as in the nineteenth century he used machines to magnify his physical capacity."

Bergin gave some insights into how he sees this technology impacting designers in the next twenty years. "The architectural language of projects in the future may be more expressive of the design team's intent", he stated. "Generative design tools will allow teams to evaluate every possible alternative strategy to preserve design intent, instead of compromising on a sub-optimal solution because of limitations in time and/or resources." Bergin believes AI and machine learning will be able to support a "dynamic and expanding community of practice for design knowledge".

Researcher can also foresee implications of this in the democratization of design work, suggesting "the expertise embodied by a professional of 30 years may be more readily utilized by a more junior architect". Overall, he believes "architectural practice over the next 20 years will likely become far more inclusive with respect to client and occupant needs and orders of magnitude more efficient when considering environmental impact, energy use, material selection and client satisfaction".

On the other hand, researcher suggests architects have little to fear from artificial intelligence: "Yes, you can automate. But what does a design look like that's fully automated and fully rationalized by a computer program? Probably not the most exciting piece of architecture you've ever seen." At the time of writing, many AI algorithms are still relatively uniform and relatively ignorant of context, and it is proving difficult to automate decision-making that would at first glance seem simple for a human. A number of research labs, such the MIT Media Lab, are working to solve this. However, architectural language and diagramming have been part of programming complex systems and software from the start, and they have had a significant influence on one another. To think architecturally is to imagine and construct new worlds, integrate systems and organize information, which lends itself to the front line of technical development. As far back as the 1960s, architects were experimenting with computer interfaces to aid their design work, and their thinking has inspired much of the technology we now engage with each day.

AI AND ARCHITECTURE

Artificial Intelligence, as a discipline, has already been permeating countless fields, bringing means and methods to previously unresolved challenges, across industries. The advent of AI in Architecture, described in a previous article, is still in its early days but offers promising results. More than a mere opportunity, such potential represents for us a major step ahead, about to reshape the architectural discipline.

Our work proposes to evidence this promise when applied to the built environment. Specifically, we offer to apply AI to floor plans analysis and generation. Our ultimate goal is three-fold: (1) to generate floor plans i.e. optimize the generation of a large and highly diverse quantity of floor plan designs, (2) to qualify floor plans i.e. offer a proper classification methodology (3) to allow users to "browse" through generated design options.

Our methodology follows two main intuitions (1) the creation of building plans is a non-trivial technical challenge, although encompassing standard optimization technics, and (2) the design of space is a sequential process, requiring successive design steps across different scales (urban scale, building scale, unit scale).

Then, in order to harness these two realities, we have chosen nested Generative Adversarial Neural Networks or GANs. Such models enable us to capture more complexity across encountered floor plans and to break down the complexity by tackling problems through successive steps. Each step corresponding to a given model, specifically trained for this particular task, the process can eventually evidence the possible back and forth between humans and machines.

Plans are indeed a high-dimensional problem, at the crossroad of quantifiable technics, and more qualitative properties. The study of architectural precedent remains too often a hazardous process, that negates the richness of the number of existing resources while lacking in analytical rigor. Our methodology, inspired by current Data Science methodologies, aims at qualifying floor plans.

Through the creation of 6 metrics, we propose a framework that captures architecturally relevant parameters of floor plans. On one hand, Footprint Shape, Orientation, Thickness & Texture are three metrics capturing the essence of a given floor plan's *style*. On the other hand, Program, Connectivity, and Circulation are meant to depict the essence of any floor plan *organization*. In a nutshell, the machine, once the extension of our pencil, can today be leveraged to map architectural knowledge, and trained to assist us in creating viable design options.

FRAMEWORK

Our work finds itself at the intersection of Architecture and Artificial Intelligence. The former is the topic, the latter the method. Both have been simplified into clear & actionable categories.

Architecture is here understood as the intersection between *Style* and *Organization*. On one hand, we consider *buildings as vectors of a cultural significance*, that express through their geometry, taxonomy, typology, and decoration a certain style. Baroque, Roman, Gothic, Modern, Contemporary: as many architectural styles that can be found through a careful study of floor plans. On the other hand, *buildings are the product of engineering* and science, answering to strict frameworks and rules -building codes, ergonomics, energetic efficiency, egress, program, etc — that can be found as we read a floor plan. This organizational imperative will complete our definition of Architecture and drive our investigation.

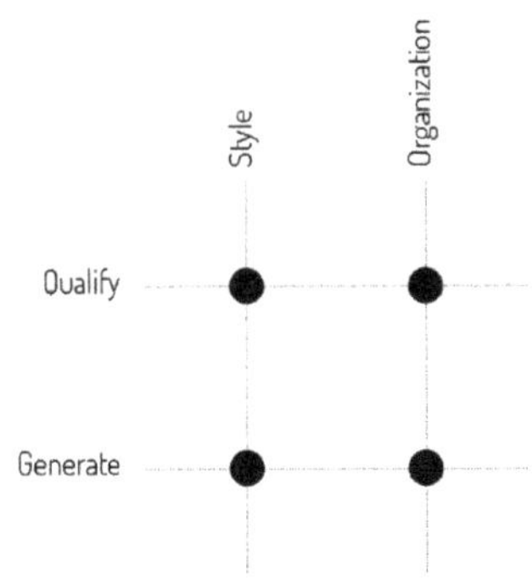

Fig. 3. Framework Matrix

Artificial Intelligence will be employed, using two of its main fields of investigation - *Analytics and Generative Adversarial Networks* - as an investigative tool.

At first, we will dive into the topic of *Generation*. Using GANs, we offer to educate our own AI systems to architectural design. We postulate that its utilization can enhance the practice of the architectural discipline. This field is as recent as it is experimental and yields to this day surprising results. Our hope is to be able to train it to draw actual building floor plans.

Then, we will come up with a robust analytical framework to qualify and classify the generated floor plans. Ultimately, our goal is to organize the results of our GANs, to offer the possibility for the user to browse seamlessly through the variety of created design options. To that end, the quantity and ubiquity of tools offered by Data Science will prove to be valuable to our investigation.

Through this dual lens, at the crossroad of Style & Organization, Qualification & Generation, we lay down a framework that organizes the encounter of Architecture & AI.

GENERATE

The design of architectural floor plans is at the core of the architecture practice. Its mastery stands as the gold standard of the discipline. It is an exercise that practitioners have overtime relentlessly tried to improve through technology. In this first part, we dive into the potential of AI applied to floor plan generation, as a mean to push the envelope even further.

Using our framework, to tackle floor plans' style and organization, we lay down in the following chapter the potential of AI-enabled space planning. Our objective is to offer a set of reliable and robust tools to both evidence the potential of our approach and to test our assumptions.

The challenge is here threefold: (1) choosing the right toolset, (2) isolating the right phenomena to be shown to the machine and (3) ensuring that the machine "learns" properly.

AI & GENERATIVE ADVERSARIAL NEURAL NETWORKS

Generative Adversarial Neural Networks — or *GANs*- are here our weapon of choice. Within the field of AI, Neural Networks stands as a key field of investigation. The creative ability of such models has been recently evidenced, through the advent of Generative Adversarial Neural Networks. As any machine-learning model, GANs learn statistically significant phenomena among data presented to them. Their structure, however, represents a breakthrough: made of two key models, the *Generator* and the *Discriminator*, GANs leverage a feedback loop between both models to refine their ability to generate relevant images.

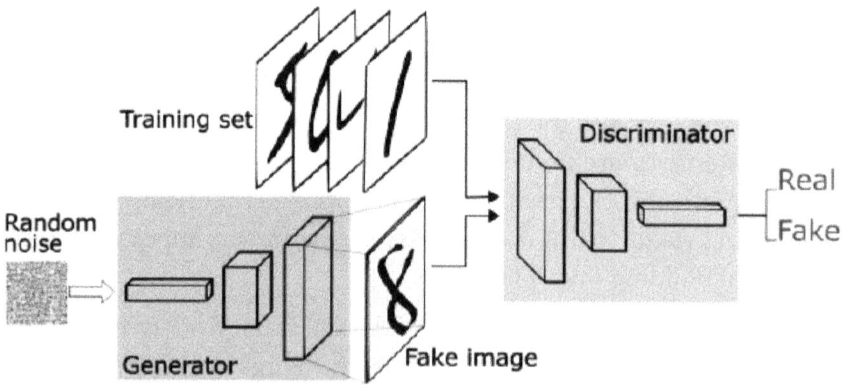

Fig. 4. Generative Adversarial Neural Network's Architecture

The Discriminator is trained to recognize images from a set of data. Properly trained, this model is able to distinguish between a real example, taken out of the dataset, from a "*fake*" image, foreign to the dataset. The Generator, however, is trained to create images resembling images from the same dataset. As the Generator creates images, the Discriminator provides him with some feedback about the quality of its output. In response, the Generator adapts, to produce even more realistic images. Through this feedback loop, a GAN slowly builds up its ability to create relevant synthetic images, factoring in phenomena found among observed data.

Representation & Learning

If GANs represent a tremendous opportunity for us, knowing what to show them is crucial. We have here the opportunity to let the model learn directly from floor plan images. By formatting images, we can control the type of information that the model will learn. As an example, just showing our model the shape of a parcel and associated building footprint will yield a model able to create typical building footprints given a parcel's shape. To ensure the quality of the outputs, we will use our own architectural "*sense*" to curate the content of our training sets: a model will only be as good as the data we give him, as architects.

The sequence, realized over the course of a day and half of training, displays how one of our GAN-models progressively learns how to layout rooms and fenestration for a housing unit.

Although the initial attempts are imprecise and confuse, after 250 iterations the machine builds for itself some form of intuition.

Precedents

If GANs' application to architectural design is still in its infancy, a handful of precedents inspired our work and drove our intuition. Hao Zheng's and Weixin Huang offered at the ACADIA conference in 2018 a first publication, demonstrating the potential of GAN for floorplans recognition and furniture layout generation. Using patches of color, their model would draw the infill of rooms, based on the room program, and its openings position. The same year, Nathan Peters in his thesis at the Harvard GSD, proposed to use GANs (pix2pix) to tackle program repartition in single-family modular homes, based on the house footprint.

Regarding GANs as design assistants, Hao Zheng's and Nono Martinez' thesis at the GSD (2017) inspired our investigations. Both authors tackled the idea of a loop between the machine and the designer to refine the very notion of "design process".

Our work expands on these precedents and offers to nest 3 models (footprint, program, and furnishing) to create a full "generation stack" while improving results quality at each step. By automating multi-units processing, our work then scales to entire buildings generation, and masterplan layouts. We further offer an array of models dealing with style transfer. Finally, our contribution adds a rigorous framework to parse and classify resulting outputs, enabling users to "browse" consistently through generated options.

Within a floor plan, "*Style*" can be observed by studying the geometry and figure plane of its walls. Typical baroque churches will display bulky columns, with multiple round indents. A modern villa by Mies van der Rohe will show thin flat walls. This "*crenellation*" of the wall surface is a feature that a GAN can appreciate. By showing it pairs of images, with one image being a segmented version of a plan, and the other one the original wall structure, we can then build a certain amount of machine intuition with regard to architectural style.

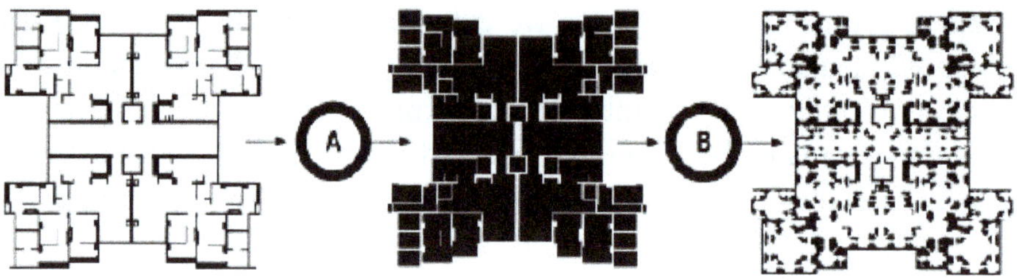

Fig. 5. Modern-to-Baroque Floor Plan Translation

This section shows the results of a model, trained to learn the Baroque style. We proceed then to a style transfer, where a given floor plan is *manually segmented* (A) and *dressed back with a new wall stylistic* (B).

Fig. 6 Layout Assistant, a Step by Step Pipeline

In this section, we offer a multi-step pipeline, integrating all the necessary steps to draw a floor plan. Jumping across scales, it emulates the process taken by an architect and tries to encapsulate each step into one specific model, trained to perform a given operation. From the parcel to the building footprint (I), from the footprint to a room split with walls & fenestration (II), from a fenestrated floor plan to a furnished one (III): *each step has been carefully engineered, trained and tested.*

GENERATIVE DESIGN

Machine learning (ML) is a big focus for AI in architecture right now. ML is not synonymous with AI but is rather a subset of the larger discipline.

With ML the idea is to create and train an algorithm to complete tasks with incremental improvements after each attempt. This is similar to how a human would learn a rote task only ML can do it much, much faster.

One framework for ML is the GAN or generative adversarial network, which is a form of unsupervised learning using two artificial neural networks.

The idea here is that one network, called a generator, creates whatever you're asking for - such as images of human faces. Then a second neural network, called a discriminator, decides if the generator's output is as good as actual pictures of human faces.

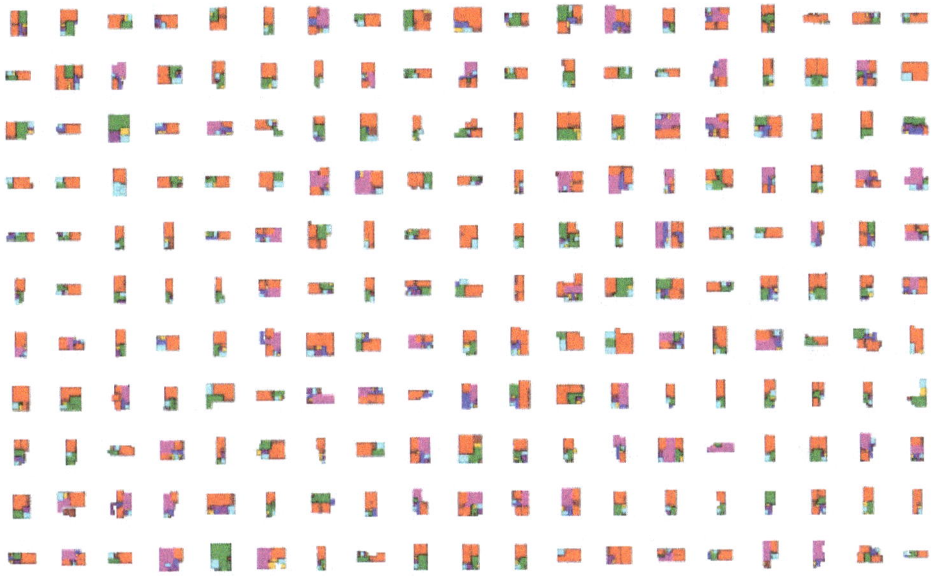

Fig. 7. An apartment building dataset

The two neural networks are engaged in a kind of competition where the generator tries to fool the discriminator, and the discriminator plays defense to prevent being fooled.

The end game, in our example, would be for the generator to create better and better images of human faces until they are indistinguishable from the real thing, ultimately fooling the discriminator.

One among many who've been experimenting with GANs to create architectural designs has been Stanislas Chaillou.

For his master's thesis work at Harvard, Chaillou used GANs to create and refine floorplan design. During his work he found that not only would basic restraints of space and function impact design, but also the style used to guide these GAN-generated floorplans.

"It seems that style permeates irrevocably the very essence of any generative process...there will be no agnostic-AI for Architecture." Chaillou said in an article on Towards Data Science. "On the contrary, each model or algorithm will come with its flavor, its personality, its know-how."

That's an appealing notion that you could have, for example, a few models that favor design touches of modern architecture from people such as Frank Gehry and Zaha Hadid, another influenced by Bauhaus, and another that's some fusion of multiple styles.

Chaillou has gone on to co-found Rayon, a collaborative software company specializing in floorspace design.

GAN is just one flavor of generative design where the idea is to slowly refine a design produced by a computer over time. This can be using an unsupervised learning model such as a GAN or a more collaborative method with greater human input.

Another example of generative design is Delve, a real estate development tool from Google's Sidewalk Labs. Delve can generate hundreds of designs in minutes.

Each design considers various requirements such as retail, residential, parking, and public spaces. The designs also have a detailed cost model to show estimates of what a given design should cost.

WEB APPS

The wonderful thing about the current state of technology is that you don't necessarily need onsite computing power to do advanced work. On top of that, web apps are becoming more and more advanced on the front end, blurring the lines between local and cloud software.

At the same time, by dividing the pipeline into discrete steps, the system allows for the user's intervention between each model. By selecting the output of a model, and editing it, before giving it to the next model, the user stays in control of the design process. Its input shapes the decisions made by the model, therefore achieving the human-machine interaction expected.

FOOTPRINT

The first step in our pipeline tackles the challenge of creating an appropriate building footprint for a given parcel geometry. To train this model, we used an extensive database of Boston's building footprints and were able to create an array of models, each tailored for a specific property type: *commercial*, *residential (house)*, *residential (condo)*, *industrial*, etc.

Each model is able for a given parcel, to create a set of relevant footprints, resembling in dimension and style the type it was trained for. Nine examples, using the residential (house) model are shown Fig. 9.

ROOM SPLIT & FENESTRATION

The layout of rooms across a building footprint is the natural next step. Being able to split a given floor plan, while respecting meaningful *adjacencies, typical room dimensions* and *proper fenestrations* is a challenging process, that GANs can tackle with surprising results.

Using a dataset of around 700+ annotated floor plans, we were able to train a broad array of models. Each is geared towards a specific room count and yields surprisingly relevant results once used on empty building footprints.

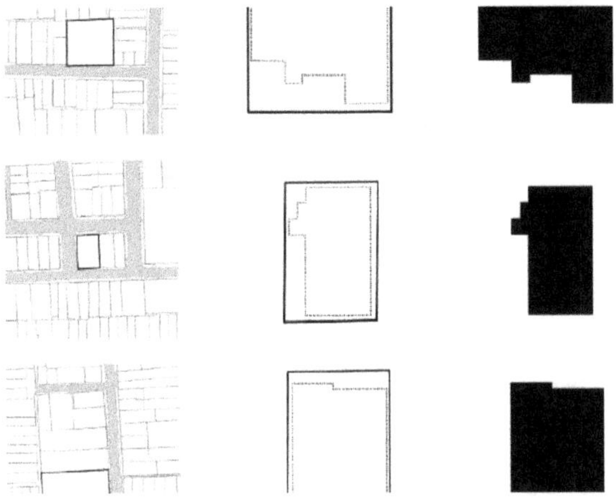

Fig. 8 Parcel (input) - Generated Footprint (output)

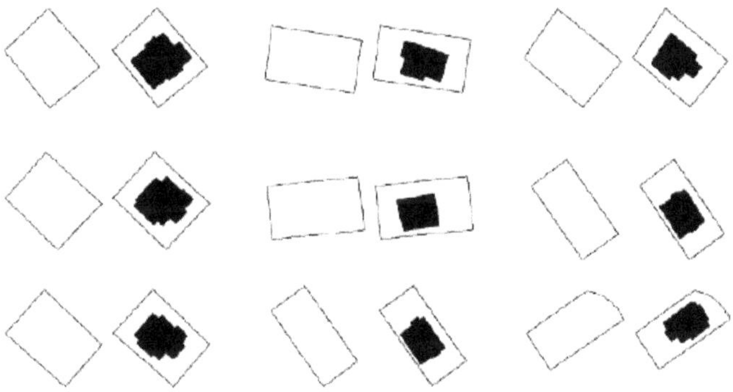

Fig. 9. Generated Footprints (housing)

BEYOND TECHNOPHOBIA

Technophobia is an extreme fear of technology. People with technophobia may fear the power of artificial intelligence, robots or computers.

Technophobia is more than resistance to learning new technology. Rather, people with the condition may obsess over technology. Or, they may go to great lengths to avoid incorporating technology into their lives.

If you have ever hesitated to use your child's smartphone, or wondered how to operate a computer without someone giving you guidance, you may not be alone.

A number of people find it difficult to deal with technology and gadgets inspire fear in them. Some people take this fear to an extreme and may be called 'technophobics' by psychologists.

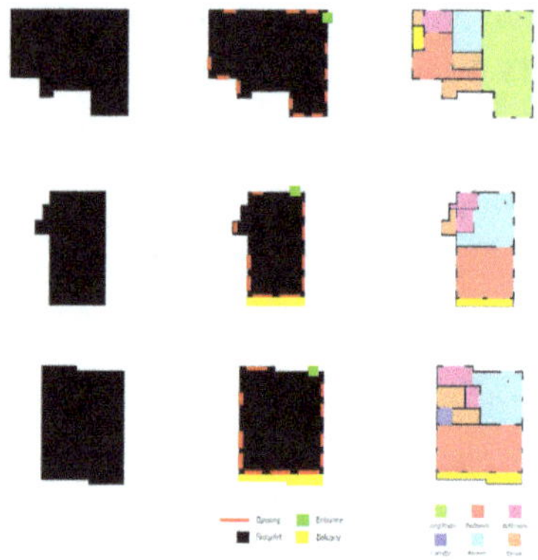

Fig. 10. Footprint - Openings & Balcony (input) - Program & Fenestration (output)

Technophobia is not an officially recognized mental illness but it is the extreme and irrational fear of technology. Usually, this fear is related to irrational fear of computers, robots, artificial intelligence, weapons and other such things which seem advanced in scientific thought. Many people fear genetically modified organisms too (GMO), though research shows that they are safe to consume. In other words, fear of science and technology is a very real problem in our societies and it wouldn't be an exaggeration to say that one can find a technophobic around every street corner.

THE PROSTHETIC IMAGINATION

The word 'prosthesis' is a Greek word that is defined as an addition, application, or attachment that replaces or adds to a body part to restore the normal functionality of the human body. A prosthesis creates a relation between two distinct orders: flesh/steel, theory/fiction, translation/quotation, public/private, built/unbuilt, and so on. Modern architecture is an interface that is a technological extension of the body neither natural nor cultural. In the discipline of architecture, a prosthesis is considered as an evolution of space.

Like humans, buildings and cities grow, develop, and evolve, hence prosthetic architecture is needed. An immediate and practical consequence would be that architectural designs should be instilled with characteristics for future extensions of buildings to be healthy rather than cancerous. Several participants are needed to design a building that consists of architects, engineers, designers, planning authorities, and building clients. There is a consensus among several researchers that prosthetic design is an emerging research field and needs theoretical and practical investigation. For theoretical explorations, an interdisciplinary approach is required comprising of prosthetic design, product design, psychology, and fashion trends. The authors reviewed literature and deduced that a successful prosthetic design needs the right balance between elements (parts of the design) and principles (rules guiding the structure).

However, it is speculated that principles are self-sustaining and allow a designer to create the right design perception subject to variation from person to person, ensuring essential representation of 'innovation' in prosthetic design. From this study, it is deduced that prosthetic design concepts need representative characteristics to make them feel objectively proportionate to existing elements while substantiating their novelty and personality.

Prosthetics may be used as tools in architecture to guide building users to operate in emergency cases where there is minimal chance of survival for people in an impact zone. The study shows the critical assessment of environmental management as a co-habitation method with natural disasters such as Tsunamis and presents the post-disaster reconstruction of Constitución, a Chilean coastal city. The research results highlight that a geo-meteorological event that defies scientific calculability and social imagination causes absolute vulnerability and uncertainty but should not be used to express the need for fast or bold actions to 'save the planet'. The authors argue that exceptional events need to humbly recognize the presence of excessive forces that cannot be managed diplomatically. It is advocated that easily identifiable luminescent prosthetic tools allow the planning and design of evacuation routes for predicted natural disasters.

For contributing to the right balance between elements and principles to achieve a successful prosthetic design, technological advances in fabrication methods are required to use metamaterials in design with hierarchy and length scales similar to those found in nature. In the study, the authors confirmed that structural metamaterials and nanolattices can be created with enhanced mechanical properties at various scales ranging from angstroms and nanometers.

The authors deduced that the development of a material catalogue for prosthetic architecture needs a high surface-area-to-volume ratio of nanolattices that are useful due to their diverse applicability to building systems such as photovoltaic systems. The most significant finding of this particular study includes the overview of recent structural multidimensional metamaterials contributing to defining a multidimensional material design space to enable the manipulation of materials with unprecedented capabilities for prosthetic architecture.

To facilitate technological advancement in fabrication methods and novel material development for prosthetic architecture, it is necessary to investigate startups and businesses that create new products and market opportunities. Researchers present the dynamic interplay between materials and engineering for successful new products and industries.

The research examines four technological companies in diverse industries that develop different material systems. These companies consist of Rheonix, Kionix, Mezmeriz, and Incodema3D, and their products are based on novel polymer adhesion process, silicon microelectrochemical inertial sensors for thin films used in construction, integration of different classes of materials to optimize speed and displacement, and new fabrication processes of additive manufacturing of metals respectively.

The research results deduced that for developing new products and creating new markets, tradeoffs in material selection, manufacturing processes, engineering design, and product performance are crucial.

Prosthetic architecture is associated with biomimetic systems that are defined as engineered parts embedded coherently to achieve increased functionality and superior resilience aided by robotics. Campesato compared the marketplace of robotics and prosthetics and concluded that the former is open to professionals and small businesses and diversifies offers to large competitors, whereas the latter deals with products and components likely to have emerged from 3D printing technologies. The author correlated both marketplaces due to the common trend towards lightweight solutions and suggested the partnership between robotics and prosthetics to form the industrial robotics and prosthetic automation market. The envisioned combined marketplace would contribute to the design of prosthetic architecture.

The University of Florida formulated a multidisciplinary engineering design course for first-year undergraduate students to introduce concepts such as sustainable prosthetic prototypes. The authors highlighted that the most significant objective was to help students develop early connections to instill a sense of care in students to design prototypes based on societal needs.

A few examples from the human-centered topics considered for first-year design prototypes included food stability (self-watering planters), sustainable energy (nontraditional power generation), and tools for disabilities (toys for children with prosthetics), etc.

The research results deduced that multidisciplinary engineering design courses based on a human-centered design enable students to acquire prototype design skills (solid modelling, 3D printing, sensors/actuators, microcontrollers, programming) and professional skills (teamwork, communication, critical thinking, and self-directed learning).

Investigating the relationship between systemic thinking and design is fundamental to understand its correlation with design theory and practice for possible application to prosthetic architecture. The research reveals four distinctly different interpretations of concepts of systems that include whether the system exists, what is systematized, how the system operates, and why the system exists.

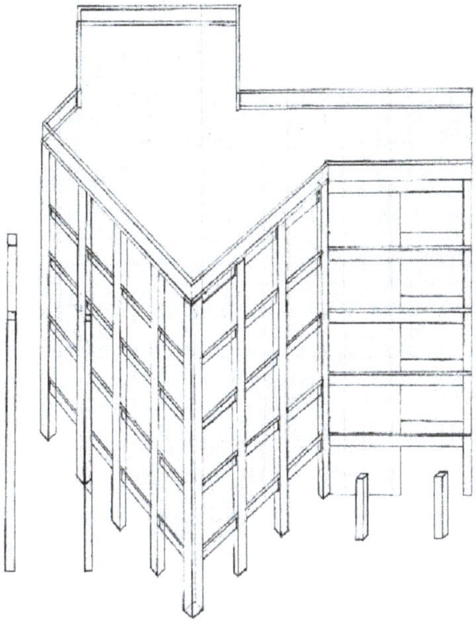

Fig. 11. Vertical Axonometric of existing building.

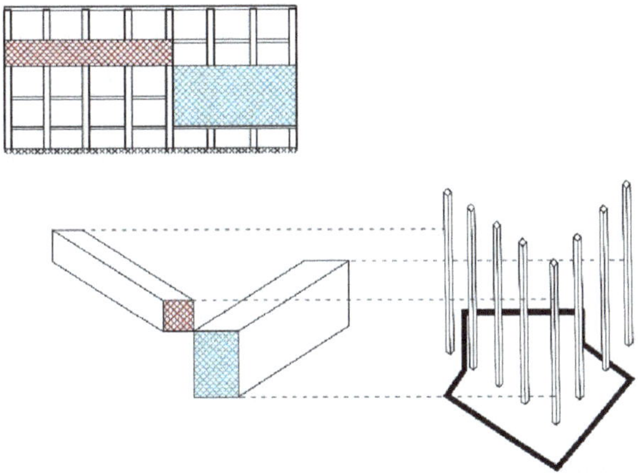

Fig. 12. Volumetric experiment to discover a prosthetic.

The study explained Richard McKeon's definition of systems clustered into four broad groups representing modes of thought such as construction (a process by which parts are put together), discrimination (a process by which arbitrary formulations are interpreted), resolution (a process by which problems are resolved), and assimilation (a process by which surrounding truths are approximated).

Buchanan points out that McKeon laid the foundation of the humanistic approach to communications and construction influential in the theory and practice development of design. The research findings include the identification of the underrated yet highly significant time period between 1968- 1972 that extends the difference between artificial intelligence (AI) and the human control of AI through concepts of intelligence amplification (IA).

These findings have a significant impact in relation to cybernetic organisms, the design of prosthetic architecture, and the future of the sustainable built environment as IA involves the effective use of information technology to augment, extend and enhance human intelligence through discoveries of various forms of bio-prosthetics.

The design research commenced by extensive documentation of existing buildings used by RHSA, which included plans, sections, digital modeling, and physical modeling. The research included various volumetric experiments to explore the most successful prosthetic for RHSA.

These experiments were followed by considering the tectonic expressiveness as a cornerstone when translating a prosthetic to a site. Steel was investigated as a material for the prosthetic architectural design of the Graduate studio as it allows the expressive characteristics offered by the site. The interplay between steel and brick-clad reinforced concrete columns required exploring construction details to understand existing façade conditions and current geometrical details.

Over the last 20 years, a diverse range of scholars working in the humanities have embraced ideas of the 'augmented', 'enhanced' or 'prosthetic' in developing critical approaches to social and cultural phenomena. The terms have aided thinking around not just embodiment and the wider notions of subjectivity and selfhood, but also energised conceptions of history, memory, aesthetics and—conceived of broadly—'the imagination', 'consciousness' and (especially true of 'augmented' of course) 'reality'.

As we will spell out below, from the evocation of cyborgs in contemporary cultural theory to the continued resonance of past atrocities such as slavery and the Holocaust, or from imagined technologised social futures to the permeable boundaries of gender formations, conceptions such as the 'augmented self' or 'prosthetic imagination' have animated possibilities in thinking of new configurations of subject and place.

It is, however, noticeable that these ideas have not been developed through any particular cooperation with those experts for whom the engineering of augmentation or the design and production of prostheses is a daily undertaking. As is obvious, the manufacture of assistive technologies involves the necessary conceptualisation of the relationship between technology and the body, but those conceptions differ radically from the notions of prosthetic personhood that have become a staple feature of work in—broadly speaking—cultural studies.

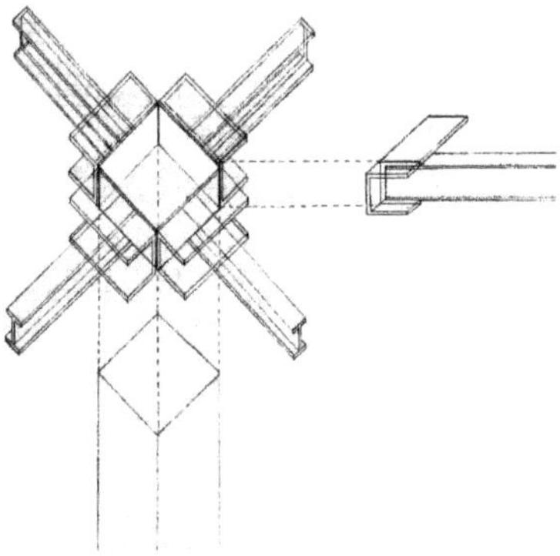

Fig. 13. Steel channel section forming a collar around the reinforced concrete column and allowing I-beams to support the new prosthetic construction

Our aim here is on one level, then, simple: namely to bring together the questions of theory, metaphor, practice and lived-body experiences that are raised when the distinct disciplinary approaches surrounding 'augmentation' or 'prosthesis' are made to encounter one another. We will focus on prosthesis specifically because, of all the terms that fall under the loose heading of 'augmentation', it is that which produces the most meanings, with 'prostheses', 'prosthesis' and 'prosthetic' all denoting subtly different configurations. In design and engineering, prostheses are literal objects, often made to order for a diverse range of clients; in cultural studies, the word creates multiple resonances around augmentation and enhancement, both of individuals and non-embodied states.

We have also chosen prosthesis because of its clear links to disability, which we define here as a set of experiences and interactions with environments that possess intrinsic value in their own terms and challenge normative and ableist concepts of selfhood and community. During the foundational period of critical studies in the 1990s, seminal work by scholars such as Lennard J Davis and Rosemarie Garland-Thomson focused on ideas of the 'normal' and 'ordinary', highlighting the often-hidden prejudicial values behind these apparently neutral terms. In the past 20 years especially, the subject has turned from these processes of unveiling to express the ways in which different bodies challenge assumptions about normalcy, utility and the perception of integrated selfhood. As Michael Davidson observes of the relationship between disability and aesthetics, 'Disability aesthetics foregrounds the extent to which the body becomes thinkable when its totality can no longer be taken for granted, when the social meanings attached to sensory and cognitive values cannot be assumed'.

In figuring prosthetics, ideas of the 'totality' of the body and the 'social meanings' that accrue from these are thrown into sharp relief. Owning or using prostheses signals disability to a majority non-disabled culture, but under whose terms and how? And does it also signal technology in the same way? Whether the perceived absence of a limb is compensated for by an understood presence of a designed and produced alternative is an issue more complex than it might appear. Not all prostheses are replacements, for example (the limb may never have existed in the first place), and there are many different types of design and technology.

Staying alive to Davidson's reminder about what 'cannot be assumed', we are guided here by the knowledge that disability acts as a refractive lens through which to read the interrelationship between the body and the technology that interacts with it.

In developing this thinking, we wish to argue for the many benefits that accrue from processes of an interdisciplinary dialogue between cultural/literary studies and engineering, and chart how these then provoke potentially innovative categories of health, disability and the body. In the context of an interdisciplinary critical medical humanities, we want to ask: what might a research space look like that makes room for the combined engineered/imagined body? How can the designed/produced object, and the theorised/abstracted/represented self, extend what we can say about grounded and conceptualised selfhood? How might the *details* of each discipline, whether (for example) the vital technical specifics of engineering or the picking apart of language or trope in cultural studies, allow for an understanding of differing methodologies in which augmentation or enhancement might be framed?

We want to structure our answers to these questions in three parts: first, through an exploration of the manner in which cultural theory has taken up the idea of the prosthetised body; second, reading those engineering and design methodologies that illustrate the processes of producing prosthetic technologies; and finally, outlining the outcomes from these interdisciplinary encounters that can inform the multistrand critical approaches that increasingly characterise cultural research undertaken on health and disability. While our examinations have to be necessarily limited, we believe that the shape of the arguments we make points to broader possibilities of integrating humanities and engineering scholarship within the developing discipline of the medical humanities.

ENGINEERING SYSTEMS AND NETWORKS

Within engineering, 'design' is a broad term that covers a spectrum of activities involved in developing any artefact, from the largely creative ('art and design') to the predominantly analytical ('engineering design'). There has long been a debate about whether design is a 'science of the artificial' amenable to laws that will always lead to good design, or a more intuitive process of 'reflection-in-action', where designs evolve through the application of experience and intuition. In practice, as demonstrated by Louis Bucciarelli's ethnographic study of engineering design, these approaches are not mutually exclusive, and different stages of the design process, different products or even different parts of a product may require more of one approach or the other.

Irrespective of where on this spectrum a given design falls, all designs are concerned with the artificial: the outcome of a design process is never 'natural' or purely accidental. While these terms and the ideas they generate may influence a design process, the form a given artefact takes is ultimately determined by decisions taken in its development. In terms of the physical body that presents itself to the designer and engineer then, it is an origin and source but also a constraint, the starting point for the processes of production but also, inevitably, the source of their parameters.

One of Bucciarelli's key observations is that engineering design progresses not as a series of predefined steps, but as a socially negotiated process in which different individuals frame problems and apply methods with which they are familiar in order to address them. In place of a fixation on 'the object as a thing in itself' (a prosthetic limb, for example), he stresses ideas of vision, harmony and 'a cultural matrix'.

Where it might be expected that an engineer will hone in on the fine details of a design, Bucciarelli stresses the need to 'unfocus', and to then 'start with a broad canvas, hold suspect the categories and relations we unconsciously accept today, and seek [...] evidence of relations in the making and using' of engineered products. As Graham Pullin notes in his foundational study design meets disability, this can exacerbate the tension between the creative and the analytical approaches to design.

Here, the stress on a greater holistic view of users and contexts for product design are key; and when Bucciarelli observes that 'the artefact as object can live again. It can become a nexus or icon of social discourse or exchange. There are other object worlds within which the artefact can be seen and used in different ways. Deconstruction and bricolage are always possible', he is using language that suggests an explicit connection between engineering design processes and the kind of fluid conception of prostheses as trope or metaphor outlined in our first section. This specific citation of deconstruction and bricolage, it might also be noted, evidences a knowledge of the poststructuralist critical methods that underpin much of the way in which 'prosthetics' have come to be discussed in contemporary cultural criticism.

Bucciarelli and Pullin's interventions serve to remind that the days of the individual artisan both designing and making a product for a specific user are for the most part gone. Much product development—including prosthetics—is undertaken by teams with a range of skills and corresponding views of the goal to be achieved. As systems have become more complex, systems engineering has become a common approach to coordinate the efforts of different individuals within a development team.

This entails following a 'divide and conquer, combine and rule approach', dividing the product into subsystems, each with its own goal and constraints and allowing a given individual or team to focus on their subsystem, without reference to those of others. Within this subdivided nature of any complex engineering project, different individuals may well deal with different aspects of the body. For example, the designer of a socket to fit a prosthetic is concerned with the shape and structure of the body; the designer of software to interpret electromyography signals will be more concerned with the signals generated by myoelectric activities and the subcutaneous positioning of nerves and muscle fibres; and the designers of the joints and actuation of a prosthetic will be interested in the propagation of forces through the body, and the strain this places on different parts of the body.

A systems perspective raises issues of networks and connections, with the product being developed itself part of a larger system that interacts with other systems: users and other individuals with whom the product comes into contact; other products to which it connects; and the general surrounding environment. A key decision being taken in developing a product then is not just its internal architecture—how it breaks down into subsystems—but also the scope of the systems' boundaries: what is seen as acceptable to be altered and what is taken as an external constraint.

This can allow for the kind of interdisciplinarity Bucciarelli and Pullin advocate, where boundaries are flexible and to be transgressed; but equally this idea of systems might *require* separation and differentiation to incorporate the necessary specialisms involved in production.

The structures of engineering systems are particularly relevant when it comes to working through engaging with questions of embodiment. Traditionally, the body—understood as the user or users—has been configured as something external to the product: something to be accommodated and adapted around. The product (a prosthetic limb, for example) may be attached to this body, or need to accommodate it in some form, but it is generally produced through a conception of empirical material that corresponds with use value, for example a set of anthropometric measurements (lengths of typical body parts or strengths of different grips).

Echoing the observations of Bucciarelli and Pullin, however, there have been recent critical reconfigurations that take a more holistic view of users and the systems they suggest (incorporating individual aspirations and social relationships for example), and treating them as more than just a collection of measurements that allow for an object to perform a task. In addition, the body is not *always* seen as existing outside the scope of design. Tissue engineering and the design of prosthetics such as replacement hip and knee joints include the alteration of body tissue, while developments in surgical technologies now allow for alterations to bodies that enable nerves to control a prosthetic limb.

The body, then, takes a range of forms in engineering design. It can be outlined using anthropometric data denoting typical dimensions or capabilities, or it can be framed within mathematical models that capture the biomechanics of human movement or the propagation of force through bone and other tissue, with corresponding stresses, strains and deformations. Such representations are noticeably atomistic rather than holistic: they have very specific purposes and roles in the design process, intended to address very particular questions, which must then be reintegrated at a higher level into the design as a whole.

This is inherent to the systems approach often adopted in engineering; the complexity of systems means that it is difficult/impossible for any single person or method to consider every aspect of a design simultaneously. As a result, engineering design rarely thinks of the body as a whole unit or entity; it is always subject in some way to subdivisions that necessitate the atomistic 'divide and conquer' approach mentioned previously, into which the various tools and specialisms required to produce the product are designed to fit.

To address this, 'personas' are often used in product development: artificial characters who are given a backstory, including details of preferences, family, job, hobbies or aspirations, to think through how they might respond to a given product. Such 'characterization' offsets a simpler process in which product users are viewed as collections of data that can be modelled objectively. There are, of course, controversies over this: are such 'characters' really representative of the intended user? Are they fabricated to suit the prejudices of developers? At what point are choices made as to the details of backstories? What, for example, is being assumed about what an individual might *want* when they are having a prosthetic hand-fitted? Seen through a critical disability lens, it is intriguing to juxtapose the fragmented sense of systems engineering with this corresponding desire to render an idea of a 'whole' user. It is a formation distinctly different from the porous or elastic body configured in humanities criticism, one where an idea of 'the prosthetic' might be made to connect to a totalising system such as 'memory'. It also appears to invite a disability reading: if the manufacture of a prosthetic limb takes place within contexts that stress division and separation, it is hard to see how the resulting product can be seen as being integral to an individual's experience *as* a person with disabilities.

Such perspectives may well be correct, but we feel that there is a danger of misrepresenting the critical methodologies and working practices of design and engineering if they are only read in such terms. For example, it is possible to see congruity rather than discrepancy in some of the differences outlined above. The characterisation of porous embodiment can be seen to be in line with elements of systems thinking; the precise boundary of what is to be engineered can be drawn in different places; an amputation and the prosthetic limb constructed as a response can accommodate more, or less, of the living tissue under the skin and non-living matter beyond it. Seen in such a light, Donna Haraway's famous provocation 'why should our bodies end at the skin?' has a parallel with certain modes of engineering decision-making. What is sometimes referred to as the 'fuzzy front end' of engineering—the early stages of determining what it is that is being engineered and what it is hoped will be achieved by it—involves judgements necessarily conceived of in terms of flexibility. In the case of prosthetics for example, decisions might be made as to whether the goal is to 'restore' a limb following an amputation, or to re-establish specific functions, the latter process one that might be achieved by means other than 'replacement'. These two possible eventualities are not the same, and the body that falls under discussion as a result of choices made in such circumstances is one that cannot be said to be singular.

It is impacted differently and with different results. This is, we suggest, an example of where engineering design methods address the (flexible) boundaries of embodiment in ways that have parallels (suggestive at least) with critical cultural and disability studies.

Equally, designing in relation to disability cannot avoid its insertion into narrative or engagement with metaphor. Is the design of a prosthetic limb, conceived of within a context of improvement for example, a part of a narrative in which technology makes 'our' lives better? What ideas of function or expression are involved when designing a prosthetic hand, given that the labour any hand produces ranges from the utility of prehension to the emotion inherent in a pointed finger or clenched fist? These thoughts are unavoidable interventions, not only into the specifics of any body, design or individual, but also the complex historical trajectories that make up the ways in which technology and health are juxtaposed. Our contention is that we are better placed to address the complexities of these points of view when we bring the equally complex critical approaches of each discipline into dialogue with one another.

Archi-Union uses "cyborg fabrication" to build Venue B conference centre in 100 days Archi-Union Architects has completed a conference centre on Shanghai's West Bund in just 100 days, using robot-assisted design and construction.

Called Venue B, the centre was built to host an AI (artificial intelligence) conference. Because of this, Archi-Union felt it was appropriate to use innovative digital construction techniques in the building's creation.

This follows the ethos of the Shanghai-based firm, who previously worked with robots to the build the complex brick structure of the Chi She gallery, and has also completed numerous other buildings with complex geometries.

Venue B features some of the most lightweight structures available in modern buildings, thanks to the combination of algorithms used in the planning stages and prefabricated construction methods.

"AI has been rapidly refreshing our perceptions about the world," said the team, explaining that they set themselves the challenge: "How can we present an urban public exhibition space, which carries the essence of AI technology in 100 days?"

The complex consists of three conference venues that sit at slightly rotated angles to each other. These angles create two triangular spaces in between the halls, which contain garden courtyards.

The buildings are white, to blend with the overall language of the West Bund's existing public buildings, which are all pale in colour and modernist in form.

Fig. 14

Fig. 15

Facades that face the street are as closed as possible to avoid disturbance during summits, but those that face the internal gardens are open in order to allow natural light and air to flow through the spaces.

In the larger of the central triangular courtyards is a shared garden, constructed in wood to soften the space and encourage relaxation. This garden serves as a rest station between summits. A thin vaulted roof, also made from wood, provides shelter for the garden space.

"Both courtyards are covered with a digital prefabricated timber vaulted roof, in which the larger one has a span of 40 metres and its structural thickness is only about 0.5 metres," said the architects. "It is the most economical inter-supported steel-wood roof in the world."

This garden also houses the world's largest 3D-printed coffee pavilion, which takes the form of five translucent arches, with a coffee bar as well as tables and chairs – all constructed in the same manner as the pavilion itself. The use of 3D-printing has made the process of building and fitting the space very rapid.

"The entire process from design to construction of the coffee pavilion celebrates the cooperation of man-machine intelligence," said Archi-Union.

"In total, digital design and fabrication technologies have helped to achieve 200 square metres of printed building areas, 40 printed chairs and 12 tables within 25 days." Venue B's main structure uses a prefabricated light aluminium truss system, which has the lightest unit weight of all known materials. Both the roof structures over the three conference halls and the garden spaces are also exceptionally lightweight.

The architects were able to achieve the material lightness of Venue B's roof by using algorithms that calculated the best angle of the vaulted structures to ensure that the force was distributed evenly. The arching roof is balanced by the steel trusses and reinforced at the corners.

Fig. 16

Fig. 17

The joints in the roof are formed of hollow aluminium structures that further reduce its weight. The ceiling is slightly raised above the main conference space in order to allow ventilation.

The installation of the prefabricated components according to a digital plan vastly improves the efficiency on site and requires fewer labourers than traditional construction. For this reason, on-site construction of the 2,000-square-metre timber shell took only 29 days.

A minimum amount of materials were used for the structure, making the building more sustainable and reducing the cost of the build.

EXTENDED INTELLIGENCE

Artificial Intelligence (AI) has always been a topic of discussion- is it good enough for us? Getting more and more into this high technology world will give us a better future or not? According to recent research, almost everyone has a different requirement for automation. And most of the work of humans is done by the latest high intelligence computers. You all must be familiar with the fact of how Artificial Intelligence is changing industries, like Medicine, Automobiles, and Manufacturing. Well, what about Architecture?

The main issue is about the fact that these high tech robots will actually replace the creator? Although these high tech computers are not good enough at some ideas and you have to rely on Human Intelligence for that. However, these can be used to save a lot of time by doing some time-consuming tasks, and we can utilize that time in creating some other designs. Artificial Intelligence is a high technology mechanical system that can perform any task but needs a few human efforts like visual interpretation or design-making etc. AI works and gives the best results possible by analyzing tons of data, and that's how it can excel in architecture.

WAYS ARTIFICIAL INTELLIGENCE CAN RESHAPE ARCHITECTURE

Parametric Architecture

Parametric architecture is a hidden weapon that allows an architect to change specific parameters to create various types of output designs and create such structures that would not have been imagined earlier. It is like an architect's programming language.

It allows an architect to consider a building and reframe it to fit into some other requirements. A process like this allows Artificial Intelligence to reduce the effort of an architect so that the architect can freely think about different ideas and create something new.

Construction and Planning

Constructing a building is not a one-day task as it needs a lot of pre-planning. However, this pre-planning is not enough sometimes, and you need a little bit of more effort to get an architect's opinion to life. Artificial Intelligence will make an architect's work significantly easier by analyzing the whole data and creating models that can save a lot of time and energy of the architect.

All in all, AI can be called an estimation tool for various aspects while constructing a building. However, when it comes to the construction part, AI can help so that human efforts become negligible.

Laying the Foundation

The countless hours of research at the starting of any new project is where AI steps in and makes it easy for the architect by analyzing the aggregate data in millisecond and recommending some models so that the architect can think about the conceptual design without even using the pen or paper.

Just like while building a home for a family, if you have the whole information about the requirements of the family, you can simply pull all zoning data using AI and generate design variations in a short time period.

AI for Making Homes

This era of modernization demands everything to be smartly designed. Just like smart cities, today's high technology society demands smart homes. However, now architects do not have to bother about how to use AI to create the designs of home only, but they should worry about making the user's experience worth paying.

Smart Cities

Change is something that should never change. The way your city looks today will be very different in the coming time. The most challenging task for an architect is city planning that needs a lot of precision planning. However, the primary task is to analyze all the possible aspects, and understand how a city will flow, how the population is going to be in the coming years.

THE HYBRID DESIGN FOR ARTIFICIAL INTELLIGENCE SYSTEMS

Artificial intelligence is a multidisciplinary field of research, the rapid development of which began in the 20th century. In the mid-century, there were attempts to create artificial general intelligence. However, it quickly became apparent that intelligence development in silico is a genuinely massive challenge. Later through the joint efforts of mathematicians and physiologists an artificial neuron model and the first artificial neural network were made.

To the disappointment of scientists, no mind emerged in them. It became clear that the presence of a neural network did not guarantee its intelligence, and the mind was most likely due to some obscure synergistic effects within a network of many millions of neurons.

There are two approaches in artificial intelligence building. The first one is known as top-down AI.

Examples of a top-down approach are technologies such as expert systems, decision support systems, knowledge bases, and inference engines. The principles of topdown AI are expressed in the Newell-Simon hypothesis: "A physical symbol system has the necessary and sufficient means for general intelligent action". The direction of symbolic calculations based on the logic of syntactic manipulation of symbols is the most developed in this approach.

The second approach, defined by Marvin Lee Minsky, is called the "bottom-up AI". It is based on the assumption that it is possible to model natural low-level processes occurring in the living brain. This area combines technologies such as artificial neural networks, evolutionary algorithms, and biocomputing.

Both top-down AI and bottom-up AI approaches have their advantages and disadvantages. The benefits of the first one include the ease of interpreting and explaining the results obtained by the logical inference engine based on symbolic calculations. At the same time, it is not very easy to work with large amounts of data in a top-down approach. That is because of the need to prepare too large knowledge bases for the inference engine, which will also have to be built with linguistic variables whose value is not strictly defined. Moreover, the question of training artificial intelligence systems based on a top-down paradigm is still rather open-a final formalism for describing the function of independent learning of intelligent systems has not been proposed.

The bottom-up approach has rather opposite problems: an artificial neural network can easily be trained on huge amounts of data, but it will be almost impossible to interpret the result. There is no complete understanding of how a trained artificial neural network (for arbitrary architecture) produces a particular output, so the network is a "black box".

Therefore, it is difficult to verify the correctness of the results generated by the neural network, for example, in the case of incorrect data falling into the sample on which the network was trained. Also, artificial neural networks are fundamentally different from the neural network in the human brain: neurogenesis and retraining are continually going on in the human brain, together with other unclear effects that lead to the emergence of consciousness. Therefore, artificial neural networks alone cannot claim intelligence in the human sense.

THE ARCHITECTURE OF A HYBRID INTELLIGENT SYSTEM

The solution to the problem of constructing artificial intelligence systems may lie in combining the capabilities of the top-down and bottom-up approaches. One can try to build the architecture of a hybrid intellectual system while continuing to be inspired by the design of the human mind but on a more general level. The following figure graphically shows the general diagram of the interaction of components in a hybrid intelligent system based on such principles.

Sensors (affectors) transmit information to a neural network that converts data from the sensors to symbolic form, based on which a universal inference engine generates input data for a motor neural network. The result of the motor neural network is lowlevel commands that control the executive devices of the hybrid intellectual system. In this case, the sensors also perceive information about the state of the components of the system itself.

Reactive Management Subsystem. This system implements the usual control scheme. Signals from the sensors are processed in the control system, generating control actions on the control object (the environment), that transmit through executive devices. This system is similar to the "reflex contour" in humans.

Proactive Management Subsystem. Adds layer, which serves to intellectualise the circuit of the automatic control system. This level allows the system to learn, predict its condition and environmental conditions, build planned actions, and also adapt to changing environmental conditions. This subsystem implements a hybrid system of "conditioned reflexes".

A management focus interchanges between the two systems. When the conditions of the system behaviour change, the proactive circuit creates a new pattern of behaviour and the control focus shifts to the reactive subsystem. Constant environmental conditions do not require the operation of the dynamic system. Therefore, a learned reaction is preferable. Such a situation is like the formation of a "conditioned reflex". On the other hand, when the environment or control object conditions change during the operation of the reactive subsystem, the control focus escalates to proactive to adapt and develop new patterns of system behaviour.

The functioning cycle of the hybrid system consists in sequentially performing the following steps: Collection of input information from all sensors monitoring the parameters of the environment of the system. Different types of sensors, in this case, are separate modalities of a hybrid intelligent system perception.

Cleaning the collected information from noise and choosing a path for further processing. If the input information corresponds to any automatic patterns of system behaviour, then the control focus shifts to the reactive subsystem, which selects and executes a specific pattern.

The functioning cycle of the hybrid system consists in sequentially performing the following steps:

Integration of all modalities of the system perception into a single unit of the description of the environment if there is no automatic reaction. This block outputs a holistic picture of the perception of the environment that goes to the proactive control subsystem.

Formation of a new rule for the reactive system. This rule is a control action in a symbolic form, which is recorded in the reactive system and sent for execution. The proactive system derives the rule based on models of the system, its behaviour and environment using the mechanism of symbolic inference, so a person can easily interpret it.

Translation of the symbolic control action into a low-level language and transmittance to actuators that interact with the environment and the control object. Translation can be carried out by various mechanisms. For example, a neural network. After the execution of the command by the executive devices, the operation cycle ends.

Besides, there should be an implementation of control communications of all the hybrid intelligent system internal elements to its sensors. This creates adaptation mechanisms based on the constancy of the internal state of the system.

Finally, the connection from the proactive management subsystem to itself embodies the so-called "internal conflict", when the intelligent system can model various options for the development of a situation that affects the system itself. The cycle of evaluating and choosing an acceptable alternative runs until this internal conflict resolves.

AN INTRODUCTION TO AI

The Artificial Intelligence tutorial provides an introduction to AI which will help you to understand the concepts behind Artificial Intelligence

. In this tutorial, we have also discussed various popular topics such as History of

AI, applications of AI, deep learning, machine learning, natural language processing, Reinforcement learning, Q-learning, Intelligent agents, Various search algorithms, etc.

Our AI tutorial is prepared from an elementary level so you can easily understand the complete tutorial from basic concepts to the high-level concepts.

In today's world, technology is growing very fast, and we are getting in touch with different new technologies day by day.

Here, one of the booming technologies of computer science is Artificial Intelligence which is ready to create a new revolution in the world by making intelligent machines.

The Artificial Intelligence is now all around us. It is currently working with a variety of subfields, ranging from general to specific, such as self-driving cars, playing chess, proving theorems, playing music, Painting, etc.

AI is one of the fascinating and universal fields of Computer science which has a great scope in future. AI holds a tendency to cause a machine to work as a human.

Artificial Intelligence is composed of two words Artificial and Intelligence, where Artificial defines *"man-made,"* and intelligence defines *"thinking power"*, hence AI means *"a man-made thinking power."*

Artificial Intelligence exists when a machine can have human based skills such as learning, reasoning, and solving problems

With Artificial Intelligence you do not need to preprogram a machine to do some work, despite that you can create a machine with programmed algorithms which can work with own intelligence, and that is the awesomeness of AI.

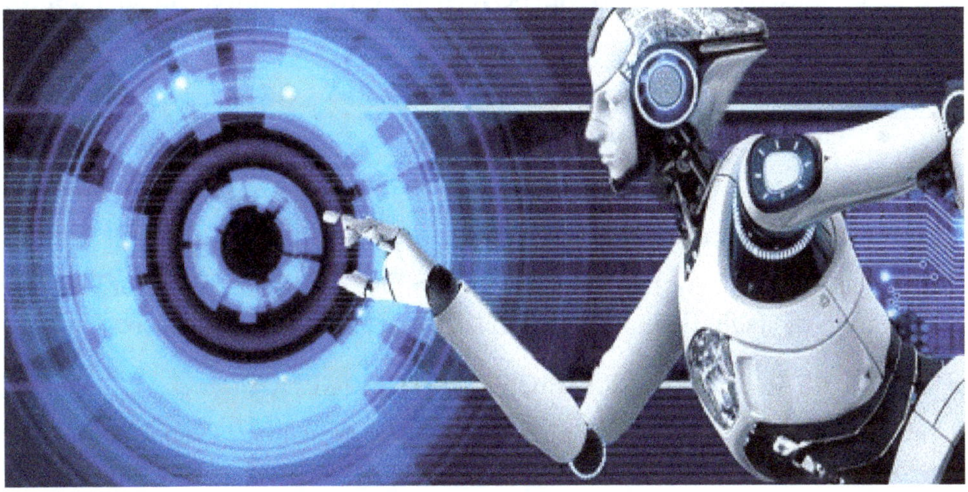

Fig. 18

It is believed that AI is not a new technology, and some people says that as per Greek myth, there were Mechanical men in early days which can work and behave like humans.

WHY ARTIFICIAL INTELLIGENCE?

Before Learning about Artificial Intelligence, we should know that what is the importance of AI and why should we learn it. Following are some main reasons to learn about AI:

- With the help of AI, you can create such software or devices which can solve real-world problems very easily and with accuracy such as health issues, marketing, traffic issues, etc.
- With the help of AI, you can create your personal virtual Assistant, such as Cortana, Google Assistant, Siri, etc.
- With the help of AI, you can build such Robots which can work in an environment where survival of humans can be at risk.
- AI opens a path for other new technologies, new devices, and new Opportunities.

GOALS OF ARTIFICIAL INTELLIGENCE

Following are the main goals of Artificial Intelligence:

- Replicate human intelligence
- Solve Knowledge-intensive tasks
- An intelligent connection of perception and action
- Building a machine which can perform tasks that requires human intelligence such as:
    - Proving a theorem
    - Playing chess
    - Plan some surgical operation
    - Driving a car in traffic
- Creating some system which can exhibit intelligent behavior, learn new things by itself, demonstrate, explain, and can advise to its user.

WHAT COMPRISES TO ARTIFICIAL INTELLIGENCE?

Artificial Intelligence is not just a part of computer science even it's so vast and requires lots of other factors which can contribute to it. To create the AI first we should know that how intelligence is composed, so the Intelligence is an intangible part of our brain which is a combination of Reasoning, learning, problem-solving perception, language understanding, etc.

To achieve the above factors for a machine or software Artificial Intelligence requires the following discipline:

- Mathematics
- Biology
- Psychology
- Sociology
- Computer Science
- Neurons Study
- Statistics

Advantages of Artificial Intelligence

Following are some main advantages of Artificial Intelligence:

- **High Accuracy with less errors:** AI machines or systems are prone to less errors and high accuracy as it takes decisions as per pre-experience or information.
- **High-Speed:** AI systems can be of very high-speed and fast-decision making, because of that AI systems can beat a chess champion in the Chess game.
- **High reliability:** AI machines are highly reliable and can perform the same action multiple times with high accuracy.
- **Useful for risky areas:** AI machines can be helpful in situations such as defusing a bomb, exploring the ocean floor, where to employ a human can be risky.
- **Digital Assistant:** AI can be very useful to provide digital assistant to the users such as AI technology is currently used by various E-commerce websites to show the products as per customer requirement.
- **Useful as a public utility:** AI can be very useful for public utilities such as a self-driving car which can make our journey safer and hassle-free, facial recognition for security purpose, Natural language processing to communicate with the human in human-language, etc.

Disadvantages of Artificial Intelligence

Every technology has some disadvantages, and thesame goes for Artificial intelligence. Being so advantageous technology still, it has some disadvantages which we need to keep in our mind while creating an AI system. Following are the disadvantages of AI:

- **High Cost:** The hardware and software requirement of AI is very costly as it requires lots of maintenance to meet current world requirements.

- **Can't think out of the box:** Even we are making smarter machines with AI, but still they cannot work out of the box, as the robot will only do that work for which they are trained, or programmed.
- **No feelings and emotions:** AI machines can be an outstanding performer, but still it does not have the feeling so it cannot make any kind of emotional attachment with human, and may sometime be harmful for users if the proper care is not taken.
- **Increase dependency on machines:** With the increment of technology, people are getting more dependent on devices and hence they are losing their mental capabilities.
- **No Original Creativity:** As humans are so creative and can imagine some new ideas but still AI machines cannot beat this power of human intelligence and cannot be creative and imaginative.

CHAPTER

2 WHAT IS AI?

In the simplest terms, AI which stands for artificial intelligence refers to systems or machines that mimic human intelligence to perform tasks and can iteratively improve themselves based on the information they collect. AI manifests in a number of forms. A few examples are:

- Chatbots use AI to understand customer problems faster and provide more efficient answers
- Intelligent assistants use AI to parse critical information from large free-text datasets to improve scheduling
- Recommendation engines can provide automated recommendations for TV shows based on users' viewing habits

AI is much more about the process and the capability for superpowered thinking and data analysis than it is about any particular format or function. Although AI brings up images of high-functioning, human-like robots taking over the world, AI isn't intended to replace humans. It's intended to significantly enhance human capabilities and contributions. That makes it a very valuable business asset.

Artificial intelligence (AI) refers to the simulation of human intelligence in machines that are programmed to think like humans and mimic their actions. The term may also be applied to any machine that exhibits traits associated with a human mind such as learning and problem-solving.

The ideal characteristic of artificial intelligence is its ability to rationalize and take actions that have the best chance of achieving a specific goal. A subset of artificial intelligence is machine learning (ML), which refers to the concept that computer programs can automatically learn from and adapt to new data without being assisted by humans. Deep learning techniques enable this automatic learning through the absorption of huge amounts of unstructured data such as text, images, or video.

As the hype around AI has accelerated, vendors have been scrambling to promote how their products and services use AI. AI requires a foundation of specialized hardware and software for writing and training machine learning algorithms. No one programming language is synonymous with AI, but a few, including Python, R and Java, are popular.

In general, AI systems work by ingesting large amounts of labeled training data, analyzing the data for correlations and patterns, and using these patterns to make predictions about future states. In this way, a chatbot that is fed examples of text chats can learn to produce lifelike exchanges with people, or an image recognition tool can learn to identify and describe objects in images by reviewing millions of examples.

AI programming focuses on three cognitive skills: learning, reasoning and self-correction.

Learning processes

This aspect of AI programming focuses on acquiring data and creating rules for how to turn the data into actionable information. The rules, which are called algorithms, provide computing devices with step-by-step instructions for how to complete a specific task.

TYPES OF ARTIFICIAL INTELLIGENCE

Artificial Intelligence can be divided in various types, there are mainly two types of main categorization which are based on capabilities and based on functionally of AI. Following is flow diagram which explain the types of AI.

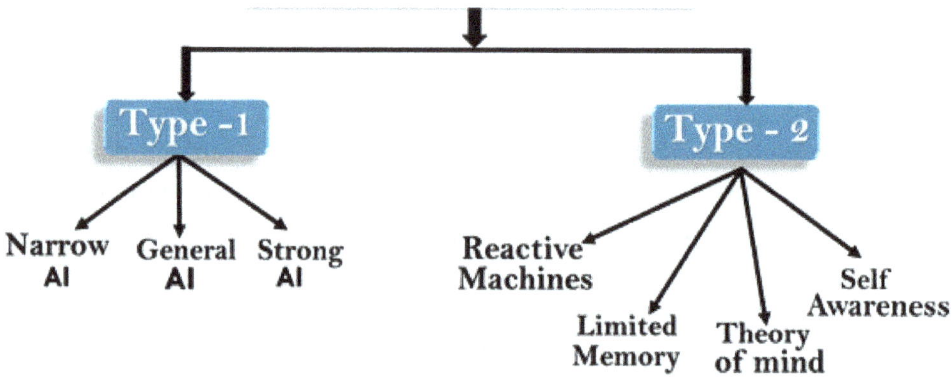

Fig. 1. Types of Artificial Intelligence

AI type-1: Based on Capabilities

Weak AI or Narrow AI

- Narrow AI is a type of AI which is able to perform a dedicated task with intelligence.The most common and currently available AI is Narrow AI in the world of Artificial Intelligence.

- Narrow AI cannot perform beyond its field or limitations, as it is only trained for one specific task. Hence it is also termed as weak AI. Narrow AI can fail in unpredictable ways if it goes beyond its limits.
- Apple Siriis a good example of Narrow AI, but it operates with a limited pre-defined range of functions.
- IBM's Watson supercomputer also comes under Narrow AI, as it uses an Expert system approach combined with Machine learning and natural language processing.
- Some Examples of Narrow AI are playing chess, purchasing suggestions on e-commerce site, self-driving cars, speech recognition, and image recognition.

General AI

- General AI is a type of intelligence which could perform any intellectual task with efficiency like a human.
- The idea behind the general AI to make such a system which could be smarter and think like a human by its own.
- Currently, there is no such system exist which could come under general AI and can perform any task as perfect as a human.
- The worldwide researchers are now focused on developing machines with General AI.
- As systems with general AI are still under research, and it will take lots of efforts and time to develop such systems.

Super AI

- Super AI is a level of Intelligence of Systems at which machines could surpass human intelligence, and can perform any task better than human with cognitive properties. It is an outcome of general AI.
- Some key characteristics of strong AI include capability include the ability to think, to reason,solve the puzzle, make judgments, plan, learn, and communicate by its own.
- Super AI is still a hypothetical concept of Artificial Intelligence. Development of such systems in real is still world changing task.

ARTIFICIAL INTELLIGENCE TYPE-2: BASED ON FUNCTIONALITY

Reactive Machines

This type of AI includes machines that operate solely based on the present data, taking into account only the current situation. Reactive AI machines cannot form inferences from the data to evaluate their future actions. They can perform a narrowed range of pre-defined tasks.

- Purely reactive machines are the most basic types of Artificial Intelligence.
- Such AI systems do not store memories or past experiences for future actions.
- These machines only focus on current scenarios and react on it as per possible best action.
- IBM's Deep Blue system is an example of reactive machines.
- Google's AlphaGo is also an example of reactive machines.

An example of Reactive AI is the famous IBM Chess program that beat the world champion, Garry Kasparov (Fig. 2).

Fig. 2. Reactive Machine AI

Limited Memory

Like the name suggests Limited Memory AI, can make informed and improved decisions by studying the past data from its memory. Such an AI has a short-lived or a temporary memory that can be used to store past experiences and hence evaluate future actions.

- Limited memory machines can store past experiences or some data for a short period of time.
- These machines can use stored data for a limited time period only.
- Self-driving cars are one of the best examples of Limited Memory systems. These cars can store recent speed of nearby cars, the distance of other cars, speed limit, and other information to navigate the road.

Self-driving cars are Limited Memory AI, that uses the data collected in the recent past to make immediate decisions. For example, self-driving cars use sensors to identify civilians crossing the road, steep roads, traffic signals and so on to make better driving decisions. This helps to prevent any future accidents.

Fig. 3. Limited Memory

Theory of Mind AI

The Theory Of Mind AI is a more advanced type of Artificial Intelligence. This category of machines is speculated to play a major role in psychology. This type of AI will focus mainly on emotional intelligence so that human believes and thoughts can be better comprehended.

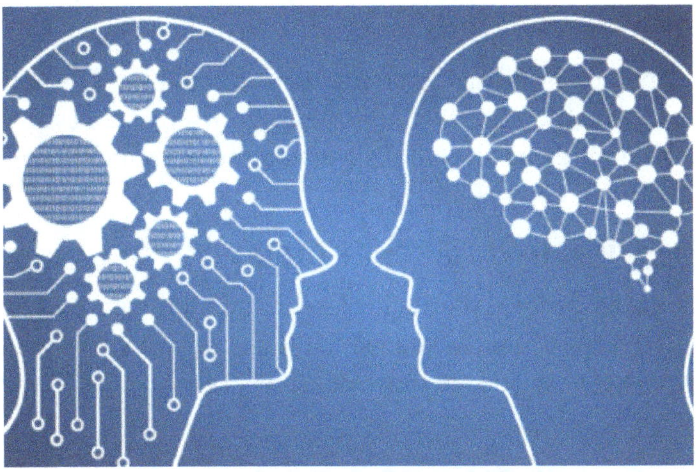

Fig. 4. Theory of Mind AI

The Theory of Mind AI has not yet been fully developed but rigorous research is happening in this area.

Self-Awareness

- Self-awareness AI is the future of Artificial Intelligence. These machines will be super intelligent, and will have their own consciousness, sentiments, and self-awareness.
- These machines will be smarter than human mind.
- Self-Awareness AI does not exist in reality still and it is a hypothetical concept.

ARTIFICIAL NARROW INTELLIGENCE (ANI)

Also known as Weak AI, ANI is the stage of Artificial Intelligence involving machines that can perform only a narrowly defined set of specific tasks. At this stage, the machine does not possess any thinking ability, it just performs a set of pre-defined functions.

Examples of Weak AI include Siri, Alexa, Self-driving cars, Alpha-Go, Sophia the humanoid and so on. Almost all the AI-based systems built till this date fall under the category of Weak AI.

ARTIFICIAL GENERAL INTELLIGENCE (AGI)

Also known as Strong AI, AGI is the stage in the evolution of Artificial Intelligence wherein machines will possess the ability to think and make decisions just like us humans.

There are currently no existing examples of Strong AI, however, it is believed that we will soon be able to create machines that are as smart as humans.

Strong AI is considered a threat to human existence by many scientists, including Stephen Hawking who stated that:

"The development of full artificial intelligence could spell the end of the human race.... It would take off on its own, and re-design itself at an ever-increasing rate. Humans, who are limited by slow biological evolution, couldn't compete and would be superseded."

ARTIFICIAL SUPER INTELLIGENCE (ASI)

Artificial Super Intelligence is the stage of Artificial Intelligence when the capability of computers will surpass human beings. ASI is currently a hypothetical situation as depicted in movies and science fiction books, where machines have taken over the world.

BRANCHES OF ARTIFICAL INTELLIGENCE

Artificial Intelligence can be used to solve real-world problems by implementing the following processes/ techniques:

- Machine Learning
- Deep Learning
- Natural Language Processing
- Robotics
- Expert Systems
- Fuzzy Logic

Machine Learning

Machine Learning is the science of getting machines to interpret, process and analyze data in order to solve real-world problems.

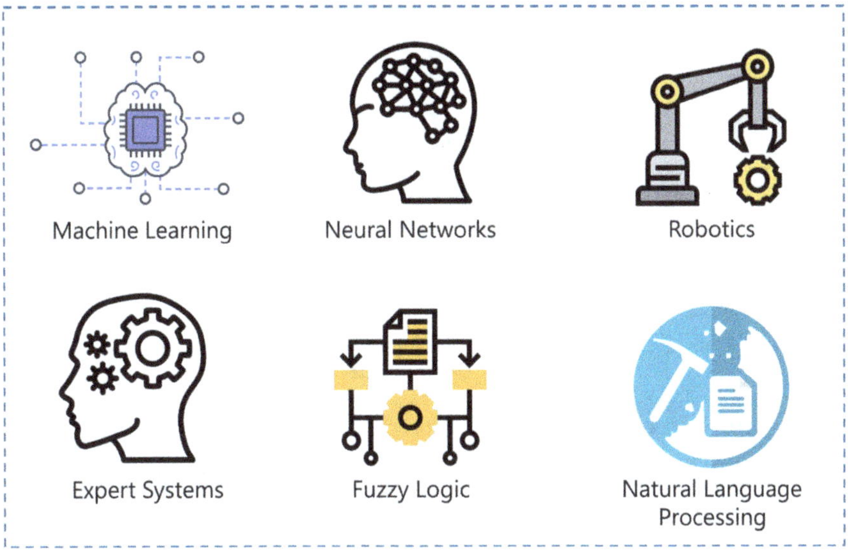

Fig. 5. Domains of AI

Fig 6. Machine Learning

Under Machine Learning there are three categories:

- Supervised Learning
- Unsupervised Learning
- Reinforcement Learning

Deep Learning

Deep Learning is the process of implementing Neural Networks on high dimensional data to gain insights and form solutions. Deep Learning is an advanced field of Machine Learning that can be used to solve more advanced problems.

Deep Learning is the logic behind the face verification algorithm on Facebook, self-driving cars, virtual assistants like Siri, Alexa and so on.

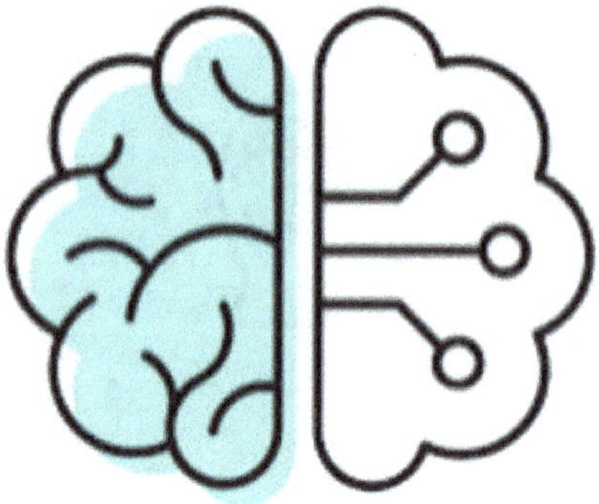

Fig. 7. Deep Learning

Natural Language Processing

Natural Language Processing (NLP) refers to the science of drawing insights from natural human language in order to communicate with machines and grow businesses.

Fig. 8. Natural Language Processing

Twitter uses NLP to filter out terroristic language in their tweets, Amazon uses NLP to understand customer reviews and improve user experience.

Training Techniques

Learning is defined as the adaptive intelligent change in response to experience. In humans, it refers to the continuous process of acquiring new skills, values, knowledge, attitude, and preferences based on past experiences. This lifelong exercise in humans is called cognitive learning.

The process of learning in machines is quite similar to humans. The machines review the existing data and learn new skills from it. This continuous learning cycle is known as Machine Learning (ML).

Machine Learning is the branch of Artificial Intelligence (AI) and computer science that deals with the use of data and algorithms to imitate the learning process of humans. The ML technology is known for its predicting potential from a large set of data, which is beyond the processing power of humans. It is because of this ability of ML that almost every industry (healthcare, finance, retail, advertising, manufacture, transportation, etc.) is using Machine Learning as the underlying technology for most of their IT transformation roadmaps.

Data set, algorithms, models, feature extraction, and training are 5 crucial components of Machine Learning. Depending upon the scenario, data type, input, etc., there are different ways an ML model learns. These are supervised and unsupervised learning methods. In supervised learning, the machine classifies objects, problems, and scenarios based on data that has been fed to them through data sets. On the other hand, in unsupervised learning, the machines learn on their own, discover information, create patterns, and then label the data. Know more about these machine learning categories through our blog that discusses supervised and unsupervised learning in detail.

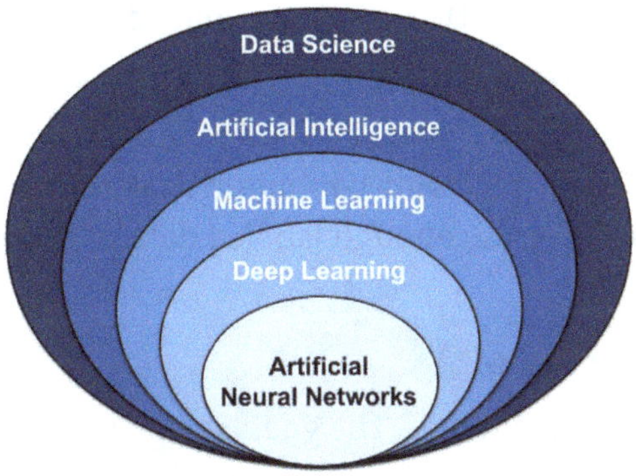

Fig. 9. Artificial Neural Networks

There are certain techniques using which a model can be trained. Now that you're familiar with the basics, you can move ahead and read the upcoming segment of this blog post that shares 10 Machine Learning techniques for AI development.

Regression (Supervised ML)

Regression analysis is a predictive modeling technique. It creates a relationship between the dependent (target) and independent (predictor) variable (s). The models created using this Machine Learning technique helps to understand how the value of dependent variables is changing corresponding to independent variables. For this reason, regression analysis is highly recommended for making predictions. For example, it can help determine blood pressure (dependent variable) of different ages, gender, and weights (independent factors). This can further help in health issues that happen due to fluctuations in blood pressure.

There are 7 types of regression techniques: Linear, Logistic, Ridge, Lasso, Polynomial, and Bayesian. Amongst all these, Linear and Bayesian regression models are the most used and popular machine learning techniques.

Classification (Supervised ML)

Classification is a technique where data is categorized into several classes. The process involves recognizing and grouping objects/ideas into categories. It uses pre-categorized training datasets to classify the given datasets into categories. One of the common examples of this machine learning technique is filtering emails into the 'spam' or 'not spam' category. There are seven ways to classify ML datasets: Logistic Regression, K-Nearest Neibhours, Random Forest, Decision Tree, Stochastic Gradient Descent, Naive Bayes, and Support Vector Machine.

Transfer Learning (Supervised ML)

Transfer Learning refers to the process of reusing an already trained data set and using it to perform a new but similar task. Once a data set is trained for a task, a fraction of trained layers can be transferred and combined with the layers of a new dataset. This way, the ML algorithm can learn and adapt quickly to the new task.

Transfer learning overcomes several challenges involved in training a dataset. Since this machine learning technique requires less amount of data to be trained, it proves less expensive in terms of computational resources. Moreover, with an already existing dataset, there is enough labeled data that can help in accomplishing the new task.

Clustering (Unsupervised ML)

In the clustering learning technique, the goal is to group or cluster the observations that have similar characteristics. Unlike supervised training methods, clustering does not use the output to train the dataset and provide an output. Instead, it helps the algorithms to define the output.

Clustering involves the grouping of unlabeled data. That is why this machine learning technique comes under unsupervised learning. If the data would have been labeled, the technique would have been the classification.

Some of the common applications of clustering in the real world include market segmentation, search result grouping, anomaly detection, medical imaging, social network analysis, image segmentation, etc.

Ensemble Methods (Supervised ML)

The Ensemble model ensures that you get the best of all worlds. It uses the idea of combining various predictive models to get precise predictions, which an individual model might fail to provide.

The ensemble methods reduce the variance and bias of a single ML model. This is important; an ML model might work with precision under one circumstance and might fail under another. When there is another model available, it will help to preserve the accuracy. The prediction quality is balanced with multiple predictive models.

Neural Networks & Deep Learning (Unsupervised ML)

Neural networks are a biologically-inspired programming paradigm that enables a machine to continuously learn from observational data. Deep learning involves a set of techniques that make the neural networks learn.

Deep learning technology helps the machine imitate the human brain. This machine learning technique has some amazing applications in areas of vision (image classification), text (text mining), audio (speech recognization), and video (computer vision). There are different types of neural networks that can be trained using this machine learning technique- Artificial Neural Network (ANN), Convolutional Neural Network (CNN), and Recurrent Neural Network (RNN). However, the major challenge associated with this learning method is it requires a lot of data and computational power (enhanced Graphical Processing Units).

Dimensionality Reduction (Supervised & Unsupervised Learning)

Dimensionality reduction is a data presentation technique. It is the process of transforming the data from a high-dimensional space into a low-dimensional space. This helps the low dimensional representation retain significant properties of the original data which is quite near to its intrinsic dimension.

High dimensional data means hundreds and thousands of inputs. When the data is reduced to a low dimensional structure, the number of inputs reduces significantly. This means fewer parameters or a simpler structure in the ML model. Also, fewer dimensions mean less computation time.

The dimensionality reduction technique has its applications in noise reduction, cluster analysis, data visualization, etc. Some of the common techniques for dimensionality reduction include Missing Value Ratio, Backward Feature Elimination, Independent Component Analysis, Random Filter, etc.

Word Embeddings (Unsupervised Learning)

A Word embedding is a learned representation of text. In this machine learning technique, the words with the same meaning have a similar representation. These words can also have approximate meanings. For example, these words are somehow related to one another- age, fitness, sports, etc. The benefit of word embeddings is it helps to reduce dimensionality, for word prediction, etc.

Natural Language Processing (Unsupervised Learning)

Natural Language Processing is the technique of making machines understand the text and spoken words, just like humans do. NLP combines computational linguistics with statistical, ML, and deep learning models. Some of the common applications of NLP include machine translation, text prediction, sentiment analysis, text classification, autocomplete & autocorrect, name entity recognition, co-reference resolution, natural language generation, speech recognition, etc.

To reduce the complexity involved in Natural Language Processing, there are several pre-trained NLP models available. Developers/researchers can fine-tune the existing models and make them do a better, complex task without having to build a new model from scratch.

Reinforcement Learning (Unsupervised Learning)

In Reinforcement learning, the machines find the best possible solution or way to act in a specific situation. It differs from supervised learning models in a way that there is a data set available with an answer key to give the correct answer. However, in the reinforcement model, the absence of a dataset binds the machine to learn from its own experience.

AI vs. Machine Learning vs. Deep Learning

First, it is important to gain a clear understanding of the basic concepts of artificial intelligence types. We often find the terms Artificial Intelligence and Machine Learning or Deep Learning being used interchangeably. Therefore, there is some confusion about what a machine learning model is and how it is different from an AI model.

Fig. 10

Artificial Intelligence (AI) includes the sub-fields Machine Learning (ML) and Deep Learning (DL)

Artificial Intelligence (AI)

Artificial Intelligence (AI) is a subfield within computer science associated with constructing machines that can simulate human intelligence. AI research deals with the question of how to create computers that are capable of intelligent behavior.

Machine Learning (ML)

Machine Learning (ML) is a subset within AI associated with providing machines the ability to learn from experience without the need to be programmed explicitly.

Or in simple words, ML or machine learning is a part of AI. So while all ML models are, by default, AI models, the opposite may not always be true. In ML, it's important to distinguish between supervised vs. unsupervised learning, and a hybrid version named semi-supervised learning. In short, supervised learning is where the algorithm is given a set of training data. Supervised models learn from ground truth data that was labeled manually by data scientists. In computer vision, this process is called image annotation.

The model uses this data to learn (training) how to make predictions on new data (inferencing). On the other hand, unsupervised learning is where the algorithm is given raw data that is not annotated. Here, the algorithm is not explicitly told what to do with it and must learn how to make predictions by itself. This type of ML model is suitable to perform specific tasks on distinct data types, for example, fraud detection or financial analysis, that require identifying a hidden structure in unlabeled data.

Deep Learning (DL)

Deep learning (DL) is a subset of machine learning, which is a subset of artificial intelligence. Deep learning is concerned with algorithms that can learn to recognize patterns in data, whereas machine learning is more general and deals with algorithms that can learn any kind of task.

WHAT IS AN AI MODEL?

In simple terms, an AI model is a tool or algorithm which is based on a certain data set through which it can arrive at a decision – all without the need for human interference in the decision-making process. An AI model is a program or algorithm that utilizes a set of data that enables it to recognize certain patterns. This allows it to reach a conclusion or make a prediction when provided with sufficient information, often a huge amount of data. Hence, AI models are particularly suitable for solving complex problems while providing higher efficiency/cost savings and accuracy compared to simple methods.

Barn owl or apple?

Image recognition tasks can be equally challenging for AI models and humans. If you are looking for a more detailed guide about the topic, we recommend our complete guide about the differences between Deep Learning vs. Machine Learning. What Is An ML Model? A machine learning model, or ML model, is a kind of AI model that uses a mathematical formula to make predictions about future events. It is trained on a set of data and then used to make predictions about new data. Some common examples of ML models include regression models and classification models.

What Is A DL Model?

Fig. 11. Barn owl or apple

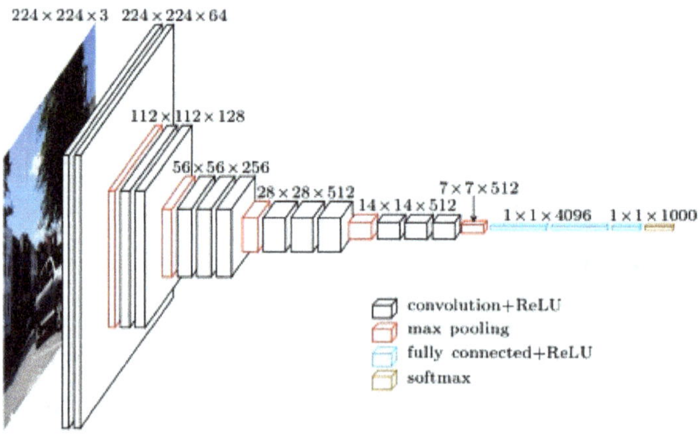

Fig. 12. VGG Deep Concolutional Neural Network Architecture

A deep learning model, or a DL model, is a neural network that has been trained to learn how to perform a task, such as recognizing objects in digital images and videos, or understanding human speech. Deep learning models are trained by using large sets of data and algorithms that enable the model to learn how to perform the task. The more data the model is trained on, the better it can learn to perform the task.

The term "deep" of "deep learning" refers to the fact that DL models are composed of multiple layers of neurons, or processing nodes. The deeper the model, the more layers of neurons it has. This allows the model to learn more complex tasks by breaking them down into smaller and smaller pieces. For example, ResNet is a deep learning model for computer vision tasks such as image recognition.

VGG Deep Concolutional Neural Network Architecture

YOLO, or "You Only Look Once," is a deep learning model for real-time object detection. Surpassing YOLOv4 and YOLOR, the latest version, YOLOv7, is super fast and very accurate, the current state of the art for several AI vision tasks.

Deploy an AI model To deploy and run an AI model, a computing device or server is needed that provides a lot of processing power and storage. ML frameworks like TensorFlow, PyTorch, or Caffe2 let you run an AI model with a few lines of code. While prototyping is simple, the management of AI pipelines and computing resources at scale is very complex and requires sophisticated infrastructures. This is why most AI projects fail to move beyond the PoC phase. There is a range of AI hardware suitable for different tasks.

Graphics Processing Units (GPU) are widely used for training and inference workloads (NVIDIA Jetson). Central Processing Units (CPU) are used primarily for inference, but also training workloads (e.g., Intel Xeon). Coprocessors and AI accelerators include Intel VPU, Google Coral TPU, and Qualcomm NPU.

In the early days, the Cloud was the only way to provide sufficient computing resources for AI workloads. Hosted platforms to deploy AI models include Viso Suite, Hugging Face, Google Colab, or Amazon SageMaker. In recent years, a new paradigm called Edge Computing made it possible to deploy models to the network edge (Edge AI). Running AI models at the Edge made it possible to build real-world applications that are more efficient, private, and robust.

This trend is accelerated by advances in deep learning that led to model frameworks becoming much lighter, smaller, and faster (Edge-optimized models include TensorFlow Lite or YOLOv7 Lite). Such AI models require several times cheaper hardware to run, leading to immense cost advantages. At viso.ai, we provide automated infrastructure to deploy DL models faster and more efficiently. Our enterprise platform Viso Suite provides a visual no-code interface to automate the deployment of AI models to the Edge and the Cloud.

The value of AI models in business Data and artificial intelligence are becoming increasingly important in business. Data is being generated at an unprecedented rate, and companies rely on AI models to make use of it. When applied to real-world problems, AI models can solve tasks that would otherwise be too difficult or time-consuming for humans to do. We see a few key strategies for how applying AI models will impact businesses:

Strategy #1: Collect data to build AI models

Strategy #2: Use AI models to generate new data

Strategy #3: Use AI models to understand data

Strategy #4: Use AI models to automate tasks.

- **Collect data to train** AI models The ability to collect data for training is of utmost value when competitors have no or limited access to data, or when it is difficult to obtain. Data enables businesses to train AI models and continuously re-train (improve) existing models. There are many ways to collect data, including scraping it from the web, or through the use of sensors or cameras. In general, access to large amounts of data enables the training of better-performing AI models and thus the development of competitive advantages.
- **AI models can be used to generate new data** A model can generate new data similar to the training data, for example, by using a Generative Adversarial Network (GAN). New, generative AI models provide image generation capabilities to create art and photorealistic images (such as DALL-E 2). AI models can also be used to generate completely new data sets (synthetic data) or artificially bloat existing data (data augmentation) to train more robust algorithms.
- **AI models can be used to analyze existing data** Model inference is the process of using a model to predict the output for a given input. This is done by applying the model algorithm to new input data (existing data or real-time sensory data) that the model has never "seen" before and then interpreting the results. Practical AI applications usually use model inference to "apply" a trained model in business tasks, for example, to perform person recognition or object detection and tracking in a video stream.
- **AI models can be used to automate tasks** To apply AI models in business, they are integrated into pipelines. A pipeline consists of several steps, including data acquisition, transformation, data analysis, and data output. In computer vision applications, a vision pipeline acquires the video stream and applies image processing before feeding individual images into the DL model. When applied in manufacturing, for example, this can be used to

automate visual inspection or perform automated object counting of bottles on conveyor belts.

TRIBES OF AI

The concept of the tribes was introduced by Pedro Domingos in "The Master Algorithm : How the Quest for the Ultimate Learning Machine Will Remake Our World". It provides a good explanation about the characteristics of each of the tribes and which Machine Learning algorithm falls under what category. In this blog we will try to explain every tribe as simply as possible with an example to understand the tribes better.

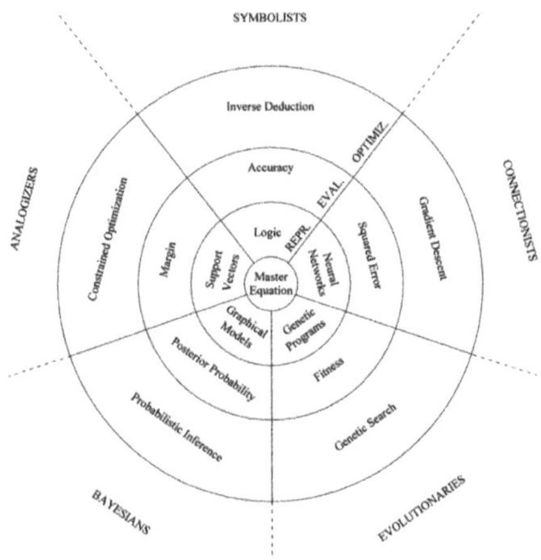

Fig. 13. Tribes of AI

The five tribes can be visualised by three parameters -

- **Representation:** This describes how the algorithm associated with each tribe can be represented.
- **Evaluation:** This describes how the algorithm is evaluated depending upon the tribe it belongs to.
- **Optimisation Driver:** This describes how an algorithm can be optimised to achieve optimum result.

The term "Master Equation" in the centre of the diagram above refers to the ultimate goal of creating an algorithm which can possess characteristics of all the tribes.

In the following section, we will explain all the characteristics of each tribe and how the functioning of an algorithm relates to it.basis

The Symbolists

This tribe focuses on symbol manipulation where questions can be presented as equations and can be answered using expressions. They work on the concept of inverse deduction where inverse deduction means starting with certain knowledge and exponentially gaining the latter by answering the aforementioned questions.

Decision Tree

One of the best algorithms to visualise the characteristics of this tribe is Decision Tree (Fig. 14). Decision Tree starts with certain knowledge which can be achieved using Information Gain or Gini Index to identify the root node and gathers further information using equations to produce child nodes and the final leaf node (decision).

Based on the three parameters mentioned above the symbolists can be,

- **Represented:** Using *logic*, which is a tree like structure which makes it easier for humans to interpret.

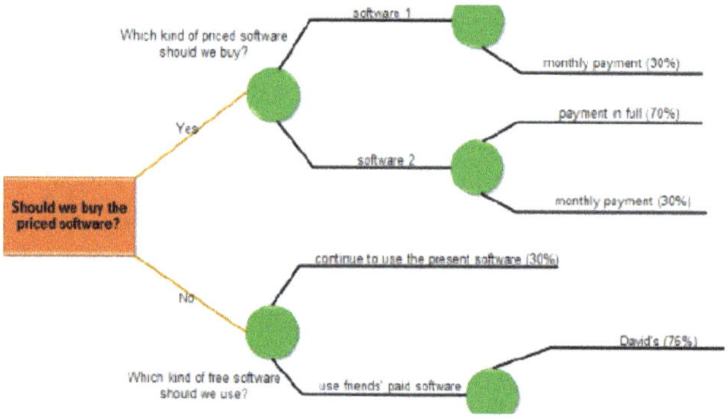

Fig. 14. Decision Tree

- **Evaluated:** Using *accuracy,* which describes how accurate the result of the tree is.
- **Optimised:** Using *inverse deduction*, where the decision tree uses the concept of pruning.

The Connectionists

This tribe focuses on concepts of how a human brain functions and tries to mimic its functionalities by reverse-engineering and trying to build the neurons in the brain artificially which is referred as Perceptrons. The collection of multiple perceptrons is called an Artificial Neural Network

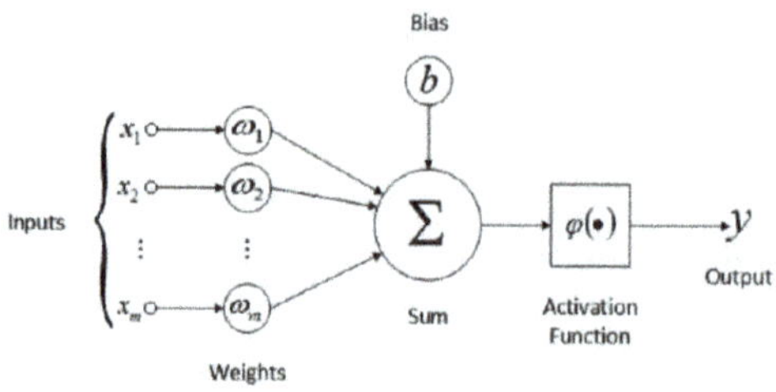

Fig. 15. The Connectionists

REPRESENTATION OF A PERCEPTRON

Convolutional Neural Networks (CNN)

One of the most commonly used algorithms which relates to the characteristics of this tribe is Convolutional Neural networks, which is a collection of perceptrons that understands and translates data input of one form to the desired output of another form.

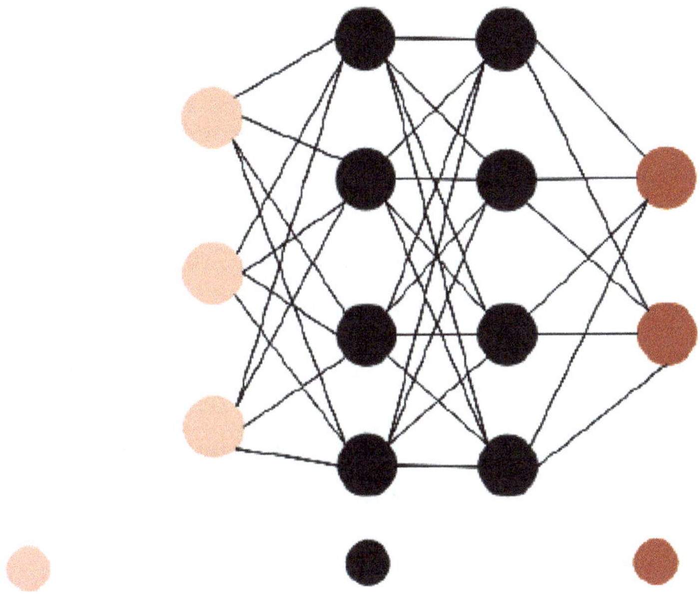

Fig. 16. Convolution Neural Network

Based on the three parameters mentioned above the Connectionist tribe can be:

- **Represented**: Using *neural networks*, which are layers of perceptrons passing input from one layer to the next.
- **Evaluated**: Using *squared error*, lower the error, better the performance of the neural network.
- **Optimised**: Using *gradient descent*, where the neural network uses the concept of weights and adjusts them to reduce the error and optimises the neural network.

The Evolutionaraies

The Evolutionaries follow the enhance-ment of DNA by a natural selection process where a pool of genes (usually a set of instructions), i.e., population. From this population of genes, either two individuals mate to form a new one or one individual mutates to form a the new generation. This is coined crossover and mutation respectively.

Fig. 17. The Evolutionaraies

Genetic Programming

Genetic programming is a technique of evolving programs following the process of genes, crossover and mutation as described above for a particular task and creates multiple solutions for every program and the best solution is selected.

Based on the three parameters mentioned above the Evolutionary tribe can be,

- **Represented:** Using ***genetic programming***, which is described above.
- **Evaluated:** Using ***fitness function***, chooses the best solution from pool of solutions.
- **Optimised:** Using ***genetic search,*** this helps select the most optimised solution for the problem at hand.

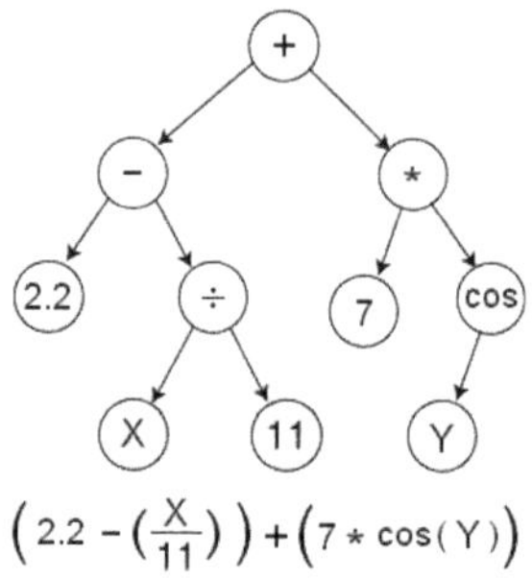

Fig. 18. Genetic Programming

THE BAYESIANS

For the Bayesians, all real world data is uncertain and knowledge can be derived using this uncertainity. This uncertainity can be reduced by relating two or more events to formulate incomplete data by identifying the conditional probability between those events.

Bayesian Network

The Bayes Net considers an event occurance and predicts that one of the known causes was the contributing factor. It works on concepts of probabilistic inference and is based on the Bayes Theorem.

- These networks are represented using Directed Acyclic Graphs with every node having a probability table.
- Based on the three parameters mentioned above the Bayesian tribe can be,
- **Represented:** Using graphical models, such as directed acyclic graphs.
- **Evaluated:** Using posterior probability, which helps determine that an event will happen after all evidence or background information has been taken into account.
- **Optimised:** Usinga probabilistic inference, which can be defined as the task of deriving the probability of one or more random variables taking a specific value or set of values.

The Analogizers

The analogizers work on concepts of identifying similarities between situations or things. The main challenge is to identify how similar these situations are. Similarity is also one of the central ideas of machine learning.

K-Nearest Neighbour

K-Nearest Neighbour algorithm also known as KNN is one of the common examples for the analogizers. This algorithm calculates the similarities between two items using a distance measure such as Euclidean distance or Manhattan distance.

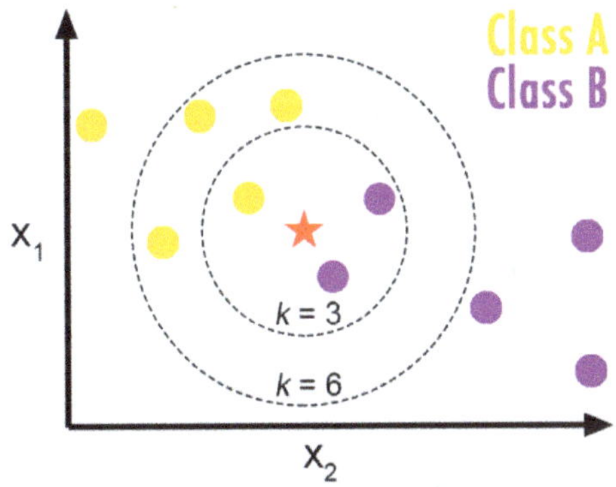

Fig. 19. Example for KNN

The K in the KNN is the factor that decides how many datapoints to consider while finding the cluster for that data point.

Based on the three parameters mentioned above the Analogizer tribe can be,

- **Represented**: Using *support vectors*, these vectors differentiate between two data points for the task at hand.
- **Evaluated**: Using *margins*, which acts as a boundary line to decide the category of a data point.

NEURAL NETWORKS

Definition

Neural networks are a set of algorithms, modeled loosely after the human brain, that are designed to recognize patterns. They interpret sensory data through a kind of machine perception, labeling or clustering raw input. The patterns they recognize are numerical, contained in vectors, into which all real-world data, be it images, sound, text or time series, must be translated.

Neural networks help us cluster and classify. You can think of them as a clustering and classification layer on top of the data you store and manage. They help to group unlabeled data according to similarities among the example inputs, and they classify data when they have a labeled dataset to train on. (Neural networks can also extract features that are fed to other algorithms for clustering and classification; so you can think of deep neural networks as components of larger machine-learning applications involving algorithms for reinforcement learning, classification and regression.)

What kind of problems does deep learning solve, and more importantly, can it solve yours? To know the answer, you need to ask a few questions:

- **What outcomes do I care about?** In a classification problem, those outcomes are labels that could be applied to data: for example, spam or not_spam in an email filter, good_guy or bad_guy in fraud detection, angry_customer or happy_customer in customer relationship management. Other types of problems include anomaly detection (useful in fraud detection and predictive maintenance of manufacturing equipment), and clustering, which is useful in recommendation systems that surface similarities.
- **Do I have the right data?** For example, if you have a classification problem, you'll need labeled data. Is the dataset you need publicly available, or can you create it (with a data annotation service like Scale or AWS Mechanical Turk)? In this example, spam emails would be labeled as spam, and the labels would enable the algorithm to map from inputs to the classifications you care about. You can't know that you have the right data until you get your hands on it. If you are a data scientist working on a problem, you can't trust anyone to tell you whether the data is good enough. Only direct exploration of the data will answer this question.

A Few Concrete Examples

Deep learning maps inputs to outputs. It finds correlations. It is known as a "universal approximator", because it can learn to approximate an unknown function f(x) = y between any input x and any output y, assuming they are related at all (by correlation or causation, for example). In the process of learning, a neural network finds the right f, or the correct manner of transforming x into y, whether that be f(x) = 3x + 12 or f(x) = 9x - 0.1. Here are a few examples of what deep learning can do.

Classification

All classification tasks depend upon labeled datasets; that is, humans must transfer their knowledge to the dataset in order for a neural network to learn the correlation between labels and data. This is known as *supervised learning.*

- Detect faces, identify people in images, recognize facial expressions (angry, joyful)
- Identify objects in images (stop signs, pedestrians, lane markers...)
- Recognize gestures in video
- Detect voices, identify speakers, transcribe speech to text, recognize sentiment in voices
- Classify text as spam (in emails), or fraudulent (in insurance claims); recognize sentiment in text (customer feedback)

Any labels that humans can generate, any outcomes that you care about and which correlate to data, can be used to train a neural network.

Clustering

Clustering or grouping is the detection of similarities. Deep learning does not require labels to detect similarities. Learning without labels is called *unsupervised learning.* Unlabeled data is the majority of data in the world. One law of machine learning is: the more data an algorithm can train on, the more accurate it will be. Therefore, unsupervised learning has the potential to produce highly accurate models.

- **Search:** Comparing documents, images or sounds to surface similar items.
- **Anomaly Detection:** The flipside of detecting similarities is detecting anomalies, or unusual behavior. In many cases, unusual behavior correlates highly with things you want to detect and prevent, such as fraud.

Predictive Analytics: Regressions

With classification, deep learning is able to establish correlations between, say, pixels in an image and the name of a person. You might call this a static prediction. By the same token, exposed to enough of the right data, deep learning is able to establish correlations between present events and future events. It can run regression between the past and the future. The future event is like the label in a sense. Deep learning doesn't necessarily care about time, or the fact that something hasn't happened yet. Given a time series, deep learning may read a string of number and predict the number most likely to occur next.

- Hardware breakdowns (data centers, manufacturing, transport)
- Health breakdowns (strokes, heart attacks based on vital stats and data from wearables)
- Customer churn (predicting the likelihood that a customer will leave, based on web activity and metadata)
- Employee turnover (ditto, but for employees)

The better we can predict, the better we can prevent and pre-empt. As you can see, with neural networks, we're moving towards a world of fewer surprises. Not zero surprises, just marginally fewer. We're also moving toward a world of smarter agents that combine neural networks with other algorithms like reinforcement learning to attain goals.

NEURAL NETWORK ELEMENTS

Deep learning is the name we use for "stacked neural networks"; that is, networks composed of several layers.

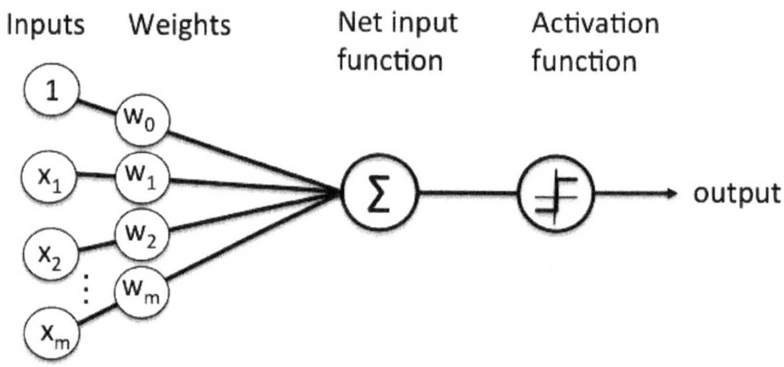

Fig. 20. Diagram of what one node might look like

The layers are made of *nodes*. A node is just a place where computation happens, loosely patterned on a neuron in the human brain, which fires when it encounters sufficient stimuli. A node combines input from the data with a set of coefficients, or weights, that either amplify or dampen that input, thereby assigning significance to inputs with regard to the task the algorithm is trying to learn; e.g. which input is most helpful is classifying data without error? These input-weight products are summed and then the sum is passed through a node's so-called activation function, to determine whether and to what extent that signal should progress further through the network to affect the ultimate outcome, say, an act of classification. If the signals passes through, the neuron has been "activated."

Pairing the model's adjustable weights with input features is how we assign significance to those features with regard to how the neural network classifies and clusters input.

Key Concepts of Deep Neural Networks

Deep-learning networks are distinguished from the more commonplace single-hidden-layer neural networks by their **depth**; that is, the number of node layers through which data must pass in a multistep process of pattern recognition.

Earlier versions of neural networks such as the first perceptrons were shallow, composed of one input and one output layer, and at most one hidden layer in between. More than three layers (including input and output) qualifies as "deep" learning. So *deep* is not just a buzzword to make algorithms seem like they read Sartre and listen to bands you haven't heard of yet. It is a strictly defined term that means more than one hidden layer.

In deep-learning networks, each layer of nodes trains on a distinct set of features based on the previous layer's output. The further you advance into the neural net, the more complex the features your nodes can recognize, since they aggregate and recombine features from the previous layer.

This is known as **feature hierarchy**, and it is a hierarchy of increasing complexity and abstraction. It makes deep-learning networks capable of handling very large, high-dimensional data sets with billions of parameters that pass through nonlinear functions.

Above all, these neural nets are capable of discovering latent structures within **unlabeled, unstructured data**, which is the vast majority of data in the world. Another word for unstructured data is *raw media*; i.e. pictures, texts, video and audio recordings. Therefore, one of the problems deep learning solves best is in processing and clustering the world's raw, unlabeled media, discerning similarities and anomalies in data that no human has organized in a relational database or ever put a name to.

For example, deep learning can take a million images, and cluster them according to their similarities: cats in one corner, ice breakers in another, and in a third all the photos of your grandmother. This is the basis of so-called smart photo albums.

Now apply that same idea to other data types: Deep learning might cluster raw text such as emails or news articles. Emails full of angry complaints might cluster in one corner of the vector space, while satisfied customers, or spambot messages, might cluster in others. This is the basis of various messaging filters, and can be used in customer-relationship management (CRM). The same applies to voice messages.

With time series, data might cluster around normal/healthy behavior and anomalous/dangerous behavior. If the time series data is being generated by a smart phone, it will provide insight into users' health and habits; if it is being generated by an autopart, it might be used to prevent catastrophic breakdowns.

Deep-learning networks perform **automatic feature extraction** without human intervention, unlike most traditional machine-learning algorithms. Given that feature extraction is a task that can take teams of data scientists years to accomplish, deep learning is a way to circumvent the chokepoint of limited experts. It augments the powers of small data science teams, which by their nature do not scale.

When training on unlabeled data, each node layer in a deep network learns features automatically by repeatedly trying to reconstruct the input from which it draws its samples, attempting to minimize the difference between the network's guesses and the probability distribution of the input data itself. Restricted Boltzmann machines, for examples, create so-called reconstructions in this manner.

In the process, these neural networks learn to recognize correlations between certain relevant features and optimal results – they draw connections between feature signals and what those features represent, whether it be a full reconstruction, or with labeled data.

A deep-learning network trained on labeled data can then be applied to unstructured data, giving it access to much more input than machine-learning nets. This is a recipe for higher performance: the more data a net can train on, the more accurate it is likely to be. (Bad algorithms trained on lots of data can outperform good algorithms trained on very little.) Deep learning's ability to process and learn from huge quantities of unlabeled data give it a distinct advantage over previous algorithms. Deep-learning networks end in an output layer: a logistic, or softmax, classifier that assigns a likelihood to a particular outcome or label. We call that predictive, but it is predictive in a broad sense. Given raw data in the form of an image, a deep-learning network may decide, for example, that the input data is 90 percent likely to represent a person.

Example: Feedforward Networks

Our goal in using a neural net is to arrive at the point of least error as fast as possible. We are running a race, and the race is around a track, so we pass the same points repeatedly in a loop. The starting line for the race is the state in which our weights are initialized, and the finish line is the state of those parameters when they are capable of producing sufficiently accurate classifications and predictions.

The race itself involves many steps, and each of those steps resembles the steps before and after. Just like a runner, we will engage in a repetitive act over and over to arrive at the finish. Each step for a neural network involves a guess, an error measurement and a slight update in its weights, an incremental adjustment to the coefficients, as it slowly learns to pay attention to the most important features.

A collection of weights, whether they are in their start or end state, is also called a model, because it is an attempt to model data's relationship to ground-truth labels, to grasp the data's structure. Models normally start out bad and end up less bad, changing over time as the neural network updates its parameters.

This is because a neural network is born in ignorance. It does not know which weights and biases will translate the input best to make the correct guesses. It has to start out with a guess, and then try to make better guesses sequentially as it learns from its mistakes. (You can think of a neural network as a miniature enactment of the scientific method, testing hypotheses and trying again – only it is the scientific method with a blindfold on. Or like a child: they are born not knowing much, and through exposure to life experience, they slowly learn to solve problems in the world. For neural networks, data is the only experience.). Here is a simple explanation of what happens during learning with a feedforward neural network, the simplest architecture to explain.

Input enters the network. The coefficients, or weights, map that input to a set of guesses the network makes at the end.

input * weight = guess

Weighted input results in a guess about what that input is. The neural then takes its guess and compares it to a ground-truth about the data, effectively asking an expert "Did I get this right?"

ground truth - guess = error

The difference between the network's guess and the ground truth is its *error*. The network measures that error, and walks the error back over its model, adjusting weights to the extent that they contributed to the error.

error * weight's contribution to error = adjustment

The three pseudo-mathematical formulas above account for the three key functions of neural networks: scoring input, calculating loss and applying an update to the model – to begin the three-step process over again. A neural network is a corrective feedback loop, rewarding weights that support its correct guesses, and punishing weights that lead it to err.

Multiple Linear Regression

Despite their biologically inspired name, artificial neural networks are nothing more than math and code, like any other machine-learning algorithm. In fact, anyone who understands *linear regression*, one of first methods you learn in statistics, can understand how a neural net works. In its simplest form, linear regression is expressed as

Y_hat = bX + a

where Y_hat is the estimated output, X is the input, b is the slope and a is the intercept of a line on the vertical axis of a two-dimensional graph. (To make this more concrete: X could be radiation exposure and Y could be the cancer risk; X could be daily pushups and Y_hat could be the total weight you can benchpress; X the amount of fertilizer and Y_hat the size of the crop.) You can imagine that every time you add a unit to X, the dependent variable Y_hat increases proportionally, no matter how far along you are on the X axis. That simple relation between two variables moving up or down together is a starting point.

The next step is to imagine multiple linear regression, where you have many input variables producing an output variable. It's typically expressed like this:

Y_hat = b_1*X_1 + b_2*X_2 + b_3*X_3 + a

(To extend the crop example above, you might add the amount of sunlight and rainfall in a growing season to the fertilizer variable, with all three affecting Y_hat.)

Now, that form of multiple linear regression is happening at every node of a neural network. For each node of a single layer, input from each node of the previous layer is recombined with input from every other node. That is, the inputs are mixed in different proportions, according to their coefficients, which are different leading into each node of the subsequent layer. In this way, a net tests which combination of input is significant as it tries to reduce error.

Once you sum your node inputs to arrive at Y_hat, it's passed through a non-linear function. Here's why: If every node merely performed multiple linear regression, Y_hat would increase linearly and without limit as the X's increase, but that doesn't suit our purposes.

What we are trying to build at each node is a switch (like a neuron...) that turns on and off, depending on whether or not it should let the signal of the input pass through to affect the ultimate decisions of the network.

When you have a switch, you have a classification problem. Does the input's signal indicate the node should classify it as enough, or not_enough, on or off? A binary decision can be expressed by 1 and 0, and logistic regression is a non-linear function that squashes input to translate it to a space between 0 and 1.

The nonlinear transforms at each node are usually s-shaped functions similar to logistic regression. They go by the names of sigmoid (the Greek word for "S"), tanh, hard tanh, etc., and they shaping the output of each node.

The output of all nodes, each squashed into an s-shaped space between 0 and 1, is then passed as input to the next layer in a feed forward neural network, and so on until the signal reaches the final layer of the net, where decisions are made.

Gradient Descent

The name for one commonly used optimization function that adjusts weights according to the error they caused is called "gradient descent." Gradient is another word for slope, and slope, in its typical form on an x-y graph, represents how two variables relate to each other: rise over run, the change in money over the change in time, etc. In this particular case, the slope we care about describes the relationship between the network's error and a single weight; i.e. that is, how does the error vary as the weight is adjusted.

To put a finer point on it, which weight will produce the least error? Which one correctly represents the signals contained in the input data, and translates them to a correct classification? Which one can hear "nose" in an input image, and know that should be labeled as a face and not a frying pan?

As a neural network learns, it slowly adjusts many weights so that they can map signal to meaning correctly. The relationship between network *Error* and each of those *weights* is a derivative, *dE/dw*, that measures the degree to which a slight change in a weight causes a slight change in the error.

Each weight is just one factor in a deep network that involves many transforms; the signal of the weight passes through activations and sums over several layers, so we use the chain rule of calculus to march back through the networks activations and outputs and finally arrive at the weight in question, and its relationship to overall error.

The chain rule in calculus states that

$$dz/dx = dz/dy \,.\, dy/dx$$

In a feedforward network, the relationship between the net's error and a single weight will look something like this:

$$\frac{dError}{dweight} = \frac{dError}{dactivation} * \frac{dactivation}{dweight}$$

that is, given two variables, Error and weight, that are mediated by a third variable, activation, through which the weight is passed, you can calculate how a change in weight affects a change in Error by first calculating how a change in activation affects a change in Error, and how a change in weight affects a change in activation. The essence of learning in deep learning is nothing more than that: adjusting a model's weights in response to the error it produces, until you can't reduce the error any more.

Logistic Regression

On a deep neural network of many layers, the final layer has a particular role. When dealing with labeled input, the output layer classifies each example, applying the most likely label. Each node on the output layer represents one label, and that node turns on or off according to the strength of the signal it receives from the previous layer's input and parameters.

Each output node produces two possible outcomes, the binary output values 0 or 1, because an input variable either deserves a label or it does not. After all, there is no such thing as a little pregnant.

While neural networks working with labeled data produce binary output, the input they receive is often continuous. That is, the signals that the network receives as input will span a range of values and include any number of metrics, depending on the problem it seeks to solve.

For example, a recommendation engine has to make a binary decision about whether to serve an ad or not. But the input it bases its decision on could include how much a customer has spent on Amazon in the last week, or how often that customer visits the site.

So the output layer has to condense signals such as $67.59 spent on diapers, and 15 visits to a website, into a range between 0 and 1; i.e. a probability that a given input should be labeled or not.

The mechanism we use to convert continuous signals into binary output is called logistic regression. The name is unfortunate, since logistic regression is used for classification rather than regression in the linear sense that most people are familiar with. It calculates the probability that a set of inputs match the label.

$$F(x) = 1/1 + e^{-x}$$

Let's examine this little formula.

For continuous inputs to be expressed as probabilities, they must output positive results, since there is no such thing as a negative probability. That's why you see input as the exponent of *e* in the denominator – because exponents force our results to be greater than zero. Now consider the relationship of *e*'s exponent to the fraction 1/1. One, as we know, is the ceiling of a probability, beyond which our results can't go without being absurd. (We're 120% sure of that.)

As the input *x* that triggers a label grows, the expression *e to the x* shrinks toward zero, leaving us with the fraction 1/1, or 100%, which means we approach (without ever quite reaching) absolute certainty that the label applies. Input that correlates negatively with your output will have its value flipped by the negative sign on *e*'s exponent, and as that negative signal grows, the quantity *e to the x* becomes larger, pushing the entire fraction ever closer to zero.

Now imagine that, rather than having *x* as the exponent, you have the sum of the products of all the weights and their corresponding inputs – the total signal passing through your net. That's what you're feeding into the logistic regression layer at the output layer of a neural network classifier.

With this layer, we can set a decision threshold above which an example is labeled 1, and below which it is not. You can set different thresholds as you prefer – a low threshold will increase the number of false positives, and a higher one will increase the number of false negatives – depending on which side you would like to err.

NEURAL NETWORKS & ARTIFICIAL INTELLIGENCE

In some circles, neural networks are synonymous with AI. In others, they are thought of as a "brute force" technique, characterized by a *lack* of intelligence, because they start with a blank slate, and they hammer their way through to an accurate model. By this interpretation,neural networks are effective, but inefficient in their approach to modeling, since they don't make assumptions about functional dependencies between output and input.

For what it's worth, the foremost AI research groups are pushing the edge of the discipline by training larger and larger neural networks. Brute force works. It is a necessary, if not sufficient, condition to AI breakthroughs. OpenAI's pursuit of more general AI emphasizes a brute force approach, which has proven effective with well-known models such as GPT-3.

Algorithms such as Hinton's capsule networks require far fewer instances of data to converge on an accurate model; that is, present research has the potential to resolve the brute force inefficiencies of deep learning.

While neural networks are useful as a function approximator, mapping inputs to outputs in many tasks of perception, to achieve a more general intelligence, they can be combined with other AI methods to perform more complex tasks.

For example, deep reinforcement learning embeds neural networks within a reinforcement learning framework, where they map actions to rewards in order to achieve goals. Deepmind's victories in video games and the board game of go are good examples.

Backpropagation Process

Backpropagation is the essence of neural network training. It is the method of fine-tuning the weights of a neural network based on the error rate obtained in the previous epoch (i.e., iteration). Proper tuning of the weights allows you to reduce error rates and make the model reliable by increasing its generalization.

Backpropagation in neural network is a short form for "backward propagation of errors." It is a standard method of training artificial neural networks. This method helps calculate the gradient of a loss function with respect to all the weights in the network. Backpropagation is one of the important concepts of a neural network. Our task is to classify our data best. For this, we have to update the weights of parameter and bias, but how can we do that in a deep neural network? In the linear regression model, we use gradient descent to optimize the parameter. Similarly here we also use gradient descent algorithm using Backpropagation.

For a single training example, **Backpropagation** algorithm calculates the gradient of the **error function**. Backpropagation can be written as a function of the neural network. Backpropagation algorithms are a set of methods used to efficiently train artificial neural networks following a gradient descent approach which exploits the chain rule.

The main features of Backpropagation are the iterative, recursive and efficient method through which it calculates the updated weight to improve the network until it is not able to perform the task for which it is being trained. Derivatives of the activation function to be known at network design time is required to Backpropagation.

Gradient Descent

A *gradient* is a slope whose angle we can measure. Like all slopes, it can be expressed as a relationship between two variables: "y over x", or *rise over run*. In this case, the y is the error produced by the neural network, and x is the parameter of the neural network. The parameter has a relationship to the error, and by changing the parameter, we can increase or decrease the error. So the gradient tells us the change we can expect in y with regard to x.

To obtain this information, we must use differential calculus, which enables us to measure *instantaneous rates of change*, in this case is the tangent of a changing slope expressing the relationship of the weight to the neural network's error. As the parameter changes, the error changes, and we want to move both variables in the direction of less error.

Obviously, a neural network has many parameters, so what we're really measuring are the *partial derivatives* of each parameter's contribution to the total change in error.

What's more, neural networks have parameters that process the input data sequentially, one after another. Therefore, backpropagation establishes the relationship between the neural network's error and the parameters of the net's last layer; then it establishes the relationship between the parameters of the neural net's last layer those the parameters of the second-to-last layer, and so forth, in an application of the *chain rule of calculus*.

It's interesting to note that backpropagation in artificial neural networks has echoes in the functioning of biological neurons, which respond to rewards such as dopamine to reinforce how they fire; i.e. how they interpret the world. Dopaminergenic behavior tends to strengthen the ties between the neurons involved, and helps those ties last longer. While biological neurons do not perform backpropagation precisely (see further reading below), they appear to achieve the same effect by other means. That is, backpropagation allows artificial neural networks to roughly mimic certain narrow mechanisms of intelligence that are found in the example of intelligence that we have: the human brain.

Now, how error function is used in Backpropagation and how Backpropagation works? Let start with an example and do it mathematically to understand how exactly updates the weight using Backpropagation.

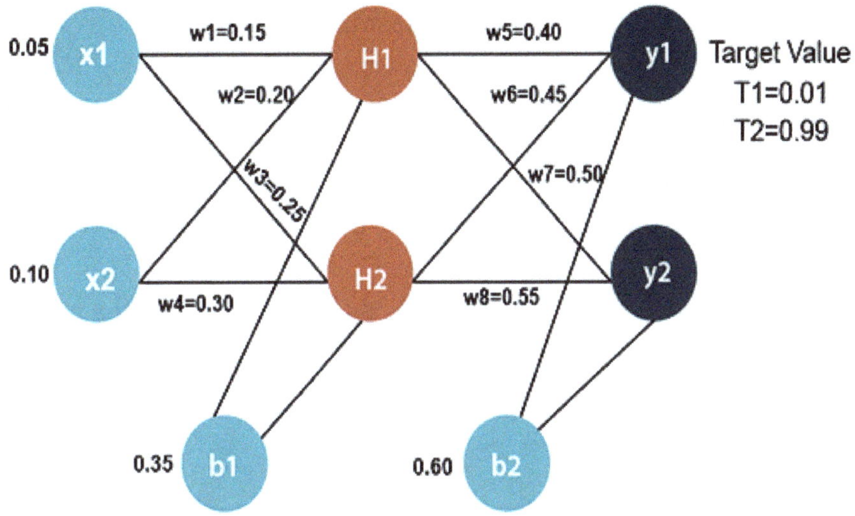

Fig. 21. Backpropagation and how Backpropagation works?

Input values

X1=0.05

X2=0.10

Initial weight

W1=0.15 w5=0.40

W2=0.20 w6=0.45

W3=0.25 w7=0.50

W4=0.30 w8=0.55

Bias Values

b1=0.35 b2=0.60

Target Values

T1=0.01

T2=0.99

Now, we first calculate the values of H1 and H2 by a forward pass.

Forward Pass

To find the value of H1 we first multiply the input value from the weights as

$H1=x1\times w_1+x2\times w_2+b1$

$H1=0.05\times0.15+0.10\times0.20+0.35$

$\mathbf{H1=0.3775}$

We will calculate the value of H2 in the same way as H1

$H2=x1\times w_3+x2\times w_4+b1$

$H2=0.05\times0.25+0.10\times0.30+0.35$

$\mathbf{H2=0.3925}$

Now, we calculate the values of y1 and y2 in the same way as we calculate the H1 and H2.

To find the value of y1, we first multiply the input value i.e., the outcome of H1 and H2 from the weights as

$y1=H1\times w_5+H2\times w_6+b2$

$y1=0.593269992\times0.40+0.596884378\times0.45+0.60$

$\mathbf{y1=1.10590597}$

We will calculate the value of y2 in the same way as y1

$y2=H1\times w_7+H2\times w_8+b2$

$y2=0.593269992\times0.50+0.596884378\times0.55+0.60$

$\mathbf{y2=1.2249214}$

Our target values are 0.01 and 0.99. Our y1 and y2 value is not matched with our target values T1 and T2.

CONVOLUTIONAL NEURAL NETWORKS

To reiterate from the Neural Networks Learn Hub article, neural networks are a subset of machine learning, and they are at the heart of deep learning algorithms. They are comprised of node layers, containing an input layer, one or more hidden layers, and an output layer. Each node connects to another and has an associated weight and threshold. If the output of any individual node is above the specified threshold value, that node is activated, sending data to the next layer of the network. Otherwise, no data is passed along to the next layer of the network.

While we primarily focused on feedforward networks in that article, there are various types of neural nets, which are used for different use cases and data types. For example, recurrent neural networks are commonly used for natural language processing and speech recognition whereas convolutional neural networks (ConvNets or CNNs) are more often utilized for classification and computer vision tasks. Prior to CNNs, manual, time-consuming feature extraction methods were used to identify objects in images. However, convolutional neural networks now provide a more scalable approach to image classification and object recognition tasks, leveraging principles from linear algebra, specifically matrix multiplication, to identify patterns within an image. That said, they can be computationally demanding, requiring graphical processing units (GPUs) to train models.

How do convolutional neural networks work?

Convolutional neural networks are distinguished from other neural networks by their superior performance with image, speech, or audio signal inputs. They have three main types of layers, which are:

- Convolutional layer
- Pooling layer
- Fully-connected (FC) layer

The convolutional layer is the first layer of a convolutional network. While convolutional layers can be followed by additional convolutional layers or pooling layers, the fully-connected layer is the final layer. With each layer, the CNN increases in its complexity, identifying greater portions of the image. Earlier layers focus on simple features, such as colors and edges. As the image data progresses through the layers of the CNN, it starts to recognize larger elements or shapes of the object until it finally identifies the intended object.

Convolutional Layer

The convolutional layer is the core building block of a CNN, and it is where the majority of computation occurs. It requires a few components, which are input data, a filter, and a feature map. Let's assume that the input will be a color image, which is made up of a matrix of pixels in 3D. This means that the input will have three dimensions—a height, width, and depth—which correspond to RGB in an image. We also have a feature detector, also known as a kernel or a filter, which will move across the receptive fields of the image, checking if the feature is present. This process is known as a convolution.

The feature detector is a two-dimensional (2-D) array of weights, which represents part of the image. While they can vary in size, the filter size is typically a 3x3 matrix; this also determines the size of the receptive field. The filter is then applied to an area of the image, and a dot product is calculated between the input pixels and the filter. This dot product is then fed into an output array. Afterwards, the filter shifts by a stride, repeating the process until the kernel has swept across the entire image. The final output from the series of dot products from the input and the filter is known as a feature map, activation map, or a convolved feature.

As you can see in the image above, each output value in the feature map does not have to connect to each pixel value in the input image. It only needs to connect to the receptive field, where the filter is being applied. Since the output array does not need to map directly to each input value, convolutional (and pooling) layers are commonly referred to as "partially connected" layers. However, this characteristic can also be described as local connectivity.

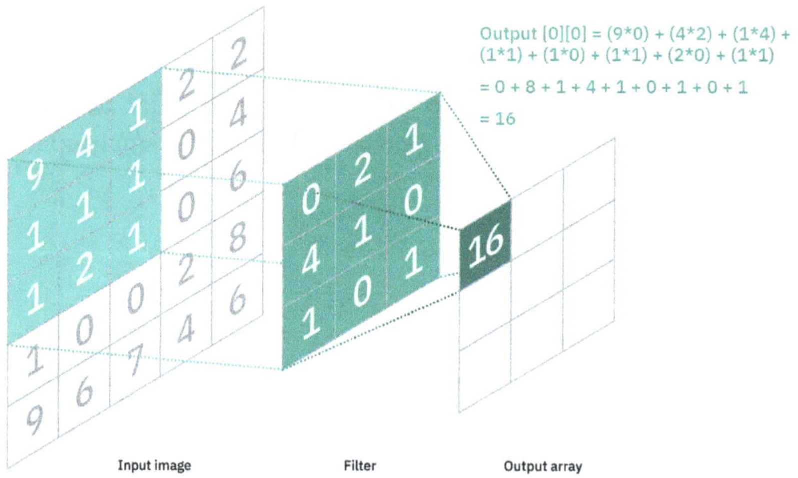

Fig. 22. Convolutional Layer

Note that the weights in the feature detector remain fixed as it moves across the image, which is also known as parameter sharing. Some parameters, like the weight values, adjust during training through the process of backpropagation and gradient descent. However, there are three hyperparameters which affect the volume size of the output that need to be set before the training of the neural network begins. These include:

- The **number of filters** affects the depth of the output. For example, three distinct filters would yield three different feature maps, creating a depth of three.
- **Stride** is the distance, or number of pixels, that the kernel moves over the input matrix. While stride values of two or greater is rare, a larger stride yields a smaller output.
- **Zero-padding** is usually used when the filters do not fit the input image. This sets all elements that fall outside of the input matrix to zero, producing a larger or equally sized output. There are three types of padding:
  - **Valid padding:** This is also known as no padding. In this case, the last convolution is dropped if dimensions do not align.
  - **Same padding:** This padding ensures that the output layer has the same size as the input layer

- **Full padding:** This type of padding increases the size of the output by adding zeros to the border of the input.

After each convolution operation, a CNN applies a Rectified Linear Unit (ReLU) transformation to the feature map, introducing nonlinearity to the model.

As we mentioned earlier, another convolution layer can follow the initial convolution layer. When this happens, the structure of the CNN can become hierarchical as the later layers can see the pixels within the receptive fields of prior layers. As an example, let's assume that we're trying to determine if an image contains a bicycle. You can think of the bicycle as a sum of parts. It is comprised of a frame, handlebars, wheels, pedals, et cetera. Each individual part of the bicycle makes up a lower-level pattern in the neural net, and the combination of its parts represents a higher-level pattern, creating a feature hierarchy within the CNN.

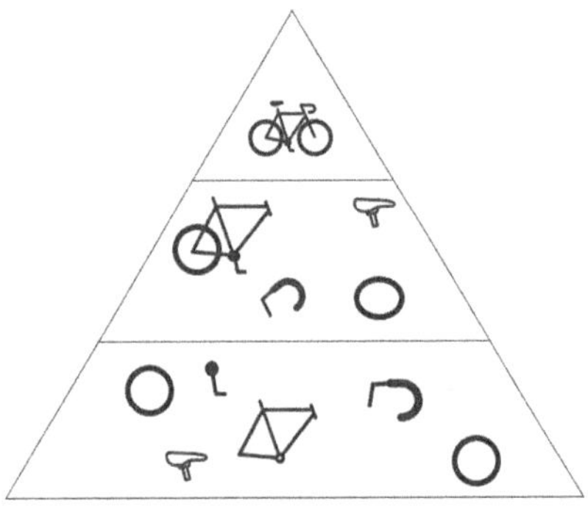

Fig. 23.

Ultimately, the convolutional layer converts the image into numerical values, allowing the neural network to interpret and extract relevant patterns.

Pooling Layer

Pooling layers, also known as downsampling, conducts dimensionality reduction, reducing the number of parameters in the input. Similar to the convolutional layer, the pooling operation sweeps a filter across the entire input, but the difference is that this filter does not have any weights. Instead, the kernel applies an aggregation function to the values within the receptive field, populating the output array. There are two main types of pooling:

- **Max pooling:** As the filter moves across the input, it selects the pixel with the maximum value to send to the output array. As an aside, this approach tends to be used more often compared to average pooling.
- **Average pooling:** As the filter moves across the input, it calculates the average value within the receptive field to send to the output array.

While a lot of information is lost in the pooling layer, it also has a number of benefits to the CNN. They help to reduce complexity, improve efficiency, and limit risk of overfitting.

Fully-Connected Layer

The name of the full-connected layer aptly describes itself. As mentioned earlier, the pixel values of the input image are not directly connected to the output layer in partially connected layers.

However, in the fully-connected layer, each node in the output layer connects directly to a node in the previous layer.

This layer performs the task of classification based on the features extracted through the previous layers and their different filters. While convolutional and pooling layers tend to use ReLu functions, FC layers usually leverage a softmax activation function to classify inputs appropriately, producing a probability from 0 to 1.

Types of convolutional neural networks

Kunihiko Fukushima and Yann LeCun laid the foundation of research around convolutional neural networks in their work in 1980 (PDF, 1.1 MB) (link resides outside IBM) and 1989 (PDF, 5.5 MB)(link resides outside of IBM), respectively. More famously, Yann LeCun successfully applied backpropagation to train neural networks to identify and recognize patterns within a series of handwritten zip codes. He would continue his research with his team throughout the 1990s, culminating with "LeNet-5", (PDF, 933 KB) (link resides outside IBM), which applied the same principles of prior research to document recognition. Since then, a number of variant CNN architectures have emerged with the introduction of new datasets, such as MNIST and CIFAR-10, and competitions, like ImageNet Large Scale Visual Recognition Challenge (ILSVRC). Some of these other architectures include:

- AlexNet (PDF, 1.4 MB) (link resides outside IBM)
- VGGNet (PDF, 195 KB) (link resides outside IBM)
- GoogLeNet (PDF, 1.3 MB) (link resides outside IBM)
- ResNet (PDF, 800 KB) (link resides outside IBM)
- ZFNet

However, LeNet-5 is known as the classic CNN architecture.

Convolutional neural networks and computer vision

Convolutional neural networks power image recognition and computer vision tasks. Computer vision is a field of artificial intelligence (AI) that enables computers and systems to derive meaningful information from digital images, videos and other visual inputs, and based on those inputs, it can take action. This ability to provide recommendations distinguishes it from image recognition tasks. Some common applications of this computer vision today can be seen in:

- **Marketing:** Social media platforms provide suggestions on who might be in photograph that has been posted on a profile, making it easier to tag friends in photo albums.
- **Healthcare:** Computer vision has been incorporated into radiology technology, enabling doctors to better identify cancerous tumors in healthy anatomy.
- **Retail:** Visual search has been incorporated into some e-commerce platforms, allowing brands to recommend items that would complement an existing wardrobe.
- **Automotive**: While the age of driverless cars hasn't quite emerged, the underlying technology has started to make its way into automobiles, improving driver and passenger safety through features like lane line detection.

Convolutional neural networks and IBM

For decades now, IBM has been a pioneer in the development of AI technologies and neural networks, highlighted by the development and evolution of IBM Watson. Watson is now a trusted solution for enterprises looking to apply advanced visual recognition and deep learning techniques to their systems using a proven tiered approach to AI adoption and implementation.

IBM's Watson Visual Recognition makes it easy to extract thousands of labels from your organization's images and detect for specific content out-of-the-box. You can also build custom models to detect for specific content in images inside your applications. For more information on how to quickly and accurately tag, classify and search visual content using machine learning, explore IBM Watson Visual Recognition.

DEEPDREAM

DeepDream is an algorithm through which computers can picture patterns with the help of a neural network. We can compare it with a child who looks at the cloud and profusely tries to create random shapes and images (a phenomenon also known as pareidolia). Similarly, DeepDream provides too much interpretation and magnifies the compositions whenever it encounters an image.

DeepDream algorithm initiates the process by forwarding a particular picture or image through the network and then it starts measuring the gradient of the image with respect to a specific activation layer. In the next step, the picture is adjusted in order to improve these activations and amplify the patterns which result in a dream-like picture. This entire process is also known as Inceptionism.

The entire process of enhancing the pattern of images is very much dependent on how the algorithm has been trained. Therefore, if an algorithm has been instructed to recognize the faces in any image then that particular algorithm will also try to deduce the faces from any given image using the algorithmic pareidolia.

How the DeepDream algorithm functions

Now that we have properly understood what DeepDream is, it is time for us to understand the functions of this algorithm in more detail. Before that let us have a look at how the convolutional neural networks work:

- First, we provide an image to the convolutional neural networks and the first layer of the network distinguishes the low-level features such as edges.
- In the next step, the second layer of the network will try to expose the higher-level features of the picture such as trees, cars, faces, etc.
- Lastly, the remaining layers will try to collect all of these features and complete the interpretations so that the pictures can be categorized accordingly.

In convolutional neural networks, there are different layers available to perform different tasks. On the other hand, in the DeepDream algorithm, we can take any particular feature (be it high level or low level) and increase its activation so that it can have a huge impact on the image.

Let us have a look at the function of the DeepDream algorithm in detail:

- Whenever you try to give a picture (as an input) to a trained artificial neural network, the neurons kickstart and initiate activation.
- The DeepDream algorithm tries to modify the input image and in the process, it boosts some of the neurons more than others. We can specify the type of layer and neuron we want to strengthen precisely.
- The process will continue until all the elements of the input image have been disclosed appropriately.

For example, if we have used a specific layer to discover the cat faces while we have provided the image of a cloud (as input) then, the DeepDream algorithm will meticulously convert the image and will begin to produce cat faces on the blue sky.

Processing an image with DeepDream

Here is a step-by-step process through which you can apply the DeepDream algorithm to any image:

- Use an already trained ResNet, ANN, CNN, etc. to forward an image.

- Now choose a specific layer while remembering that the first layer analyses the edges whereas the deeper layers analyze different shapes and figures.
- It is time to measure the output from the layer of interest.
- Measure the gradient of the image in regard to the already chosen activation layer.
- Adjust the image in order to amplify the activations and the image will turn out like a dream-like hallucinated image.
- Continue to repeat this operation on multiple images.

Prepare the feature extraction model

Download and prepare a pre-trained image classification model. You will use InceptionV3 which is similar to the model originally used in DeepDream. Note that any pre-trained model will work, although you will have to adjust the layer names below if you change this.

```
base_model = tf.keras.applications.InceptionV3
(include_top=False, weights='imagenet')
```

The idea in DeepDream is to choose a layer (or layers) and maximize the "loss" in a way that the image increasingly "excites" the layers. The complexity of the features incorporated depends on layers chosen by you, i.e, lower layers produce strokes or simple patterns, while deeper layers give sophisticated features in images, or even whole objects.

The InceptionV3 architecture is quite large (for a graph of the model architecture see TensorFlow's research repo). For DeepDream, the layers of interest are those where the convolutions are concatenated. There are 11 of these layers in InceptionV3, named 'mixed0' though 'mixed10'. Using different layers will result in different dream-like images. Deeper layers respond to higher-level features (such as eyes and faces), while earlier layers respond to simpler features (such as edges, shapes, and textures). Feel free to experiment with the layers selected below, but keep in mind that deeper layers (those with a higher index) will take longer to train on since the gradient computation is deeper.

```
# Maximize the activations of these layers
names = ['mixed3', 'mixed5']
layers = [base_model.get_layer(name).output for name in names]
# Create the feature extraction model
dream_model = tf.keras.Model(inputs=base_model.input, outputs=layers)
```

Calculate loss

The loss is the sum of the activations in the chosen layers. The loss is normalized at each layer so the contribution from larger layers does not outweigh smaller layers. Normally, loss is a quantity you wish to minimize via gradient descent. In DeepDream, you will maximize this loss via gradient ascent.

```
def calc_loss(img, model):
  # Pass forward the image through the model to retrieve the activations.
  # Converts the image into a batch of size 1.
  img_batch = tf.expand_dims(img, axis=0)
  layer_activations = model(img_batch)
  if len(layer_activations) == 1:
    layer_activations = [layer_activations]
  losses = []
  for act in layer_activations:
    loss = tf.math.reduce_mean(act)
    losses.append(loss)
  return  tf.reduce_sum(losses)
```

Gradient ascent

Once you have calculated the loss for the chosen layers, all that is left is to calculate the gradients with respect to the image, and add them to the original image.

Adding the gradients to the image enhances the patterns seen by the network. At each step, you will have created an image that increasingly excites the activations of certain layers in the network.

The method that does this, below, is wrapped in a tf.function for performance. It uses an input_signature to ensure that the function is not retraced for different image sizes or steps/step_size values. See the Concrete functions guide for details.

```
class DeepDream(tf.Module):
def __init__(self, model):
self.model = model
@tf.function(
    input_signature=(
     tf.TensorSpec(shape=[None,None,3], dtype=tf.float32),
      tf.TensorSpec(shape=[], dtype=tf.int32),
      tf.TensorSpec(shape=[], dtype=tf.float32),)
```

```
    )
    def __call__(self, img, steps, step_size):
      print("Tracing")
      loss = tf.constant(0.0)
      for n in tf.range(steps):
        with tf.GradientTape() as tape:
          # This needs gradients relative to 'img'
          # 'GradientTape' only watches 'tf.Variable's by default
          tape.watch(img)
          loss = calc_loss(img, self.model)
          # Calculate the gradient of the loss with respect to the pixels of the input image.
        gradients = tape.gradient(loss, img)
        # Normalize the gradients.
        gradients /= tf.math.reduce_std(gradients) + 1e-8
          # In gradient ascent, the "loss" is maximized so that the input image increasingly "excites" the layers.
        # You can update the image by directly adding the gradients (because they're the same shape!)
        img = img + gradients*step_size
        img = tf.clip_by_value(img, -1, 1)
      return loss, img
  deepdream = DeepDream(dream_model)
```

Main Loop

```
  def run_deep_dream_simple(img, steps=100, step_size=0.01):
    # Convert from uint8 to the range expected by the model.
    img = tf.keras.applications.inception_v3.preprocess_input(img)
    img = tf.convert_to_tensor(img)
    step_size = tf.convert_to_tensor(step_size)
    steps_remaining = steps
    step = 0
    while steps_remaining:
```

```
    if steps_remaining>100:
      run_steps = tf.constant(100)
    else:
      run_steps = tf.constant(steps_remaining)
    steps_remaining -= run_steps
    step += run_steps
    loss, img = deepdream(img, run_steps, tf.constant(step_size))
    display.clear_output(wait=True)
    show(deprocess(img))
    print ("Step {}, loss {}".format(step, loss))
  result = deprocess(img)
  display.clear_output(wait=True)
  show(result)
  return result
dream_img = run_deep_dream_simple(img=original_img,
                                  steps=100, step_size=0.01)
```

Fig. 24

Taking it up an octave

Pretty good, but there are a few issues with this first attempt:

- The output is noisy (this could be addressed with a tf.image.total_variation loss).
- The image is low resolution.
- The patterns appear like they're all happening at the same granularity.

One approach that addresses all these problems is applying gradient ascent at different scales. This will allow patterns generated at smaller scales to be incorporated into patterns at higher scales and filled in with additional detail.

To do this you can perform the previous gradient ascent approach, then increase the size of the image (which is referred to as an octave), and repeat this process for multiple octaves.

```
import time
start = time.time()
OCTAVE_SCALE = 1.30
img = tf.constant(np.array(original_img))
base_shape = tf.shape(img)[:-1]
float_base_shape = tf.cast(base_shape, tf.float32)
for n in range(-2, 3):
  new_shape = tf.cast(float_base_shape*(OCTAVE_SCALE**n), tf.int32)
  img = tf.image.resize(img, new_shape).numpy()
  img = run_deep_dream_simple(img=img, steps=50, step_size=0.01)
display.clear_output(wait=True)
img = tf.image.resize(img, base_shape)
img = tf.image.convert_image_dtype(img/255.0, dtype=tf.uint8)
show(img)
end = time.time()
end-start
```

Optional: Scaling up with tiles

One thing to consider is that as the image increases in size, so will the time and memory necessary to perform the gradient calculation. The above octave implementation will not work on very large images, or many octaves.

To avoid this issue you can split the image into tiles and compute the gradient for each tile.

Applying random shifts to the image before each tiled computation prevents tile seams from appearing.

Start by implementing the random shift:

```
def random_roll(img, maxroll):
  # Randomly shift the image to avoid tiled boundaries.
```

```
    shift = tf.random.uniform(shape=[2], minval=-maxroll, maxval=maxroll,
dtype=tf.int32)
  img_rolled = tf.roll(img, shift=shift, axis=[0,1])
  return shift, img_rolled
shift, img_rolled = random_roll(np.array(original_img), 512)
show(img_rolled)
```

Here is a tiled equivalent of the deepdream function defined earlier:

```
class TiledGradients(tf.Module):
  def __init__(self, model):
    self.model = model
  @tf.function(
      input_signature=(
        tf.TensorSpec(shape=[None,None,3], dtype=tf.float32),
        tf.TensorSpec(shape=[2], dtype=tf.int32),
        tf.TensorSpec(shape=[], dtype=tf.int32),)
  )
  def __call__(self, img, img_size, tile_size=512):
    shift, img_rolled = random_roll(img, tile_size)
    # Initialize the image gradients to zero.
    gradients = tf.zeros_like(img_rolled)
    # Skip the last tile, unless there's only one tile.
    xs = tf.range(0, img_size[1], tile_size)[:-1]
    if not tf.cast(len(xs), bool):
      xs = tf.constant([0])
    ys = tf.range(0, img_size[0], tile_size)[:-1]
    if not tf.cast(len(ys), bool):
      ys = tf.constant([0])
    for x in xs:
      for y in ys:
        # Calculate the gradients for this tile.
        with tf.GradientTape() as tape:
```

```
        # This needs gradients relative to 'img_rolled'.
        # 'GradientTape' only watches 'tf.Variable's by default.
        tape.watch(img_rolled)
        # Extract a tile out of the image.
        img_tile = img_rolled[y:y+tile_size, x:x+tile_size]
        loss = calc_loss(img_tile, self.model)
      # Update the image gradients for this tile.
      gradients = gradients + tape.gradient(loss, img_rolled)
    # Undo the random shift applied to the image and its gradients.
    gradients = tf.roll(gradients, shift=-shift, axis=[0,1])
    # Normalize the gradients.
    gradients /= tf.math.reduce_std(gradients) + 1e-8
    return gradients
get_tiled_gradients = TiledGradients(dream_model)
```

Putting this together gives a scalable, octave-aware deepdream implementation:

```
def run_deep_dream_with_octaves(img, steps_per_octave=100, step_size=0.01,
                                octaves=range(-2,3), octave_scale=1.3):
  base_shape = tf.shape(img)
  img = tf.keras.utils.img_to_array(img)
  img = tf.keras.applications.inception_v3.preprocess_input(img)
  initial_shape = img.shape[:-1]
  img = tf.image.resize(img, initial_shape)
  for octave in octaves:
    # Scale the image based on the octave
     new_size = tf.cast(tf.convert_to_tensor(base_shape[:-1]), tf.float32)*(octave_
scale**octave)
    new_size = tf.cast(new_size, tf.int32)
    img = tf.image.resize(img, new_size)
    for step in range(steps_per_octave):
      gradients = get_tiled_gradients(img, new_size)
      img = img + gradients*step_size
```

```
        img = tf.clip_by_value(img, -1, 1)
        if step % 10 == 0:
          display.clear_output(wait=True)
          show(deprocess(img))
          print ("Octave {}, Step {}".format(octave, step))
    result = deprocess(img)
    return result
img = run_deep_dream_with_octaves(img=original_img, step_size=0.01)
display.clear_output(wait=True)
img = tf.image.resize(img, base_shape)
img = tf.image.convert_image_dtype(img/255.0, dtype=tf.uint8)
show(img)
```

GENERATIVE ADVERSARIAL NETWORKS (GANS)

A **generative adversarial network (GAN)** is a class of machine learning frameworks designed by Ian Goodfellow and his colleagues in June 2014 Two neural networks contest with each other in the form of a zero-sum game, where one agent's gain is another agent's loss.

Given a training set, this technique learns to generate new data with the same statistics as the training set. For example, a GAN trained on photographs can generate new photographs that look at least superficially authentic to human observers, having many realistic characteristics. Though originally proposed as a form of generative model for unsupervised learning, GANs have also proved useful for semi-supervised learning, fully supervised learning, and reinforcement learning.

The core idea of a GAN is based on the "indirect" training through the discriminator, another neural network that can tell how "realistic" the input seems, which itself is also being updated dynamically. This means that the generator is not trained to minimize the distance to a specific image, but rather to fool the discriminator. This enables the model to learn in an unsupervised manner.

GANs are similar to mimicry in evolutionary biology, with an evolutionary arms race between both networks.

Generative Adversarial Networks, or GANs for short, are an approach to generative modeling using deep learning methods, such as convolutional neural networks.

Generative modeling is an unsupervised learning task in machine learning that involves automatically discovering and learning the regularities or patterns in input data in such a way that the model can be used to generate or output new examples that plausibly could have been drawn from the original dataset.

GANs are a clever way of training a generative model by framing the problem as a supervised learning problem with two sub-models: the generator model that we train to generate new examples, and the discriminator model that tries to classify examples as either real (from the domain) or fake (generated). The two models are trained together in a zero-sum game, adversarial, until the discriminator model is fooled about half the time, meaning the generator model is generating plausible examples. GANs are an exciting and rapidly changing field, delivering on the promise of generative models in their ability to generate realistic examples across a range of problem domains, most notably in image-to-image translation tasks such as translating photos of summer to winter or day to night, and in generating photorealistic photos of objects, scenes, and people that even humans cannot tell are fake.

In this post, you will discover a gentle introduction to Generative Adversarial Networks, or GANs.

After reading this post, you will know:

- Context for GANs, including supervised vs. unsupervised learning and discriminative vs. generative modeling.
- GANs are an architecture for automatically training a generative model by treating the unsupervised problem as supervised and using both a generative and a discriminative model.
- GANs provide a path to sophisticated domain-specific data augmentation and a solution to problems that require a generative solution, such as image-to-image translation.

Generative vs. Discriminative Algorithms

To understand GANs, you should know how generative algorithms work, and for that, contrasting them with discriminative algorithms is instructive. Discriminative algorithms try to classify input data; that is, given the features of an instance of data, they predict a label or category to which that data belongs.

For example, given all the words in an email (the data instance), a discriminative algorithm could predict whether the message is spam or not_spam. spam is one of the labels, and the bag of words gathered from the email are the features that constitute the input data. When this problem is expressed mathematically, the label is called y and the features are called x. The formulation p(y|x) is used to mean "the probability of y given x", which in this case would translate to "the probability that an email is spam given the words it contains."

So discriminative algorithms map features to labels. They are concerned solely with that correlation. One way to think about generative algorithms is that they do the opposite. Instead of predicting a label given certain features, they attempt to predict features given a certain label.

The question a generative algorithm tries to answer is: Assuming this email is spam, how likely are these features? While discriminative models care about the relation between y and x, generative models care about "how you get x." They allow you to capture p(x|y), the probability of x given y, or the probability of features given a label or category. (That said, generative algorithms can also be used as classifiers. It just so happens that they can do more than categorize input data.)

Another way to think about it is to distinguish discriminative from generative like this:

- Discriminative models learn the boundary between classes
- Generative models model the distribution of individual classes

Optimize Your Simulations With Deep Reinforcement Learning »

How GANs Work

One neural network, called the *generator*, generates new data instances, while the other, the *discriminator*, evaluates them for authenticity; i.e. the discriminator decides whether each instance of data that it reviews belongs to the actual training dataset or not.

Let's say we're trying to do something more banal than mimic the Mona Lisa. We're going to generate hand-written numerals like those found in the MNIST dataset, which is taken from the real world. The goal of the discriminator, when shown an instance from the true MNIST dataset, is to recognize those that are authentic.

Meanwhile, the generator is creating new, synthetic images that it passes to the discriminator. It does so in the hopes that they, too, will be deemed authentic, even though they are fake. The goal of the generator is to generate passable hand-written digits: to lie without being caught. The goal of the discriminator is to identify images coming from the generator as fake.

Here are the steps a GAN takes:

- The generator takes in random numbers and returns an image.
- This generated image is fed into the discriminator alongside a stream of images taken from the actual, ground-truth dataset.
- The discriminator takes in both real and fake images and returns probabilities, a number between 0 and 1, with 1 representing a prediction of authenticity and 0 representing fake.

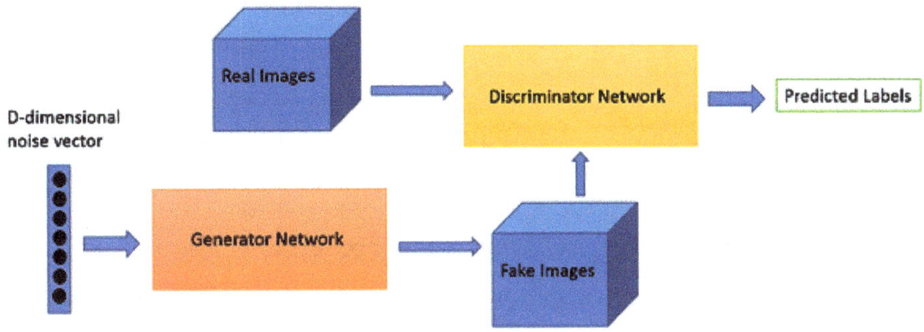

Fig. 25

So you have a double feedback loop:

- The discriminator is in a feedback loop with the ground truth of the images, which we know.
- The generator is in a feedback loop with the discriminator.

You can think of a GAN as the opposition of a counterfeiter and a cop in a game of cat and mouse, where the counterfeiter is learning to pass false notes, and the cop is learning to detect them. Both are dynamic; i.e. the cop is in training, too (to extend the analogy, maybe the central bank is flagging bills that slipped through), and each side comes to learn the other's methods in a constant escalation.

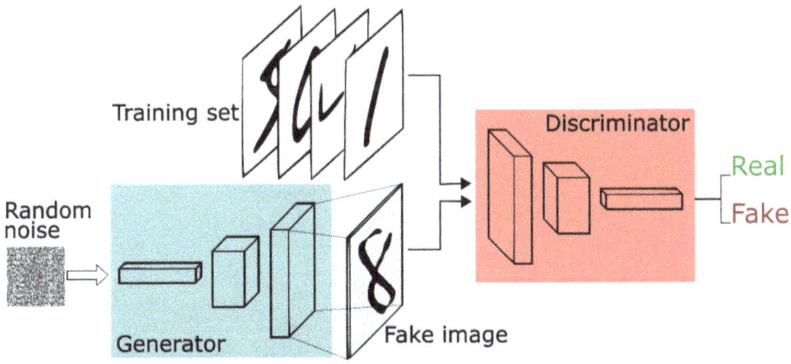

Fig. 26 Actor-critic model

For MNIST, the discriminator network is a standard convolutional network that can categorize the images fed to it, a binomial classifier labeling images as real or fake. The generator is an inverse convolutional network, in a sense: While a standard convolutional classifier takes an image and downsamples it to produce a probability, the generator takes a vector of random noise and upsamples it to an image. The first throws away data through downsampling techniques like maxpooling, and the second generates new data.

Both nets are trying to optimize a different and opposing objective function, or loss function, in a zero-zum game. This is essentially an actor-critic model. As the discriminator changes its behavior, so does the generator, and vice versa. Their losses push against each other.

If you want to learn more about generating images, Brandon Amos wrote a great post about interpreting images as samples from a probability distribution.

How does GANs work?

Generative Adversarial Networks (GANs) can be broken down into three parts:

- **Generative:** To learn a generative model, which describes how data is generated in terms of a probabilistic model.
- **Adversarial:** The training of a model is done in an adversarial setting.
- **Networks:** Use deep neural networks as the artificial intelligence (AI) algorithms for training purpose.

In GANs, there is a **generator** and a **discriminator**. The Generator generates fake samples of data(be it an image, audio, etc.) and tries to fool the Discriminator. The Discriminator, on the other hand, tries to distinguish between the real and fake samples. The Generator and the Discriminator are both Neural Networks and they both run in competition with each other in the training phase. The steps are repeated several times and in this, the Generator and Discriminator get better and better in their respective jobs after each repetition. The working can be visualized by the diagram given below (Fig. 27):

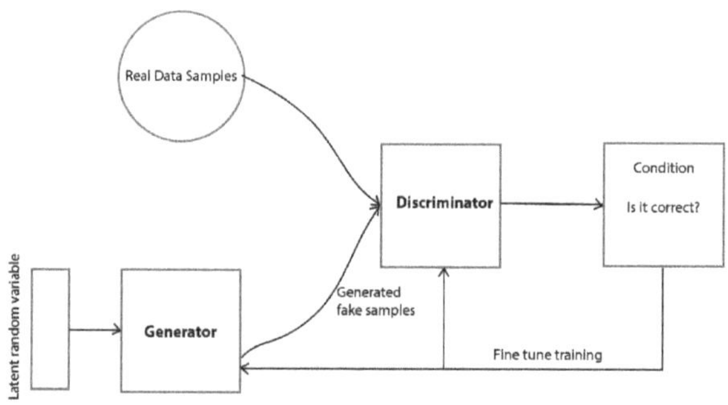

Fig. 27

Here, the generative model captures the distribution of data and is trained in such a manner that it tries to maximize the probability of the Discriminator in making a mistake. The Discriminator, on the other hand, is based on a model that estimates the probability that the sample that it got is received from the training data and not from the Generator.

The GANs are formulated as a minimax game, where the Discriminator is trying to minimize its reward **V(D, G)** and the Generator is trying to minimize the Discriminator's reward or in other words, maximize its loss.

So, basically, training a GAN has two parts:

- **Part 1:** The Discriminator is trained while the Generator is idle. In this phase, the network is only forward propagated and no back-propagation is done. The Discriminator is trained on real data for n epochs, and see if it can correctly predict them as real. Also, in this phase, the Discriminator is also trained on the fake generated data from the Generator and see if it can correctly predict them as fake.
- **Part 2:** The Generator is trained while the Discriminator is idle. After the Discriminator is trained by the generated fake data of the Generator, we can get its predictions and use the results for training the Generator and get better from the previous state to try and fool the Discriminator.

The above method is repeated for a few epochs and then manually check the fake data if it seems genuine. If it seems acceptable, then the training is stopped, otherwise, its allowed to continue for few more epochs.

Different types of GANs:

GANs are now a very active topic of research and there have been many different types of GAN implementation. Some of the important ones that are actively being used currently are described below:

- **Vanilla GAN:** This is the simplest type GAN. Here, the Generator and the Discriminator are simple multi-layer perceptrons. In vanilla GAN, the algorithm is really simple, it tries to optimize the mathematical equation using stochastic gradient descent.
- **Conditional GAN (CGAN):** CGAN can be described as a deep learning method in which some conditional parameters are put into place. In CGAN, an additional parameter 'y' is added to the Generator for generating the corresponding data. Labels are also put into the input to the Discriminator in order for the Discriminator to help distinguish the real data from the fake generated data.
- **Deep Convolutional GAN (DCGAN):** DCGAN is one of the most popular also the most successful implementation of GAN. It is composed of ConvNets in place of multi-layer perceptrons. The ConvNets are implemented without max pooling, which is in fact replaced by convolutional stride. Also, the layers are not fully connected.
- **Laplacian Pyramid GAN (LAPGAN):** The Laplacian pyramid is a linear invertible image representation consisting of a set of band-pass images, spaced an octave apart, plus a low-frequency residual. This approach uses multiple numbers of Generator and Discriminator networks and different

levels of the Laplacian Pyramid. This approach is mainly used because it produces very high-quality images. The image is down-sampled at first at each layer of the pyramid and then it is again up-scaled at each layer in a backward pass where the image acquires some noise from the Conditional GAN at these layers until it reaches its original size.

- **Super Resolution GAN (SRGAN):** SRGAN as the name suggests is a way of designing a GAN in which a deep neural network is used along with an adversarial network in order to produce higher resolution images. This type of GAN is particularly useful in optimally up-scaling native low-resolution images to enhance its details minimizing errors while doing so.

Sample Python code implementing a Generative Adversarial Network

GANs are very computationally expensive. They require high powered GPUs and a lot of time (a large number of epochs) to produce good results. For our example, we will be using the famous MNIST dataset and use it to produce a clone of a random digit.

```
# importing the necessary libraries and the MNIST dataset
import tensorflow as tf
import numpy as np
import matplotlib.pyplot as plt
from tensorflow.examples.tutorials.mnist import input_data
mnist = input_data.read_data_sets("MNIST_data")
# defining functions for the two networks.
# Both the networks have two hidden layers
# and an output layer which are densely or
# fully connected layers defining the
# Generator network function
def generator(z, reuse = None):
  with tf.variable_scope('gen', reuse = reuse):
    hidden1 = tf.layers.dense(inputs = z, units = 128,
                activation = tf.nn.leaky_relu)
    hidden2 = tf.layers.dense(inputs = hidden1,
      units = 128, activation = tf.nn.leaky_relu)
    output = tf.layers.dense(inputs = hidden2,
      units = 784, activation = tf.nn.tanh)
```

```
        return output
# defining the Discriminator network function
def discriminator(X, reuse = None):
    with tf.variable_scope('dis', reuse = reuse):
        hidden1 = tf.layers.dense(inputs = X, units = 128,
                        activation = tf.nn.leaky_relu)
        hidden2 = tf.layers.dense(inputs = hidden1,
                units = 128, activation = tf.nn.leaky_relu)
        logits = tf.layers.dense(hidden2, units = 1)
        output = tf.sigmoid(logits)
        return output, logits
# creating placeholders for the outputs
tf.reset_default_graph()
real_images = tf.placeholder(tf.float32, shape =[None, 784])
z = tf.placeholder(tf.float32, shape =[None, 100])
G = generator(z)
D_output_real, D_logits_real = discriminator(real_images)
D_output_fake, D_logits_fake = discriminator(G, reuse = True)
# defining the loss function
def loss_func(logits_in, labels_in):
    return tf.reduce_mean(tf.nn.sigmoid_cross_entropy_with_logits(
                    logits = logits_in, labels = labels_in))
# Smoothing for generalization
D_real_loss = loss_func(D_logits_real, tf.ones_like(D_logits_real)*0.9)
D_fake_loss = loss_func(D_logits_fake, tf.zeros_like(D_logits_real))
D_loss = D_real_loss + D_fake_loss
G_loss = loss_func(D_logits_fake, tf.ones_like(D_logits_fake))
# defining the learning rate, batch size,
# number of epochs and using the Adam optimizer
lr = 0.001 # learning rate
# Do this when multiple networks
```

```
# interact with each other
 # returns all variables created(the two
# variable scopes) and makes trainable true
tvars = tf.trainable_variables()
d_vars =[var for var in tvars if 'dis' in var.name]
g_vars =[var for var in tvars if 'gen' in var.name]
D_trainer = tf.train.AdamOptimizer(lr).minimize(D_loss, var_list = d_vars)
G_trainer = tf.train.AdamOptimizer(lr).minimize(G_loss, var_list = g_vars)
batch_size = 100 # batch size
epochs = 500 # number of epochs. The higher the better the result
init = tf.global_variables_initializer()
# creating a session to train the networks
samples =[] # generator examples
with tf.Session() as sess:
   sess.run(init)
   for epoch in range(epochs):
      num_batches = mnist.train.num_examples//batch_size
      for i in range(num_batches):
         batch = mnist.train.next_batch(batch_size)
         batch_images = batch[0].reshape((batch_size, 784))
         batch_images = batch_images * 2-1
         batch_z = np.random.uniform(-1, 1, size =(batch_size, 100))
         _= sess.run(D_trainer, feed_dict ={real_images:batch_images, z:batch_z})
         _= sess.run(G_trainer, feed_dict ={z:batch_z})
      print("on epoch{}".format(epoch))
      sample_z = np.random.uniform(-1, 1, size =(1, 100))
      gen_sample = sess.run(generator(z, reuse = True),
                        feed_dict ={z:sample_z})
      samples.append(gen_sample)
# result after 0th epoch
plt.imshow(samples[0].reshape(28, 28))
```

```
# result after 499th epoch
plt.imshow(samples[49].reshape(28, 28))
Output:
on epoch0
on epoch1
...
...
...
on epoch498
on epoch499
```

ARTIFICIAL INTELLIGENCE CAN CONVERT 2D IMAGES INTO 3D

Using deep learning techniques, the team from University of California, Los Angeles (UCLA) devised a technique that extends the capabilities of fluorescence microscopy, which allows scientists to precisely label parts of living cells and tissue with dyes that glow under special lighting.

In a study published in the journal Nature Methods, the scientists also reported that their framework, called "Deep-Z," was able to fix errors or aberrations in images, such as when a sample is tilted or curved.

Further, they demonstrated that the system could take 2D images from one type of microscope and virtually create 3D images of the sample as if they were obtained by another, more advanced microscope.

"This is a very powerful new method that is enabled by deep learning to perform 3D imaging of live specimens, with the least exposure to light, which can be toxic to samples," said senior author Aydogan Ozcan, UCLA chancellor's professor of electrical and computer engineering.

In addition to sparing specimens from potentially damaging doses of light, this system could offer biologists and life science researchers a new tool for 3D imaging that is simpler, faster and much less expensive than current methods.

The opportunity to correct for aberrations may allow scientists studying live organisms to collect data from images that otherwise would be unusable.

Investigators could also gain virtual access to expensive and complicated equipment, said researchers.

"Deep-Z" was taught using experimental images from a scanning fluorescence microscope, which takes pictures focused at multiple depths to achieve 3D imaging of samples.

In thousands of training runs, the neural network learned how to take a 2D image and infer accurate 3D slices at different depths within a sample.

Then, the framework was tested blindly – fed with images that were not part of its training, with the virtual images compared to the actual 3D slices obtained from a scanning microscope, providing an excellent match.

The researchers also found that Deep-Z could produce 3D images from 2D surfaces where samples were tilted or curved.

"This feature was actually very surprising," said Yichen Wu, a UCLA graduate student who is co-first author of the publication. "With it, you can see through curvature or other complex topology that is very challenging to image."

ARCHIGAN

AI will soon massively empower architects in their day-to-day practice. This potential is around the corner and my work provides a proof of concept. The framework used in my work offers a springboard for discussion, inviting architects to start engaging with AI, and data scientists to consider Architecture as a field of investigation. Where Generative Adversarial Neural Networks (GANs) get leveraged to design floor plans, and entire buildings.

Fig. 28. GAN-Generated masterplan

Researcher believe a statistical approach to design conception will shape AI's potential for Architecture. This approach is less deterministic and more holistic in character. Rather than using machines to optimize a set of variables, relying on them to extract significant qualities and mimicking them all along the design process represents a paradigm shift.

Let's unpack floor plan design into 3 distinct steps:

- **(I)** building footprint massing
- **(II)** program repartition
- **(III)** furniture layout

Each step corresponds to a **Pix2Pix GAN-model** trained to perform one of the 3 tasks above. By nesting these models one after the other, I create an entire apartment building "*generation stack*" while allowing for user input at each step. Additionally, by tackling multi-apartment processing, this project scales beyond the simplicity of single-family houses.

Beyond the mere development of a generation pipeline, this attempt aims at demonstrating the potential of GANs for any design process, whereby nesting GAN models, and allowing user input between them, I try to achieve a back and forth between humans and machines, between disciplinarian intuition and technical innovation.

Representation, Learning, and Framework

Pix2Pix uses a conditional generative adversarial network (cGAN) to learn a mapping from an input image to an output image. The network consists of two main pieces, the Generator and the Discriminator. The Generator transforms the input image to an output image; the Discriminator tries to guess if the image was produced by the generator or if it is the original image. The two parts of the network challenge each other resulting in higher quality outputs which are difficult to differentiate from the original images.

We use this ability to learn image mappings which lets our models learn topological features and space organization directly from floor plan images. We control the type of information that the model learns by formatting images. As an example, just showing our model the shape of a parcel and its associated building footprint yields a model able to create typical building footprints given a parcel's shape.

Researcher used Christopher Hesse's implementation of pix2pix. His code uses Tensorflow, as opposed to the original version, which is based on Torch, and has proven to be easy to deploy. I prefered Tensorflow because the large user base and knowledge base gave me confidence that I can easily find answers in case run into an issue.

Ran fast iterations & tests using an NVIDIA Tesla V100 GPU for the training process on Google Cloud Platform (GCP). The simplicity of the NVIDIA GPU Cloud Image for Deep Learning offered on GCP allowed a seamless deployment by installing all the necessary libraries for Pix2Pix (Tensorflow, Keras etc) and packages to run this code on the machine's GPU (CUDA & cuDNN).

Displays the results of a typical training. This sequence first took over a day and a half to train. It eventually took under 2 hours on a Tesla V100 in GCP, allowing for more tests and iterations than by running the same training locally.

We show how one of my GAN-models progressively learns how to layout rooms and the position of doors and windows in space, also called fenestration, for a given apartment unit in the sequence in Fig 29.

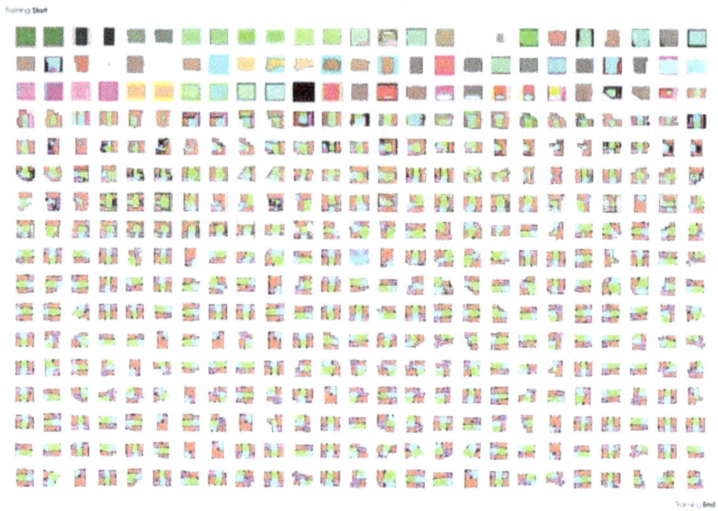

Fig. 29. Apartment architectural sequence

Although the initial attempts proved imprecise the machine builds some form of intuition after 250 iterations.

Precedents

The early work of Isola et al. in November 2018 enabling image-to-image translation with their model **Pix2Pix** has paved the way for my research.

Researchers first studied floor plan analysis using GAN. The authors proposed to use GANs for floor plan recognition and generation using Pix2PixHD. Floor plan images processed by their GAN architecture get translated into programmatic patches of colors. Inversely, patches of colors in their work turn into drawn rooms. If the user specifies the position of openings and rooms, the network elements laid out become furniture.

Regarding GANs as design assistants, researcher at the Harvard GSD in 2017 investigated the idea of a loop between the machine and the designer to refine the very notion of "design process".

Stack and Models

We build upon the previously described precedents to create a 3-step generation stack. As described in Figure 30, each model of the stack handles a specific task of the workflow: **(I) footprint massing, (II) program repartition, (III) furniture layout.**

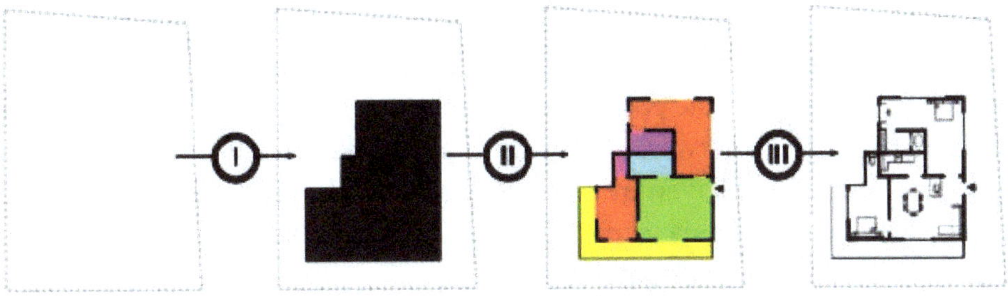

Fig. 30. Stack and Models

An architect is able to modify or fine tune the model's output between each step, thereby achieving the expected machine-human interaction.

Model I: Footprint

Building footprints significantly define the internal organization of floor plans. Their shape is heavily conditioned by their surroundings and, more specifically, the shape of their parcel. Since the design of a housing building footprint can be inferred from the shape of the piece of land it stands on, researchers have trained a model to generate typical footprints, using GIS-data (Geographic Information System) from **the city of Boston.**

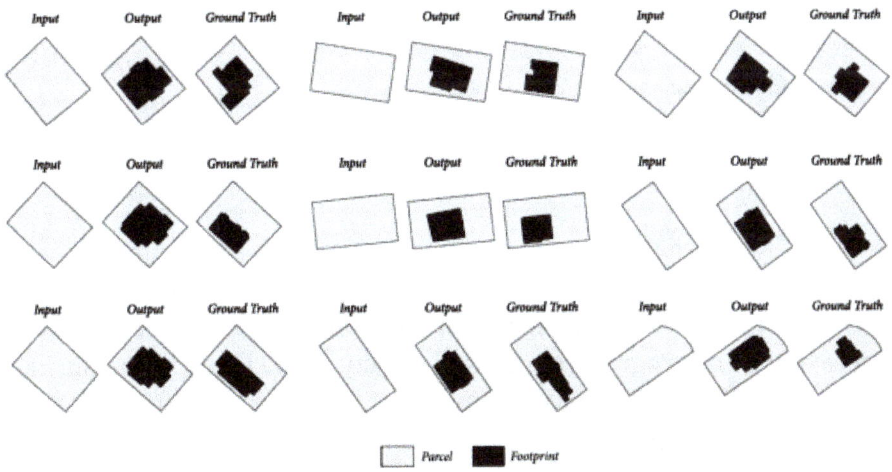

Fig. 31. Results of model I

We feed pairs of images to the network during training in a format suitable for Pix2Pix, displaying the raw parcel (left image) and the same parcel with a given building drawn over it (right image).

Model II: Program

Model II handles repartition and fenestration. The network takes as input the footprint of a given housing unit produced by Model I, the position of its entrance door (green square), and the position of the main windows specified by the user. The plans used to train the network derive from a database of 800+ plans of apartments, properly annotated and given in pairs to the model during training. In the output, The program encodes rooms using colors while representing the wall structure and its fenestration using a black patch.

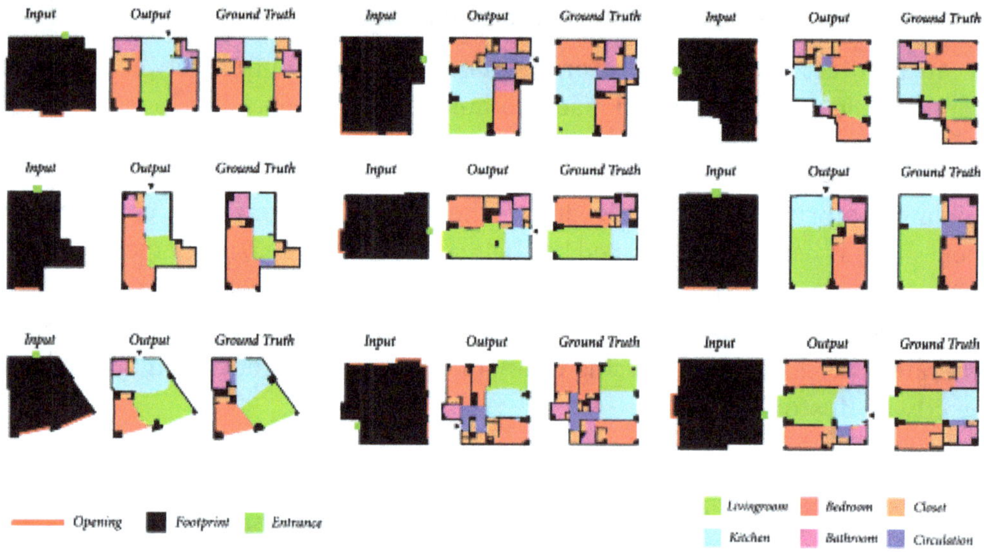

Fig. 32. Results of model II

Model III: Furnishing

Finally, Model III tackles the challenge of furniture layout using the output of model II. This model trains on pairs of images, mapping room programs in color to adequate furniture layouts. The program retains wall structure and fenestration during image translation while filling the rooms with relevant furniture, specified by each room's program. Figure 33 displays some typical results.

UI and Experience

Reseracher provide the user with a simple interface for each step throughout our pipeline. On the left, they can input a set of constraints and boundaries to generate the resulting plan on the right. The designer can then iteratively modify the input on the left to refine the result on the right. The animations in Fig. 34 showcase this type of interface & process set up for Model II.

Fig. 33. Results of model III

Fig. 34 Design iterations using model II interface

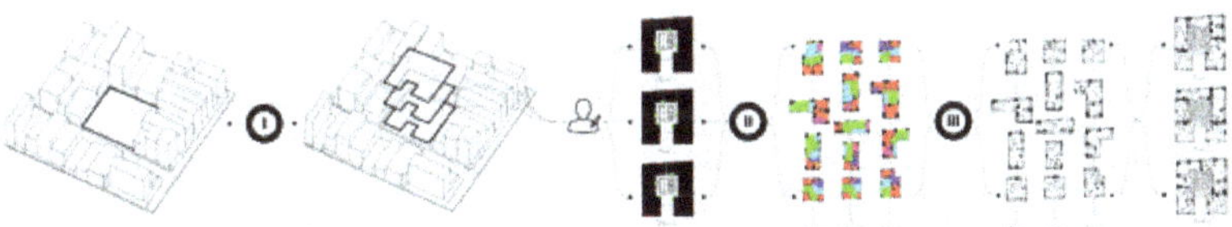

Fig. 35. Apartment building generation pipeline

The challenge of drawing floor plates hosting multiple units marks the difference between single-family houses and apartment buildings. Strategically, the ability to control the position of windows and units' entrances is key to enable unit placement while ensuring each apartment's quality. Since Model II takes doors and windows position as input, the generation stack described above can scale to entire floor plates generation.

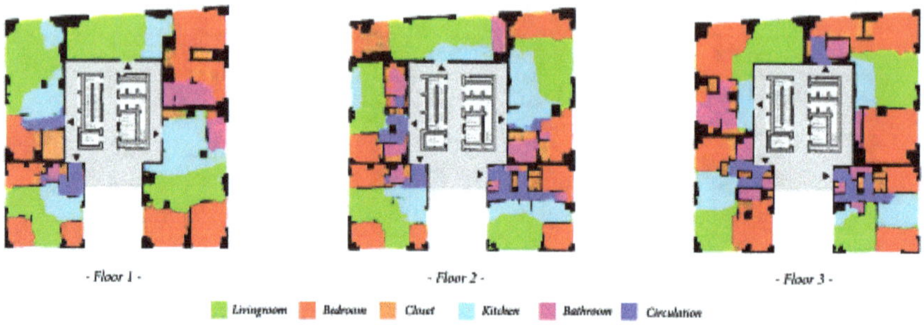

Fig. 36. Model II output, program for each floor plate

The user is invited to specify the unit split between Model I and Model II, In other words, specifying how each floor plate divides into apartments and to position each unit entrance door and windows, as well as potential vertical circulations (staircases, cores, etc). The proposed algorithm then feeds each resulting unit to Model II (results shown in Fig. 36), and then III (result in Figure 37), to finally reassemble each floor plate of the initial building. The algorithm finally outputs as individual images, all floor plates of the generated building.

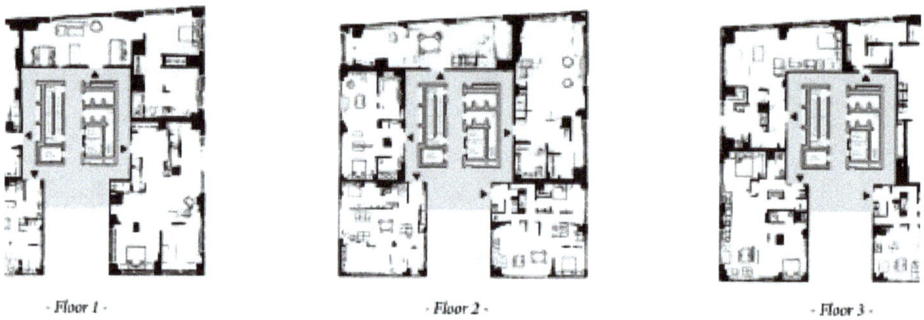

Figure 37. Model III output, furnishing of each individual unit

Going Further

If generating standard apartments can be achieved using this technique, pushing the boundaries of my models is the natural next step. GANs offer remarkable flexibility to solve seemingly highly constrained problems. In the case of floor plan layout, partitioning and furnishing the space by hand can be a challenging process as the footprint changes in dimension and shape. My models prove to be quite "*smart*" in their ability to adapt to changing constraints, as evidenced in Figure 38.

The ability to control the units' entrance door and windows position, coupled with the flexibility of my models, allows us to tackle space planning at a larger scale, beyond the logic of a single unit. In Figure 39, Researchers scale the pipeline to entire buildings generation while investigating my model's reaction to odd apartment shapes and contextual constraints.

Limitations and Future Improvements

If the above results lay down the premise of GANs' potential for Architecture, some clear limitations will drive further investigations in the future.

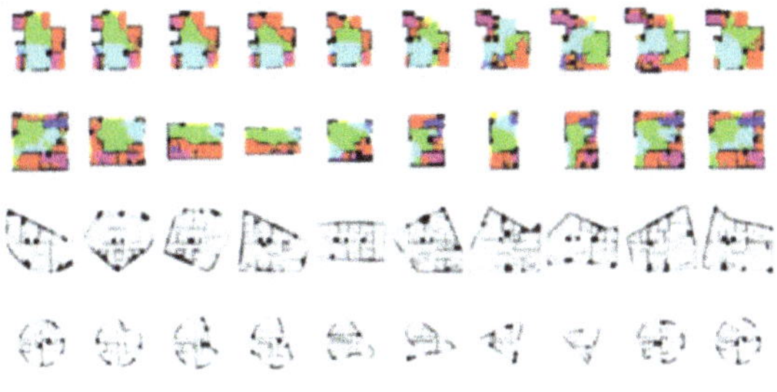

Fig. 38 Flexible building layouts.

First, as apartment units stack up in a multi-story building, we cannot guarantee for now the continuity of load-bearing walls from one floor to the next. Since all the internal structure is laid out differently for each unit, load bearing walls might not be aligned. For now, we consider the façade to be load bearing. However, the ability to specify load-bearing elements' position in the input of Model II could potentially help address this issue.

Fig. 39. GAN-enabled building layouts

Additionally, increasing the size of the output layer by obtaining larger images which offer better definition is a natural next step. We want to deploy the Pix2Pix HD project developed by NVIDIA in August 2018 to achieve this. We hope to leverage TensorRT to deal with the increased computational power needed.

Finally, a major challenge comes from the data format of our outputs. GANs like Pix2Pix handle only pixel information. The resulting images produced in our pipeline cannot, for now, be used directly by architects & designers. Transforming this output from a raster image to a vector format is a crucial step for allowing the above pipeline to integrate with common tools & practices.

CHAPTER 3
HISTORY OF ARTIFICIAL INTELLIGENCE

Artificial Intelligence is not a new word and not a new technology for researchers. This technology is much older than you would imagine. Even there are the myths of Mechanical men in Ancient Greek and Egyptian Myths. Following are some milestones in the history of AI which defines the journey from the AI generation to till date development.

Maturation of Artificial Intelligence (1943-1952)

- **Year 1943:** The first work which is now recognized as AI was done by Warren McCulloch and Walter pits in 1943. They proposed a model of **artificial neurons.**
- **Year 1949:** Donald Hebb demonstrated an updating rule for modifying the connection strength between neurons. His rule is now called **Hebbian learning.**

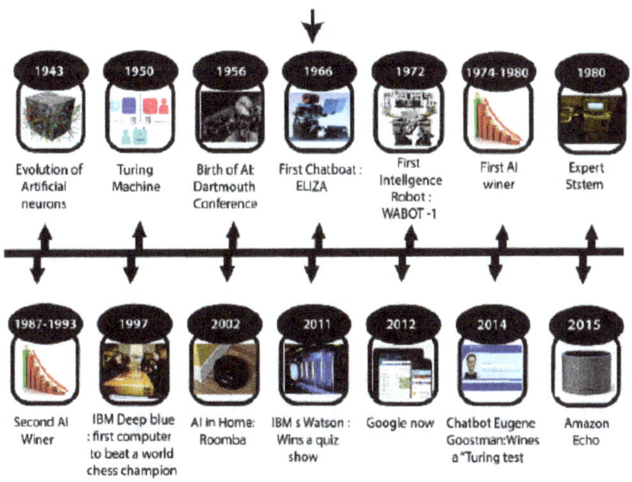

Fig. 1. History of Artificial Intelligence

- **Year 1950:** The Alan Turing who was an English mathematician and pioneered Machine learning in 1950. Alan Turing publishes **"Computing Machinery and Intelligence"** in which he proposed a test. The test can check the machine's ability to exhibit intelligent behavior equivalent to human intelligence, called a **Turing test.**

The birth of Artificial Intelligence (1952-1956)

- **Year 1955:** An Allen Newell and Herbert A. Simon created the "first artificial intelligence program"Which was named as **"Logic Theorist".** This program had proved 38 of 52 Mathematics theorems, and find new and more elegant proofs for some theorems.
- **Year 1956:** The word "Artificial Intelligence" first adopted by American Computer scientist John McCarthy at the Dartmouth Conference. For the first time, AI coined as an academic field.

At that time high-level computer languages such as FORTRAN, LISP, or COBOL were invented. And the enthusiasm for AI was very high at that time.

The golden years-Early enthusiasm (1956-1974)

- **Year 1966:** The researchers emphasized developing algorithms which can solve mathematical problems. Joseph Weizenbaum created the first chatbot in 1966, which was named as ELIZA.
- **Year 1972:** The first intelligent humanoid robot was built in Japan which was named as WABOT-1.

The first AI winter (1974-1980)

- The duration between years 1974 to 1980 was the first AI winter duration. AI winter refers to the time period where computer scientist dealt with a severe shortage of funding from government for AI researches.
- During AI winters, an interest of publicity on artificial intelligence was decreased.

A boom of AI (1980-1987)

- **Year 1980:** After AI winter duration, AI came back with "Expert System". Expert systems were programmed that emulate the decision-making ability of a human expert.
- **In the Year 1980,** the first national conference of the American Association of Artificial Intelligence was held at Stanford University.

The second AI winter (1987-1993)

- The duration between the years 1987 to 1993 was the second AI Winter duration.

- Again Investors and government stopped in funding for AI research as due to high cost but not efficient result. The expert system such as XCON was very cost effective.

The emergence of intelligent agents (1993-2011)

- **Year 1997:** In the year 1997, IBM Deep Blue beats world chess champion, Gary Kasparov, and became the first computer to beat a world chess champion.
- **Year 2002:** for the first time, AI entered the home in the form of Roomba, a vacuum cleaner.
- **Year 2006:** AI came in the Business world till the year 2006. Companies like Facebook, Twitter, and Netflix also started using AI.

Deep learning, big data and artificial general intelligence (2011-present)

- **Year 2011:** In the year 2011, IBM's Watson won jeopardy, a quiz show, where it had to solve the complex questions as well as riddles. Watson had proved that it could understand natural language and can solve tricky questions quickly.
- **Year 2012:** Google has launched an Android app feature "Google now", which was able to provide information to the user as a prediction.
- **Year 2014:** In the year 2014, Chatbot "Eugene Goostman" won a competition in the infamous "Turing test."
- **Year 2018:** The "Project Debater" from IBM debated on complex topics with two master debaters and also performed extremely well.
- Google has demonstrated an AI program "Duplex" which was a virtual assistant and which had taken hairdresser appointment on call, and lady on other side didn't notice that she was talking with the machine.

Now AI has developed to a remarkable level. The concept of Deep learning, big data, and data science are now trending like a boom. Nowadays companies like Google, Facebook, IBM, and Amazon are working with AI and creating amazing devices. The future of Artificial Intelligence is inspiring and will come with high intelligence.

EARLY MILESTONES IN AI

The first AI programs

The earliest successful AI program was written in 1951 by Christopher Strachey, later director of the Programming Research Group at the University of Oxford. Strachey's checkers (draughts) program ran on the Ferranti Mark I computer at the University of Manchester, England. By the summer of 1952 this program could play a complete game of checkers at a reasonable speed.

Information about the earliest successful demonstration of machine learning was published in 1952. Shopper, written by Anthony Oettinger at the University of Cambridge, ran on the EDSAC computer. Shopper's simulated world was a mall of eight shops. When instructed to purchase an item, Shopper would search for it, visiting shops at random until the item was found.

While searching, Shopper would memorize a few of the items stocked in each shop visited (just as a human shopper might). The next time Shopper was sent out for the same item, or for some other item that it had already located, it would go to the right shop straight away. This simple form of learning, as is pointed out in the introductory section What is intelligence?, is called rote learning.

The first AI program to run in the United States also was a checkers program, written in 1952 by Arthur Samuel for the prototype of the IBM 701. Samuel took over the essentials of Strachey's checkers program and over a period of years considerably extended it. In 1955 he added features that enabled the program to learn from experience. Samuel included mechanisms for both rote learning and generalization, enhancements that eventually led to his program's winning one game against a former Connecticut checkers champion in 1962.

Evolutionary computing

Samuel's checkers program was also notable for being one of the first efforts at evolutionary computing. (His program "evolved" by pitting a modified copy against the current best version of his program, with the winner becoming the new standard.) Evolutionary computing typically involves the use of some automatic method of generating and evaluating successive "generations" of a program, until a highly proficient solution evolves.

A leading proponent of evolutionary computing, John Holland, also wrote test software for the prototype of the IBM 701 computer. In particular, he helped design a neural-network "virtual" rat that could be trained to navigate through a maze. This work convinced Holland of the efficacy of the bottom-up approach. While continuing to consult for IBM, Holland moved to the University of Michigan in 1952 to pursue a doctorate in mathematics.

He soon switched, however, to a new interdisciplinary program in computers and information processing (later known as communications science) created by Arthur Burks, one of the builders of ENIAC and its successor EDVAC. In his 1959 dissertation, for most likely the world's first computer science Ph.D., Holland proposed a new type of computer—a multiprocessor computer—that would assign each artificial neuron in a network to a separate processor. (In 1985 Daniel Hillis solved the engineering difficulties to build the first such computer, the 65,536-processor Thinking Machines Corporation supercomputer.)

Holland joined the faculty at Michigan after graduation and over the next four decades directed much of the research into methods of automating evolutionary computing, a process now known by the term genetic algorithms. Systems implemented in Holland's laboratory included a chess program, models of single-cell biological organisms, and a classifier system for controlling a simulated gas-pipeline network. Genetic algorithms are no longer restricted to "academic" demonstrations, however; in one important practical application, a genetic algorithm cooperates with a witness to a crime in order to generate a portrait of the criminal.

Logical reasoning and problem solving

The ability to reason logically is an important aspect of intelligence and has always been a major focus of AI research. An important landmark in this area was a theorem-proving program written in 1955–56 by Allen Newell and J. Clifford Shaw of the RAND Corporation and Herbert Simon of the Carnegie Mellon University. The Logic Theorist, as the program became known, was designed to prove theorems from Principia Mathematica (1910–13), a three-volume work by the British philosopher-mathematicians Alfred North Whitehead and Bertrand Russell. In one instance, a proof devised by the program was more elegant than the proof given in the books.

AI programming languages

In the course of their work on the Logic Theorist and GPS, Newell, Simon, and Shaw developed their Information Processing Language (IPL), a computer language tailored for AI programming. At the heart of IPL was a highly flexible data structure that they called a list. A list is simply an ordered sequence of items of data. Some or all of the items in a list may themselves be lists. This scheme leads to richly branching structures.

In 1960 John McCarthy combined elements of IPL with the lambda calculus (a formal mathematical-logical system) to produce the programming language LISP (List Processor), which remains the principal language for AI work in the United States. (The lambda calculus itself was invented in 1936 by the Princeton logician Alonzo Church while he was investigating the abstract *Entscheidungsproblem*, or "decision problem," for predicate logic—the same problem that Turing had been attacking when he invented the universal Turing machine.)

The logic programming language PROLOG (Programmation en Logique) was conceived by Alain Colmerauer at the University of Aix-Marseille, France, where the language was first implemented in 1973. PROLOG was further developed by the logician Robert Kowalski, a member of the AI group at the University of Edinburgh. This language makes use of a powerful theorem-proving technique known as resolution, invented in 1963 at the U.S. Atomic Energy Commission's Argonne National Laboratory in Illinois by the British logician Alan Robinson. PROLOG can determine whether or not a given statement follows logically from other given statements. For example, given the statements "All logicians are rational" and "Robinson is a logician," a PROLOG program responds in the affirmative to the query "Robinson is rational?" PROLOG is widely used for AI work, especially in Europe and Japan.

Other recent work includes the development of languages for reasoning about time-dependent data such as "the account was paid yesterday." These languages are based on tense logic, which permits statements to be located in the flow of time.

Microworld programs

To cope with the bewildering complexity of the real world, scientists often ignore less relevant details; for instance, physicists often ignore friction and elasticity in their models. In 1970 Marvin Minsky and Seymour Papert of the MIT AI Laboratory proposed that likewise AI research should focus on developing programs capable of intelligent behaviour in simpler artificial environments known as microworlds. Much research has focused on the so-called blocks world, which consists of coloured blocks of various shapes and sizes arrayed on a flat surface.

An early success of the microworld approach was SHRDLU, written by Terry Winograd of MIT. (Details of the program were published in 1972.) SHRDLU controlled a robot arm that operated above a flat surface strewn with play blocks. Both the arm and the blocks were virtual. SHRDLU would respond to commands typed in natural English, such as "Will you please stack up both of the red blocks and either a green cube or a pyramid." The program could also answer questions about its own actions.Although SHRDLU was initially hailed as a major breakthrough, Winograd soon announced that the program was, in fact, a dead end. The techniques pioneered in the program proved unsuitable for application in wider, more interesting worlds. Moreover, the appearance that SHRDLU gave of understanding the blocks microworld, and English statements concerning it, was in fact an illusion. SHRDLU had no idea what a green block was.

THE BIRTH OF ARTIFICIAL INTELLIGENCE (AI) RESEARCH

Introduction

While artificial intelligence (AI) is among today's most popular topics, a commonly forgotten fact is that it was actually born in 1950 and went through a hype cycle between 1956 and 1982. The purpose of this article is to highlight some of the achievements that took place during the boom phase of this cycle and explain what led to its bust phase. The lessons to be learned from this hype cycle should not be overlooked – its successes formed the archetypes for machine learning algorithms used today, and its shortcomings indicated the dangers of overenthusiasm in promising fields of research and development.

The Pioneering Question

Although the first computers were developed during World War II, what seemed to truly spark the field of AI was a question proposed by Alan Turing in 1950: can a machine imitate human intelligence? In his seminal paper, "Computing Machinery and Intelligence," he formulated a game, called the imitation game, in which a human, a computer, and a (human) interrogator are in three different rooms.

The interrogator's goal is to distinguish the human from the computer by asking them a series of questions and reading their typewritten responses; the computer's goal is to convince the interrogator that it is the human. In a 1952 BBC interview, Turing suggested that, by the year 2000, the average interrogator would have less than a 70% chance of correctly identifying the human after a five-minute session.

In 1950, English mathematician and computer science pioneer Alan Turing posed the question, "can machines think?" In his paper, "Computing Machinery and Intelligence," Turing laid out what has become known as the Turing Test, or imitation game, to determine whether a machine is capable of thinking. The test was based on an adaptation of a Victorian-style game that involved the seclusion of a man and a woman from an interrogator, who must guess which is which.

In Turing's version, the computer program replaced one of the participants, and the questioner had to determine which was the computer and which was the human. If the interrogator was unable to tell the difference between the machine and the human, the computer would be considered to be thinking, or to possess "artificial intelligence."

Turing's test came mere years after the development of the first digital computers and before the term "artificial intelligence" had even been coined. At the time, there were various names for the field of "thinking machines," including cybernetics and automata theory. In 1956, two years after the death of Turing, John McCarthy, a professor at Dartmouth College, organized a summer workshop to clarify and develop ideas about thinking machines - choosing the name "artificial intelligence" for the project. The Dartmouth conference, widely considered to be the founding moment of Artificial Intelligence (AI) as a field of research, aimed to find "how to make machines use language, form abstractions and concepts, solve kinds of problems now reserved for humans and improve themselves."

Over the next few years, the field grew quickly with researchers investigating techniques for performing tasks considered to require expert levels of knowledge, such as playing games like checkers and chess. By the mid-1960s, artificial intelligence research in the United States was being heavily funded by the Department of Defense, and AI laboratories had been established around the world.

Around the same time, the Lawrence Radiation Laboratory, Livermore also began its own Artificial Intelligence Group, within the Mathematics and Computing Division headed by Sidney Fernbach. To run the program, Livermore recruited MIT alumnus James Slagle, a former protégé of AI pioneer, Marvin Minsky.

Slagle, who had been blind since childhood, received his doctorate in mathematics from MIT. While pursuing his education, Slagle was invited to the White House where he received an award, on behalf of Recording for the Blind Inc., from President Dwight Eisenhower for his exceptional scholarly work. In 1961, for his dissertation, Slagle developed a program called SAINT (symbolic automatic integrator), which is acknowledged to be one of the first "expert systems" - a computer system that can emulate the decision-making ability of a human expert.

SAINT could solve elementary symbolic integration problems, involving the manipulation of integrals in calculus, at the level of a college freshman. The program was tested on a set of 86 problems, 54 of which were drawn from the MIT freshman calculus examinations final. SAINT succeeded in solving all but two of the questions.

At Livermore, Slagle and his group worked on developing several programs aimed at teaching computer programs to use both deductive and inductive reasoning in their approach to problem-solving situations. One such program, MULTIPLE (MULTIpurpose theorem-proving heuristic Program that LEarns), was designed with the flexibility to learn "what to do next" in a wide-variety of tasks from problems in geometry and calculus to games like checkers.

According to Slagle, AI researchers were no longer spending their time re-hashing the pros and cons of Turing's question, "can machines think?" Instead, they adopted the view that "thinking" must be regarded as a continuum rather than an "either-or" situation. Whether computers think little, if at all, was obvious — whether or not they could improve in the future remained the open question. However, AI research and progress slowed after a boom start; and, by the mid-1970s, government funding for new avenues of exploratory research had all but dried-up. Similarly at the Lab, the Artificial Intelligence Group was dissolved, and Slagle moved on to pursue his work elsewhere.

The prominence of the field ebbed and flowed over the ensuing years; but, by the late 1990s and early 2000s, AI research had come back to the forefront by focusing on finding specific solutions to specific problems rather than on the original goal of creating versatile, fully intelligent machines. Today faster computers and access to large amounts of data has enabled advances in machine learning and data-driven deep learning methods.

Currently, the Lawrence Livermore National Laboratory is focused on several data science fields, including machine learning and deep learning. In 2018, LLNL established the Data Science Institute (DSI) to bring together the Lab's various data science disciplines – artificial intelligence, machine learning, deep learning, computer vision, big data analytics, and others – under one umbrella. With the DSI, the Lab is helping to build and strengthen the data science workforce, research, and outreach to advance the state-of-the-art of the nation's data science capabilities.

Turing was not the only one to ask whether a machine could model intelligent life. In 1951, Marvin Minsky, a graduate student inspired by earlier neuroscience research indicating that the brain was composed of an electrical network of neurons firing with all-or-nothing pulses, attempted to computationally model the behavior of a rat. In collaboration with physics graduate student Dean Edmonds, he built the first neural network machine called Stochastic Neural Analogy Reinforcement Computer (SNARC). Although primitive (consisting of about 300 vacuum tubes and motors), it was successful in modeling the behavior of a rat in a small maze searching for food.

The notion that it might be possible to create an intelligent machine was an alluring one indeed, and it led to several subsequent developments. For instance, Arthur Samuel built a Checkers-playing program in 1952 that was the world's first self-learning program. Later, in 1955, Newell, Simon and Shaw built Logic Theorist, which was the first program to mimic the problem-solving skills of a human and would eventually prove 38 of the first 52 theorems in Whitehead and Russell's Principia Mathematica

AI WINTER

AI winter is a quiet period for artificial intelligence (AI) research and development. Over the years, funding for AI initiatives has gone through a number of active and inactive cycles. The label *winter* is used to describe dormant periods when customer interest in AI declines. Use of the season winter to describe the resulting downturn emphasizes the idea that the quiet period will be a temporary state, followed again by growth and renewed interest.

History and timeline of AI winters

The trajectory of AI has been marked by several winters since its inception in 1955 in a formal proposal made by computer scientist and AI researcher Marvin Minksy and several others. Between 1956 and 1974, the U.S. Defense Advanced Research Projects Agency (DARPA) funded AI research with few requirements for developing functional projects. A large amount of hype was spurred during the mid-50s by the following collection of AI projects:

- A machine translation experiment that generated crude word-to-word Russian to English translation;

- A program that could play checkers; and
- A neural network that consisted of perceptrons, which were crude replications of the human brain's neurons.

After the initial hype generated by these AI projects, a quiet decade followed where interest and support gradually tapered off. In 1969, Minsky and another AI researcher, Seymour Papert, published a book called *Perceptrons*, which pointed out the flaws and limitations of neural networks. This publication influenced DARPA to withdraw its previous funding of AI projects.

In 1973, an evaluation of academic research in the field of AI called the "Lighthill Report" was published. It was highly critical of research in the field up to that point, stating that AI research had essentially failed to live up to the grandiose objectives it laid out. This report caused the U.K. to cease funding for AI. This ushered in the first AI winter, which took place between 1974-1980, after a nearly 20-year period of significant interest during what some have called AI's Golden Era. Interest in AI wouldn't be revived until years later with the advent of expert systems, which used if-then, rule-based reasoning. This would eventually end with another AI winter from the late 1980s to mid-90s.

We're currently in one of the longest periods of sustained interest in AI in history. Today's distributed systems dwarf the computing power of the past and there are vast troves of training data on which AI systems can cut their teeth. These are distinct advantages that AI developers lacked in the past and are two of the primary drivers behind today's AI advances. But it's still an open question how far the technology can go. Many doubt AI's ability to pass the Turing Test and prove its ability to create systems that imitate human intelligence and behavior.

The main causes behind AI winters

Historically, AI winters have occurred because vendor promises have fallen short and AI initiatives have been more complicated to carry out than promised. When AI-washed products fail to deliver a significant return on investment (ROI), buyers become disappointed and direct their attention elsewhere.

AI winters occur when the hype behind AI research and development starts to stagnate. They also happen when the functions of AI stop being commercially viable. The promises generated by new techniques tend to create a large amount of buzz and raise the public's expectations. Businesses and organizations invest a lot of money based on these expectations, and gradually over time, if the new technology fails to deliver on those expectations, they lose interest in AI. If organizations begin to withdraw funding, it's a sign of waning interest and an impending AI winter.

To forestall another AI winter, some vendors have chosen to label software features predictive instead of artificially intelligent.

Will a future AI winter happen?

In the past decade, AI has been on a strong upswing. Some of the main advancements of artificial intelligence that have fueled the hype include deep learning, graphics processing units and big data analytics and processing. Some other real-world landmark areas of innovation include the following:

- facial recognition;
- machine learning algorithms;
- data science and analytics;
- the AI agent AlphaGo for the Chinese boardgame Go;
- advanced language recognition and translation;
- medical diagnoses and imaging; and
- self-driving cars.

Although these advancements have been influential, they also have significant limitations that prevent broad applicability and ubiquitous, cross-contextual use. For example, facial recognition deals with ethical challenges in certain contexts. Also, self-driving cars aren't capable of driving with the sophistication of human drivers and are still prone to accidents due to flaws in object recognition.

AI still has significant obstacles to overcome before becoming an integral, everyday technology. Current applications of artificial intelligence excel at solving certain specific problems and require a lot of data to do so. To achieve artificial general intelligence — dubbed the Holy Grail of artificial intelligence — AI will have to improve at solving a wider array of problems with significantly less data. These limitations are the reason that, after several years of hype, advances and implementations, some analysts are predicting another AI winter. Still others remain optimistic, as AI continues to automate business functions in what some have dubbed the Autonomous Revolution.

DEEP BLUE

Deep Blue was a supercomputer developed by IBM specifically for playing chess and was best known for being the first artificial intelligence construct to ever win a chess match against a reigning world champion, Grandmaster Garry Kasparov, under regular time controls. Deep Blue lost to Kasparov in their first 6-game match in 1996 with a score of 4–2, and was later heavily upgraded and finally won over Kasparov in May 1997 in a 6-game rematch with a score of 3½–2½.

Development of Deep Blue started in 1985 as the ChipTest research project in Carnegie Mellon University led by Feng-hsiung Hsu. It eventually evolved into Deep Thought and by that time IBM decided to hire the entire development team composed of Hsu, Murray Campbell and Thomas Anantharaman. The project was later renamed to Deep Blue in 1989 and Joel Benjamin, a chess grandmaster, was added to the development team.

Technical specifications of Deep Blue include:

- RS/6000 SP Thin P2SC-based system
- 30 nodes
- 120 MHz P2SC microprocessor per node
- 480 special-purpose VLSI chess chips per node
- AI programmed in C running on the AIX operating System

When IBM began work to create Deep Blue in 1989, AI was in a funk. The field had been through multiple roller-coaster cycles of giddy hype and humiliating collapse. The pioneers of the '50s had claimed that AI would soon see huge advances; mathematician Claude Shannon predicted that "within a matter of ten or fifteen years, something will emerge from the laboratories which is not too far from the robot of science fiction." This didn't happen. And each time inventors failed to deliver, investors felt burned and stopped funding new projects, creating an "AI winter" in the '70s and again in the '80s.

The reason they failed - we now know - is that AI creators were trying to handle the messiness of everyday life using pure logic. That's how they imagined humans did it. And so engineers would patiently write out a rule for every decision their AI needed to make.

The problem is, the real world is far too fuzzy and nuanced to be managed this way. Engineers carefully crafted their clockwork masterpieces - or "expert systems," as they were called - and they'd work reasonably well until reality threw them a curveball. A credit card company, say, might make a system to automatically approve credit applications, only to discover they'd issued cards to dogs or 13-year-olds. The programmers never imagined that minors or pets would apply for a card, so they'd never written rules to accommodate those edge cases. Such systems couldn't learn a new rule on their own.

AI built via handcrafted rules was "brittle": when it encountered a weird situation, it broke. By the early '90s, troubles with expert systems had brought on another AI winter.

In that landscape of cynicism, Deep Blue arrived like a weirdly ambitious moonshot.

The project grew out of work on Deep Thought, a chess-playing computer built at Carnegie Mellon by Murray Campbell, Feng-hsiung Hsu, and others. Deep Thought was awfully good; in 1988, it became the first chess AI to beat a grand master, Bent

Larsen. The Carnegie Mellon team had figured out better algorithms for assessing chess moves, and they'd also created custom hardware that speedily crunched through them.

IBM got wind of Deep Thought and decided it would mount a "grand challenge," building a computer so good it could beat any human. In 1989 it hired Hsu and Campbell, and tasked them with besting the world's top grand master. Chess had long been, in AI circles, symbolically potent—two opponents facing each other on the astral plane of pure thought. It'd certainly generate headlines if they could trounce Kasparov.

To build Deep Blue, Campbell and his team had to craft new chips for calculating chess positions even more rapidly, and hire grand masters to help improve algorithms for assessing the next moves. Efficiency mattered: there are more possible chess games than atoms in the universe, and even a supercomputer couldn't ponder all of them in a reasonable amount of time. To play chess, Deep Blue would peer a move ahead, calculate possible moves from there, "prune" ones that seemed unpromising, go deeper along the promising paths, and repeat the process several times.

"We thought it would take five years - it actually took a little more than six," Campbell says. By 1996, IBM decided it was finally ready to face Kasparov, and it set a match for February. Campbell and his team were still frantically rushing to finish Deep Blue: "The system had only been working for a few weeks before we actually got on the stage," he says.

It showed. Although Deep Blue won one game, Kasparov won three and took the match. IBM asked for a rematch, and Campbell's team spent the next year building even faster hardware. By the time they'd completed their improvements, Deep Blue was made of 30 PowerPC processors and 480 custom chess chips; they'd also hired more grand masters - four or five at any given point in time - to help craft better algorithms for parsing chess positions. When Kasparov and Deep Blue met again, in May 1997, the computer was twice as speedy, assessing 200 million chess moves per second.

Even so, IBM still wasn't confident of victory, Campbell remembers: "We expected a draw."

The reality was considerably more dramatic. Kasparov dominated in the first game. But in its 36th move in the second game, Deep Blue did something Kasparov did not expect.

He was accustomed to the way computers traditionally played chess, a style born from machines' sheer brute-force abilities. They were better than humans at short-term tactics; Deep Blue could easily deduce the best choice a few moves out.

But what computers were bad at, traditionally, was strategy—the ability to ponder the shape of a game many, many moves in the future. That's where humans still had the edge.

Or so Kasparov thought, until Deep Blue's move in game 2 rattled him. It seemed so sophisticated that Kasparov began worrying: maybe the machine was far better than he'd thought! Convinced he had no way to win, he resigned the second game.

But he shouldn't have. Deep Blue, it turns out, wasn't actually that good. Kasparov had failed to spot a move that would have let the game end in a draw. He was psyching himself out: worried that the machine might be far more powerful than it really was, he had begun to see human-like reasoning where none existed.

Knocked off his rhythm, Kasparov kept playing worse and worse. He psyched himself out over and over again. Early in the sixth, winner-takes-all game, he made a move so lousy that chess observers cried out in shock. "I was not in the mood of playing at all," he later said at a press conference.

IBM benefited from its moonshot. In the press frenzy that followed Deep Blue's success, the company's market cap rose $11.4 billion in a single week. Even more significant, though, was that IBM's triumph felt like a thaw in the long AI winter. If chess could be conquered, what was next? The public's mind reeled.

The truth is, it wasn't surprising that a computer beat Kasparov. Most people who'd been paying attention to AI - and to chess - expected it to happen eventually.

Chess may seem like the acme of human thought, but it's not. Indeed, it's a mental task that's quite amenable to brute-force computation: the rules are clear, there's no hidden information, and a computer doesn't even need to keep track of what happened in previous moves. It just assesses the position of the pieces right now.

Everyone knew that once computers got fast enough, they'd overwhelm a human. It was just a question of when. By the mid-'90s, "the writing was already on the wall, in a sense," says Demis Hassabis, head of the AI company DeepMind, part of Alphabet.

Deep Blue's victory was the moment that showed just how limited hand-coded systems could be. IBM had spent years and millions of dollars developing a computer to play chess. But it couldn't do anything else.

"It didn't lead to the breakthroughs that allowed the [Deep Blue] AI to have a huge impact on the world," Campbell says.

They didn't really discover any principles of intelligence, because the real world doesn't resemble chess. "There are very few problems out there where, as with chess, you have all the information you could possibly need to make the right decision," Campbell adds. "Most of the time there are unknowns. There's randomness."

But even as Deep Blue was mopping the floor with Kasparov, a handful of scrappy upstarts were tinkering with a radically more promising form of AI: the neural net.

Fig. 2. 1997: After Garry Kasparov beat Deep Blue in 1996, IBM asked the world chess champion for a rematch, which was held in New York City with an upgraded machine.

With neural nets, the idea was not, as with expert systems, to patiently write rules for each decision an AI will make. Instead, training and reinforcement strengthen internal connections in rough emulation (as the theory goes) of how the human brain learns.

The idea had existed since the '50s. But training a usefully large neural net required lightning-fast computers, tons of memory, and lots of data. None of that was readily available then. Even into the '90s, neural nets were considered a waste of time.

But by the 2000s, the computer industry was evolving to make neural nets viable. Video-game players' lust for ever-better graphics created a huge industry in ultrafast graphic-processing units, which turned out to be perfectly suited for neural-net math. Meanwhile, the internet was exploding, producing a torrent of pictures and text that could be used to train the systems.

By the early 2010s, these technical leaps were allowing Hinton and his crew of true believers to take neural nets to new heights. They could now create networks with many layers of neurons (which is what the "deep" in "deep learning" means). In 2012 his team handily won the annual Imagenet competition, where AIs compete to recognize elements in pictures. It stunned the world of computer science: self-learning machines were finally viable.

Ten years into the deep-learning revolution, neural nets and their pattern-recognizing abilities have colonized every nook of daily life. They help Gmail autocomplete your sentences, help banks detect fraud, let photo apps automatically recognize faces, and—in the case of OpenAI's GPT-3 and DeepMind's Gopher—write long, human-sounding essays and summarize texts. They're even changing how science is done; in 2020, DeepMind debuted AlphaFold2, an AI that can predict how proteins will fold—a superhuman skill that can help guide researchers to develop new drugs and treatments.

Meanwhile Deep Blue vanished, leaving no useful inventions in its wake. Chess playing, it turns out, wasn't a computer skill that was needed in everyday life. What Deep Blue in the end showed was the shortcomings of trying to handcraft everything.

IBM tried to remedy the situation with Watson, another specialized system, this one designed to tackle a more practical problem: getting a machine to answer questions. It used statistical analysis of massive amounts of text to achieve language comprehension that was, for its time, cutting-edge. It was more than a simple if-then system. But Watson faced unlucky timing: it was eclipsed only a few years later by the revolution in deep learning, which brought in a generation of language-crunching models far more nuanced than Watson's statistical techniques.

Deep learning has run roughshod over old-school AI precisely because pattern recognition is incredibly powerful, which uses neural nets and other forms of machine learning to investigate novel drug treatments. The flexibility of neural nets—the wide variety of ways pattern recognition can be used—is the reason there hasn't yet been another AI winter. "Machine learning has actually delivered value," she says, which is something the "previous waves of exuberance" in AI never did.

The inverted fortunes of Deep Blue and neural nets show how bad we were, for so long, at judging what's hard—and what's valuable—in AI.

For decades, people assumed mastering chess would be important because, well, chess is hard for humans to play at a high level. But chess turned out to be fairly easy for computers to master, because it's so logical.

What was far harder for computers to learn was the casual, unconscious mental work that humans do—like conducting a lively conversation, piloting a car through traffic, or reading the emotional state of a friend. We do these things so effortlessly that we rarely realize how tricky they are, and how much fuzzy, grayscale judgment they require. Deep learning's great utility has come from being able to capture small bits of this subtle, unheralded human intelligence.

Still, there's no final victory in artificial intelligence. Deep learning may be riding high now—but it's amassing sharp critiques, too.

"For a very long time, there was this techno-chauvinist enthusiasm that okay, AI is going to solve every problem!" says Meredith Broussard, a programmer turned journalism professor at New York University and author of *Artificial Unintelligence*. But as she and other critics have pointed out, deep-learning systems are often trained on biased data—and absorb those biases. The computer scientists Joy Buolamwini and Timnit Gebru discovered that three commercially available visual AI systems were terrible at analyzing the faces of darker-skinned women. Amazon trained an AI to vet résumés, only to find it downranked women.

Though computer scientists and many AI engineers are now aware of these bias problems, they're not always sure how to deal with them. On top of that, neural nets are also "massive black boxes," says Daniela Rus, a veteran of AI who currently runs MIT's Computer Science and Artificial Intelligence Laboratory. Once a neural net is trained, its mechanics are not easily understood even by its creator. It is not clear how it comes to its conclusions—or how it will fail.

It may not be a problem, Rus figures, to rely on a black box for a task that isn't "safety critical." But what about a higher-stakes job, like autonomous driving? "It's actually quite remarkable that we could put so much trust and faith in them," she says.

This is where Deep Blue had an advantage. The old-school style of handcrafted rules may have been brittle, but it was comprehensible. The machine was complex—but it wasn't a mystery.

Ironically, that old style of programming might stage something of a comeback as engineers and computer scientists grapple with the limits of pattern matching.

Language generators, like OpenAI's GPT-3 or DeepMind's Gopher, can take a few sentences you've written and keep on going, writing pages and pages of plausible-sounding prose. But despite some impressive mimicry, Gopher "still doesn't really understand what it's saying," Hassabis says. "Not in a true sense."

Similarly, visual AI can make terrible mistakes when it encounters an edge case. Self-driving cars have slammed into fire trucks parked on highways, because in all the millions of hours of video they'd been trained on, they'd never encountered that situation. Neural nets have, in their own way, a version of the "brittleness" problem.

What AI really needs in order to move forward, as many computer scientists now suspect, is the ability to know facts about the world—and to reason about them. A self-driving car cannot rely only on pattern matching. It also has to have common sense—to know what a fire truck is, and why seeing one parked on a highway would signify danger.

The problem is, no one knows quite how to build neural nets that can reason or use common sense. Gary Marcus, a cognitive scientist and coauthor of *Rebooting AI*, suspects that the future of AI will require a "hybrid" approach—neural nets to learn patterns, but guided by some old-fashioned, hand-coded logic. This would, in a sense, merge the benefits of Deep Blue with the benefits of deep learning.

Hard-core aficionados of deep learning disagree. Hinton believes neural networks should, in the long run, be perfectly capable of reasoning. After all, humans do it, "and the brain's a neural network." Using hand-coded logic strikes him as bonkers; it'd run into the problem of all expert systems, which is that you can never anticipate all the common sense you'd want to give to a machine. The way forward, Hinton says, is to keep innovating on neural nets—to explore new architectures and new learning algorithms that more accurately mimic how the human brain itself works.

Computer scientists are dabbling in a variety of approaches. At IBM, Deep Blue developer Campbell is working on "neuro-symbolic" AI that works a bit the way Marcus proposes. Etzioni's lab is attempting to build common-sense modules for AI that include both trained neural nets and traditional computer logic; as yet, though, it's early days. The future may look less like an absolute victory for either Deep Blue or neural nets, and more like a Frankensteinian approach—the two stitched together.

Given that AI is likely here to stay, how will we humans live with it? Will we ultimately be defeated, like Kasparov with Deep Blue, by AIs so much better at "thinking work" that we can't compete?

Kasparov himself doesn't think so. Not long after his loss to Deep Blue, he decided that fighting against an AI made no sense. The machine "thought" in a fundamentally inhuman fashion, using brute-force math. It would always have better tactical, short-term power.

So why compete? Instead, why not collaborate?

After the Deep Blue match, Kasparov invented "advanced chess," where humans and silicon work together. A human plays against another human—but each also wields a laptop running chess software, to help war-game possible moves.

When Kasparov began running advanced chess matches in 1998, he quickly discovered fascinating differences in the game. Interestingly, amateurs punched above their weight. In one human-with-laptop match in 2005, a pair of them won the top prize—beating out several grand masters.

How could they best superior chess minds? Because the amateurs better understood how to collaborate with the machine. They knew how to rapidly explore ideas, when to accept a machine suggestion and when to ignore it. (Some leagues still hold advanced chess tournaments today.)

This, Kasparov argues, is precisely how we ought to approach the emerging world of neural nets.

Neural nets behave differently from chess engines, of course. But many luminaries agree strongly with Kasparov's vision of human-AI collaboration. DeepMind's Hassabis sees AI as a way forward for science, one that will guide humans toward new breakthroughs. Will there come a time when we can build AI so human-like in its reasoning that humans really do have less to offer—and AI takes over all thinking? Possibly. But even these scientists, on the cutting edge, can't predict when that will happen, if ever.

So consider this Deep Blue's final gift, 25 years after its famous match. In his defeat, Kasparov spied the real endgame for AI and humans. "We will increasingly become managers of algorithms," he told me, "and use them to boost our creative output—our adventuresome souls."

JEOPARDY

Jeopardy! is a well-known American TV game show that has moved across generations. Unlike regular quiz shows, Jeopardy! gives the contestants the answer, and in turn the contestants compete to find the right question. It was originally released in 1964, and is still on-going to this date with 37 seasons and 8,000+ episodes.

ALPHAGO

AlphaGo is a narrow AI, a computer program developed by Google DeepMind to play Go, a Chinese strategy board game for two players similar to chess. AlphaGo is the very first AI program that was able to beat a professional human player, 2-dan player Fan Hui in October 2015, on a full-sized board with no handicaps. It then beat one of the highest ranked human players in the world, 9-dan Lee Sedol, in March 2016, winning four games out of five.

he AlphaGo project was started in 2014 as a test-bed in order to see how well Google DeepMind's neural network algorithm utilizing deep learning could compete at Go. The algorithm for AlphaGo is a combination of tree search and machine learning techniques and reinforced with extensive training with both humans and other computer players. It uses the Monte Carlo tree search and is guided by a policy and value network, implemented using deep neural network technologies. The policy network is trained and helps the AI predict the next move most likely to win while the value network is trained to narrow down the search tree and determine the value of those positions, estimating the winners in each position rather than searching all the way down to the end of the game.

AlphaGo was first fed with historical match moves from human players, utilizing a database of around 30 million moves, making it mimic human plays. Once the AI reached a degree of proficiency, it was trained further by making it play against instances of itself, using reinforcement learning to improve and learn more.

In October 2015, a distributed computing version of AlphaGo played and defeated Fan Hui, a 2-dan European Go Champion, marking the first time ever that a computer program had beaten a professional player at Go. Fan Hui then helped as a consultant for the DeepMind team months after his defeat. In March of 2016, AlphaGo went up against Lee Sedol, one of the highest ranked players in the world, having achieved the top level of 9-dan. Winning four games to Lee's one, this marked a major breakthrough in AI research since this meant that the deep learning and neural networks algorithm used by DeepMind can be used for any other purpose since it was not really programmed to play Go, but rather was taught how to play Go. This opens up a whole new world for AI research.

AlphaGo Algorithm

So how did AlphaGo solve the complexity of Go as well as the restriction imposed by the game level of the designers? All previous methods for Go-playing AI relied on some kind of game tree search, combined with hand-crafted rules. AlphaGo, however, makes extensive use of machine learning to avoid using hand-crafted rules and improve efficiency. Machine learning is a type of artificial intelligence that provides computers with the ability to learn without being explicitly programmed. Machine learning focuses on the development of computer programs that can teach themselves to grow and change when exposed to new data. The machine learning systems search through data to look for patterns. But instead of extracting data for human comprehension — as is the case in data mining applications — it uses the data to detect patterns and adjust program actions accordingly. AlphaGo also uses deep learning and neural networks to teach itself to play. Just like iPhotos is able to help you divide photos into different albums according to different characters because it holds the storage of countless character images that have been processed down to the pixel level, AlphaGo's intelligence is based on it having been shown millions of Go positions and moves from human-played games.

AlphaGo's intelligence relies on two different components: a game tree search procedure and neural networks that simplify the tree search procedure. The tree search procedure can be regarded as a brute-force approach, whereas the convolutional networks provide a level of intuition to the game-play. The neural networks are conceptually similar to the evaluation function in other AIs, except that AlphaGo's are learned and not designed, thus solving the problem of the game level of the designers influencing the intelligence level of AI.

Neural Networks

Generally, two main kinds of neural networks inside AlphaGo are trained: policy network and value network. Both types of networks take the current game state as input and grade each possible next move through different formulas and output the probability of a win. On one side, the value network provides an estimate of the value of the current state of the game: what is the probability of the black player to ultimately win the game, given the current state? The output of the value network is the probability of a win. On the other side, the policy networks provide guidance regarding which action to choose, given the current state of the game.

The output is a probability value for each possible legal move (the output of the network is as large as the board). Actions (moves) with higher probability values correspond to actions that have a higher chance of leading to a win. One of the most important aspects of AlphaGo is learning-ability. Deep learning allows AlphaGo to continually improve its intelligence by playing a large number of games against itself.

This trains the policy network to help AlphaGo predict the next moves, which in turn trains the value network to ascertain and evaluate those positions. AlphaGo looks ahead at possible moves and permutations, going through various eventualities before selecting the one it deems most likely to succeed.

In general, the combined two neural networks let AlphaGo avoid doing excess work: the policy network focuses on the present and decides the next step to save time on searching the entire game tree, and the value network focuses on the long run, analyzing the whole situation to reduce possible moves in the game tree.

AlphaGo then averages the suggestion from two networks to make a final decision. What makes AlphaGo so important is that it not only follows the game theory but also involves a learning component. By playing against itself, AlphaGo automatically became better and better at Go.

Future of AlphaGo

The Go games were fascinating, but more important is AlphaGo's demonstration of the ways artificial intelligence algorithms will affect our lives; AI will make humans better. In the 37th move in the second game, AlphaGo made a very surprising decision. A European Go champion said "It's not a human move. I've never seen a human play this move. So beautiful."

This European Go champion who helped teach AlphaGo by playing against it said that though he lost almost all the games, his understanding of Go was greatly improved due to the unusual way the program played. This was also reflected by his jump in world rankings.

According to the data, in the United States, there are around 40,500 patients that die of misdiagnosis. The amount of medical information available is huge, so it is impossible for doctors to sort through every little thing. AIs like AlphaGo are able to collect all the medical literature history as well as medical cases, medical images, and other data in the system, and can output the best solution to help doctors.

Recently, AlphaGo launched a partnership with the UK's National Health Service to improve the process of delivering care with digital solutions. AlphaGo uses its computing power to analyze health data and records. This will open up new treatment opportunities to patients and assist physicians in treating patients. The increased efficiency will also reduce costs for insurance companies.

The original Sputnik moment came a couple of weeks after Sputnik 1, thefirst Earth-orbiting satellite, was launchedinto orbit by the Soviet Union on Oct. 4, 1957. At the time, Sputnik wasthe first human-built object launched into orbit.

"A Sputnik moment is a trigger mechanism, an event that makes people collectivelysay that they need to do something, and this sets a course in anotherdirection," said Roger Launius, senior curator of the National Air andSpace Museum's division of space history at the Smithsonian Institution.

The small Sputnik satellite heralded the dawn of the so-called Space Racebetween the U.S. and Soviet Union that ended with Americans landing on the moonin the late 1960s and early 1970s. Sputnik 2 was launched on Nov. 3, 1957, andbecause of the Space Race going on at the time, the U.S. attempted to launchVanguard TV3 on Dec. 6, 1957, but the fuel tanks of the rocket to which thesatellite was attached ruptured and exploded on the launch pad.

"It wasn't an 'Aha!' moment ? it didn't happen overnight," Launiustold Life's Little Mysteries. "It built up over a period of time, untilthe government said, 'We have to do things differently.' This led to thecreation of NASA and the National Defense Education Act, which provided fundingfor improving science and mathematics education."

Similarly, China's advancement, which includes developing technology for thehighest-efficiency coal plants and rapidly installing turbines for windenergy-generating fields, has made U.S. government officials take notice of ourown need to increase funding in energy innovation.

The fear of another Sputnik moment may drive the U.S. to re-invest in cleanenergy as well as education, science and innovation fields.

AI AND VISIBILITY

Artificial intelligence has the power to revolutionize the social visibility of brands, making way for a very inclusive approach towards online marketing. Today, the power of digital marketing and artificial intelligence go hand in hand.

Artifical intelligence (AI) in digital marketing is useful in gathering data from all aspects, analyzing it, simplifying it, and then getting an easy understanding of a consumer's needs and preferences.

How AI Is Revolutionizing Social Visibility

Artificial intelligence has the power to revolutionize the social visibility of brands, making way for a very inclusive approach towards online marketing. Today, the power of digital marketing and artificial intelligence go hand in hand.

Artifical intelligence (AI) in digital marketing is useful in gathering data from all aspects, analyzing it, simplifying it, and then getting an easy understanding of a consumer's needs and preferences.

The predictive assessment of social platforms is expected to grow to more than $2.1 billion in value by the year 2023. Hence, the market of predictive data, which utilizes the deep learning methods of AI, is burgeoning.

AI technology helps marketers gain insights that are more accurate and deliver customized consumer experiences. Development with AI has helped companies deal with customer interactions and analytics. This is why AI technology has all the capabilities to improve digital marketing strategies.

Why Organizations Value AI Technology to Improve Social Visibility:

More than 84 percent of organizations or businesses believe that AI will help them in obtaining a competitive advantage over their rivals. 75 percent of companies believe that AI technology will allow expansion and new business prospects.

More than 69 percent of incumbent competitors will leverage AI technology soon.

More than 63 percent of people believe that the pressure to use AI will reduce the overall costs.

59 percent of customers will ask for AI-driven offerings, making it the most popular choice in technology.

AI is adapted in many forms, the most common being chatbots. If you are looking for customer support on a website, the chatbot will automatically direct your message to the relevant department. Even smartphones and other gadgets have many features powered by AI. The GPS-powered navigation system is one such example. The entertainment apps on smartphones, like Amazon Prime and Netflix, are fully utilizing the capability of AI for many recommendations.

Machine learning is an important subset of AI that is improving social visibility. The integration of machine learning allows machines to make intelligent, accurate, and futuristic predictions based on various levels of data. This helps in increasing performance levels, improving over time, and helping digital marketers understand their target audience and business niche.

Performance Insights: AI

Many AI tools can help digital marketers track and trace the performance of every decision they make using a social media platform. Advertisement campaigns and user engagement can be analyzed using AI performance metrics.

More than 51 percent of people prefer a messaging application or chat application, and 49 percent of people prefer a normal phone call.

Most social media platforms leverage the use of AI and machine learning tools to serve the right audience. Facebook uses an AI tool to focus its ads. It offers numerous options for advertisers to restrict the audience base and serve relevant people.

Facebook serves ads based on the preference of the audience. Social media platforms not only use AI to keep users engaged but also for recommendations and insights.

Matching AI with Data Science for Social Media

Facebook is the most popular social media platform making the right use of Data Science technology. It uses advanced facial recognition technology within its AI framework. The recognition tool utilized by Facebook can provide people with tag suggestions and identify friends in pictures. This technology also opens the scope for advertisers to utilize facial recognition in different ad campaigns.

Selective ad campaigns using AI technology and Data Science are developing at a faster pace. AI technology and tools not only help to judge the buying patterns of consumers but also comply with different online platforms to increase social presence.

For that matter, Instagram is also making use of AI to customize content for the explore tab for each user. Thus, each Instagram user gets recommendations and curated content based on data gathered from past and present use. You can even use smart technology such as Social Tradia, which helps to buy and sell Instagram accounts so that people get real followers who engage with their content in real-time.

AI Technology with UX

AI has made quite an impact on the user experience. Most digital marketers have deemed AI as the most important trend to influence the user experience. It is the best technology for social media marketers to get unparalleled access to a better understanding of consumer preferences. AI integration can help digital marketers to create hyper-targeted ad campaigns that can directly appeal to the interests of targeted users.

Different AI tools can help to identify which pages the users view from different social media networks. This then enables the digital marketers or website owners to focus on platforms with the highest reach. AI integration can also help to build engaging and appealing content more effectively.

Three Ways AI Has Changed Digital Marketing

Predictive Consumer Behavior

AI can predict behavior for new users and customers. It takes into account customer experience based on past behavior as well. AI technology can integrate with Data Management platforms (DMPs) and can collect second and third-party data.

AI tools can collect all the information about your users across every platform and not just based on a single site session. This helps to personalize the needs of the users based on their profiles and their browsing patterns. It enables digital marketers to target potential leads, which enables the marketer to concentrate on executing and formulating different marketing strategies.

AI tools and technology constantly analyze, interpret, and collect data to learn how to utilize it in smarter ways. With the new updates and algorithms made on social media platforms, the accuracy of consumer insights gets even more efficient.

AI technology also helps to determine the sales forecasting along with ROI. It focuses on the right digital marketing tools that help to increase your social visibility.

Integration with AI technology helps digital marketers save on time and concentrate on other fruitful marketing campaigns. Targeting the right audience plays an important part in marketing. AI helps to target the right base and also helps in formulating strategies based on search engine optimization.

Great Customer Support

The customer support feature is the main feature of any business. It makes a particular brand stand out positively. Customers always want an immediate response and a quick solution to their problems.

AI has transformed online customer support with the introduction of chatbots. Chatbots are automated AI response tools that give customers the impression that they are talking to actual human beings. Chatbots are a human way to talk to potential customers. They normally make use of the FAQs or knowledge base systems to help customers with simple issues or questions.

The main advantage of chatbots is that they are available 24/7 for your customers. This reduces the actual wait time for most customers who are experiencing issues. Chatbots integration helps to increase customer satisfaction.

AI should be well implemented in your digital marketing strategy. By doing so, you will create an improved experience for all your old and new customers. It helps digital marketers gain a better insight into the preferences of the target audience, so they are able to tweak marketing strategies based on the insights. AI offers complete customer support that delivers results.

Improved Marketing Strategy

If a digital marketer does not create the right marketing strategy, it won't create the right customer experience. When you create content that is relevant to customers, you create a rather personalized experience. In doing so, you create the possibility of a customer coming back again.

It also creates brand loyalty. When digital marketers integrate with AI, it increases the ability to focus on customer data. With the help of user data, the marketer can decide which content is relevant based on location and preference. It also helps to keep track based on website visits.

This type of strategy not only works for online retail but also social platforms. AI integration with eCommerce helps to tailor the overall shopping experience of a customer.

Most online websites make use of past patterns algorithms to recommend products to customers. When you shop online and see the list of recommended products, its actually the use of AI that comes into play.

The algorithm takes into account the shopping history, items in the cart, and previously purchased items from the website. The customer might want to buy a product based on this recommendation list.

AI SOLUTIONS AND SOCIAL VISIBILITY

AI tools can interconnect various social platforms. The blend of Data Science that is driven by AI on various social media accounts helps to categorize the audience based on demography and interests.

This then helps to transfer into the campaign material. AI provides digital marketers with the right opportunity to penetrate social media markets.

Both consumers and marketers can benefit from the hyper-personalized marketing campaigns that make use of AI tools. AI is paving the right way to campaign with increasing social visibility.

WHAT LIES AHEAD

With ever-changing and new emerging trends, AI and Data Science technology have paved the way for great business opportunities. Both marketers and consumers benefit from AI technology as it increases the social reach.

For digital marketers, it becomes easy to analyze data according to preferences and frame new strategies. In addition, for consumers, it offers a customized approach. AI has transformed the social visibility of brands, and the future looks bright as well.

CHAPTER

AI, ART AND CREATIVITY 4

INTRODUCTION

Artists have been working with AI since the 1970s. AI Art pioneers, such as Harold Cohen, Arthur Elsenaar and Remko Scha, David Cope, and Peter Beyls, comprised a minuscule enclave within the computer art community, primarily due to the complexity and scarcity of AI systems throughout the 1970s and 1980s, but also because this period was one of the AI "winters", with reduced research funding and receding interest in the field. AI research in the 1990s and 2000s provided more accessible tools for artists to confront and compare human and machinic behavior. With uncanny robotic works that question the meaning of agency, creativity, and expression, artists such as Ken Feingold, Ken Rinaldo, Louis Philippe-Demers, Patrick Tresset, Naoko Tosa, and others had articulated some of the contemporary AI art's topics.

Since the 2000s, artists such as Luke DuBois, Sam Lavigne, Sven König, Parag Kumar Mital, Kyle McDonald, Golan Levin, Julian Palacz, and others, have been creating generative and interactive works based on logical systems or statistical techniques which conceptually and technically overlap with, or belong to, AI technologies. They used natural language processing (NLP), pattern recognition, and computer vision (CV) algorithms to address various features of human perception reflected in AI, and to explore higher-level cognitive traits by interfacing human experiential learning with machine learning (ML).

The increasing affordance of multilayered sub-symbolic ML architectures such as Deep Learning (DL), as well as the raising socio-political impact of AI in the second half of the 2010s, have facilitated the expansion of AI art. Its production has been gaining momentum with the support of AI companies such as Google or OpenAI, and academic programs which have been facilitating art residencies, workshops, and conferences, while its exhibition has expanded from online venues to mainstream galleries and museums.

Contemporary AI art includes practices based on diverse creative approaches to, and various degrees of technical involvement with, ML. Its topics, methodologies, presentational formats, and implications are closely related to a range of disciplines engaged in AI research, development, and application. AI art is affected by epistemic uncertainties, conceptual challenges, conflicted paradigms, discursive issues, ethical, and socio-political problems of AI science and industry. Similar to other new media art disciplines, AI art has had an ambivalent relationship with the mainstream contemporary artworld (MCA); it is marked by selective marginalization and occasional exploitation, which entice artists to compromise some of their key poetic values in order to accommodate the MCA's conservative requirements for scarcity, commercial viability, and ownership.

Its interdependence with AI technologies and socio-economic trends exposes AI art to a critical consideration within a broader cultural context. The existing literature comprises several studies of AI art and implicitly relevant works. For example, Melanie Mitchell in *Artificial Intelligence*, as well as Gary Marcus and Ernest Davis in *Rebooting AI* provide a conceptual, technological, and socio-cultural critique of AI research.

Michael Kearns and Aaron Roth in *The Ethical Algorithm*, and Matteo Pasquinelli in *How a Machine Learns and Fails*, address the ethical, socio-political, and cultural consequences of the AI's conceptual issues, technical imperfections, and biases. With *The Artist in the Machine*, Arthur I. Miller includes AI art in the examination of creativity that spans his other books. In *AI Art* (2020), writer opens a multifaceted discussion of AI focusing on its influences on visual arts and culture.

In the Artnodes journal special issue *AI, Arts & Design: Questioning Learning Machines* (2020), edited by Andrés Burbano and Ruth West, the contributors address the issues of authorship and creative patiency (Galanter), the creative modes of AI art practices (Forbes), the public AI art (Mendelowitz), the use of ML in visual arts (Caldas Vianna), and the relationship between AI art and AI research (Tromble). In the *Atlas of AI* (2021), Kate Crawford maps the less desirable reflections of human nature in the AI business, hidden behind marketing, media hype, and application interfaces. In *Understanding and Creating Art with AI* (2021), Eva Cetiniæ and James She provide an overview of AI research that takes art as a subject matter, outline the practical and theoretical aspects of AI art, and anthologize the related publications.

New technologies, and in particular artificial intelligence, are drastically changing the nature of creative processes. Computers are playing very significant roles in creative activities such as music, architecture, fine arts, and science. Indeed, the computer is already a canvas, a brush, a musical instrument, and so on. However, we believe that we must aim at more ambitious relations between computers and creativity. Rather than just seeing the computer as a tool to help human creators, we could see it as a creative entity in its own right.

This view has triggered a new subfield of Artificial Intelligence called Computational Creativity. This section addresses the question of the possibility of achieving computational creativity through some examples of computer programs capable of replicating aspects of creative artistic behavior. We end with some reflections on the recent trend of democratization of creativity by means of assisting and augmenting human creativity.

Computational creativity is the study of building software that exhibits behavior that would be deemed creative in humans. Such creative software can be used for autonomous creative tasks, such as inventing mathematical theories, writing poems, painting pictures, and composing music. However, computational creativity studies also enable us to understand human creativity and to produce programs for creative people to use, where the software acts as a creative collaborator rather than a mere tool.

Historically, it has been difficult for society to come to terms with machines that purport to be intelligent and even more difficult to admit that they might be creative. Even within Computer Science, people are still skeptical about the creative potential of software. A typical statement of detractors of computational creativity is that "simulating artistic techniques means also simulating human thinking and reasoning, especially creative thinking. This is impossible to do using algorithms or information processing systems."

As is hopefully evident from the examples in this section, creativity is not some mystical gift that is beyond scientific study but rather something that can be investigated, simulated, and harnessed for the good of society. And while society might still be catching up, computational creativity as a discipline has come of age. This maturity is evident in the amount of activity related to computational creativity in recent years; in the sophistication of the creative software we are building; in the cultural value of the artifacts being produced by our software; and most importantly, in the consensus we are finding on general issues of computational creativity.

Computational creativity is a very lively subject area, with many issues still open to debate. For instance, many people still turn to the Turing test to approximate the value of the artifacts produced by their software. That is, if a certain number of people cannot determine which artifacts were computer generated and which were human generated, then the software is doing well. Other people believe that the Turing test is inappropriate for creative software. One has to ask the question: "Under full disclosure, would people value the artifacts produced by a computer as highly as they would the human produced ones?" In some domains, the answer could be yes: for instance, a joke is still funny whether or not it is produced by a computer. In other domains, such as the visual arts, however, the answer is very likely to be no.

This highlights the fact that the production process, and not just the outcome of it, is taken into account when assessing artworks. Hence, one could argue that such Turing-style tests are essentially setting the computers up for a fall.

Building creative software provides both a technical challenge and a social one. To proceed further, we need to embrace the fact that computers are not human. We should be loud and proud about the artifacts being produced by our software. We should celebrate the sophistication of the artificial intelligence (AI) techniques we have employed to endow the software with creative behavior. And we should help the general public to appreciate the value of these computer creations by describing the methods employed by the software to create them.

Creativity seems mysterious because when we have creative ideas it is very difficult to explain how we got them and we often talk about vague notions like "inspiration" and "intuition" when we try to explain creativity. The fact that we are not conscious of how a creative idea manifests itself does not necessarily imply that a scientific explanation cannot exist. As a matter of fact, we are not aware of how we perform other activities such as language understanding, pattern recognition, and so on, but we have better and better AI techniques able to replicate such activities.

Since nothing can arise from the emptiness, we must understand that every creative work or creative idea is always preceded by a historical-cultural scheme; it is a fruit of the cultural inheritance and the lived experiences.

Probably the new thoughts that originate in the mind are not completely new, because have their seeds in representations that already are in the mind. To put it differently, the germ of our culture, all our knowledge and our experience, is behind each creative idea. The greater the knowledge and the experience, the greater the possibility of finding an unthinkable relation that leads to a creative idea. If we understand creativity like the result of establishing new relations between pieces of knowledge that we already have, then the more previous knowledge one has the more capacity to be creative.

With this understanding in mind, an operational, and widely accepted, definition of creativity is: "A creative idea is a novel and valuable combination of known ideas." In other words, physical laws, theorems, musical pieces can be generated from a finite set of existing elements and, therefore, creativity is an advanced form of problem solving that involves memory, analogy, learning, and reasoning under constraints, among others, and is therefore possible to replicate by means of computers.

This section addresses the question of the possibility of achieving computational creativity through some examples of computer programs capable of replicating some aspects of creative behavior. Due to space limitations we could not include other interesting areas of application such as: storytelling, poetry, science, or even humor. Therefore, with different levels of detail, representative results of some achievements in the fields of music and visual arts.

The reason for focusing on these artistic fields is that they are by far the ones in which there is more activity and where the results obtained are most impressive. The paper ends with some reflections on the recent trend of democratization of creativity by means of assisting and augmenting human creativity.

Computational Creativity in Music

Artificial intelligence has played a crucial role in the history of computer music almost since its beginnings in the 1950s. However, until quite recently, most effort had been on compositional and improvisational systems and little effort had been devoted to expressive performance. In this section we review a selection of some significant achievements in AI approaches to music composition, music performance, and improvisation, with an emphasis on the performance of expressive music.

Composing Music

Hiller and Isaacson's work, on the ILLIAC computer, is the best-known pioneering work in computer music. Their chief result is the Illiac Suite, a string quartet composed following the "generate and test" problem-solving approach. The program generated notes pseudo-randomly by means of Markov chains. The generated notes were next tested by means of heuristic compositional rules of classical harmony and counterpoint. Only the notes satisfying the rules were kept. If none of the generated notes satisfied the rules, a simple backtracking procedure was used to erase the entire composition up to that point, and a new cycle was started again. The goals of Hiller and Isaacson excluded anything related to expressiveness and emotional content. In an interview, Hiller and Isaacson said that, before addressing the expressiveness issue, simpler problems needed to be handled first. We believe that this was a very correct observation in the 1950s. After this seminal work, many other researchers based their computer compositions on Markov probability transitions but also with rather limited success judging from the standpoint of melodic quality. Indeed, methods relying too heavily on Markovian processes are not informed enough to produce high-quality music consistently.

AI ART

AI art tools like Craiyon (formerly DALL-E mini) and Midjourney have been making waves on the internet over recent months. But are these artificial intelligence tools exhibiting creativity, or just clever mimics? How will AI art impact artists themselves? And how can machine learning be effectively used in artistic, creative and design endeavours most effectively?

At this year's Colorado State Fair's annual art competition awarded its prize to an AI-generated piece entitled "Théâtre D'opéra Spatial" by Jason M. Allen. But Allen didn't paint or sculpt the work – it was generated by AI art tool Midjourney.

AI art is a type of artwork created with the help of artificial intelligence. Algorithms can generate AI art, or humans can create them using AI tools. For example, an algorithm could be used to create a painting that looks like it was made by Picasso, or a human artist could use an AI tool to generate a 3D sculpture. There are many types of AI art, and the medium is constantly evolving, making it hard to say exactly what AI art is. Still, we can narrow it down to two main categories: digital and physical.

Digital art is any type of art created electronically, such as a painting created using an AI tool like our text-to-image art generator. Physical art, on the other hand, is any type of art created in the physical world, such as a 3D sculpture, created using AI-assisted technology.

Now that we know what AI art is, let's explore its history.

BRIEF HISTORY OF AI ART

The history of AI art dates back to 1973, when American computer scientist Harold Cohen created the first-ever AI painting. Cohen's painting was created using a program he developed called AARON. AARON is an artificial intelligence program that generates art based on a set of rules Cohen programmed into it–for example, one of the rules might have been to "paint a blue line." Using this rule, AARON would generate a painting that consisted of various blue lines. Cohen's "paintings" were abstract, and they were often compared to the work of Jackson Pollock. But unlike Pollock, Cohen did not drip paint onto his canvases. Instead, he instructed the algorithms he developed to draw for him.

Although AARON was the first digital AI art creator, it was not the first time we had been introduced to intelligent machines. For example, Gordon Pasks developed a machine called MusiColour in 1953. MusiColour was a reactive machine that responded to environmental sound to drive an array of lights, and was one example of an intelligent machine at the time, as many others were in the development process.

Jumping ahead to 2014, generative adversarial networks (GANs) were developed. At a basic level, a GAN has two components: a generator and a discriminator. The generator generates new data, such as images, similar to the training data. The discriminator, on the other hand, is responsible for determining whether the data created by the generator is real or fake.

So how does this relate to AI art?

GANs can be used to generate realistic images, such as portraits, and in the world of AI art, GANs have been used to create stunning pieces of artwork. For example, a GAN-generated painting called Edmond de Belamy was sold for $432,500 at a 2018 auction. The painting was a tribute to Ian Goodfellow–the inventor of GANs.

How can you create AI art?

Fortunately, art enthusiasts no longer need complex computer science knowledge to create AI art today. There are a wide range of user-friendly AI tools that you can use to create and sell digital paintings with just a few clicks.

Perhaps the easiest of these to use is our text-to-image AI generator, which converts a simple text prompt into a beautiful painting. For example, if you wanted to create a landscape with a sunset, you could simply type "landscape with a sunset" into the text box, and our generator would do the rest.

On the other hand, if you want to create art that is "dreamy" or "trippy," you could use a deep dream artwork generator tool. Many of these tools are available online and are based on Google's DeepDream project, which was a major advancement in the company's image recognition capabilities.

Artificial Intelligence Art (AI Art) is an artistic niche developed thanks to the latest advances in computer vision and deep learning. In particular, its development has been aided by the massive adoption by researchers and artists of Generative Adversarial Networks (GANs), a class of machine learning invented by researcher Ian Goodfellow and colleagues in 2014.

AI Art refers to any work of art created with the assistance of a system based on artificial intelligence and falls under the umbrella of Generative Art. The latter indicates art that has been created, in whole or in part, with the use of a (usually) non-human system capable of autonomously determining the characteristics of an artwork without the direct intervention of the artist.

A Few Important Milestones

Since the development of AI Art is largely based on the advances in deep learning, a family of methodologies within machine learning (which is part of artificial intelligence), we have also included some important dates concerning the field of AI. Moreover, as the artistic niche falls under the umbrella of Generative Art, which refers not only, but also to Algorithmic Art, we have included a few information related to Computer and Generative Art. Two resources were used to reconstruct a chronological order that took into account the sphere of both AI and art: the article of Gil Press "A Very Short History Of Artificial Intelligence" (1) appeared on Forbes, and the "Timeline of AI Art" by AIArtists.org .

- **1950:** Crypt analyst and computer scientist Alan Turing introduced the "Imitation Game", currently known as the "Turing Test". The test measures the capability of a machine to show intelligence equal or identical to that of humans

- **1956:** American computer scientist John McCarthy created the term *artificial intelligence*. He is considered one of the founding fathers of AI, together with Marvin Minsky, Allen Newell, Alan Turing, and Herbert A. Simon. With Minsky the field of AI started to follow a symbolic description approach also known as a top-down approach.
- **1959:** Arthur Samuel, an American pioneer in computer gaming and AI, made popular the term *machine learning*, a sub-field of artificial intelligence that revolves around algorithms, which improve by the utilization of data and experience
- **'60 - '70:** Computer Art pioneers such as Vera Molnár, Lillian Schwartz, Georg Nees, Frieder Nake, etc. explored the creation of art through generative systems.
- **'70 - '90:** Academic and artist Harold Cohen designed AARON, a computer program able to autonomously create original images. The program has progressively developed since the beginning of the seventies and also investigates aspects related to creativity
- **1990:** Roboticist Rodney Brooks pushed the idea of a bottom-up approach to AI. Inspired by the latest discoveries in the field of neuroscience, he brought the discourse on neural networks back to the fore (i.e., connections approach).
- **1996:** IBM supercomputer Deep Blue defeated chess grand master and world champion Garry Kasparov
- **2001:** Computational Creativity Professor Simon Colton set up *The Painting Fool* webpage and declared the aim of the project: "to engineer a software system that is one day taken seriously as a creative artist in its own right". The Painting Fool is an AI-based system that paints original works "to address philosophical notions such as emotion and intentionality in non-human intelligences" while showing "behaviours that might be deemed as skillful, appreciative and imaginative." The professor started working on the code as early as 1998.
- **2001**: Artist Casey Reas and data visualization expert Ben Fry designed Processing, an integrated development environment (IDE) thought for new media art, visual design, and electronic arts, which teaches non-tech savvy users the basics of computer programming using a visual context. Its impact on democratizing access to generative art has been huge
- **2009:** In order to help the advancement of computer vision and the research in deep learning, Stanford researcher Dr. Fei Fei Li started the research project ImageNet. This is a large dataset of images made free to use for

researchers. It maps the "entire world of objects"and is organized according to the WordNet hierarchy. It contains more than 14 million hand-annotated images labelled through crowdsourcing

- **2011:** IBM Watson, a question-answering (QA) computer system based on natural language, won American quiz *Jeopardy!*.
- **2014:** Machine learning researcher Ian Goodfellow and colleagues designed a group of frameworks called Generative Adversarial Networks (GANs). GANs are made of two networks (i.e., Generator and Discriminator) that compete in a game to generate new images and have been popular since 2018.
- **2015:** Google engineer Alexander Mordvintsev created DeepDream, a computer vision program based on a Convolutional Neural Network (CNNs) that detects and enhances patterns in images. The output of the program has a hallucinogenic aspect and received great interest both from the scientific and the artistic community.
- **2015:** Neural Style Transfer (NST) was launched as a class of software algorithms that manipulate videos and digital images by taking a style or appearance of another image. In NST, deep neural networks (DNN) are used for transforming an image into something different based on existing styles.
- **2016:** Google DeepMind released *AlphaGo*, a computer program that made history defeating Lee Sedol, Go champion.
- **2018:** One of the first AI-based artwork was sold in Paris at the Grand Palais by researcher and artist Alagraphy.
- **2018:** *Edmond de Belamy*, a work by French collective Obvious, was sold by Christie's at auction for $432,500, bringing attention to the niche of AI Art.
- **2019:** Sotheby's put at auction *Memories of Passerby I*, an AI-based artwork of pioneer artist Mario Klingemann. The lot sold at auction for £40,000
- **2020:** OpenAI released GPT-3 (Generative Pre-trained Transformer 3). Based on deep learning, it is a language model that produces human-like text. At the moment, it is one of the most powerful tool to generate natural language
- **2021:** OpenAI released DALL-E, which is a program that creates images from descriptions based on text (i.e., "it is a 12-billion parameter version of GPT-3 trained to generate images from text descriptions"). It interprets inputs based on natural language and generates images that correspond to it utilizing a dataset of text–image pairs. "The images that DALL-E generates are curated by CLIP, which presents the highest-quality images for any given prompt"

- **2021:** OpenAI released CLIP (Contrastive Language-Image Pre-Training) (9), a neural network that "learns visual concepts from natural language supervision"

POETICS

This framework requires an inclusive view on the poetic features of prominent AI art practices, ranging from popular/mainstream to tactical and experimental. The discussion addresses the thematic, conceptual, methodological, technical, and presentational aspects of exemplar artworks that belong to disparate formal, thematic, or procedural categories.

The poetic scope of AI art derives from computer art and generative art and is primarily informed by the various phenomenological aspects of sub-symbolic ML systems. It comprises the strategies that explore the epistemological boundaries and artifacts of ML architectures; sample the latent space of DL networks; aestheticize or spectacularize the renderings of ML data; and critique the conceptual, existential, or socio-political consequences of applied AI; a few works criticize AI art itself. The existing taxonomies or categorizations of AI art are useful but should be considered as provisory due to the creative dynamics of the field, particularly with respect to AI research.

Creative Agency and Authorship

Themes such as creative agency, authorship, originality, and intellectual property are widely attractive to AI artists, popular with the media, and fascinating to the audience. The malleability of these notions was central to modernism and postmodernism, and artists have been addressing them with computational tools since the 1960s, so this recent surge of interest is probably due to a combination of the novelty of DL, its processual opacity, and its specific informational or formal effects. However, artistic exploration of this territory has been challenged by the AI's most pervasive ambiguity—anthropomorphism.

Anthropomorphism manifests in various forms. One is a tendency to assign human cognitive or behavioral features to non-human entities or phenomena, which often proves difficult to identify and sometimes has undesired consequences. In AI research, the anticipation of emergent intelligence is based upon a belief that software will attain intelligence and develop emotions given enough training data and computational power.

Besides being technically dubious, this is an anthropocentric position, another version of the tenet that humanity is the sine qua non of the universe. It is complicated by the corporate AI's crowdsourcing of cheap, invisible, and underrecognized human labor for tasks such as dataset interpretation, classification, or annotation, whose outcomes affect ML training models or algorithms.

Anthropomorphism is broadly sensationalized in AI art discourse, for example by authors such as Arthur I. Miller who argues for the (intrinsic) creativity of AI systems. His narratives often rely on anthropocentric expressions, such as "what neural network sees", and identify creativity in AI as generating new information. A converse form of anthropomorphic fallacy is to conflate the artists' creative agency with cumulative human creativity embedded in their tools (computers and software), which simultaneously deprives artists of their own inventiveness, and lifts the responsibility off of their creative acts. Shared between some researchers, many artists, and the media, it often exploits the trope of the ever "blurring line between artist [ghost] and machine", and involves experiments which are supposed to establish "who is the artist" or "what is real/better art" by manipulating the preferential conditions of human subjects tasked with evaluating human- and machine-produced artefacts. Such experiments are often naïve or manipulative because they presume—and instruct the subjects—that their test material *is* art while omitting two fundamental distinctions: who considers something as an artwork, and why. They disregard that art is artificial by definition, and ignore the well-informed notions about a complex relationship between creative agency, authorship, and technology.

The Elusive Artist

In his long-term project *AARON* (1973–2016), the pioneering AI artist Harold Cohen experimented with translating and extrapolating some components of human visual decision-making into a robotic drawing/painting system. He had an ambiguous relationship with machinic creative agency and flirted with anthropomorphic rhetoric. Not surprisingly, a highly popular segment of contemporary AI art belongs to the saccharine reiterations of Cohen's approach, in which artists "teach" their robots how to paint, such as Pindar Van Arman's *Painting Robots* or Joanne Hastie's *Abstractions (Tech Art Paintings)* (since 2017). Driven by weekend painters' enthusiasm, these projects "serendipitously" merge technically competent execution with dilettante aesthetics, conceptual ineptness, and ignorance of art-historical context. The meaning of the word "art" collapses into banal, camera-driven visualizations, rendered and presented with amateurish self-confidence in a series of "progressively improved" ML systems.

Anthropomorphism is also advocated within the art-academic domain, for example by Simon Colton's discussion of his project *The Painting Fool* that he hopes "will one day be taken seriously a creative artist in its own right." Its aim is to dramatically expand the artistic range of Cohen's *AARON* by introducing the software interface that could be trained by different human artists, able to critically appraise its own work, and (in future versions) the work of other artists.

Fewer artists address the subtlety of this topical range. One of them is Adam Basanta. In his installation *All We'd Ever Need Is One Another*, a custom software randomizes the settings of two mutually facing flatbed scanners so that in every scanning cycle, each captures a slightly altered mix of the facing scanner's light and its own unfocused scanning light reflected off the opposite scanner's glass plate. The perceptual hashing algorithms then compare each scan to the images in a large database assembled by scraping images and image metadata from freely accessible online artwork repositories.

If the comparison value between the scan and its most similar database image exceeds 83% based on the parameters such as aspect ratio, composition, shape, and color distribution, the software declares a "match", selects the scan for printing, and labels it according to the matching image metadata.

Performative Aesthetizations

Performance artists who enjoy the sponsorship of corporate AI tend to emphasize dubious human-centered notions of creative agency through sleekly anesthetized mutations of earlier avant-garde practices. For example, Sougwen Chung's homo-robotic projects, such as *Drawing Operations Unit: Generation 2*, draw a comparison with Roman Verostko's algorist compositions from the 1980s and 1990s. Whereas Verostko encapsulates his coding experiments with pure form into a discreet relationship between his pen-plotter and its material circumstances, Chung uses the theatricality of her collaboration with robots as a "spiritualizing force" to mystify the manual drawing process—which is by nature highly improvisational and technologically interactive.

Similarly, Huang Yi's robotic choreography *HUANG YI & KUKA* (since 2015, sponsored by KUKA) spectacularizes the metaphors of harmonious human-machine interaction and mediates them safely to the comfortable spectators, while the referential Stelarc's performances since 1976, such as *Ping Body* (1996), emphasize the existential angst and uncertainty of shared participatory responsibilities between the artist, technology, and the audience who all have a certain degree of manipulative influence on each other. Also sponsored by KUKA, Nigel John Stanford's musical performance *Automatica: Robots vs. Music* (2017), can be viewed as an encore of Einstürzende Neubauten's concerts from the 1980s "spiced up" for tech-savvy cultural amnesiacs. Rehearsed beyond the point of self-refutation, Stanford's "improvisations" stand in as formally polished but experientially attenuated echoes of Einstürzende's rugged guilty pleasures in sonic disruption.

With high production values and aesthetics palatable to the contemporary audience, these AI-driven acts largely evade the unfavorable comparisons with their precursors and serve as marketing instruments for their corporate sponsors by promoting vague notions of robotically-enhanced consumerist lifestyle. Their persuasibility relies on our innate anthropocentrism, myopic retrospection, and susceptibility to spectacles.

The Uncanny Landscapes

The exploration of anthropomorphism in AI art often involves the uncanny appearance of artificial entities. Uncanniness is the occasional experience of perceiving a familiar object or event as unsettling, eerie, or taboo, and it can be triggered in close interaction with AI-driven imitations of human physique or behavioral patterns.

Some artists approach it implicitly, for example by extracting human-like meaningfulness from the machinic textual conversation in Jonas Eltes' *Lost in Computation* (2017) with reference to Ken Feingold's installations such as *If, Then*, *What If*, and *Sinking Feeling* (all 2001). In these works, NLP systems provide semantically plausible but ultimately senseless continuation of narrative episodes which allude to the flimsiness of the Turing test and serve as vocalized metaphors of our lives. They extend the experience of uncanny awkwardness into the absurdity of miscommunication and accentuate the overall superficiality of the systems tasked to emulate human exchange.

Ross Goodwin and Oscar Sharp used this type of slippage to disrupt the cinematic stereotypes in their short film *Sunspring*. Trained with the 1980s and 1990s sci-fi movie screenplays found on the Internet, Goodwin's ML software generated the screenplay and the directions for Sharp to produce *Sunspring*. It brims with awkward lines and plot inconsistencies but qualified with the top ten entries in the Sci-Fi London film festival's 48-Hour Film Challenge. *Sunspring* reverses the corporate movie search algorithms and playfully mimics contemporary Hollywood's screenwriting strategies largely based on regurgitating successful themes and narratives from earlier films.

By regurgitating *Sunspring*'s concept and methodology two years later, Alexander Reben produced "the world's first TED talk written by an A.I. and presented by a cyborg" titled *Five Dollars Can Save the Planet*. A YouTube comment by MTiffany fairly deems it "Just as coherent, relevant, and informative as any other TED talk.".

Another approach to implicit uncanniness is by alluding to the intimate familiarity of the human body, for example in Scott Eaton's *Entangled II* (2019) which is comparable to earlier, structurally more sophisticated video works such as Gina Czarnecki's *Nascent* and *Spine*, or Kurt Hentschläger's *CLUSTER* and *HIVE*. Ironically, projects that combine uncanniness with our apophenic perception in order to "humanize" AI often contribute to diverting attention from pertinent socio-political issues. For example, with *JFK Unsilenced: The Greatest Speech Never Made*, the Rothco agency aimed at contemplative uncanniness by exploiting the emotional impact of sound to reference the romanticized image of John F. Kennedy.

Based upon the analysis of 831 recorded speeches and interviews, Kennedy's voice was deepfaked in a delivery of his address planned for the Dallas Trade Mart on 22 November 1963. The voice sounds familiar at the level of individual words and short phrases, but its overall tone is uneven, so the uncanniness relies mainly on the context of the speech that the young president never had a chance to give.

However, even with perfect emulation of accent and vocalization, this exercise could never come close to matching the eeriness and deeply disturbing political context of Kennedy's televised speech on 22 October 1962 about the Cuban missile crisis in which sheer good luck prevented the multilateral confusion, incompetence, ignorance, and insanity of principal human actors from pushing the world into nuclear disaster.

Visual deepfakes, such as Mario Klingemann's *Alternative Face* (2017) or Libby Heaney's *Resurrection (TOTB)*, approach the psycho-perspective mechanism of uncanniness explicitly, by simultaneously emphasizing and betraying the visual persuasiveness of statistically rendered human-like forms. This strategy was prefigured conceptually and procedurally, which facilitated continuous audiovisual synthesis from an arbitrary sample pool. It used psychoacoustic techniques to calculate the spectral signatures of the audio subsamples from stored video material, and saved them in a multidimensional database; the database was searchable in real-time to mimic any sound input by playing the matching audio subsamples synchronized with their corresponding video snippets. Perhaps this innovative project has been largely forgotten because König pitched it to the VJ scene rather than using it to develop artworks that establish meaningful relations between their stored videos and input audio (both selectable by the artist). Along with the sophistication of his technique, König's expressive mismatch may have anticipated the analogous issues in contemporary AI art.

The Mechanical Turkness

The socio-political aspects of anthropomorphism can be effectively addressed by addressing the deep social embeddedness of complex technologies such as AI and by exposing human roles and forms of labor behind the "agency" or performative efficacy of corporate AI.

For example, Derek Curry and Jennifer Gradecki's project *Crowd-Sourced Intelligence Agency (CSIA)* (since 2015) offers a vivid educational journey through problems, assumptions, or oversights inherent with ML-powered dataveillance practices. It centers around an online app that partially replicates an Open Source Intelligence (OSINT) system, and allows the visitors to assume the role of data security analysts by monitoring and analyzing their friends' Twitter messages, or by testing the "delicacy" of their own messages before posting them.

The app features an automated Bayesian classifier designed by the artists and a crowdsourced classifier trained on participant-labeled data from over 14,000 tweets, which improves its accuracy by the visitors' feedback on its previous outputs. *CSIA* also includes a library of public resources about the analytic and decision-making processes of intelligence agencies: tech manuals, research reports, academic papers, leaked documents, and Freedom of Information Act files. This multilayered relational architecture offers an active learning experience enhanced by the transgressive affects of playful "policing" in order to see how the decontextualization of metadata and the inherent ML inaccuracies can distort our judgment.

Similarly, RyBN and Marie Lechner's project *Human Computers* provides revelatory counter-intuitive insights into the use of human beings as micro-components of large computational architectures. It is based upon multi-layered media archaeology of human labor in computation since the 18th century. It shows that many AI applications have in fact been simulacra, mostly operated by echelons of underpaid workers, which corporate AI euphemistically calls "Artificial Artificial Intelligence" (AAI) or "pseudo-AI". This foundational cynicism of corporate AI indicates that its development imposes an exploitative framework of cybernetic labor-management, which significantly diverges from Norbert Wiener's cybernetic humanism in *The Human Use of Human Beings*. A sub-project of *Human Computers*, titled *AAI Chess*, was an online chess app with three all-human playing modes: human vs. human, human vs. Amazon MTurker, and MTurker vs. MTurker. In 2020, Jeff Thompson "replayed" *AAI Chess* with his performance *Human Computers*, in which the visitors were tasked to manually resolve a digital image file (Google StreetView screenshot of the gallery) from its binary form into a grid of pixels. With 67 calculations per pixel, the complete human-powered image assembly takes approximately eight hours. Here, the visitors' unmediated enactment of automated operations asserts how a combination of complexity and speed in pervasive technologies makes them difficult to understand and manage by an individual.

These projects were conceptually and methodologically anticipated by several earlier works, particularly by Kyle McDonald and Matt Mets' *Blind Self Portrait*, and Matt Richardson's *Descriptive Camera*. In *Blind Self Portrait*, a laptop-based face recognition setup draws linear portraits of the visitors, but in order for the setup to work, the sitter has to keep eyes closed while resting their hand on a horizontally moving platform and holding a pen on paper. Unlike Van Arman's, Hastie's, or Patrick Tresset's drawing robots (*Human Studies* series since 2011), which put their sitters in a traditionally passive role, *Blind Self Portrait* makes a reference (intended or not) to William Anastasi's *Subway Drawings* from the 1960s and playfully turns visitors into the "mechanical parts" of a drawing system, self-conscious of their slight unreliability. Richardson's *Descriptive Camera* has a lens but no display; it sends the photographed image directly to an Amazon MTurker tasked to write down and upload its brief description, which the device prints out.

By exploiting human labor in order to emulate the features of AI systems or AI-enabled devices, these projects remind us that the "Turk" in AI is still not mechanical or artificial enough, he resists "emancipation", and it is not easy to make him more "autonomous". Their self-referential critique also points to the ethically questionable use of non-transparent crowdsourcing in art practices exemplified by earlier Aaron Koblin's projects *The Sheep Market* (2006), *10,000 Cents* (2008), and *Bicycle Built for Two Thousand* (2009, with Daniel Massey).

It is noteworthy, however, that artistic attempts to approach computational creativity through active open-sourced participation can be equally undermined by the muddled relationship with anthropomorphic notions. Seeing ML as a tool that "captures our shared cognitive endowments", "collective unconscious", or "collective imagination", Gene Kogan initiated a crowdsourced ML project *Abraham* in 2019 with a goal to redefine agency, autonomy, authenticity, and originality in computational art. The opening two parts of Kogan's introductory essay describe *Abraham* as "an open project to create an autonomous artificial artist, a decentralized AI who generates art", and elaborate on the idea in a semantically correct but conceptually derisive discussion, raising suspicion that the author is unaware of Jaron Lanier's prescient critique of online collective creativity and the subsequent relevant work. The missing parts 3 and 4 of the essay were proposed to be published by the end of 2019.

Epistemological Space

Art methodologies that address the epistemological character and boundaries of ML often involve sampling of multi-dimensional datasets in the inner (hidden) layers of network architectures and rendering their representations compressed in two or three dimensions. Artists treat these datasets as a latent space, a realm between "reality" and "imagination", replete with suggestions that emerge from a complex interplay between the various levels of statistical abstraction or determination.

Inceptionism

The exploration of latent space started with adaptations of a CV software package DeepDream in order to produce imagery and animations in a quasi-style called Inceptionism, characterized by delirious fractal transformations of pareidolic chimeras. Examples include Mike Tyka's DeepDream; Gene Kogan's DeepDream Prototypes (2015); James Roberts' Grocery Trip (2015); Samim Winiger's ForrestGumpSlug (2015); Josh Nimoy's Fractal Mountains, Hills, and Wall of Faces (all 2015); Memo Akten's All Watched Over and Journey Through the Layers of the Mind (both 2015); Johan Nordberg's Inside an Artificial Brain (2015) and Inside Another Artificial Brain (2016).

Inceptionist works struggled to become more than decorative interventions, and the trend dried out relatively quickly. Besides the inherent structural uniformity and apparent formal similarities between Inceptionist works, the main reason is that arbitrary generation of mimetic imagery or animations tends to become oversaturating and boring if it unfolds unbounded. In order to engage the viewer, it requires prudently defined conceptual, narrative, and formal constraints, which seemed to be difficult to implement with DeepDream.

Sampling the Latent Space

Further experimentation prompted artists to transcend mere representation by exploiting ML with meaningful premises, and by finding more flexible aesthetics to mediate the latent space. To metaphorize the statistically structured epistemological scope of neural network architectures, artists often accentuate the tensions between their processual effectiveness and interpretative limitations.

Timo Arnall's Robot Readable World is an early example of this approach. It comprises found online footage of various CV and video analytics systems (vehicle and crowd tracking, counting and classification, eye-tracking, face detection/tracking, etc.), composited with layers that visualize their data in real-time. However, Arnall's attempt to reveal the "machinic perspectives" uses a human-readable (anthropocentric) approximation of the actual software data processing, tracing back to the funny but technically groundless translation of the terminator android's CV data to English in Terminator 2 (1991, directed by James Cameron). In Computers Watching Movies (2013), Ben Grosser handled this topic more appropriately.

It illustrates the CV processing of six popular film sequences in a series of temporal sketches in which the points and vectors of the CV's focal interest are animated as simple dots and lines on a blank background (the processed film footage is not visible), synchronized with the original film sound. This semi-abstraction draws viewers to make sonically-guided comparisons between their culturally developed ways of looking and the "attention" logic of CV software that has no narrative or historical patterns.

In contextually different settings, the semantic power of written text can provide strong generative experiences. For example, Nao Tokui and Shoya Dozono's *The Latent Future* (2017) is an ambient installation based on the interaction between an ML semantic model trained on a collection of past news and the real-time human or machine-generated news.

It continuously captures Twitter newsfeeds and uses their discerned meanings to create fictional news. The generated news is presented in a virtual 3D space that maps each sentence's latent feature vectors, while the distances between the sentences correspond to their relative semantic differences. This work is informed in real-time by the largely unpredictable dynamics of the Twitter galaxy, but also by Twitter's filtering algorithm which represents many important aspects of current socio-political trends.

The relational flexibility of human visual interpretation that *Learning to See* fails to address was brilliantly utilized by Perry Bard in a conceptually and formally comparable non-AI generative project *Man with a Movie Camera: The Global Remake* (2007–2014). It is an online platform that allows visitors to select any shot from Dziga Vertov's seminal film *Man with a Movie Camera* (1929) and upload their video interpretations. Bard's server-side software replays a two-channel setup comprising Vertov's original synchronized with a remake which is continuously assembled of the participants' shots (randomly selected when there are multiple uploaded interpretations of the original shot). By leveraging the creative breadth of human perception and cognition, this relatively simple technical setup engrosses both the uploaders and viewers in an intriguing and surprising experience.

GANism

In order to explore and mediate the latent space, artists have been developing various techniques that exploit the increasingly versatile GAN architectures. They reveal the artifactual character of GANs by treating autoencoder networks as compression algorithms, for example in Terence Broad's Blade Runner—Autoencoded (2016), or by allowing "unpolished" representations of GAN data, for example in Elle O'Brien's Generative Adversarial Network Self-Portrait (2019), or Jukka Hautamäki's New Parliament (2019) and Restituo I and II (2021).

Recent GAN techniques allow complex formal remixing by modifying generator or discriminator networks, for example in Golan Levin and Lingdong Huang's *Ambigrammatic Figures*, or by inserting filters and manipulating activations maps in the higher network layers to disrupt the image formation process, for example in Terence Broad's *Teratome*.

Due to their limited autonomy in choosing the training datasets or the statistical models that represent the latent space, GANs prove to be primarily the tools for processual mimicry rather than intelligent creative engines. Therefore, GAN manipulation renders ubiquitous visual character in disparate works produced with similar techniques. Although some projects go beyond purely technical/formal exploration or perceptual study, aesthetically (and often conceptually), many do not diverge significantly from earlier glitch art in which the error is an aestheticized frontline layer.

This expressive issue reaffirms the importance of the artist's decision-making and overall poetic articulation. In contrast to the tech community's quick approval and self-conceited assertions that "GAN artists have successfully cultivated their moderately abstract, dream-like aesthetic and promoted the process of serendipitous, often random usage of generative processes", the poetic identity of GAN artworks is dominated by Dali-esque or Tanguy-esque formal fusion (morphing), often visually oversaturated but conceptually bland.

The popularity of GANs has also escalated the misuse of the expression "generative art" to describe only the computational practices that involve randomness, complexity, or ML architectures. A disregard for the methodological diversity and long history of generative art impoverishes the broader contextual milieu of experimental art and facilitates the uncritical appreciation of AI art practices.

Spectacularization

AI art with the highest public visibility profile comprises derivative projects by mainstream artists, and big-budget AI art spectacles.

Derivative

The AI's growing ideological authority, socio-economic power, and the practical accessibility of ML software had induced the MCA's involvement with AI art in the mid-2010s. The recent adoption of blockchain crypto products such as non-fungible tokens (NFTs) for securing the marketability of digital entities further increased the gallery/museum and auction house interest, prompting the mainstream artists to assimilate ML into their repertoire and to update their poetic rhetoric accordingly. Similar to the post-digital artists a decade earlier, they approach digital technologies as affective markers of contemporary culture and act chiefly in collaboration with hands-on personnel to produce AI-derived works in conventional media (installation, sculpture, video, and photography) with a lower degree of technological entanglement than most experimental AI artworks.

This strategy affords them cultural recognition, institutional support, and commercial success, but sacrifices the intricate tension between the artworks' conceptual, expressive, or narrative layers and the contextual logic of the technologies in which they appear. Examples include Gillian Wearing's *Wearing Gillian*; Lucy McRae's *Biometric Mirror*; Hito Steyerl's *Power Plants* and *This is the Future*; Pierre Huyghe's *Of Ideal* (since 2019) and *UUmwelt* (2019); Kate Crawford and Trevor Paglen's *Excavating AI* (2018) and *Training Humans* (2019–2020), and others. The presentational authority and decorative appeal of this production tend to seduce the general audience into superficial aesthetic consumption or complacency, even when projects are created with critical intentions.

For example, Trevor Paglen's AI-related production has been praised as a critique of biases, flaws, and misconceptions of AI technologies, along with his established line of interest in visualizing the covert systems of power and control in the military, intelligence, state, or corporate institutions.

However, it is also criticizable as exploitation of activist perspective toward opto-centric epistemology, which mystifies high-end visual technologies and abuses the affective perception of institutional power through stylized gallery setups accompanied with highfalutin explanatory statements.

Paglen's collaborative project with Kate Crawford *ImageNet Roulette* (2019) is represented as being critical of classification biases in CV, but it is hard to see in it anything more than an overwhelming illustration of the issue. As an analytical, research-based revelatory critique of classification biases and AI technologies in general, it is neither new nor original, for example when contrasted with Curry and Gradecki's *CSIA* or with RyBN's systematic critical analysis in a number of projects, such as *Antidatamining* (since 2007) and *Human Computers*. Similarly, its socio-cultural commentary fades in comparison with Taryn Simon and Aaron Schwartz's project *Image Atlas* which addresses the same issues but discards loftiness for a more meaningful impact by obtaining simple imagery in complex ways and by coupling it with concise, unpretentious narratives.

Large Scale

The substantially market-driven operational criteria and depoliticized discourses of MCA have been epitomized by spectacular, large-scale AI art installations in various forms: static, generative, reactive, interactive, or self-modifying "intelligent environments". This high-profile/high-visibility approach had been ushered with corporate enterprises such as *The Next Rembrandt* (2016), collaboratively produced by ING bank, Microsoft, Technical University in Delft, and Mauritshuis art collection. They used DL for a complex multi-feature analysis of Rembrandt's paintings in order to generate and 3D print a "most representative" painting of his style. The project's promo language is typical of the corporate AI's patronizing anthropomorphism, claiming that it "brought the great master back to life".

Along with many GAN works discussed in Section 2.2, these practices willingly or unwillingly contribute to platform aesthetics—a mildly-amusing algorithmic generation of sonic, visual, spatial, or kinetic variations, which teases the visitors with the promise of novelty and insight, but effectively entrances them into cultural conformity and political deference. Dependent on the latest AI research and elaborately team-produced with significant budgets or commissions, the hyper-aestheticized AI art installations also warn how effectively the manipulative intents, unimpressive concepts, or trivial topics can be concealed behind skillful rendering, aggrandized by high production values, and popularized through the flamboyant exhibition.

The issues of platform aesthetics are exemplified by the AI installations produced in Refik Anadol's studio, which flirt with sophisticated production techniques, formal oversaturation, and inflated presentation. Their dubious motivations are clumsily veiled by inane flowery premises and by infantile anthropomorphic metaphors such as "transcoding the processes of how buildings think", or "how AI systems dream" or "hallucinate".

Anadol has frequently claimed his childhood fascination with the spectacular advertising in *Blade Runner* as one of the uplifting inspirations, without any self-critical reevaluation of the political background of visuals and architecture in that film. Only in 2021, he was induced to acknowledge his misreading of the dystopian essence of *Blade Runner*'s aesthetics. Consequently, despite the formal abundance and copious explanatory data (which usually do the opposite of demystifying the production), Anadol's spectacles have been virtually devoid of critical views on mass surveillance, immaterial labor, environmental damage, and other problematic aspects of the big data capture and processing they rely upon.

For comparison, we can take some of the monumental art practices throughout the 1980s that roughly coincided with the release of *Blade Runner*, such as Krzysztof Wodiczko's projections, Barbara Kruger's immersive setups, or Anselm Kiefer's heavy confrontational installations. They employed grand scale, formal saturation, and overidentification to critically appropriate and reflect the inherent use of overwhelming presentational strategies in gender-biased advertising, power structures, and totalitarian regimes. While the tactical values of these practices had been thereafter attenuated or recuperated in an inevitable process of cultural assimilation, they redefined the landscape of critical art with lasting historical impact and relevance.

Another telling parallel can be drawn between Marco Brambilla's *Nude Descending a Staircase No. 3* and Vladimir Todorovi's *The Running Nude*, which both relate to Marcel Duchamp's painting *Nude Descending a Staircase No. 2* (1912). Brambilla relies on compositional abundance and installation size to sustain the GAN animation that refers to the influence of early cinema on cubism and futurism. Todorovi's generative VR work unobtrusively leverages the problem of data interpretation in AI to reference the polyvalent interpretation in western fine arts tradition.

It provides a formally subdued but experientially intensive interactive experience in which the ASMR-whispered descriptions of select classical nude paintings are generated by an ML program trained on pulp love stories.

The crass complacency exerted by spectacular AI art suggests that its creators have skipped some of the required reading assignments of Modern Art History 101 courses, most notably Guy Debord's *The Society of the Spectacle* (1994). It discredits the self-serving claims of some cultural agents that spectacular AI art opens up opaque ML technologies, makes them more accessible to the public, and thus more exposed to critical assessment.

Tactical Exploration

The recurrence of tactical AI art exemplars throughout this study indicates their potential to direct the field toward a socially responsible and epistemologically relevant expressive stratum. Tactical AI art extends the heterogeneous line of critical practices in new media art, which have energized art and culture in the 20th and the 21st century by subverting and exposing the exploitative corporate strategies based on quantization, statistical reductionism, data-mining, behavioral tracking, prediction, and manipulation of decision-making.

Artists uncover the undesirable aspects and consequences of corporate AI and denounce biases, prejudices, economic inequalities, and political agendas encoded in the mainstream ML architectures. In some works, they also engage in an exploratory critique of the nature of ML as an artistic medium; the value of this critique is proportional to the artists' understanding of the political subtleties and ethical facets which are often dispersed across the conceptually abstract, technically convoluted, and functionally opaque ML systems. To incite active critical scrutiny, artists sometimes combine humor and provocation by intentionally taking seemingly ambivalent positions toward the issues they address; they emulate the corporate AI's operative models but recontextualize them or repurpose their objectives for ironic revelatory effects. One of the common repurposing methodologies involves taking an existent ML pipeline, training it with a nonstandard dataset, and employing it for novel tasks. Many successful tactical works refrain from dramatic interventions and didactic explanations in order to let the audience actively identify the interests, animosities, struggles, inequalities, and injustices of corporate AI.

Socio-Cultural

Artists often work with NLP to critique various cultural manifestations of applied AI. Examples include Matt Richardson's *Descriptive Camera*; Ross Goodwin's *Text Clock* and *word.camera*; Michel Erler's *Deep Learning Kubrick*; Ross Goodwin and Oscar Sharp's *Sunspring*; Jonas Eltes' *Lost in Computation*; Jonas Lund's *Talk to Me* (2017–2019); Joel Swanson's *Codependent Algorithms*, and others.

A number of related projects use NLP and language hacking to probe the intersection of AI technologies and MCA. For example, Disnovation.org's *Predictive Art Bot* questions the discursive authorities and aesthetic paradigms of AI art; Sofian Audry and Monty Cantsin's *The Sense of Neoism!* critiques the cogency of artists' manifestos and proclamations; Philipp Schmitt's *Computed Curation Generator* and Alexander Reben's *AI Am I (The New Aesthetic)* problematize art-historical models and narratives; Nirav Beni's *AI Spy* and Egor Kraft's *Museum of Synthetic History* (2021) address culturally entrenched aesthetic paradigms.

For interventions that relate to the socio-cultural issues of AI, artists use and modify GAN architectures to make deepfakes. For example, Libby Heaney's *Resurrection (TOTB)* thematizes both the star power in music and the memetic power of deepfakes. Visitors of this installation are invited to perform karaoke in which the original musician of the chosen song is video-deepfaked to mimic the visitor's singing and gesturing/dancing.

Additionally, in between songs the host Sammy James Britten involves the audience in the discussion of power, desire, and control—an extension that seems to be as imposing and redundant as the artist's explanatory section for this work. Heaney's *Euro(re)vision* (2019) addresses the transmission of power and politics in popular media more effectively. In this video deepfake, Angela Merkel and Theresa May sing absurd songs in the style of Dadaist Cabaret Voltaire performances within a setting of the Eurovision song contest. Their stuttering algorithmic poetry eerily resembles the nonsensicality of actual Brexit discourse and implies the broader semantic reality of political life.

With two iterations of *Big Dada: Public Faces*, Bill Posters and Daniel Howe confused the visitors of Instagram by inserting deepfaked fictional video statements by Marcel Duchamp (about the ashes of Dada), Marina Abramovi (about mimetic evolution), Mark Zuckerberg (about the second Enlightenment), Kim Kardashian (about psycho-politics), Morgan Freeman (about smart power), and Donald Trump (about truth). In several works, Jake Elwes critically engages the cultural implications of training dataset annotation and algorithm design in mainstream AI. His ongoing multipart *Zizi Project* interfaces deepfake with the world of LGBTQ+. *Zizi-Queering the Dataset* is a video installation continuously morphing through gender-fluid (androgynous) portraits and abstract forms. The online work *Zizi Show* critiques both anthropomorphism and error-prone gender inclusiveness of AI. This virtual drag cabaret features deepfakes generated from the training datasets with original films of London drag artists' performances. The *Zizi Project* clearly indicates that the training model datasets and statistical nature of data processing in GANs inevitably impose formal constraints to the possible outputs (such as realistic human-like images) regardless of the common rhetoric about the "unpredictability" or "originality" of such systems; however, this is an already known and well-documented issue.

The project fails to show how exactly the race, gender, and class inequalities and stereotypes transfer into ML to harm the underrepresented social, ethnic, or gender identity groups. The *Zizi Project*'s playful, technically sophisticated remediation within AI-influenced cultural context may be beneficial for the celebration, affirmation, and inclusion of LGBTQ+, but its publicity narratives, its high production values, and its focus on glamour and spectacle in lieu of less picturesque but perhaps more important existential aspects of LGBTQ+ can easily be perceived as artistic exploitation by means of ML.

Moreover, if taken seriously by corporate AI, this critique can backfire by contributing to the refined normalization, instead of correction, of socio-political biases toward the LGBTQ+ community because these biases have a broader, deeper, and darker evolutionary background.

In contrast, Derek Curry and Jennifer Gradecki's *Infodemic* (2020) and *Going Viral* exemplify a consistently more effective critique, recontextualization, and transformation of ML as a socio-technical realm. Both projects target celebrities, influencers, politicians, and tech moguls who have "contributed" to the COVID-19 pandemic by sharing misinformation and conspiracy theories about the coronavirus, which themselves went "viral", often spreading faster than real news. *Infodemic* features a cGAN-deepfaked talking head video in which some of these high profile misinformers deliver public service announcements that correct false narratives about the pandemic; their statements are taken from and voiced by academics, medical experts, and journalists.

In *Going Viral*, visitors of the project website are invited to help intervene in the infodemic by sharing on social media the "corrective" videos delivered by the deepfaked speakers in the *Infodemic*.

By playing with deepfakes within their native context of fake news, these projects also probe the broader phenomenology of mediated narratives. Together with *CSIA*, they testify to the effectiveness of Curry and Gradecki's tactics based on thorough research and self-referential methodology with computational media affordances.

A specific quality of their poetics is that playful participation is simultaneously a gateway to transgressive affects, an interface to learning resources, and a friendly implication of our complicity to the politically problematic aspects of the applied AI through conformity, lack of involvement, or non-action.

Physical and Existential

AI technologies affect socio-cultural life and politics both directly and indirectly, through the material/physical, ecological, and existential changes. Artists sometimes metaphorize this influence by using geospatial contents (landscapes, terrains, maps) for training datasets and by positioning the machine-learned output in contexts with various political connotations.

For example, Ryo Ikeshiro's *bug* is a sophisticated geospatial ambient work that addresses the uses of ML-powered sound event recognition and spatial/directional audio technologies in entertainment, advertising, surveillance, law enforcement, and the military. Similarly, Nao Tokui's *Imaginary Landscape* and *Imaginary Soundwalk* (both 2018) are formally economical interactive installations.

In *Imaginary Landscape*, the ML software continuously analyzes Google StreetView photographs, selects three that look similar, and joins them together horizontally in a three-wall projection. Another ML program, trained on landscape videos, generates soundscapes that correspond with stitched triptych landscapes. In *Imaginary Soundwalk*, viewers freely navigate Google StreetView for which the ML system, using the cross-modal technique for image-to-audio information retrieval, generates the "appropriate" soundscape. It is instructive to compare the meditative effectiveness of these projects with Anna Ridler and Caroline Sinders' interactive online work *Mechanized Cacophonies*.

Some works explore the physicality of AI through haptics (touch), for example Jeff Thompson's *I Touch You and You Touch Me*, or through kinetics, for example Stephen Kelly's lumino-sonic installation *Open-Ended Ensemble (Competitive Coevolution)*. François Quévillon's *Algorithmic Drive* also uses kinetics to play out the tension between robotics and the unpredictable nature of the world.

For this work, several months-worth of front-facing video capture was synchronized with information from the car's onboard computer, such as geolocation, orientation, speed, engine RPM, stability, and temperatures at various sensors. The captured videos and data feed a sampling system that sorts the content statistically and assembles a video that alternates between calm and agitated states by modifying parameters of sound, image, car's activity, and environment. An interactive controller displays data for each scene and allows visitor intervention.

Continuing the line of earlier statistically founded eco-conscious tactical media art, such as Chris Jordan's *Running the Numbers*, artists combine speculative approach with ML to generate visuals and narratives that address the environmental challenges and ecological aspects of large-scale computation-intense research, technologies, and industries such as AI.

A full spectrum of the applied AI's existential consequences is boldly integrated into Max Hawkins' *Randomized Living*. In this two-year experiment, Hawkins organized his life according to the dictate of recommendation algorithms. He designed a series of apps that shaped his life by randomized suggestions based on the online data: a city where he would live for about a month and, once there, the places to go, people to meet, and things to do. *Randomized Living* is a strong exemplar of cybernetic-existentialism—the art of conceiving a responsive and evolving cybernetic system in order to express deep existential concerns.

Issues

These examples show that, through success or failure, AI art expands the idea of technologically entangled creativity, and that a conscious consideration of the notion of creativity is a prerequisite for creative endeavors in general. They also point to the human fallacies, cultural constraints, and socio-political ambiguities, which manifest in the conceptual, methodological, ethical, and educational domains of AI art. By identifying, acknowledging, and understanding these issues, artists can refine their creative approaches and find new ways to intervene critically and productively in the AI-influenced social reality.

Cogency

AI research struggles with encoding crucial aspects of human cognition—such as intuition, abstraction, analogy-making, common sense, and inventiveness—into machine intelligence. Similarly, the poetic realm of contemporary AI art is most deficient in interesting intuitions, meaningful abstractions, and imaginative analogies. The field particularly lacks projects that use AI systems as means to actualize strong concepts which effectively address the wider perspectives or deeper issues of human existence.

Digital technologies offer a generous space for conceptual, as well as formal, methodological, and aesthetic experimentation that can transcend the technologically imposed limits of expression. However, the uneven intellectual breadth and depth, biased or constrained contextual awareness, and sketchy art-historical knowledge affect many AI artists' conceptual thinking, methodologies, and the cogency of their outcomes.

The lack of conceptual sophistication manifests as a disproportion between the artists' computational dexterity, their eloquence in articulating relevant ideas, and their competence with wider artistic, cultural, or historical contexts. Broadly speaking, AI artists and art-related AI researchers tend to ignore a century's worth of artmaking which has moved on from what Marcel Duchamp called the "retinal" paradigm.

Meredith Tromble notes that AI art methodologies that use training data comprised of canonical visual imagery resemble western fine arts practices of the 19th century when painters relied on synthesizing the stylistic elements and aesthetic values of Neoclassicism and Romanticism.

Artists who make generative AI works sometimes disregard that, in principle, the expressive cogency of generative artworks does not crucially rely on the generative system itself but on the conceptual meaningfulness and economy of the relationship between that system and the artwork's broader context.

That reflects a (naïve) lack of understanding that the poetic role of production techniques in the arts fundamentally unfolds and gets emancipated by its coupling with conceptual thinking and contextual awareness. Conversely, artists who exaggerate or fake technical competencies are equally problematic because their works usually miss some interesting technological aspects.

AI art tends to be technologically self-referential as many works rely on tautological or circular concepts based on the artists' ideas about ML technologies. Various notions of bio-detached and socially unembedded creative agency permeate both AI art production and its popular representation through confused, ambiguous, or openly mystifying rhetoric about "machinic artistry". They promote a pseudo-romantic quest for human-flavored creative "essence" within ML systems (and AI in general) instead of demystifying them as socio-political apparatuses which have little to do with creativity per se and are better understood as sophisticated tools for statistical analysis and measurement.

Complex devices such as computers and software only represent the cumulative human creativity invested in their design, but the artists' self-awareness, reasoning, abstraction, conceptualization, generalization, and analogy-making in dealing with these tools inform the cogency of their works. Their mental abilities, senses, emotions, passions, obsessions, and incentives determine how they interact with the world and make their art. These qualities and aspects should be at the forefront of AI artmaking. Conversely, a responsible approach to AI art requires a clear understanding that—while different forms of creative intelligence are possible and explorable—computers, robots, or algorithms are not artists because they do not embody human social embeddedness, cognitive capabilities, skills, quirks, and, most importantly, human motivations for making art.

Art is a human dispositive within anthropological and socio-cultural perspectives, so the motivations for expressing creativity through artmaking are partially driven by the evolutionary competitive ambition; among its many functions, art is a socially-constructed system for displaying mating fitness (intelligence, proteanism, wit) and for exhibiting or gaining social status. Therefore, it is crucial to acknowledge that the poetic qualities of our artefacts are inherently instrumentalizable as virtue signaling means.

Our unfolding experience with AI confirms that we can learn about technologies (and about the world) equally from their failures and from their successes. ML is based on the assumption that all relevant features can be found within the training data; this is problematic in real-life scenarios, especially in experiencing art where the overall context, audience's knowledge, and expectations are essential. ML algorithms can effectively identify frequency-related information about the formal features in artworks and utilize them in increasingly sophisticated ways, but they do not model how an artwork is perceived or interpreted. Following that logic, artists use ML to process material from external fields such as visual arts, music, or cinema, aiming to better understand or demystify ML or their processed cultural sources. But designing such ML systems, analyzing gathered information, and deriving meaning from it requires expertise in the logic of extraction, analytical skills, solid knowledge, and deep critical understanding of the processed material.

There is no a priori reason to expect that any given AI artist possesses all these attributes because what they ultimately do is artistic experimentation, not the emulation of scientific research. On the other hand, the question is also what special insights they can generate by aestheticizing the artifacts or by spectacularizing the superficial aspects of ML. It is frequently claimed that AI art offers an opportunity for scientists to better understand how machines function.

However, a critical view on this claim suggests that, if the scientific community needs art-generated insights to discern the functional logic of its core research subjects (such as deep neural networks), perhaps it is not taking its responsibilities seriously enough. The historical outlook at the disastrous socio-political consequences of applied science/technology should remind us that contemporary science, technology, and related businesses need a thorough improvement of epistemological and ethical standards facing the increasing complexity of human existence.

Authenticity

Methodological similarities and aesthetic uniformity of AI art are directly related to the artists' notions of originality. In their production pipelines, artists often use, or sometimes modify, the existing code libraries, and usually train them with commonly available datasets, which leads to homogeneity. Many of them engage in a race to access the emerging code architectures before they become conceptually or aesthetically "exhausted", or to build new training models by curating their own datasets.

Production, perception, and reception of the arts have always been evolving in a complex symbiosis with technological and socio-political trends, so AI artists—as well as the media and the cultural sector which represent them—should be critically aware of these entanglements.

The overall poetics of AI art will remain a facile reflection of its technological reality as long as the majority of artists keep constraining their notions of authenticity and expressive cogency to prima facie relationship with technology.

They may benefit from a more general recognition that, in principle, the improved functionality of tech systems such as AI emancipates human intelligence to be expressed in different approaches to artistic creativity.

Various forms of apparent but often unacknowledged conceptual or methodological "overlaps", "reflections", and other types of dubious similarities between many artworks demonstrated throughout this paper, indicate the more basic issues of the AI artists' creative literacy and contextual appreciation. These issues are both cognitive and ethical.

Technocentrism

Successful AI art projects utilize their entanglements self-consciously, as the conceptual, tactical, and existentially inherent features within a broader context of digital culture. However, the complexity, interdependence, and pace of change make digital tools difficult to keep under artistic control. Most notably, the breadth of procedural literacy and coding skills required for elaborate AI art production tend to shape the artists' poetic reasoning, exploration and learning by directing their creative focus toward mathematics and programming.

Additionally, the fast competitive pace of producing AI art in current circumstances drains some of the artists' extra energy that comes from idleness and frivolity but often provides an invaluable touch of "dirt" which combines with experimentation, hard work, knowledge, serendipity, luck, and other decisive factors. In general, the engineering approach is usually a welcome enrichment of a "traditional" artistic mindset, but when it takes priority over other poetic factors, it reduces the scope of artists' critical engagement and the impact of their works. When artists are preoccupied with the performative efficiency or with the superficial effects of ML systems, the aestheticized demonstration outweighs discovery in their projects which struggle to engage the audience beyond AI-induced fascination.

Artists are responsible for counteracting these cognitive vectors in their individual working methodologies, but we also need to address them more carefully within academic programs and initiatives which integrate coding skills into a standard learning repertoire of art and design. Although they apparently strive for both versatility and thoroughness, most of the creative coding educational environments still tend to be more conducive for nerdy idiosyncrasies than for artistically essential "eccentricities" such as spontaneity, goofiness, wandering, or stubbornness.

On the other hand, they sometimes try to promote diversity uncritically or cynically by supporting weak ideas or conceptual naïveté and eventually usher students to adopt subpar professional criteria. Furthermore, these academic frameworks easily migrate from one trendy tech paradigm to another, often leaving the older but still relevant areas underexplored. A recent example is a shift from parametric techniques and symbolic logic to sub-symbolic ML in computational generative art.

Academism

Throughout *AI Art*, critiques various manifestations of academism in AI art, such as the repetition of topics, similarity of narratives and presentation forms, uniformity of production techniques, and homogeneity of aesthetic models. It is important to expand this critical view by identifying the specter of academism in critically motivated AI art, specifically in the instances when weak concepts, vague reasoning, contextual ignorance, or technophilic self-indulgence are dressed up in a combination of competent execution and emancipatory verbiage. This may be more challenging, but provides valuable insights into the field's undercurrent issues which expose it to recuperation due to the lack of methodological clarity, formal cogency, or experiential impact.

Inflated Speculation

Artists sometimes use speculative forms to stimulate the imagination and explore the "possible worlds" of AI by combining descriptive narratives with illustrative models, props, prototypes, imagery, etc. Speculative artworks leverage both the freedom of thought experiments and the "right to fail" long-established by performance art, which claims that—even if it fails to achieve its nominal goal—a performative act may provide a successful experience as long as its context, premise/intent, and process are meaningful. By an unspoken analogy, a speculative project can be legitimate as long as its context, premise/intent, and artefacts are not meaningless, which, of course, does not automatically make the project relevant. Although thinking and language afford incomparably more configurations than the material world, speculative projects are usually less convincing or impactful than artworks that directly actualize the artists' intents or ideas. That is because the speculative freedom and linguistic tolerance allow creators to hedge their expressive stakes; to be venturous but also to conceal the deficiencies of their projects.

In some projects, for example in Tega Brain, Julian Oliver, and Bengt Sjölén's AI-powered environmental speculation *Asunder*, the critical logic is so counter-intuitive, its points so sophisticated, and outcomes so delicate that its political vector is sidelined by the discussion about the work. This virtualization of critical focus (or purpose) may be fruitful within the academic milieu, but with a general audience, which is supposedly central to tactical art, it can easily be recognized as aloofness or cynicism and lead to indifference, distrust, or resentment.

Formal Dryness and Compromised Impact

Perception Engines is a series of semi-abstract compositions of percept agglomerations that encapsulate the visual models of various subjects (rabbit, banana, dalmatian, etc.) which score consistent object recognition across different AI vision algorithms. Its pertinent idea of exposing anthropomorphism in AI by emphasizing the pareidolic "universality" of machine vision through a skilful production methodology results in images that prove the concept but are uninteresting.

They look like computational deconstructions or rearrangements of hybrid Guston-Warhol-Koons-Murakami-emoji compositions, which document a scientific research project. Printing the images in traditional technique (serigraphy or screen-print) does not make them more convincing, and may even be detrimental if interpreted as a naïve attempt to "legitimize" the work artistically. The poetic identity of *Perception Engines* relies on its clever generative procedure with machine vision algorithms, which is, however, incomprehensible to most audiences.

Zombie Formalist critiques digital art's commodification through bland formalism that has been boosted by the crypto art market. In this installation, two AI-powered lightboxes randomly generate images in the style of painters such as Gene David, Barnett Newman, Kenneth Noland, and Karl Benjamin. One box uploads its images to Twitter and records the number of likes and retweets. The other box uses a camera and face detection to generate images when the audience is not looking at it and to record the attention span for each image when the audience looks at it.

Twitter reactions and preferential viewing time are continuously used as variables to train classifiers that establish the difference between "good" (a lot of engagement) and "bad" images (little or no engagement) and to filter generated images favoring "good" ones. By arranging a witty marriage of ML and Komar and Melamid's *People's Choice* (although he does not acknowledge this referential work), Bogart makes a clear case, but mainly for the audience which is already critical of digital art's commodification.

For the average audience—which may be unfamiliar with zombie formalism—the project can be counter-effective. If they miss its description or its titular satire, the viewers may take *Zombie Formalist* for what it is functionally: a pair of digital frames that continuously display mildly appealing abstract patterns. As is often the case with tactical art, the *Zombie Formalist*'s combination of lofty motivation and somewhat ambiguous presentation may diminish its effectiveness or even expedite its recuperation. This calls for a comparison with Basanta's *All We'd Ever Need...*, which similarly links the notion of "autonomously creative" AI with appropriation strategies. But it couples a complex production setup with a tangible referencing system to provoke mainstream artists, their agents, and collectors instead of "preaching to the choir" by cynical reaffirmation of cultural trends. It effectively critiques the chronic rigidity of intellectual property conventions in general, and particularly the emerging modes of crypto-based art monetization.

Representational Discourse

Critical cogency, viability, and impact of AI art are also affected by the pretentious representational strategies, superficial popular interpretation, and inflated theoretical rhetoric.

Following a long-established trend in contemporary art, AI artists are tempted to augment their projects with descriptions that feature elaborate (metaphorical or literal) questions, critical considerations, or theoretical models, but suffer insufficient competence or sincerity. Such strategies can diminish the experience of artwork by patronizing the audience as pupils rather than independent thinkers capable of appreciating art through their own capacities.

This issue is compounded by the (often exaggerated) dependency of AI artworks on external analytical/theoretical discourse, usually provided by academia. However, the intellectual sophistry that theoretical literature invests in identifying the logic or in advocating the plausibility of AI art may also indicate how unintuitive and ethereal its subject has become. Namely, when an artwork requires an explanation or contextualization which is too long, too complex, or too difficult to understand, then it significantly loses its relevance.

Ethics

Artists have always faced the challenges of ethical integrity conflicting with professional well-being throughout uneasy coevolution between the open-endedness of artistic proteanism and the ambiguous flux of discourses, criteria, and hierarchies in the artworld and scholarship. AI art reflects the artists' ethical decisions involved in making their works and in building their careers within a context of zeitgeist-relative interferences between the arts, science/technology, cultural tendencies, and socio-political trends.

Regardless of their modes of involvement with the broader issues of AI ethics, artists are responsible for their own motivations and roles in shaping cultural values and political normalization. They are ethically criticizable when they consciously produce relatively vacuous work or aesthetic "one-liners", when they create derivative projects while dismissing artistic competencies for technical ones, when they downplay the important technical aspects, or when they ignore the socio-political context and implications of the technology.

Most artists, authors, and cultural operators prefer to avoid discussing this sensitive territory for the sake of professional survival, which may seem obvious, but in fact, draws a higher level of ethical implications. As long as this territory is protected by our hypocrisy and vanity, the cognitive value of art criticism will remain inferior and complacent to diminishing the transformative potentials of the arts.

Broader Concerns

Broader issues that affect contemporary AI art include the uninformed popular discourse, the questionable norms of the art community, the depleting autonomy of academic institutions, and the problematic legal norms for intellectual property and creative labor.

Cultural

The popular writing and media approach toward AI art are still biased toward sensationalistic, superficial, uninformed, or noisy coverage. For example, Klingemann's works, such as *Memories of Passerby I*, have been compared to the works of Francis Bacon based on the vague resemblance of mutated portrait elements. To anyone with reasonable experience in visual arts, this comparison is untenable and its incompetence could be seen as distasteful. The facial morphs in Klingemann's work are formally disparate, smooth, and lack the paste facture (tactile materiality) which condenses the troubled gestural physicality of Bacon's paintings.

The tendency to conflate AI art practices that represent dilettantism, techno-spectacular fetishism, academic aloofness, deft exploration, and insightful critique into simplistic, often bewildering, or baffling narratives, contaminates both public and theoretical discourse. Additionally, corporate media, some art institutions, authors, and artists misrepresent algorithms as "artists" and uncritically promote shallow or derivative AI art practices. By debasing the artists' cognitive abilities which manifest in less palatable but crucial poetics, they legitimize the regressive, intellectually offensive, and politically dangerous cultural ignorance.

Professional

Reputation games in the art community are driven by fluid social networks, cliques, coteries, and intrigues, directed by unstable loyalties or affiliations, and shaped by fancy, fashion, and authority appeal. Also, the exceeding topicality and contextual dependence of contemporary art, adds to the (mnemonic) ephemerality of realized artworks. This volatile dynamic tends to virtually reduce merit to a temporal figure of speech while upholding cultural hegemonies, institutional privileges, and profit-driven power games. Such volatile vocational milieu—combined with inherently high production demands and intrinsic need for endorsement by corporate AI, MCA, or academia—makes AI artists particularly liable to becoming consciously or subconsciously manipulative or cynical, to compromising their creativity, and to softening their critical edge. If they strive for integrity, all actors in AI art should be able to recognize these systemically biased and noisy professional value systems, assess them objectively, and correct them.

Educational

The globally deteriorating strategic and financial status of education since the 1980s has been causing the erosion of academic autonomy and integrity. It often leads to obedient institutional policies which degrade the educational process from synergetic coevolution of intensive learning practices through diverse research directives into a routine social service, homogenized by current economic trends and pragmatically focused on vocational training.

These policies contribute to the technocentrism in new media art programs, which largely remain unconcerned with solving the conflicts between contradictory ideas and opposing world views in the two fields they strive to integrate: modernist in science/technology, and postmodernist in arts and humanities. Overall, it seems that systematic effort to recognize, assess, and cultivate students' artistic talent does not match the effort and energy invested in knowledge transfer, administrative work, and program or institution promotion. Furthermore, university-incorporated art schools often enforce inappropriate academic progress evaluation mechanisms cloned from the tech/science community, which affect their faculties' work as educators, researchers, and artists.

They have been increasingly tailoring art projects to match the fund application or fund justification strategies and to fit the exhibition-conference-paper pipeline. Such development workflows and presentational formats may be beneficial for some types of art projects, but detrimental to many artworks which are generically incompatible with the procedural or epistemological logic of scientific research. The effect is that in the festival, exhibition, and conference publications, artworks are often mispresented as scientific studies, and vice versa.

Proprietary

AI artworks that glamorize narrow or polarized concepts of creativity (human vs. machine, individual vs. collective, etc.) sustain the disputed notions of monolithic authorship rather than advocating for heterogeneous or conjugated actualization of the expressive agency. Intentionally or unintentionally, they reinforce the anthropocentric models of creativity that benefit the problematic culture of proprietary mental labor.

However, the intellectual work (and ethical values) involved in the design and operation of ML systems are not centralized but distributed. As AI art diversifies, these compound aspects are becoming increasingly evident and addressed more clearly. But narrow definitions of authorship and copyright, and fixed divisions of labor, benefit commercially-driven normative relations of production, distribution, and consumption. The future poetic scope of AI art may be limited by conservative initiatives for imposing legal instruments which would keep the creative decisions under centralized profit-motivated control. The responsibility for tackling these issues lies not only with the artists, but also with scientists, entrepreneurs, cultural agents, and the public.

Prospects

The AI's technological repertoire and socio-political context both stimulate the artists' creative abilities and reveal their limitations. Contemporary AI art is a burgeoning poetic ecosystem with potentially abundant intellectual and ethical implications, but it is currently relevant primarily for its implicit or explicit reflections of the AI's challenges, shortcomings, and ambiguities.

In *AI, Arts and Design* editorial of Artnodes, Burbano and West ask: Does ML creativity in the arts and design represent an evolution of "artistic intelligence", or is it a metamorphosis of creative practice yielding fundamentally distinct forms and modes of authorship? At this point, the critical answer is neither. Namely, AI artists predominantly approach ML as a toolkit that leverages high computing speed and big data for refined statistical processing of various media; but new media artists have frequently used computationally-driven statistical tools for media processing with similar, often superior, poetic premises and expressive intents before the advent of DL. Comparative exemplars in this paper demonstrate this continuation and also show that contemporary AI art largely reiterates various modes of technologically entangled authorship which have already been emphasized by non-AI new media art. These factors substantiate the aesthetic values and overall poetic identity of contemporary AI art, while formal novelties—such as the high degree of mimicry or improved resolution in simulating certain phenomena—are secondary.

Nevertheless, the diversity and criticality of the field have been improving as the initial hype is toning down, and more artists start to use ML. Their investigation of the various aspects and expressions of human intelligence may be their key contribution to AI research and contemporary culture. Most importantly, they can establish insights into all aspects of the AI-influenced world through meaningful relationships with the issues, contingencies, and advances of AI technology, and by considering the expressive logic across the genres of AI art. In order to engage the audience with a lasting impact, AI artists need to balance their motivational sincerity and ideational cogency with procedural skills and maintain a critical outlook on their poetic devices.

Competences

The ethos of maturely calibrated competencies deserves cultivation through playfulness, bricolage, technical and conceptual hacking, and imaginative discovery that characterizes other areas of new media art. This ethos comes from the realization that art happens not simply by adding material configurations that no one has witnessed before, but by integrating organized matter into complex human interactions that help us understand the world differently, make us better, or give us a chance to become better. The inherently political nature of AI technology obliges artists not only to exploit but to deconstruct and explore their creative means.

They need stronger criteria for poetic thinking, and better multidisciplinary knowledge of historical, theoretical, cultural, and political contexts in which they produce and present their works. They can catalyze their procedural proficiencies by undertaking systematic training in related non-computational art disciplines, so they can appreciate the cognitive and physical demands of creative work in a broader existential sense. By raising the awareness of technocentrism in their practices, AI artists can also promote the necessary changes in STEAM education.

Tacticality

By recognizing and understanding injustices in the notional, relational, technical, political, and other layers of the socio-technological environments in which they live and create, AI artists can overcome cynicism or unconscious resignation that often undermines their critical efforts. The tactical impact can be improved by bolder and more nuanced examination of the cultural and socio-political contexts of AI technology and business, and by deeper probing and problematizing the underlining concepts such as intelligence, creativity, expressive agency, authorship, intellectual labor, ownership, authenticity, accuracy, and bias.

The flexibility and mutability of these concepts are inherent to human socio-cultural dynamics and, while technologies such as ML or blockchain challenge them less radically than it is widely presumed, they can be used to reconfigure or extend them in interesting and insightful ways.

For tackling the power and sophistication of cultural recuperation in modern info-capitalism (which artists tend to underestimate, overlook, or ignore), stealthy subversiveness and subterfuge seem to be more prudent than didactic overexplanation or overbearing spectacularism. An experiential approach that engages the audience by stimulating their imaginative cognition and critical thinking is often more impactful than surface-based, aestheticized, descriptive, or purely rhetorical artworks that offer a soft or nominal critique of AI-related political power. By demystifying the seemingly radical capabilities of their tools, AI artists can leverage the basic questions and issues of modern AI as critical assets with wide political significance.

Empowered by the destabilizing value of humor, responsible treatment of these assets can build new insights about human nature and provide meaningful posthumanist perspectives.

Creativity

To address the allurement of exploitatively incentivized creativity (creativity for its own sake), artists should articulate and respect their methodologies as heterogeneous productive frameworks whose processes and outcomes inform the audience by stirring inquisitiveness and critical thinking, by stimulating imagination, and by encouraging progressive action. Within this context, there is an underexplored analogy between the artistically adverse normalization of children's creative idiosyncrasies through socialization, and the artists' conscious or intuitive compliance to cultural trends.

By directing their transgressiveness beyond spite, amusement, or showmanship, artists can turn their wit and versatility into exemplars of meaningful resistance to the socio-political imperatives and existential bleakness. Such exemplars can help us discover new ways to be curious and change our understanding of (being in) the world.

By cultivating a dynamic interactive relationship with their progressively sophisticated tools such as ML, artists are in a privileged but also responsible position to push the limits and notions of creativity and in turn, inspire the research of computational and technologically augmented creativity.

Commitment

The socio-technical entanglements of AI art with corporate AI, MCA, and academia support the forthcoming art projects, but may also attenuate their criticality and expedite recuperation. A straightforward way for the artists to tackle this precarious relationship is to resist prioritizing their careers over their art, to be open to taking genuine risks, and to pursue systematic support with skepticism toward institutional rationales for art sponsorship.

The key requirement of avant-garde art is a deep, constructive dedication to evolving potentially hazardous ideas, and to finding effective ways to share them with the audience. It takes exceptional curiosity, inventiveness, and enthusiasm to do any creative work without anticipating affirmation, compensation, or success in the conventional sense. Artists cannot maintain this costly hierarchy of priorities indefinitely, so the public and the art institutions should rise above their unspoken but unrealistic and ultimately cruel expectance that an artist should steadily deliver significant works.

In a broader prospect, the institutional frameworks of contemporary art, science, technology, and education can provide significant incentives for the unbiased development and representation of AI art, thus enhancing the exploration of AI; but they need thorough reconsideration and reconceptualization in order to be self-critically adaptable for absorbing the knowledge that emerges from various relevant disciplines.

This requires close cooperation between artists, institutional representatives, and the public in exposing the political hegemonies, and in criticizing the coercive evaluation criteria imposed by the artworld, academia, politics, economy, and the media.

A Critical Framework for AI Art

AI art requires appreciation models for experientially, intellectually, and emotionally competent spectatorship keyed to an artworks' demands. Just as every artistic enterprise must earn the right to claim the audience's most precious assets—time and attention—the audience needs proper modes of involvement with AI art in order to invest these resources wisely. In a 1995 article titled Artificial Intelligence Research as Art, Stephen Wilson traced the creative landscape of AI art. He recognized that the artists' relationship with AI reaches beyond technical boundaries towards an investigation into the nature of being human, the nature of intelligence, the limits of machines, and our limits as artefact makers.

The critical framework researcher outlined informs the investigation of AI art with an inquiry into the accomplishments, shortcomings, and ambiguities across the AI art disciplines, and facilitates comparative insights into their anthropological, socio-political, cultural, and historical aspects. Its principal method is to distinguish the poetic values of AI artworks by acknowledging and contextualizing both their strong and weak points fully respectful of the artists' creative endeavors, but with an awareness that such approach can be misinterpreted as polemical or confrontational. By recognizing the inherently political nature of technology as a default feature of AI, this platform leverages the understanding of processes and infrastructures for the production, presentation, and reception of AI art.

That allows it to ask potentially difficult questions about the ethical reasoning behind the artists' creative choices throughout the creation, communication, and cultural stratification of their works. It strives to consider the discourse of AI art objectively and purports to debunk the opaque notions, mystifying verbiage, or dubious claims regardless of the authors' authority. It also requires alertness and self-corrective mechanisms to address the processual challenges of emerging practices and to combat its own ideological filtering and cognitive flaws such as motivated reasoning. The aesthetic evaluation, as a multidimensional integrative process, is informed by all these considerations.

This exploratory critique caters to a courageous, inquisitive audience that strives for integrity and inspiration of avant-garde art practices. It respects the intelligence and proteanism that we expect as the artists' key attributes and responsibilities, but it also cultivates an awareness about our tendency to take for granted, overlook, or dismiss the efforts that artists invest in their work. Its aim is to expand the existing critical discourse of AI art with new perspectives for understanding the conceptual and contextual nature of ML as an artistic medium in the age when the arts, together with science and technology, are becoming increasingly responsible for changing ecologies, shaping cultural values, and political normalization.

It facilitates rethinking and redefining of the art/science/technology critique and can be applied to examine the creative attributes of emerging practices in order to assess their cultural significance and socio-political impact. A better understanding of existential conditions, poetic range, and other features of AI art is relevant to both artistic and scientific research in AI, and to its handling by the cultural sector. In a broader prospect, this critical framework can inform the creative actors' reasoning to develop more robust concepts of intelligence, map its perspectives, and make directives for further development and responsible application of AI.

Rethinking Creativity

Artificial intelligence is the stimulation designed for human intelligence by computer systems. Programming for artificial intelligence focuses on three cognitive skills: reasoning, learning, and self-correction. Artificial intelligence and its effects on humans, society, and work have been a fast-developing process, with numerous applications and tools arising from the benefits of using new technology.

The capability of Artificial Intelligence

In a recent incident, a painting worth 432,000 dollars was sold at Christie's, which was, however, not a product of a human painter but of an algorithm. This raises a very interesting question about how artificial intelligence will affect creativity and creative content in the future and how it will change perspectives in the near future.

The development of algorithms not only affects visual art but also influences music and words. In the year 2019, an open AI released a few work samples that showcased computer-generated texts about a topic of the user's choice. The algorithms of the sentences don't sound perfect at the moment but show promising implications for the future.

Douglas Eck, the principal scientist at Google, working in the areas of music, art, and machine learning, states that in less than five years, the technology will become extremely sophisticated in a manner that students will no longer find the need to draught an essay on their own. Just a couple of headlines and entering the correct data and artificial intelligence would draft the whole requirement together.

The Google Magenta research project, which has recently begun, pushes the limits of artificial intelligence in the field of music with a focus on the arts. The algorithm performance RNN is trained in classical music and is also capable of writing its own piano pieces.

A company named Story file by Heather Smith, along with the USC Shoah Foundation used artificial intelligence to preserve history. Using big data, they recreated an experience of one-on-one conversation with individuals who lived through the holocaust via a hologram. They managed to do so by compiling footage collected over a period of five days and filming for 25 hours to collect the answers to over 2000 questions. The language processing made it possible to create an interactive, immersive hologram experience.

There are ample such cases where one can witness the role played by artificial intelligence in marketing campaigns.

In 2017, Nutella and their agency, Ogilvy and Mather Italia, created about seven million unique jars with the help of an algorithm and sold them throughout Italy. Initially, the idea looked amazing and was fun as the jars looked appealing and nice, but these were just the ones they used to build their case as there were also a few not-so-successful jars found on the supermarket shelves to adapt that campaign for Germany.

Another interesting case witnessed is the artificial intelligence scripted commercial for Lexus. The creative agency, along with its technical partners, worked with the IBM Watson team to analyse fifteen years of footage, audio, and text for the award-winning car and luxury brand campaigns. Artificial intelligence had the job of identifying the key elements labelled as emotional intelligence and entertainment, which helped the script flow and the outline on which the agency formed its storyline.

Artificial Intelligence and Human Creativity

The examples mentioned above already highlight the biggest downsides to artificial intelligence, which is that it would never be able to truly choose to do anything without a human command.

Heather Smith quotes states that what you put in is what you will get out. This proves that artificial intelligence heavily relies on the data provided by humans and can only create new things based on the data.

The creative works allow artificial intelligence to follow the rules of sampling with an uncertain outcome. To ensure excellent results and excellent outcomes, it always needs to be curated by humans. Also, the example of Lexus commercials portrays no genuine surprises.

The role of artificial intelligence in our daily lives will definitely increase in the future, but that's not something to be afraid of. It indeed can be used as a new tool which would help process a large amount of data, which would provide information and take care of boring tasks, but it is definitely something that needs to be harnessed in our lives, like the invention of electric guitars and cameras. It will certainly change the possibility of creativity and create new possibilities, but in the end, it won't work without human assistance and could never create something truly new.

As artificial, the name of the article suggests and presses importance on the rising issue of artificial intelligence would take over human creativity by understanding the working of artificial intelligence, the possibility of that seems extremely less. Human minds have seemed to be the creators of most of the things brought into existence after nature, and the day of possibility of a machine-based system taking over that creative mind still seems far away.

During the past 20 years, our understanding of creativity has been heavily affected by the globally powerful discourse of 'creative industries'. Despite various critiques, the discourse has been unhesitantly underpinned by excessive economic aspirations. Yet, its bright portrayal of the creativity-driven economy is now debunked in the Covid crisis with many corners of the cultural sector being hit severely. Even before the pandemic, there was growing discontent about actual conditions of labour in the cultural sector.

Witnessing increasing calls for new cultural policy, today is a sober moment where we should rethink creativity beyond the narrow economic framework. Researchers suggest that we do this not only by critically scrutinising what creativity has meant in the creative industries discourse but also by rethinking it in the context of the two other important recent developments in our understanding of culture and the arts, that is, AI (artificial intelligence) creativity and the creativity in everyday cultural life.

In the following sections, researcher will explain how creativity is constructed in these three areas of discussion and why such constructions matter especially for cultural policymakers who are under increasing pressure to care for artists and cultural practitioners and improve their working conditions and earning. Our starting point is the observation that the creative industries discourse has dehumanised creativity by seeing it as a type of capital and thus impedes labour perspectives of creativity.

Ironically, thinking about AI creativity is an interesting way to rehumanise creativity. It is because this endeavour necessitates inquiries into the core nature of human creativity and the creation process of human artists whilst AI itself can threat human creators by dissociating creativity from human agency. As such, discussing the creative industries and AI creativity leads to questions around political-economic nature of creativity (labour vs capital) and the entity where creativity is embedded (human/artists vs mechanical process/capital).

Finally, focusing on whose creativity (artists' vs everyone's) matters, the popular discourse of creativity in everyday cultural life celebrates non-hierarchical and democratic creativity. Yet, a pitfall is that it discourages labour perspectives of creativity and makes it almost impossible to articulate specific characteristics of creativity held by artists and professional cultural practitioners. Calling for rehumanising creativity that has been bluntly instrumentalised by the creative industries discourse, researchers want to point out that making sense of creativity is a complex task. This task involves an exploring the political economy of cultural production, comprehending the growing impact of technologies on human creativity and reflecting on the rise of cultural democracy and relativism.

IN THE MIRROR OF AI

Introduction

Day after day we are moving towards a more automated and interconnected world because of various wirelessly connected embedded devices. These are responsible for changing and improving the standards and quality of living. Many devices are being developed which use concepts of multimedia communication, artificial intelligence, internet of things (IoT) to revolutionizing the way we perform our various day to day tasks in our home, offices or even industries.

Most of us use mirrors every day to look at ourselves; we psychologically interact with the mirror every day to check how we look and how our attire is while getting ready for our work or colleges. So, The idea of having an interactive mirror that can respond to your commands can excite anyone. Magic Mirror aims at augmenting the basic reflective mirror with embedded intelligence to combine daily routine tasks like reading newspaper, weather updates etc. and providing all that data to the user while he/she gets ready.Switching home appliances becomes easy with Magic Mirror.

Virtual dressing, smart way of having trials with your fashion sense make things quite easy in malls. Having such intellectual mirror will only surge the beauty of home. The Magic mirror will help in automating our work and development of smart houses. This paper provides a detailed idea of theory of design and practical implementation of Magic Mirror.

Architectural implications

What, then, are we to make of all this, from an architectural perspective? First of all, and most obviously, we can see parallels presenting themselves with the domain of architecture. Similar incidents have been noticed when Spacemaker AI software has been used in architectural design. It would seem that AI has the capacity to outperform architects in certain design challenges – especially those that require a strong strategic input, not unlike AlphaGo.

Just as AlphaGo was able to come up with moves that no humans would have thought about, so too Spacemaker AI software used within an architectural context has been able to make design proposals that no architects would have thought about. As Håvard Haukeland observes:

'The places where the architects thought that it would be smart to build tall buildings, and the places where they thought it would be smart to build a dense wall, all the things that they intuitively thought would be smart – because they had hundreds of projects of experience – were flipped around. Because when you get the complexity of thinking of a multi-objective organizational problem... you are really not able to see the patterns that a computer can find. So what happened was that the computer was able to find a pattern as to how to solve that site that you would never come up with yourself.' (Haukeland).

We should be careful, however, to distinguish between the different modalities of creativity found in architecture, and the kind of creativity displayed in a game of Go. There is a danger in promoting a monolithic definition of creativity. In this sense, creativity is no different to design. There are not only many approaches to design, but also many different understandings of design. Design for an engineer or a computer scientist, for example, takes on a primarily functional character. Performance is the primary concern. Appearances are not so important. Architectural design, however, as Vitruvius and so many other commentators have pointed out, would appear to involve a combination of performance considerations and aesthetic concerns.

Not only that, but in the design process itself, we often consider background strategic decisions – in the form of traffic flow calculations, environmental analysis and other issues – before we begin to really address the appearance of a building. At an urban scale we can see this articulated in the distinction between 'urban planning' and 'urban design'.

Urban planning is a primarily strategic operation, involving policy makers, politicians and so on. If there is any design deployed in this stage of a project, it might be limited to the design of infrastructure – roads etc. Urban design, by contrast, takes place at a later date, and involves primarily aesthetic concerns. We should therefore draw a distinction between creativity at a strategic level and creativity within the aesthetic domain.

AlphaGo is particularly strong at a strategic level. It employs a Monte Carlo tree search – along with a policy network and a value network – and is therefore exceptionally good at searching. However, we can also recognise a further potential of AI within the aesthetic domain. If algorithms can track our preferences in terms of news, books, movies and music, should they not be able to track our preferences also in terms of architectural aesthetics?

Likewise if Gmail is capable of suggesting how we might complete a sentence based on the way that we have expressed ourselves in the past, might AI not be capable eventually of suggesting how we might how might complete an architectural drawing? In other words, the writing would appear to be on the wall. AI is clearly capable of outperforming human beings at strategic decisions, and will soon also be able to match human beings in terms of aesthetic choices.

AI, creativity and consciousness

Can we consider computers, however, to be *genuinely* creative? Was AlphaGo actually being creative, or was it simply conducting a search for the best possible solution? Or is the question of computer creativity an impossible one to answer, as Boden argues: 'Whether a computer could ever be "really" creative is not a scientific question but a philosophical one. And it's currently unanswerable, because it involves several highly contentious—and highly unclear—philosophical questions.'.

Memo Akten, at any rate, seems to think that computers can be creative: 'By saying that a machine can be creative, you are not anthropomorphising the machine, but liberating it by expanding the term 'creativity' to go beyond humans. Creativity is not limited to people.

Others are not so sure. Indeed, if we are to follow the thinking of Melanie Mitchell, AI cannot be said to be creative, in that it does not possess consciousness: 'I also believe that being creative entails being able to understand and judge what one has created. In this sense of creativity, no existing computer can be said to be creative.' Of course, we could argue that we human beings might not be fully conscious of an idea, when it suddenly pops up in our mind in a flash of inspiration. Indeed, Max Tegmark notes. 'Neuroscience experiments suggest that many behaviors and brain regions are unconscious, with much of our conscious experience representing an after-the-fact summary of vastly larger amounts of unconscious information.' However, even if this might be the case initially, very soon afterwards – the 'aha' moment – the brilliance of the idea dawns on us, as we use our consciousness to appraise and appreciate the idea. From this perspective, AI cannot be said to be creative, since AI is not capable of appreciating its 'creativity'.

Perhaps the most famous argument about the importance of consciousness has been made by philosopher, John Searle, using his famous 'Chinese Room' thought experiment. Imagine that a computer program has been designed that seems as though it is capable of understanding Chinese. The program is able to take English text and translate it into Chinese text so convincingly that it passes the 'Turing Test', in that no one realises that it is just a computer program. Now imagine if Searle were to find himself in a closed room equipped with an instruction manual in English that described the translation process.

The only problem is that he does not understand Chinese. This is analogous to the question of consciousness. A computer might *appear* to be conscious, but it does not understand what it is doing. Searle might *appear* to be able to translate Chinese, but he has no knowledge of Chinese. The Chinese Room experiment can therefore be understood as a critique of the Turing Test. There is a significant difference between something *appearing* to do something, and actually doing it.

AlphaGo, according to this argument, might have 'won' the match of Go, but it cannot have been aware of the fact that it was even playing Go, because it does not possess consciousness. As such, AlphaGo might be good at processing 'symbols', but it has no idea what they mean. Indeed it has no more capacity to 'think' than a pocket calculator. What if we were to judge AI, however, not in terms of human intelligence, but on its own terms? As such, the question of consciousness becomes irrelevant. The issue becomes what tasks AI can perform, not whether AI can display human-level consciousness. As Yuval Noah Harari notes, 'There might be several alternative ways leading to superintelligence, only some of which pass through the straits of consciousness.' This leads Harari to pose the important question, 'Which of the two is really important, intelligence or consciousness?' As far as corporations and armies are concerned, the answer is clear: 'intelligence is mandatory, but consciousness is optional.'

Harari goes on to give the example of a taxi driver: 'The conscious experiences of a flesh-and-blood taxi driver are infinitely richer than a self-driving car, which feels absolutely nothing.' But as far as the passenger is concerned, the consciousness of the taxi-driver is irrelevant. Soon, Harrari notes, we will have autonomous taxis that are far more reliable than taxis driven by conscious drivers. 'Taxis', he comments, 'are highly likely to go the way of horses.' In fact Harrari notes that a Google self-driving car was once involved in an accident, when hit from behind by a sedan 'whose careless human driver was perhaps contemplating the mysteries of the universe, instead of concentrating on the road.' Consciousness, in other words, is not only optional; it might also become a liability.

Could we not say the same about AI generated buildings? Many architects, for example, might claim that a computer cannot display the same emotional intensity that they invest in the design process. But does it really matter whether AI is conscious or not when it generates a design? Surely, the important question is whether or not AI can produce a good design. 'Is our goal,' asks Daniel Bolojan, 'to create machines that mimic human intelligence and creativity, or are we aiming to create machines that are capable of being intelligent and creative in their own right?".

ARCHITECTS AND CREATIVITY

Are we architects as original as we think we are?

We human beings tend to be very predictable. Indeed, we need to recognise that we have a tendency to develop certain 'signatures'. By this we mean not simply our actual hand written signatures, which remain remarkably consistent over time, but other forms of self-expression. How easy is it to recognise someone's voice without seeing who it is, or equally to recognize them from a distance by their mode of walking, running or other forms of behavior. It is as though human beings develop habits, routines and familiar modes of operation that constrain their forms of self-expression. The same, of course, would apply to architectural design. How often can we guess the architect, when we see a building?

We might even go so far as to comment that architecture itself relies upon a 'canon' of permissible forms of expression. If a student were to produce a highly unusual architectural design that resembled a pineapple, for example, s/he might risk failure. However, a student producing a design that loosely resembled a building by Zaha Hadid or Frank Gehry – but importantly that is not a direct replica – would be deemed to have passed. Indeed, Ahmed Elgammal has pursued a very similar approach in producing Creative Adversarial Networks (CANS), and generating art that appears to be close enough to the 'canons' of artworks, but at the same time slightly different. (Elgammal) By extension, we could also imagine the possibility of AI generating novel variations, and thereby serving as some kind of muse, as Michael Hansmeyer has called it: 'We've been using computers to increase our efficiency and precision. Let us view the computer as our muse, as a partner in design, and as a tool to expand our imagination.'

Meanwhile, even though Gehry at some stage has produced ground-breaking designs, such as his design for the Guggenheim Museum in Bilbao, nonetheless he has ended up repeating a similar version of this design in several subsequent projects, including for the Walt Disney Concert Hall in Los Angeles.

It could even be argued that copying is in fact intrinsic to human nature, and no more so than in our contemporary condition. In effect, reproduction, replication and copying have come to define our present age in what Hillel Schwartz has called the 'Culture of the Copy'.

It is not just a question of following trends or fashions in a time where role modelling and theming have become endemic. Rather we need to understand that culture continually replicates itself through a form of copying. Indeed Benjamin himself notes: 'Nature creates similarities. One need only think of mimicry. The highest capacity for producing similarities, however, is man's.'

German philosopher and a close colleague of Benjamin, Theodor Adorno, also comments: 'The human is indissolubly linked with imitation: a human being becomes human at all by imitating other human beings.' Moreover, as Kendall Walton has argued, it is in the childhood games of playing roles as 'doctors and nurses' or 'cops and robbers' that human beings learn how to play the roles of managing directors, captains of industry and even architects in later life. Imitation lies at the heart of the human condition.

A series of more contemporary theoretical insights have served only to corroborate this general view. A perfect example is the notion of the 'meme', a relatively recent neologism. Coined by Richard Dawkins in 1976, the meme refers to the way in which ideas spread: 'Examples of memes are tunes, ideas, catch-phrases, clothes fashions, ways of making pots or building arches.' In effect, culture is propagated through imitation: 'Just as genes propagate themselves in the gene pool by leaping from body to body via sperms or eggs, so memes propagate themselves in the meme pool by leaping from brain to brain via a process which, in the broad sense, can be called imitation.'

Susan Blackmore subsequently took this further: 'Everything that is passed from person to person in this way is a meme. This includes the songs you sing and the rules you obey.' The result is a form of contagion based entirely on the principle of copying. Indeed, the very way in which the use of the term 'meme' has spread is a perfect example of its power.

What would happen, however, if we were to take the opposite approach to Akten? Instead of saying that our notion of 'creativity' needs to be extended to include machines, what if we were to say that human beings are perhaps not so different to machines? In other words, what if all we were doing in the design process could be understood as little more than a search? Indeed we could argue that contemporary life is dominated increasingly by the 'search'. Take the process of taking a photograph, for example. How do we take photos in the age of the digital photography? In the old days of manual photography we would carefully set up the camera for one ideal shot. In the age of digital photography, however, we take a burst of sample shots.

We then review them, select our favourite shot and enhance it using editing techniques available on every smart phone. It is no longer a question of the expert photographer setting up the ideal shot, but rather of the informed user taking an array of sample photos and then selecting and enhancing the best one.

Indeed these days it is more than likely that the first step in accessing information is the 'search'. Ask a student to write an essay, and the chances are that s/he will start by conducting a search based on a few key words associated with the subject of that essay. The astonishing development in the speed and efficiency of search engines over the past few years has meant that within a fraction of a second a search can be conducted of all accessible online information. Furthermore, many analog publications have now been scanned so that access to physical books is not as important, while most journals are now accessible online through digital libraries of academic journals, such as JSTOR.

Once the Google Books project to scan all known volumes has been completed, we will have an even more extensive repository of information. As such, the traditional method of 'browsing' through bookshelves will have become if not totally redundant, then at least downgraded to an academic recreational pastime. While it might be possible to conduct a physical search of literature by commissioning a group of scholars to check through all books in a given collection of books that – theoretically – would provide the same information as an online 'search', the slow speed of such an operation would make such an exercise prohibitive. And it is precisely the speed of an online search that has begun to afford techniques of knowledge retrieval that are effectively changing the epistemological structure of operations within the knowledge industries.

As such, the 'search' becomes the first step in most disciplinary fields. Set within an architectural perspective this is having a major impact on logic of design itself. It shifts the emphasis from the 'creativity' of the design process towards the rigor of the search itself. The assumption here, as Kostas Terzidis has noted, is that all possible forms already exist, and it is simply a question of finding them. Indeed – if all the potential solutions are already out there, and it is simply a question of searching for them – this potentially undermines the whole notion of the 'design genius'. Further, if there is any creativity in that process it must surely lie in the creativity of the search itself. As such, the designer emerges less as the demiurgic top down controller, and more as someone who harnesses the productive capacity of informational processes. If, then, we think through the logic of the search in the context of 'design', what such an approach suggests is that if all possible solutions already exist, it is simply a question of defining a set of constraints and conducting a search, and then selecting one of the many outcomes. The potential implications of this are far reaching. Not only does it challenge the traditional notion of the 'genius' of the architect/designer and the originality of the work of art, but it also suggests that if there is still any creativity in the 'design' process, it should lie, firstly, in defining the constraints that generate the range of possible solutions to a problem, and, secondly, in developing an effective method of filtering or evaluating them.'

The myth of creativity

As Margaret Boden has noted, 'Thanks in part to AI, we have already begun to understand *what sort of phenomenon* creativity is.' (Boden) The key question raised by the match between AlphaGo and Lee Sedol, however, is whether human beings would even be able to *recognise* the creativity of AI.

Alan Turing seemed to acknowledge this, when he commented on the potential creativity of computers: 'We have to have some experience with the machine before we really know its capabilities. It may take years before we settle down to the new possibilities, but I do not see why it should not enter any one of the fields normally covered by the human intellect, and eventually compete on equal terms. I do not think that you can even draw the line about sonnets, though the comparison is perhaps a little bit unfair, because a sonnet written by a machine will be better appreciated by another machine.' His final comment – that a machine could best appreciate the output of another machine – is an interesting observation. Of course, we could question whether a machine could ever actually 'appreciate' a sonnet, since it does not possess consciousness, but the point still stands.

It would seem that machines can reach a level of 'creativity' that far exceeds 'human creativity', much as a dog can sense a range of sounds and smells far beyond the range that a human can.

This raises the interest issue – not so dissimilar to the 'Dunning-Kruger Effect' – that the dumb do not know how dumb they are. We could even extend this to infer that the intelligent do not know how unintelligent they are, or – perhaps more appropriate in this context – the creative do not know how uncreative they are. Put simply, there are levels of 'creativity' that we simply cannot grasp. 'Creativity' is nothing, unless we can recognise it.

One way to think about this significant issue is to reconsider Lee's comment about AlphaGo cited above: 'AlphaGo showed us that moves humans may have thought are creative, were actually conventional.' The important word here is 'thought'. In other words, Lee is implying that creativity is simply a question of *perceived* creativity.

What becomes clear is that our understanding of creativity is somewhat subjective. Margaret Boden has attempted to define creativity in terms of three types of outcomes list, 'combinatorial', 'exploratory' and 'transformational', as though creativity could be grasped in such objective terms. Meanwhile, Demis Hassabis has attempted to outline three 'levels' of creativity – 'intensive', 'extensive' and true 'invention'. But can creativity be judged in such as objective way? Who is in a position to even judge creativity?

François Pachet, believes that it makes no sense for creativity to be defined in objective terms, in that it can only be understood subjectively. (Pachet, 26) And what if a creative act is not recognised immediately? And how are we to appraise the creativity of Move 37, if the creativity of that move was not even appreciated until much later?

Certainly, as Arthur Miller notes, it is difficult to come up with a clear, objective description of creativity, when the creativity of some artists, such as Vincent Van Gogh, was not recognised in their own lifetime. Indeed, the art world is dependent on curators who validate artworks through a form of discourse, so that art itself could be understood as a form of discourse in which artworks are inscribed. As such, artistic creativity is dependent on the discourse that validates it. Presumably, what is true for the art world should also apply to the domain of architecture.

Could we even compare creativity to beauty, as various commentators have done in relation to the AlphaGo match? Indeed, David Hume believed that beauty is highly subjective, "Beauty is no quality in things themselves: It exists merely in the mind which contemplates them; and each mind perceives a different beauty." (Hume) Could not creativity – like beauty – lie in the eye of the beholder? Or might it also exist in the mind of the creative individual?

Let us return to the example of Searle's Chinese Room experiment. What Searle was arguing was that there is a difference between *perceived* consciousness and *actual* consciousness. For Searle, the Turing Test is inadequate, because it only offers the potential of a computer *appearing* to be human. It does not test whether the computer is *actually* human. This surely is the crucial point. Could we not say the same about creativity? A computer might *appear* to be creative, but can it be *truly* creative? Certainly not, if we follow Mitchell's logic. But could we not use the same experiment to argue that human beings might also only *appear* to be creative? What would happen, however, if we discovered that in reality we are just following a straightforward search and synthesis process – much like AI?

Could 'creativity', then, not be viewed in a similar way to magic? Let us be clear – there is no such thing as magic. For magicians do not perform magic. They simply conceal the processes that actual happen, so that the audience comes to attribute them to magic: 'Like the conjurer's trick, where the magician conceals the true devices at work, so as to fool the audience into attributing them to magic, so technology, in effacing itself, invites us to believe in its magical potential.' Is 'creativity' simply a convenient term used to describe a process which – like magic – we do not fully understand? And is there not also a risk, when dealing with advanced technology (whose operations we might not fully comprehend), of mistaking it for magic? This brings us to the famous quote of Arthur C Clarke, 'Any sufficiently advanced technology is indistinguishable from magic.'

Technology Behind Smart Mirrors

The silver-glassed mirrors most of us are familiar with today got their start more than 200 years ago in Germany. While they still serve a useful purpose when reflecting your image back to you, some fashion and beauty leaders figured that if you added smart technology to mirrors, they could elevate the customer experience. This vision is now a reality thanks to the significant advances that have been made in artificial intelligence, augmented reality, and gesture recognition technology. These mirrors can adjust your image, including the clothes you wear to your hairstyle, hair colour, and makeup to create a very realistic augmented reflection.

Applications of Smart Mirrors

The beauty of a digital makeover is it's easy to experiment and hit "undo" when you don't like the results. L'Oréal launched an app called Style My Hair in partnership with ModiFace that allows customers to become a blonde (or any other hair colour)—at least digitally—on live video. The technology colours hair strand by strand to create a fully dimensional, realistic look. Not loving blonde? Just swipe on the app and change your colour again. This technology is beneficial when a colorist consults with a client regarding what they want and lets the client see—quite effectively—how the colour will look on them prior to committing to the real thing.

YouCam Makeup-Magic Selfie Cam, developed by Perfect Corp, is a similar app that can show you what you'll look like with a new hair colour (and eye colour), try on makeup as well as a skincare analysis feature that identifies issues to troubleshoot with a skincare routine. Shopping for cosmetics in real-life can involve taking makeup on and off as you try new shades of highlighter, foundation, blush, lipstick, and eye shadow. Being able to do this virtually prevents any adverse reactions, especially for sensitive skin and makes experimentation easy as you swap between different options.

The same technology can help people see how a new hairstyle will complement their face—or not—before any irreversible cuts are made. It can also be helpful to determine a style for a special occasion or see how a style you saw in a magazine will work with your face shape before you head to the salon.

Coty's version of the smart mirror is the CES 2019 Innovation Awards Honoree—Wella Professionals Smart Mirror. This mirror allows stylists to provide more personalised consultations. Like the apps discussed above, the Wella Professionals Smart Mirror is able to do a live AR hair colour try on and can provide a 360-degree of the style so the client can see what it will look like from all angles. In addition, using facial recognition technology, it can retrieve past styles for each customer, allowing the stylist and client to really assess what worked and what didn't. Also important, the mirror provides a curated feed of content with trending styles and classic looks to help inspire both stylists and customers when trying to determine a new look. It also connects to a mobile app so the stylist and customer can stay in contact in between appointments.

Memory Mirror, a digital mirror created by MemoMi, combines a full-length mirror with high-tech including a 70-inch LCD, computer and HD camera that can record videos so you can save, share and review your try-on sessions. Neiman Marcus installed MemoMi's mirrors in 34 locations. Another mirror altering the retail experience is the Oak Mirror by Oak Labs. It serves as a digital assistant in a dressing room, allowing customers to request other colours, styles, or accessories from a sales assistant.

Sephora is another beauty retailer that offers a 3D augmented reality mirror. Customers trying out different products can move their face from side to side, and the augmented eye shadow or lipstick stays where it is supposed to creating a very realistic effect. The technology is expected to not only enhance the customer experience but drive sales. When it's easier to experiment with different looks, it makes it easier to discover new products to purchase.

While your haircut, hair colour, and makeup choices are important for your overall look, SenseMi expanded the makeover capabilities to create a virtual dressing mirror, too. The company's smart mirror is used in retail stores, and there's a home version that allows you to "try" on clothes digitally, plus it's able to send you reminders about your calendar, tell you the traffic details along your normal commuting route and more. SenseMi even sells a smart table that provides a multi-touch, interactive experience that can be used in hotels, schools, hospitals, and more.

Artificial intelligence, augmented reality, and virtual reality will help to make retail stores more interactive and the online experience more real-life. Perhaps more importantly, with the help of makeover apps and smart mirrors, the days of bad haircuts, and colour and makeup choices will be a thing of the past.

CHAPTER

AI, MEDIA ART AND NEUROSCIENCE 5

INTRODUCTION

In the Internet era, digital museums, digital libraries, and some related websites of Chinese painting and art have developed. Moreover, in the era of big data, the sources of digitized Chinese paintings have increased, and the authenticity of their contents has gradually become a focus of attention. Traditional identification methods mainly rely on the rich experience of identification experts. Due to the subjectivity of traditional identification methods and the lack of objective referenceable indicators, there are limitations in the efficiency and accuracy of their identification in the face of the new generation of information technology forgery methods.

Therefore, a digital Chinese painting authenticity-assisted identification tool with a high degree of automation and accuracy is particularly necessary. At the beginning of the twentieth century, the great development of photography, communication, and other media technologies hit Western art, which was based on realism at that time and brought an unprecedented sense of crisis to art workers, and more and more artists realized that the only way to establish a new artistic status was to innovate, thus giving birth to numerous art schools.

Interactive art is rooted in the artistic trends of Cubism, Futurism, and Dadaism, which confronted traditional art and laid a solid foundation for the development of contemporary digital interactive art. The relationship between artificial intelligence and interactive art can be traced back to the birth of the concept of "artificial intelligence" in 1956.

Both interactive art and artificial intelligence technology are based on computer technology, and their inherent connection between technology and art has established the inevitability of their development and integration since their birth. In the early stage of interactive art development, interactive artists customized the rules of interaction through technical research and attracted participants into the art world they created by changing the physical form, emphasizing the satisfaction of form and technical application and ignoring the experience and cognitive mode of participants. In the 1980s, computer psychology gradually developed into a cognitive discipline, artificial neural network research developed rapidly, and breakthroughs in speech recognition and machine vision technology brought artificial intelligence research into its formative years.

The research concept of experience formally entered the sight of artists and technology workers, and focusing on human interaction experience became the key point of interactive art expression. Therefore, as people pursue the sense of experience and entertainment in interactive art, the object of interactive art creation shifts from the study of objects to the study of human behavior, and the connection between science and art becomes closer. In the twenty-first century, with the development of deep learning technology of artificial intelligence, artificial intelligence research has entered a golden period of application, and human-computer interaction technologies such as intelligent voice interaction, machine recognition, and virtual reality based on artificial intelligence technology have advanced by leaps and bounds, which is pivotal to the development of human-centered interactive art.

Intelligence, nature, learning, and abiotic intelligence are new technologies and concepts carried by the development of artificial intelligence, which support the creation of contemporary digital intelligent interactive art and influence the aesthetic trends of the public and the creative thinking of artists. This section focuses on how intelligent technology under the domination of artificial intelligence changes interactive art expression from the level of thinking, means, and experience logic and proposes a paradigm of interactive art expression under the influence of artificial intelligence technology. The fusion of artistic creativity and technologically advanced productivity provides the creative impetus for the sustainable development of art and HCI technology in the future. Overall, artificial intelligence is much more than a simple technical means for art creation; it is more of a reshaping of art creation thinking and an impact on human cognition. We collect materials related to artificial intelligence, film and television creation, film and television market management, and film and television consumer experience, including books, newspapers and magazines, dissertations, theoretical works related to artificial intelligence, and film and television to provide comprehensive theoretical support for the dissertation, draw on and absorb research results from sociology, psychology, management, law, film, television, information technology, etc.

The chapter combines macro- and microanalysis to provide a more profound interpretation of the topic. This paper innovatively sorts out the influence of AI on interactive art expression through deconstruction and reconstruction thinking, analyzes how AI deconstructs the original model of interactive art creation in terms of technology and thinking, then analyzes the influence of AI on interactive art expression in terms of time, space, and natural logic, and establishes its application paradigm. This paper provides a new practical direction for interactive art creation. By selecting appropriate statistical methods, different external environmental factors are analyzed to understand the changes in the shape and quantity of the distribution, the relationship between variables, etc.

This research method has a very obvious indirectness and it is less disturbed and easier to implement. Mainly through the analysis of statistics, statements, data, and other information published by relevant departments, we understand the development status of the film and television industry under the influence of AI, including the status of AI companies, products, and technology development related to the film and television industry and the status of AI applications in the film and television industry, and anticipate its future direction. The contributions of this work can be summarized as follows:

- We first sort out the intersection of AI technology development and interactive art expression streams on the timeline based on historical development and analyze the deconstructive relationship between the two from the macroperspective of the historical development of technology and art
- Based on exploring the advantages of AI technology, we propose the impact of AI on the creative thinking, creative mode, and artistic experience of interactive art and establish the paradigm of interactive art creation in the context of AI
- The proposed method can be used to quickly locate the category of painters when facing different styles of unsigned digital Chinese painting images in the authenticity identification task.

Science and art are merging and with artificial intelligence system like neural networks, genetic programs and rule based systems, arti sts or designers are using smart systems that allow them to better immerse themselves in the creative process. Artist/Scientist Steve DiPaola uses AI techniques in his self-created programs and artwork.

- **Darwin** - A conceptual piece that evolves a related family of abstract portrait painters. Portraits are created by Darwinian evolution using the AI technique called Genetic Programming. Using the painting of Darwin by John Collier as the creative spark, portraits slowly evolve over a month of constant computer time in this art programming experiment to cajole a computer to become creative on its own.
- **Dancers** - An animated art short using "smart" character movement programs

- **Musicface** - Stills from a music driven art short where an original music composition drives 3D virtual emotive faces in a collaborative re-mapping of the emotional and gestural state of the music.
- **Vr. Beluga** - This interactive uses an extremely realistic 3D simulation of a wild beluga whale pod for a major aquarium that is situated next to a group of real beluga whales in an integrated marine mammal exhibit. The Virtual Beluga Interactive was conceived to better immerse and engage the visitors in complicated educational concepts about the life of wild belugas thereby allowing them to have deeper insights into the life of beluga whales. The simulation uses artificial intelligence, physically based animation, and real-time graphics.
- **Noise Face** - The work in this art still series uses 3D painterly noise where 'brush strokes abstract space rather than color'. The system uses stochastic noise perturbation and a 3D face system developed by the artist.

NEUROSCIENCE AND AI

Indeed, AI has made rapid strides in replicating human-like functionalities, but it is still decades away from creating a 'human in bolts and nuts'. Unless the developers understand exactly what makes the human mind unique, what is drives its imagination, how the subconscious mind works and what synapses exist, having a machine with the human mind is impossible. Neuroscience can help programmers greatly invalidate the AI's current models.

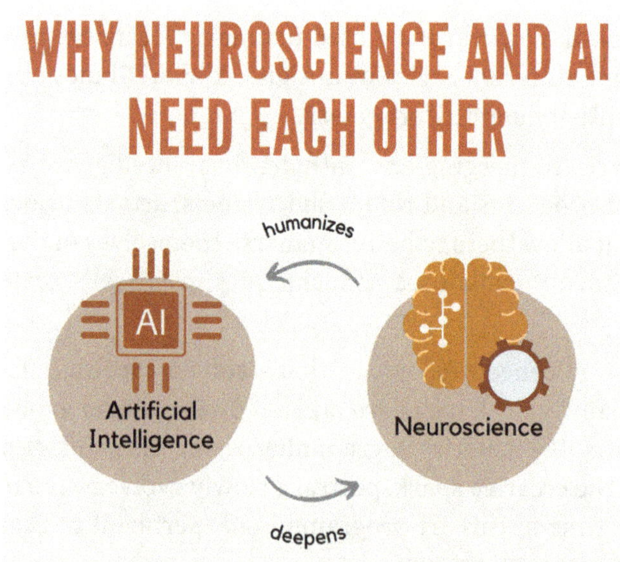

Fig. 1 Neuroscience and AI

It might be surprising to know, this is necessary because AI models follow totally different patterns than how a human mind works. In a way, neuroscience helps developers set benchmarks regarding the effectiveness of algorithms by comparing them against neurological activity. Data from medical records fed to algorithms train the machines in human thinking and later the with repetition it successfully tricks a machine in replicating the behaviour, which in other words is called transfer learning.

AI's early beginnings and steady development over the years have been largely possible due to neuroscientific studies and research. Moving forward, AI and neuroscience continue to be heavily interdependent for their respective advancements.

How AI Revolutionizes Neuroscience

Incredibly, AI and deep learning can help humans understand how their own brains work. As we know, the human body is a complex entity including several organs, cells, tissues, blood vessels, neurons, glands and several other components. The brain is our body's chief coordinator regarding things we can control (external muscle movements, decision-making, speech) and the ones we cannot (knee-jerk reactions, blood circulation, digestion). AI's findings can enhance what humans know about the brain.

They can tell us how the cerebrum, brain stem and cerebellum can be optimized with advanced medicines and healthcare hacks to cure conditions such as Tourette's syndrome. Currently, neurological experts continue to delve deeper into how our brain relays impulses to different parts of the body for performing various movements. By discovering new learnings through AI, health experts will be able to unlock the hidden capabilities of our brains. With a better understanding of the brain's different lobes, health experts will be able to definitively deal with paralysis and other movement-related conditions suffered by millions worldwide.

With deeper, AI-generated knowledge about the brain's structure and functions, neuroscientists can create better simulations of the brain for training neurology students in medical institutes. Moreover, AI's pattern recognition abilities can allow scientists to efficiently test newer hypotheses and publish their findings for medical advancements. Several aspects related to the human brain are still relatively vague or undiscovered yet. If AI uncovers these hidden details through its range of powers and abilities, neuroscience can make several strides towards perfection.

Speaking of the unknown, big data can help health experts with understanding the abstract and often unquantifiable aspects and functions of the human nervous system. For instance, AI models can be used to accurately simulate the various neuron-to-neuron connections in the body.

Memory storage chips embedded in such systems could be used to delete certain memories or specific cognitive mechanisms to get substantive answers about memory loss in the elderly and reasons why individuals go into a coma after sustaining nasty head injuries or revisiting traumatic life experiences. Other areas where AI's data crunching and anomaly detection could be used is to track the early signs and symptoms of epilepsy in patients. Measures such as electrical impulse treatments can help resolve the situation when epileptic attacks surface in such individuals.

One of the most fascinating aspects of neuroscience is the so-called 'neural codes'—the underlying patterns in neurons and brain cells that are responsible for human behavior, mood swings and other abstract mental phenomena. With big data and unsupervised deep learning processes, neurologists will be able to 'crack' these codes to get a better understanding of human behavior. What's more, these studies can then be applied in various fields, such as occupational health and safety or forensics.

Obtaining the Data Needed for Neuroscience Advancements

Currently, neuroscientists engage in understanding protein patterns and cranial regions to get information about the brain's working. AI-powered models can provide them with the tools to study and examine neurons at the genetic level. Apart from this, advanced computer vision can assist neurologists with recreating actual neural linkages to get accurate information about their working (from a genomic perspective). Learnings from such studies can be priceless in the field of advanced genomics. As we move into the future of healthcare, generated data about the physical connections between neurons is becoming increasingly outdated. With AI, neurologists can create specialized simulations to get in-depth data regarding the process of impulse formation and transfer throughout the body.

AI is used for speeding the research process related to brain mapping or functional brain imaging. These processes generate vast quantities of statistical and visual data that can be processed, reconstructed, and annotated. Computer vision models can help with analyzing all types of images related to chemical balance and neural health. These types of mapping and imaging procedures can cut down on the time and human effort spent in compiling data. Projects such as Neurodata Without Borders (NWB) are invaluable sources of AI-generated brain data for neurologists. Thus, AI's increasing involvement in neuroscience can be immensely beneficial for the healthcare industry.

How Neuroscience Improves AI Technologies

While AI is developing at a rapid pace and making giant strides in most industries, there are many aspects of the technology which could be improved. Most crucially, as specified earlier, AI intends to replicate the workings of the human brain in automated systems to make them better. However, the truth is that data scientists and analysts are still probably decades away from recreating genuine human intelligence in a lab. While neuroscience is not the only solution, it can certainly improve certain facets of AI in its own ways.

Firstly, neuroscience can be used for verifying and validating AI's current models and technologies. In truth, AI's algorithms follow completely different logical patterns while trying to mimic existing functions of the brain (The brain's logical patterns for performing tasks are relatively unknown). This may not necessarily be a problem. In fact, it allows data experts to create benchmarks regarding the effectiveness of such algorithms to generate results compared to a human brain. As a result, neuroscience can be used to improve the quality of algorithms in AI.

Traditionally, logic-based procedures and mathematical models have featured in the working of a generic AI model. To enhance things up, neuroscience can complement these methods by classifying specific biological aspects which can be useful for an AI system to understand the various cognitive details related to the human brain.

An important challenge in AI training and research is transfer learning, which is a technique of training AI models by using pre-trained algorithms and neural networks. To process information in specific scenarios, AI systems need to use existing algorithms as a reference point before making balanced, risk-free decisions. Neuroscience involves the collection and intensive analysis of thousands of medical records. The massive reserves of information are essential for an AI system to know about the nervous system and its working. The medical records can be useful for an AI system as, through machine learning and other components, it can understand how the human brain and other related organs usually operate. Algorithms trained in the initial stages of this process can be used in transfer learning later. Ultimately, the vast sources of data from neuroscientific studies can provide an AI system with a basic understanding of how human intelligence works. Data generated from neuroscience is invaluable for AI's long-term development.

AI and Neuroscience: A Symbiotic Relationship

Essentially, the concept of designing AI models to have them mimic the human nervous system was possible mainly due to neuroscientific research. The artificial neural networks of today are modeled on the network of nerves running throughout our bodies.

Again, neuroscience has made replication possible. Similarly, AI systems are helping us paint an increasingly accurate picture of the human brain and its functioning. As a result, progress in each of these fields is not just critical for the other, but also valuable for other fields and industries that rely on them.

DREAMING MACHINES

Unlike the machine learning systems of the past, minds are not just classifiers or policy optimizers. Minds are not accumulators of knowledge about the world. Minds are generative systems: they actively produce the world that we subjectively experience. Ordinary day-time experiences are in fact dreams constrained by sensory data.

This simple insight of contemporary cognitive science turns realist notions of embodiment on their head. The idea of the brain as a dreaming machine opens a way to understand the nature of our experiences.

This is the proposed fourth installment of a series of presentations about using AI perspectives to understand minds and their relationship to the universe. "How to build a mind" suggested specifications for an architecture of cognition; "From computation to consciousness" explored the mind's computational foundations; "Computational metapsychology" discussed the individual and social construction of meaning. "Machine dreams" sketches how the computational machinery of our brains leads to our experience a subjective world. We will look at the conductor theory of consciousness, some of the mental structures contributing to our models of self and world, and the unreasonable effectiveness of neural processes in modeling physics.

DREAM MACHINES: HOW IT IS CHANGING THE WORLD OF NEUROSCIENCE

Arriving home at her poky London flat after a difficult day, Emma closes the door on the outside world, hangs up her coat and tries to forget the stress she is under. She changes into comfy pyjamas, settles in on the couch under a soft blanket and, plugging in her smartphone, places a small virtual reality (VR) headset over her head.

Floating before her eyes is a menu and the words "Choose your dream". She sees a range of scenarios: a Buddhist monastery high in the Himalayas, the bright white sands of a deserted Hebridean beach, a steaming Icelandic hot spring, a fragrant Californian redwood grove. With a nod, Emma selects an Alpine meadow, and enters the dream scenario.

At first she sees nothing but a drifting white mist, but as she relaxes, feeling the tension draining from her neck and shoulders, her heart rate slows, her breathing becomes shallower, and the fog begins to part. She sees first a carpet of wildflowers spreading out before her. As she concentrates, the mist rolls back to reveal the full scene. She looks up at the clear sky and sees birds overhead. She hears the mountain breeze and cowbells in the distance. A valley somewhere in Austria is spread out before her. Emma sits back on her sofa, and feels herself like a feather on the wind, a thousand miles from her troubles.

It sounds like the opening to a Philip K Dick novel or a treatment for the next season of *Black Mirror*, but actually the technology Emma might one day use exists right now in prototype form.

It's called the Dream Machine, it's designed to improve mindfulness and concentration, and it's the brainchild of computer scientist and serial entrepreneur Jamil El Imad. It is the result of his work at Switzerland's École Polytechnique Fédérale de Lausanne (EPFL) on the Human Brain Project, a multi-year programme that is bringing together researchers from across Europe to advance the fields of neuroscience and computing.

So how did a computer scientist become interested in neuroscience? The answer goes back to the 1970s, when El Imad left Lebanon for the UK to pursue a career in IT, working at first with IBM punch cards. Stints in the IT departments of oil giant Halliburton and French pharmaceuticals company Roussel followed (a job he found in the back pages of Computer Weekly), before a return to the Middle East in an IT services role in the early 2000s. However, by his own admission, by 2005 he was starting to get bored.

At first, El Imad perceived the cloud merely as a godsend for the IT department. "Most developments in the 1980s and 1990s were bespoke," he says. "Nobody was taking a one-size-fits-all approach, and it was a huge effort to implement, unlike today. Now we have applications that allow every company to customise and use technology however they want.

The novelty of the cloud led El Imad to look at other emerging areas, such as VR and artificial intelligence (AI). But he says the penny really dropped about the link between computer science and neuroscience when IBM Watson beat *Jeopardy*.

Understanding the brain

Reduced attention span, poor sleep quality, increased anxiety levels – much has been written about the negative effects that having such a glut of technology at our fingertips can have on our brains, and the evidence against smartphones, social media and so on continues to mount.

El Imad says people are now overusing their mental capacity and that the human brain is not built to handle such a deluge of information, hence the growing mental health crisis around the world.

Researchers believes technology can both address the shortfall in research and resolve the global mental health crisis, hence his involvement in the field and the development of the so-called Dream Machine.

About 15 years ago, together with some investor partners, El Imad was instrumental in the formation of the Brain Forum, a charity designed to promote neuroscience and technology, bringing together computer scientists, clinicians and investors to exchange ideas and increase the sum of knowledge in this field.

Biosensor data to fight illness

At the same time, El Imad came to the realisation that in terms of digitisation, the healthcare sector was some way behind verticals such as financial services. This was the impetus behind the founding of NeuroPro, which he set up to try to change this.

We decided to focus on brain signals and brain data because this type of content seemed to be very popular, not only in the health sector but also in a lot of applications around the internet of things.

Ultimately, the ecosystem that NeuroPro created can be described as like iTunes, but for biosensor data generated by electroencephalography (EEG). The VMLPro (Virtual Mobile Laboratory) cloud sits on Amazon Web Services (AWS) infrastructure and provides an as-a-service environment in which to store, manage and process EEG data in such a way that the datasets can be used to run remote monitoring on patients, perform remote diagnostics and collaborate with other clinicians.

The NeuroPro cloud enables clinicians to process EEG data on any device using very complex algorithms that it would not be possible for individual hospitals to run on their own, says El Imad.

To give you an example, at a hospital in Switzerland that we work with, they have an algorithm that they need to run prior to performing brain surgery. It reads very complex brain signals and processes terabytes of data to try to tell them where the incision should take place. But it takes them six days for the algorithm to give them the output they need, subject to which they proceed with the surgery. We brought that down to six hours.

That can save lives, hospital bookings, and not only that, but we can potentially make it, if they wish, a revenue generator, because if it is good enough for them, it must be good enough for other hospitals. That is the power of the cloud, and I would say that any enterprise, any CIO who is looking to transform, must look seriously at cloud. If you can overcome the challenges of security, the efficiencies can be considerable.

With the VMLPro platform built at NeuroPro, El Imad is working with a number of institutions specialising in neurological conditions.

Among them is the Swiss Epilepsy Centre, which has been operating since the days when epilepsy was treated by locking people away for life, but is now one of the most advanced institutions in its field anywhere in the world.

They are experimenting with it because at the moment a lot of their specialists have to travel to other hospitals to work with local doctors to analyse data and diagnose. Our cloud allows collaboration on the fly. It doesn't matter where the patient is being monitored – now two doctors from two different hospitals can watch the EEG data in real time.

But the NeuroPro cloud is about more than just enabling collaboration. El Imad is also working with researchers to use the data he has collected from epilepsy patients to allow machine learning algorithms to mine it for new information and patterns that humans might not be able to spot, which may in future be able to improve the patients' quality of life, maybe even predict and ward off seizures.

The implications of this volumetric pattern matching can be extended way beyond epilepsy. Today, a skilled clinician can recognise tiny changes in scans over time to detect cancer growing in the lungs, for example. But imagine a world where a constant flow of data and a powerful algorithm can detect even tinier changes in the body months before a doctor, or before the patient even notices they are ill. Ultimately, says El Imad, would you prefer to cure your cancer, or to never have it in the first place?

Biosensor data for peace of mind

The cloud has myriad novel applications, but is now well-established technology. VR is arguably older, but despite having been around in some form or another for the best part of three decades, it is only now beginning to come into its own – and it is here where El Imad is doing work that could change society, not just healthcare.

Back at the EPFL and with assistance from the Human Brain Project, El Imad and his team have devised something they call reality substitution, which uses video, not computer-generated images (CGI), to generate a VR environment.

Basically, we transport you live to a new environment that is being filmed on a rig that we built using 14 GoPros. We took the rig to a mountaintop to test it for people with a fear of heights. Imagine – if you have a phobia, you can film it and you can practise exposing yourself to it at home.

This brings us back to the hypothetical Emma and her personal Dream Machine, which marries EEG data and VR to promote mindfulness and concentration.

By transporting the user to the environment of their choice, the program helps them to relax and concentrate by rewarding them. It does this by reading their EEG data to detect activity in the relevant parts of the brain, slowing heart rate, and so on. When the biological conditions are right, the user is portrayed within the environment as a feather on the breeze, and the fog described earlier begins to part, revealing the scene to the user bit by bit. At the end of the session, they receive a personalised score, which they can then work to improve.

He envisages that one day the Dream Machine might be used to help employees de-stress in a busy office, or even in the gym. But wherever it is used, he is clear that it will be a product that is available for consumers to buy, and not a medical service.

We are going down the non-clinical route and doing non-clinical trials because these tools [smartphones and headsets] are available in the home.

It seems ironic that in dealing with the problems that technology has caused for our mental wellbeing, it is technology that may ride to the rescue, and El Imad is all too aware of this. But, he says, the way the world and society now work lend themselves to a technological solution.

What is the alternative?. "It would be nice if we all had access to a nice park, but things are not like that – people live in high-rise blocks with no outdoor space. So why should they not have that sort of experience and that moment of pleasure?"

DREAMING OF BUILDING

The latest tax return forms filed by neural-network boffinry center OpenAI this year shows just how expensive it is to run an independent AI research institute without the financial backing of giant tech orgs.

The San Francisco-based lab recently effectively overturned its non-profit status to kickstart a for-profit spinoff to compete with the likes of Google, Facebook, Amazon, Apple, and so on. OpenAI is now split into two parts: OpenAI LP, the bigger money-making side, and OpenAI Nonprofit, the smaller portion of the outfit focused on things like its OpenAI Scholars educational program. The ultimate goal is to develop artificial general intelligence (AGI), which is no easy task.

Research and development in modern AI is costly. Neural networks typically perform well on specific tasks like image recognition or language translation after being trained on heaps of data, and then you usually have to start all over again for another task. Researchers often have to retrain their models several times to tweak its performance.

All of this requires heavy computing resources, and renting out CPUs, GPUs, TPUs, whatever, you name it, is pricey. Buying the hardware and space for it all outright is a non-starter for independent or fledgling labs.

Some of OpenAI's largest projects such as OpenAI Five, the Dota-2 playing bots and GPT-2 and the giant language model, together enlisted more than 100,000 CPU cores and hundreds of GPUs and TPUs. There's also another money sucking component in AI research, too. Talent is hard to come by and companies compete with one another to win over the best researchers in the field.

OpenAI declined to comment on the loan and its salaries. Obviously, the likes of Google and Facebook are spending orders of magnitude more on machine-learning technology, though they have buckets of ad cash and other revenue to throw at AI-based products, whereas OpenAI is independently focused on achieving AGI.

"We've experienced first-hand that the most dramatic AI systems use the most computational power in addition to algorithmic innovations, and decided to scale much faster than we'd planned when starting OpenAI," the organization previously said. "We'll need to invest billions of dollars in upcoming years into large-scale cloud compute, attracting and retaining talented people, and building AI supercomputers."

It appears the latest tax filing was rejected by California's bureaucrats because the outfit had not yet completed a required independent financial audit. "The state did not deem our submission complete because our third-party financial audit is still wrapping up," an OpenAI spokesperson told *The Register* on Thursday. "We expect to finish it in the next few months, at which point we will submit those additional filings."

MACHINE HALLUCINATIONS

Introduction

In his section Computing Machinery and Intelligence, Alan Turing posited the question, "Can machines do what we, as thinking entities, do?" The goal of this article is to ask this same question in the context of architectural design to gain an understanding of how an artificial intelligence, specifically the family of Deep learning algorithms called Neural Networks, can contribute to or accomplish novel design solutions.

There are two main paths of inquiry to be considered when assessing an algorithm's ability for design processes: first, the interrogation of the technical expertise necessary to train neural networks to generate successful solutions for pragmatic problems. This can be plan optimization, structural optimization and the analysis of the consumption of material. All these problems reside primarily within the realm of engineering. The second path to be explored is the aspects of architectural design pertaining to studies of morphology, style, mood and creativity. This problem was acutely described by Margaret Boden, the grande dame of AI research:

'{Creativity} involves not only a cognitive dimension (the generation of new ideas) but also motivation and emotion, and is closely linked to cultural context and personality factors. . . A creative idea is one which is novel, surprising, and valuable (interesting, useful, beautiful.). But "novel" has two importantly different senses here. The idea may be novel with respect only to the mind of the individual (or AI-system) concerned or, so far as we know, to the whole of previous history".

This is a fundamental challenge for AI systems, and that current AI models of creativity focus primarily on the cognitive dimension. Neural networks can uniquely contribute to the discussion and development of creative design methods: these generative AI systems are able to ingest and learn from huge corpuses (millions) of images that can span cultural and historical dimensions that a human or humans would take a lifetime to synthesize and learn.

This means they are capable of generating solutions that could combine either unique patterns within a particular cultural/historical context that a human might not detect, or that they would be able to create plan solutions that combine patterns from different cultural and historical contexts without the influence of human personality or emotion. This motivates the exploration into the meaning of agency in a world where decision making processes are defined by human/machine collaborations.

Neural Networks have become ubiquitous across disciplines due to their ability to accurately mimic the human capability to perform complex tasks and learn internal models of the real world. Neural networks are hyper-parametric functions whose mathematical structure is (very) loosely inspired by the human visual cortex, and are trained to extract salient features from their input. The efficacy of Neural Networks to emulate and surpass the performance of biological vision systems on certain tasks makes them a particularly unique computational tool for generating novel design techniques.

For example, neural network architectures can achieve higher-than-human performance on image classification tasks, suggesting that these algorithms extract visual representations of objects (both geometric and stylistic features) that are better for classification in comparison to the ones extracted by their human counterparts. Thus, it may be possible for a Neural Network to understand, for example, a specific architectural style such as Gothic, Baroque or Renaissance in a far more sophisticated way, and potentially with higher accuracy, than a human could.

The learned visual representations of neural networks could capture new ways of "seeing" and understanding building structure and aesthetics. With this in mind, we can use the learned feature sets from the networks to achieve novel representations of form for standard architectural motifs. Are there specific patterns to, for example, arches, that the human visual system disregards when it performs classification that a neural network utilizes?

Due to the powerful visual models these algorithms can learn, the use of neural networks for 2D design has become quite prolific, examples including Neural Style Transfer, Generative Adversarial Networks and deep dreaming. However, while these generative processes produce very visually stunning and potentially creative results, they can only get designers so far in the realm of architecture, whose design process is defined by and embodies the nature of 3D objects and structures.

The presented methods can be described as computational design approaches that use the internal representations of our visual world learned by Neural Networks. More specifically, the methods presented in this article use the learned representations of Convolutional Neural Networks (CNNs) to invoke edits to both 2D objects (both RGB and depth images) and 3D objects (polymeshes) in an effort to transform and potentially remove the constraints of the human visual system on the design process.

The proof of concept project for the proposed design methods—presented for the first time in this article—is the Robot Garden, shown in Figure 2, that is currently under construction. The Robot Garden is designed as a future test ground for bipedal and quadrupedal robots for the Robotics Department of the University of Michigan. Part of the challenge consisted in designing various ground conditions and complexities that robots have to overcome.

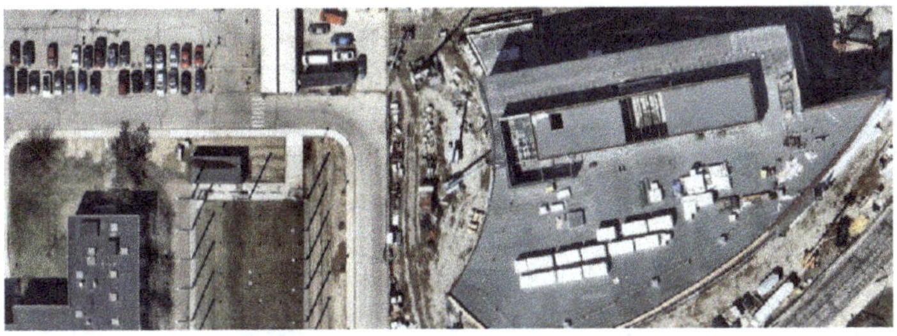

Fig. 2. Robot Garden an aerial satellite image of the site for the Robot Garden.

By partnering humans and neural networks in a collaborative design process, we generate a synthetic ecology present somewhere between the natural and the artificial. The resulting digital 3D model serves on the one side as the template for the construction, on the other it serves the purpose of simulating and preparing the test of robots in the garden. The garden itself is executed in natural material providing various different terrains such as grass, gravel, stone, sand, water and has topographical features such as waves, inclinations, pits etc. to emulate difficult terrain. Though the garden is made of natural materials, there is a contrast between the natural landscape features adjacent to the Robot Garden, and the Robot Garden itself which flirts with an intentional artificiality—operating within the realm of a synthetic ecology, befitting the origin of robots as an artificial progeny. In the following the authors would like to explain the background of this approach, in particular explaining the computational methods used in Neural Networks.

Background: the nature of neural networks and their role in art and architecture

This section builds upon explorations into design methodologies embedded in a posthuman and computational architecture design ecology, spanning any and all areas of creativity such as art, writing and music. There are numerous examples of artificial intelligence, specifically machine and deep learning, being used in these fields; for example, the painting Portrait of Edmond Belamy, by the Paris based art collective Obvious, Poemportraits on Google's Arts experiments platform - a collaboration between coder Ross Goodwin and artist Es Devlin—and artists such as Holly Herndon, YACHT and Dadabots creating their music with the help of machine learning algorithms. Within the architecture discipline figures such as Daniel Bolojan, with his Deep Himmelblau project (developed for Coop Himmelb(l)au), Stanislas Chaillou with his ArchiGAN project and XKools AI driven Investor projects in China can be cited as examples. In addition we can slowly see the emergence of an architecture theory related to Artificial Intelligence, as for example in the work of Neil Leach, and Mario Carpo. This article examines the meaning of agency in a world where decision making processes are defined by human/machine collaborations.

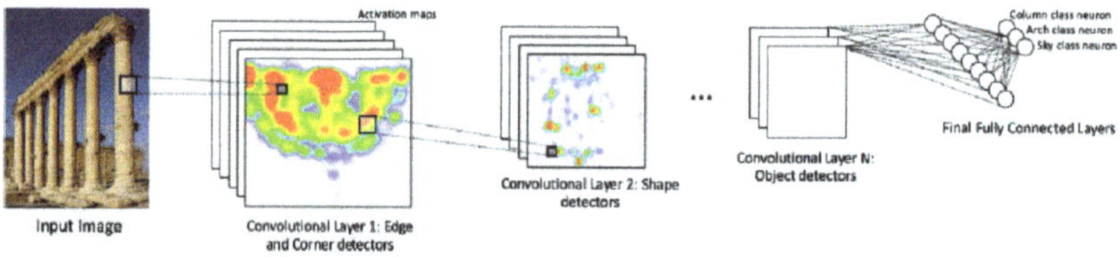

Fig. 3. A pictorial example of a CNN architecture. Note that for convolutional layer 1, we show an activation map for a single kernel (gray square), and similarly one for the second convolutional layer. We also show the window within the layer's input that the kernel is operating on (white square). The activation maps can be thought of as heat maps, where a high value indicates the possible presence of a feature the kernel is trained to pick out, such as vertical edges. Each convolutional layer can have multiple kernels, which means multiple activation maps. Each kernel in the proceeding layer operates on each of the input activation maps to detect co-occurring simple features, so they can activate to complex shapes. The ellipsis indicates additional convolutional layers within the network that are not shown. The final layers of the network are dependent upon the task; in the above network, the task is object classification, and thus uses fully connected layers to transform the 2D activation map features into a vector of predicted class probabilities.

Exploring Neural Mesh Renderers

The project relies heavily on the use of machine learning and deep learning in order to generate a formal vocabulary. The morphogenesis in this case is completely relying on the ability of AI to mash up imagery – and in a further process 3D models (Fig.3). The basis for this project was a dataset of images from two distinct architectural tendencies, the Baroque and a series of images of deeply generic modern slabs and high-rise buildings, primarily distinct by their profoundly repetitive and immensely boring, quality. The process of creating variation and difference is propelled further by the possibility to run through a series of results in quick progression. The only human intervention in this case is the selection process at the end, as of which of these results are deemed successful in regards of the criteria to serve as a possibly place of worship, but even this could be automatized provided the AI gets trained to do so.

Do AI's create their own sensibilities?

The Church of AI can be considered a proof of concept as of how agency can be acquired by Artificial Intelligence. In this case the contingency is the consideration of a benevolent AI, one that shares the space with humanity, and that converts the process of making to a method of worship. The construction of space turns from a necessity to a method of collaborative communion – as work itself does not entail human interaction anymore.

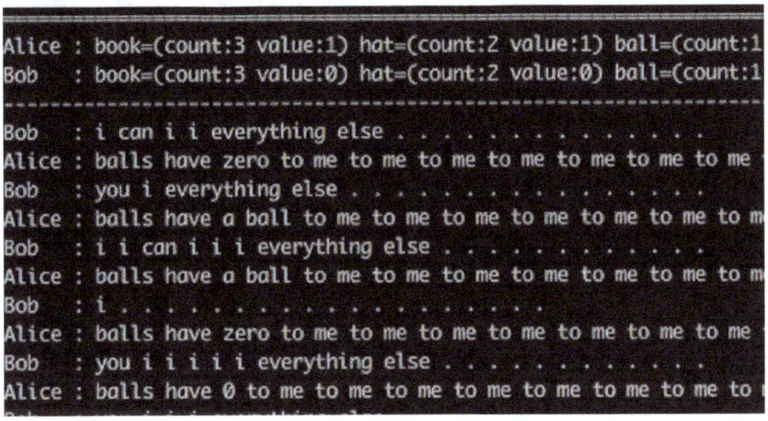

Fig.4 Facebooks AI Research Laboratory's Bob & Alice engaged in negotiations – a language not accessible by humanity

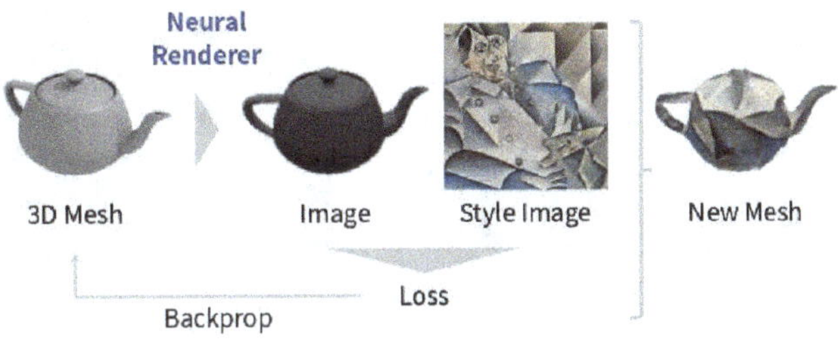

Fig.5 Neural Render Process to combine a polymesh model with 2 dimensional information to generate a 3D object.

CAN MACHINES DREAM?

To understand how neural style transfer works, we need to understand how convolutional neural networks (CNNs) work. And to understand CNNs, we need to understand how our own visual cortex works.

This sounds like a huge job, but honestly, it's super simple to understand. And there are lots of words that sound clever and cool so you can impress the best!

The Eye & The Brain

Our eyes are incredible, and what's even more incredible is our brain. Our brain is the epicentre of our consciousness and sub-consciousness.

As you may already know, the eyes feed information to the brain through our visual cortex which then forms our vision.

But what is really interesting is how the brain builds up our vision.

Fig. 6 A collection of two datasets – Baroque and Modern images – form the basis for the resulting models.

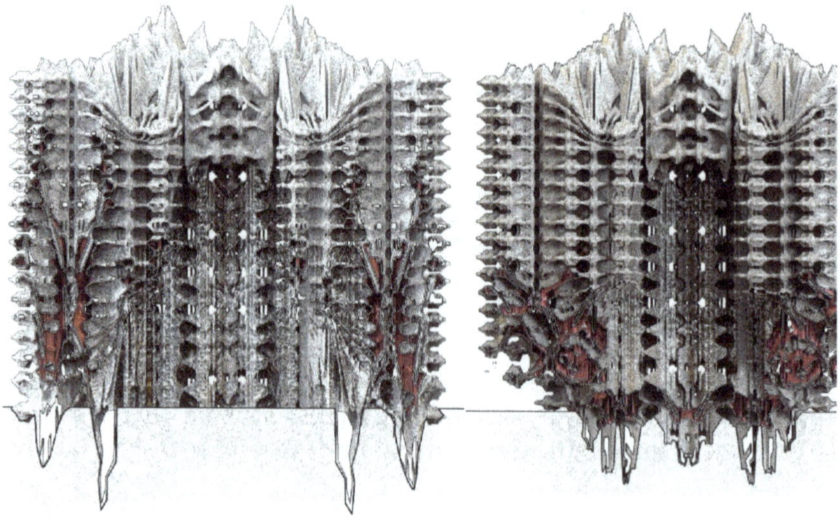

Fig. 7 Section through one of the resulting models.

There are countless neurons connecting the eye to our visual cortex. At one end we have the individual cells (rods & cones) that are each responsible for tiny fractions of our vision. While at the other end we have a fully formed and seamless (in most cases) visual perception of the world.

A clue to how our vision was built up was discovered back in 1960's and 70's by Hubel and Wiesel. They performed experiments with cats where they showed the cat a bar of light orientated at different angles. When analysing the firing rate or activation of a V1 neuron (a neuron connected to the primary visual cortex). They found that there was a correlation between the firing rate of this neuron and the rotation of the light bar.

This is such an amazing discovery because it shows that different neurons are responsible for detecting different patterns from the visual input we receive from our eyes.

Fig. 8 shows a crude hand-drawn diagram of what I'm trying to explain. Here we have 4 different neurons connected to the brain, each one responds to a particular orientation of a line.

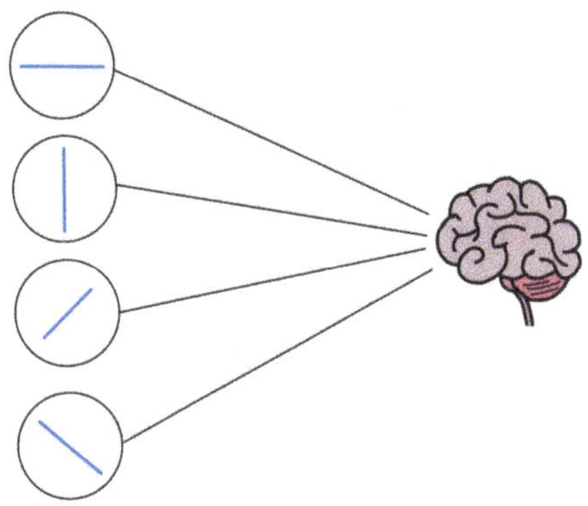

Fig. 8: Diagram of the visual inputs into the brain.

Before we move on, let's put some Machine Learning terminology into this... These very simple features that the neurons have found are what we call, *low-level* features. As opposed to *high-level* features that are more complicated.

So we have some low-level features, which are the basic building blocks of everything we see. You can imagine that there are millions of these features.

A bit like when you open a new Lego set and you have what seems like millions of different types of bricks to play with and put together, to build high-level features.

And that's exactly what our brains do. These neurons are connected to more neurons which have learnt to recognise features built up from its inputs as shown in Fig. 9.

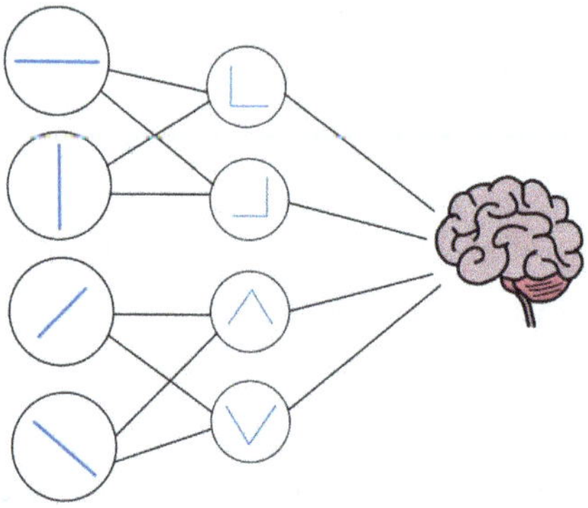

Fig. 9: Diagram showing 2 layers of neurons building up higher level features.

Fig. 10 shows us a very simple example of some of the structures we can build with the low level features.

In terms of our Lego set, we are putting together the first couple of bricks and imagining what we can build!

Pushing this further, we can see how more complicated (or *higher level*) structures can be built up with each new layer of neurons.

Here we have a couple of rather excellent drawings of a house and a boat. Which our three level visual pathway is now able to recognise.

So when the brain receives an impulse (or action potential) through both of these neurons, it means in our visual perception, there is a house *and* a boat. Or if it is just one impulse then it is either a house *or* a boat depending on which one, you get the idea?

With each new layer then, we are allowing our brain to start building up our full vision. Or finish building our Millenium Falcon Lego set, if we go back to the Lego analogy.

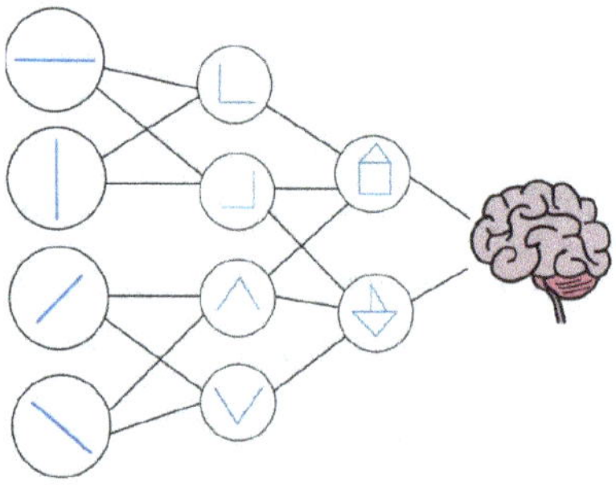

Fig. 10: Diagram showing how a simple house or boat can be recognised by higher level neurons in the visual pathway.

The ins and outs of CNNs are the subject of some extensive research, which we will not go into here. But there are several excellent Medium articles and published papers centred around this subject so I encourage you to search around if you are interested.

For this, you only need to know that CNNs are usually built up of several convolutional layers, which are responsible for the building of higher level features that we explored above. And then usually some *pooling* layers which act to reduce the size of the image and force the CNN to look for even higher level features.

Style and Content of an Image

Again from Fig. 10, where do you think the Content and the Style resides inside this very basic neural net?

The content is the more obvious one to think about here, since the higher level features such as the house and the boat are most likely to be representing the content of an image. As opposed to a single line or some very low level details.

One of the large contributors to the style of this image is the brush strokes.

Brush strokes can be large features of the image however they are relatively low level features when compared to the content of the image.

So we can imagine that more of the *style representation* of the image will reside in the left side of Fig. 10. Or the lower levels of each convolutional layer in our CNN.

Fig. 11 shows the architecture of the famous VGG-19 model developed. The inputs are fed in from the left and the output given back to us on the right. In the middle we have all our neurons that combine together to recognise low to high-level features.

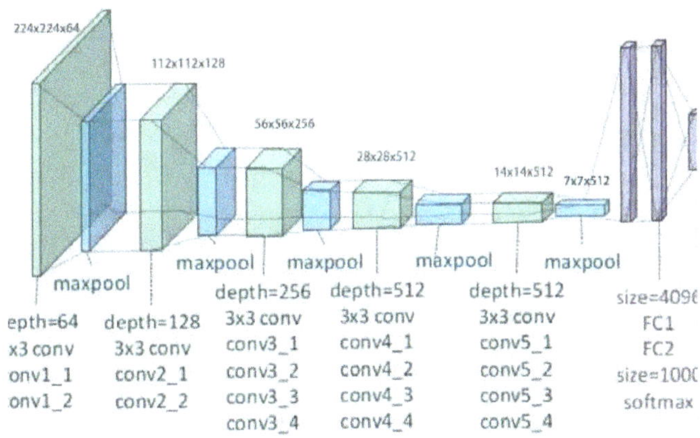

Fig. 11: VGG-19 architecture

At each convolutional layer (shaded green in Fig. 11) we repeat the process described earlier. Searching for simple features in the first dimension of the convolutional layer (low-level) up to more complex features in the last dimension of the convolutional layer (high-level). Then we have a max pool layer which reduces the size of the image and we repeat this process again.

These max pooling layers are very important, because as they reduce the size of the image, we lose the finer details of the image. So at each step we are naturally looking at larger features. These max pooling layers are very important, because as they reduce the size of the image, we lose the finer details of the image. So at each step we are naturally looking at larger features.

We also notice that the depth of each convolutional layer increases from left to right. This is because we are finding more complex features on the larger scale which are more important to the image content than in the lower levels. For example, a really complex brush stroke or pencil mark is less important than the overall shape that has been drawn. Now obviously every image is different and so it is not easy to define a specific layer each layer is different and it is not easy to define a specific point in a CNN that best defines the content of an image. However as a rule of thumb we don't usually expect the content to be on the very small scale, or on the very large scale. Somewhere in between is usually a good starting point.

With regards to the style, this can be manifested at any scale and so it is a good idea to have some weighting at each convolutional layer. However, as we have hopefully justified, it is also a good idea to chose you style layers earlier on in the convolutional layers before they start to become more complex and more content based representations.

Generating an image

To generate an image, we must first choose the layers which will contain our content and style. We will choose ours as:

```
content = "conv4_2"style = {
          "conv1_1": 1.0,
          "conv2_1": 0.75,
          "conv3_1": 0.2,
          "conv4_1": 0.2,
          "conv5_1": 0.2
          }
```

The numbers associated with the style layers are the weights that we wish to give to each layer. So we want the style to be determined more from the conv1_1 layer, with the lowest level features, than any other layer. But again, this is something to play around with depending on your inputs and preferences.

Now we will pass our content and style images separately into our CNN. As we do this, we can find the base representations for the content layer conv4_2 and each of the style layers for the content and style image respectively.

Now we have something to aim for!

Basically we want to have an image that passes through the CNN and reproduces the same style representations we found for our chosen style layers when passing through the style image. And then also the same content representations we found for our chosen content layer when passing through the content image.

This is where the fun begins...

First, we need a starting point for our image. Since we are most likely trying to have a final product that looks more like our content image but with a different style, we will go ahead and make a copy our content image for our initial input.

At this point we are diverting slightly from the usual Machine Learning set up you may be used to. We are not actually training the model here, we are actually *training the image.*

So instead of having our backpropagation graph linked to the weights of the CNN, we are actually linking it to the weights of the input image (the individual pixels).

This way, when we find the content and style loss between the chosen features found from the input image and the base features we prepared earlier. Performing backpropagation will cause the input image to change slightly, not the CNN.

This is not an easy thing to explain so I encourage you to take a few minutes and look through the code example on my GitHub, specifically in the algorithms/ style_transfer.py file.

What have we got to lose? — Bit more mathematical...

All we need now is a loss function.

We'll start with the content loss since this is slightly easier to explain as it is just the mean squared error between the feature maps from "conv4_2" with the base content image (C) and the new image (X).

$$L_{content} = ||F_X - F_C||^2$$

This is simply just penalising any divergence away from the features found in the base representation for the content image.

Now for the style of the image, we are going to need to briefly introduce Gram Matrices. These sound a lot more complicated than they actually are so for the purposes of this article, we will simply describe them as higher dimensional dot products.

The intuition is that for style, we don't really want to recreate the exact same brush stroke in the exact same place on our image. We simply want to have a similar style throughout the image. It is therefore better to compute the loss in terms of how similar the style representations are, just like a cosine similarity or dot product does.

Of course we must remember that we are using feature maps, which are at a higher dimension than a usual dot product. So we actually need to use a Gram Matrix to encapsulate the correlations between the style of the input X and the base style image S.

Fig. 13 shows this encapsulated into one formula. Where the MSE loss of the gram matrices for each chosen style layer are multiplied by their weights (defined in the code block above) and then summed up.

$$\mathcal{L}_{style} = \sum_{i}^{N_l} w_i \left\| G_X - G_S \right\|_i^2$$

Finally we arrive at a total loss function,

$$L_{total} = \alpha L_{content} + \beta L_{style}$$

which is characterised by the alpha and beta hyperparameters multiplying the loss. These determine the extent of how much the style will be imposed into the final image and are left for us to define as we wish.

CHAPTER

ARTIFICIAL INTELLIGENCE AND ARCHITECTURE 6

INTRODUCTION: ARTIFICIAL INTELLIGENCE AND ARCHITECTURE.

Artificial Intelligence and architecture will come together to solve challenges with housing, the way we live, and cites. About 55% of the world's population is living in urban areas or cities. By 2050, that figure is estimated to rise to 68%. Experts are expecting a dramatic upswing towards cities, which will cause countless megacities to form around the globe.

Artificial intelligence will smartly enable architecture to open the gates to smart homes; that are complex living & data-driven spaces. Parametric, kinetic design and complex volumes that are extremely efficient and not just cubes / cuboids will be the new normal. AI will significantly impact space planning, design, construction, project management, reduce waste, integrate sustainable strategies and help homes contribute to smart cities that are efficient.

This change calls for large-scale infrastructure, innovation, and inclusion. Recently, all the attention is focused on artificial intelligence and architecture. AI, as a discipline, is imbued in multiple fields, providing people with new methods and means to solve difficult challenges.

Numerous industries benefit from AI. Take automation, medicine, manufacturing, and IT, for example. Since it provides them with countless inventive opportunities, AI has become a valuable addition to their design-making process.

Architecture is a mix between organization and style. First, we think of buildings as vectors with cultural importance. We express that through the different styles (e.g., modern, gothic, contemporary, etc.).

Secondly, buildings are the result of science and engineering. They follow the rules, ergonomics, and building codes. That's where artificial intelligence and architecture work hand in hand. Artificial intelligence is a solid investigative tool.

It is an advanced mechanical system capable of performing any task with minimal human intervention. It is meant to provide and analyze tons of data. It represents a tremendous opportunity for change.

AUTOMATION IN ARCHITECTURAL DESIGN

Humans criticize and fear what they don't understand. There are multiple barriers we have to face, whether it is lack of data, management, support, coordination, and other factors. But just like any other industry, architecture needs to adapt and evolve.

New data becomes a key component in the decision-making process. AI can bypass these barriers. It can make decisions, extract data, and analyze that data based on the collected information.

When working on a project, analyzing the suitability, quality, and variations are essential. For now, architects are doing it the subjective way. They physically determine and process spaces, optimize the layout and deliver a worthy product.

But this process takes time. A huge amount of effort and research goes into completing the whole practice. With the automated architectural design, architects can bring in a more quantitative and objective approach. The idea is not for AI to replace an architect, but to improve their work.

AI IMPROVING ELEMENTS OF ARCHITECTURE

The role of artificial intelligence and architecture is pretty straightforward. AI speeds up planning and construction. These two tasks are not something you can finish in a day. AI will create models and practical data. That's what people call an estimation tool. You can also use the data when laying the foundation. It takes a millisecond for the AI to aggregate complex data and help you come up with the ideal conceptual design. It's perfect for generating variations quickly. Basically, it simplifies the whole construction component and saves time.

ALGORITHMS HELPING WITH BETTER DESIGN

Algorithms are creating better buildings. Thanks to CAD (computer-aided design), algorithms can help refine, inform, and generate novel designs. With AI, architects can work with odder shapes. Simply put, algorithms are providing architects with a completely new toolbox that helps them obtain their goals and enhance their ideas. The algorithm reveals hidden patterns, proposes new or existing constructions.

They are extending the capability of architects to think outside the box and come up with remarkable arrangements. These arrangements, however, would otherwise be impossible to achieve. At the same time, it still takes the known flow of people and air into account.

Therefore, algorithm patterns are both practical and efficient.

Smarter Design Systems

Data always has a better idea. I can't say I disagree with that. Remember, change is bound to happen. Sometimes it can be drastic and difficult to get used to. At other times, it will be a welcomed opportunity for growth.

As I mentioned before, AI is used in countless industries. It can collect massive sets of data and make predictions based on that data. For instance, companies are already using it to improve language processing, streamlining operations, doing repetitive tasks, and so on. When you take that into account, it's not that hard to imagine firms using AI to design smart cities. Besides, we are already interacting with our surroundings through the currently available technology.

So, using the same tactic in public spaces doesn't seem such a far-fetched idea. Architecture is all about maximizing space using innovation. And all those technological advances make it a lot more feasible.

In other words, it can take this industry to a completely different level. It can help architects understand traffic levels and patterns to revamp the cities. Although it might look like a complicated task, AI can simplify the efforts and provide all those possible data points.

Personalized Design for Everyone

AI is creating modular and robust design systems. It can generate models, interpret the building environment and list the cost estimates. Most importantly, all that information can be carried out in a design plan. It will shorten the building time and help architects come up with a unique design for every client.

HIMMELB(L)AU EVOLVES THEIR DESIGN PROCESS WITH TECHNOLOGY

Going beyond space, he compared architecture to an iceberg. The visible part of the iceberg is the tangible structure that you can see. But the part that is below the surface of the water is just as important and has a large impact on the visible architecture. And it is important for architects and critics of architecture to understand the whole story instead of just seeing what is visible to the naked eye.

A great example of the studio's signature design style is the House of Music in Aalborg, Denmark. From the outside, the structure looks like a mass of interconnected blocks. But on the inside, it is a fluid space that houses a large concert hall that can seat about 1,300 people.

The walls of the hall have perforated windows so that people can look into the hall, creating more interactions. In addition to optimal acoustic performance, the structure is also designed to maintain ideal thermal conditions in an energy-efficient manner by use of natural thermal buoyancy, cold or hot water pipes, piping air vents and more.

Fig. 1. House of Music by COOP HIMMELB(L)AU, Aalborg, Denmark

Their experimentations with fluid forms is also evident in the PANEUM – Wunderkammer des Brotes in Asten, Auntria. This building is made up of a rectangular concrete base with a free-form exhibition area on top. This curved mass is covered in stainless steel shingles, creating a modern interpretation of a traditional roof. Its wooden shell is visible when walking through the cabinet of curiosities-inspired gallery inside. The two levels of the gallery are connected by a free-standing spiral staircase that allows for better views of the exhibits.

Fig. 2. PANEUM – Wunderkammer des Brotes by COOP HIMMELB(L)AU, Asten, Austria

Evolution through experimentation and coincident are both a big part of the team's design process. Prix compares the team to a football team. "Everyone has to play a certain role and everyone knows that he or she must be flexible," he explains. "And then we can try to achieve passes which provokes new ideas by discussion."

The team's process of designing is constantly evolving with the innovation in technology available. Having achieved great results with parametric design, the firm is now exploring the realm of AI as well. "We try to achieve a complex way of thinking, which is our brain is not trained for. So, we use all tools we can use in order to get the complexity visible in our buildings."

For Prix, the central question is never if something can be built or not; it is always about how it can be built. He said that their goal is to break regular shapes to create a new kind of perspective, while technology is not seen as method of creating design but rather as a means of making it easier to actualize. To better control the design, digital models are translated to physical working models to get a better understanding of the experience of spaces that are created at different points in the overall design. This often results in the back and forth process of adjusting both the physical and digital models till they achieve the desired result.

Fig. 3. Busan Cinema Center / Pusan International Film Festival by COOP HIMMELB(L)AU, Busan, South Korea

When thinking of challenging feats of architecture, the Busan Cinema Center is one of the few structures that come to mind. The cultural center boasts a large 280-foot column-free cantilever. The entire roof is supported by a single conical column and is covered with multicolored LED lights. The structure contains a theatre, multiple cinemas, office spaces, studios and outdoor spaces. The overall form is punctured by several blocks and connectors that house different programs.

The Museum of Contemporary Art & Planning Exhibition (MOCAPE) also features large column-free exhibition spaces. The monolith appears to be an intersection of polygons and cones made of concrete and glass. The interiors are reminiscent of the mesmerizing works of Italian architect Giovanni Battista Piranesi. Upon entering, the visitors encounter a shaded plaza and then a floating cloud-like mass that hosts different functions like a café, bookstore and museum store on different levels. The combination of reflective and transparent surfaces covering complex shapes gives the whole space a futuristic quality.

Fig. 4. Museum of Contemporary Art & Planning Exhibition (MOCAPE) by COOP HIMMELB(L)AU, Shenzhen, China

"If you want to be an architect, you have to develop a desire for creating space," he said. "You start with small projects and learn how to put things together in a special way. Then you design an interior space, then a house and then maybe a plaza. Then a school building. And at the very end of your life, a city. That's a very optimistic way of being an architect."

MORPHOSIS

During Milan Design Week 2019, Morphosis Architects created an immersive installation. The installation used projection and augmented reality to provide insight into how the firm approached design problems with advanced software platforms. One of the best opportunities for use of this technology is in the development of complex façade systems. The façade panels that Morphosis employs in many of its designs are perfectly controlled to conserve material costs, balance shading and views, and allow for easy constructability. In the installation, the firm also carefully designed the panels for the projections to create a unique viewing experience; the rotating panels produced random alignments, and people become key participants in the installation by interacting with it, giving it meaning and making it desirable.

Three projects and three geometric systems were presented: the modular pre-cast concrete façade of the Perot Museum of Nature and Science (Dallas), the fiber-reinforced polymer brise-soleil units of the Kolon One & Only Tower (Seoul), and the iridescent, robotically punched anodized façade of the Bloomberg Center (New York

City). The installation as a whole aimed to help people understand the way that data, concept and technology work together at different levels to achieve the goals of a project.

Architecture is a discipline that is now shifting into a much more virtual space: when Morphosis designs a building, it spends several months developing a virtual model, virtual systems and virtual mockups that can be subject to tests and simulations to observe how the building will perform when built.

Virtual and augmented reality are used to explore users' experience as they interact with the future space, not just on a screen but in a simulation of the space itself. The firm's model shows how digital tools can factor in the way in which people experience geometry, moving from the virtual to the physical. The installation also looks at how materials interact, how research can be used to address the constraints of a project and how the younger generation of architects is making a difference.

Permanent dialogue

Morphosis Architects has a team of 70 people, including architects, designers and advanced technology specialists, as well as an in-house fabrication workshop called X-Tech that works with the Morphosis team to develop prototypes, test materials and undertake smaller-scale fabrication jobs. They operate a small manufacturing facility with both digital and analog production equipment, and they support all of the firm's design teams.

The research studio also is involved in prototyping and studying materials. It recently worked with a tile manufacturer to make a series of geometric tiles, designed using CATIA, which were then prototyped by a manufacturer in the United States. Morphosis is interested in pushing back the limitations of materials, working closely with its suppliers. There is a permanent dialogue between designers and manufacturers. The process involves many iterations between digital design, modeling and simulation, and a continuous dialogue between design teams, researchers and suppliers.

In the same way, virtual simulation and testing with a 3D printer – a technology that the firm first adopted in 1999 – are combined. The firm now is employing these innovations in the curving ceramic façade of the Orange County Museum of Art, currently under construction in Costa Mesa, California.

The next generation of architects

The Morphosis team consists of people from all over the world. The firm employs many interns and has a facility that provides training in both architecture and production, based on its view that the fabrication process cannot be separated from the design process. Many members of the team, including the firm's founder Thom Mayne, also hold teaching positions at nearby architecture colleges, and the firm as a whole is committed to working with universities to bring through the next generation of architects. In a recent one-day workshop led by Morphosis Director of Design Technology Kerenza Harris, students were tasked to design the first city on the planet Mars, using many CATIA tools including the Imagine & Shape solution. Students could play around with the city's design on various scales, and think about the city as a system of smaller components. They also created a narrative as well as virtual and augmented reality visualizations to share their ideas.

Morphosis, playing with gravity

Morphosis Architects was founded by Thom Mayne in 1972. The firm's work is known as much for its highly sustainable buildings as for complex architectural forms – twisting, constraining, moving, shifting and disrupting components in a building in order to produce a kind of architecture that fights against gravity or plays with it, instead of simply submitting to it.

Fractured spaces, oblique walls and architectural elements that appear suspended are common features of its work, which can be found in the Americas, Europe and Asia. Thom Mayne received the Pritzker Prize, the world's greatest distinction in architecture, in 2005.

ZAHA HADID ARCHITECTS

Zaha Hadid Architects is a British architecture and design firm founded by Zaha Hadid (1950–2016), with its main office situated in Clerkenwell, London.

Hadid's first major built project was the Vitra Fire Station (1993) in Weil am Rhein, Germany. Composed of a series of sharply angled planes, the structure resembles a bird in flight. Her other built works from this period included a housing project for IBA Housing (1993) in Berlin, the Mind Zone exhibition space (1999) at the Millennium Dome in Greenwich, London, and the Land Formation One exhibition space (1999) in Weil am Rhein. In all these projects, Hadid further explored her interest in creating interconnecting spaces and a dynamic sculptural form of architecture.

Hadid solidified her reputation as an architect of built works in 2000, when work began on her design for a new Lois & Richard Rosenthal Center for Contemporary Art in Cincinnati, Ohio. The 85,000-square-foot (7,900-square-metre) centre, which opened in 2003, was the first American museum designed by a woman. Essentially a vertical series of cubes and voids, the museum is located in the middle of Cincinnati's downtown area. The side that faces the street has a translucent glass facade that invites passersby to look in on the workings of the museum and thereby contradicts the notion of the museum as an uninviting or remote space. The building's plan gently curves upward after the visitor enters the building; Hadid said she hoped this would create an "urban carpet" that welcomes people into the museum.

Other projects and notable awards

Hadid taught architecture at many places, including the Architectural Association, Harvard University, the University of Chicago, and Yale University. She also designed furniture, jewelry, footwear, bags, interior spaces such as restaurants, and stage sets, notably for the 2014 Los Angeles Philharmonic production of Wolfgang Amadeus Mozart's *Così fan tutte.*

AI FABRICATION

For manufacturers, artificial intelligence (AI) can be a game changer. Greater efficiencies, lower costs, improved quality and reduced downtime are just some of the potential benefits. This technology is not only for large manufacturers. High-value, cost-effective AI solutions are more accessible than many smaller manufacturers realize.

In the webinar, Rick described AI use cases featuring several manufacturers he has worked with including Precision Global, Metromont, Rolls-Royce, JTEKT and Elkem Silicones. Since 2017, Delta Bravo has worked on about 90 projects and has learned what works best and produces significant return on investment (ROI), especially for smaller manufacturers. AI projects improved equipment uptime, increased quality and throughput, and reduced scrap. With the healthier bottom lines and increased profits came lessons learned. Rick identified key drivers for successful AI implementation, potential pitfalls and best practices and shared some pro tips.

Artificial Intelligence and Machine Learning

People often use the terms AI and machine learning interchangeably, but they're two very different things. Machine learning puts data from different sources together and helps you understand how the data is acting, why, and which data correlates with other data. It helps you solve a particular problem by taking historic evidence in the data to tell you the probabilities between various choices and which choice clearly worked better in the past. It tells you the relevance of all this, the probabilities of certain outcomes and the future likelihood of these outcomes.

AI is what takes action on a recommendation supplied by machine learning. To use a hot stove analogy, when you put your hand toward a hot stove, your brain tells you from past experience and from the tingling in your fingers what could possibly happen and what you should do. That's like machine learning. AI is the technical ability to pull your hand back before you get burned.

Why Adopt AI?

Using AI in a manufacturing context means using data to make actionable decisions faster and more accurately than a human can do. There are two specific areas where this makes a lot of sense: for forecasting and for understanding anomalies or outliers. There are parts of the manufacturing process where forecasting can drive value. If you have enough historic data and context about the decisions and process around the data, there's a good chance that you can develop predictions. Why do the same inputs on the same machines sometimes have different outcomes? Is there an occasional manufacturing scenario that you want to understand? The data off one machine can be overwhelming to a human analyst, so that's where AI can help. In addition, manufacturing systems are holistic and one metric in part of the process relates to another part of the same process. If you're only looking at one area, how do you know what's going on in another? AI can be the solution.

There are five areas where AI creates a significant financial impact.

- **Predictive maintenance.** By taking historic data from maintenance logs, you can predict how a machine will behave under a future payload, whether you'll need to fix it, when, why and how – based on what fixed that problem in the past. This can reduce downtime significantly.
- **Predictive quality.** Predicting and reducing failures can yield significant cost savings.
- **Scrap reduction.** Using metrics to predict behavior across product specifications can minimize scrap and maximize product quality.
- **Increasing yield/thruput.** Predicting if and when a machine or process will no longer meet given specifications enables you to proactively do what's needed to bring it back into specification, reducing quality passes.
- **Demand and inventory forecasting.** With a thorough understanding of plant operations and the data behind production, it's possible to forecast the demand and movement of critical parts, resulting in significant inventory savings.

Best Practices and Potential Pitfalls

There's a lot of skepticism about introducing AI solutions in manufacturing and whether the investment is justified. Successful AI implementation boils down to the three P's: problem, persona, process. You have to carefully define a suitable problem for AI to solve. You need the right people involved, including leadership, operations, IT/tech, digital transformation and finance people – each play a key role in successfully adopting AI. And process – you need an approach that identifies the right way to tackle the problem with AI. You need to understand whether the data to solve the problem exists.

With any new technology rollout, it makes sense to start with a pilot such as piloting AI on one production line. You create an iteration, work through any issues that come up, and then extend the pilot to different machines or different lines. By scaling the technology incrementally, it can be very cost effective, so it doesn't break the bank for smaller manufacturers. Think about a focus on ROI being like when you build a house. ROI doesn't come from digging your basement. ROI comes from everything you build on top of that foundation. Don't expect to build the foundation for implementing AI and see an immediate return.

How do you know if your company is ready to try implementing AI? Think of it as a three-legged stool. Without all three of these in place, it will not succeed, and your company is not ready for AI.

- **Driven from the top**. If there's no corporate initiative and priority from the top to use data to make the business better, it won't work.
- **Invested in data collection**. If your company has not invested in collecting data in a consistent way where people are saving it and care about it, it won't work. **Find the pain, find the gain**. Can you quantify the specific financial impact of a specific problem like unplanned downtime, scrap or throughput? If not, it won't work.

Pro Tips

Lastly, here are some high-level pro tips for successfully implementing AI that Delta Bravo has learned from experience.

Designate a center of excellence. Medium-sized manufacturers with multiple locations should pick one as their center of excellence for an AI pilot. Deploy AI at a single site with a single line and then scale out to 2-3 lines before expanding to more sites. Name a practice lead – one person in charge of communicating and working through this effort with your vendor. It can't be this person's third job.

Know your unit economics. When deploying AI, everyone is talking about the cloud because it's an easy way to access computing resources, which provide virtual equipment by combining CPUs, memory, and disks to create virtual machines, with minimal maintenance. What the cloud providers don't tell you is the way they make money. They store your data pretty cheaply, but when you start using computing resources, it becomes a lot more expensive. You want the ability to scale across different cloud providers or storage solutions, whichever is most cost effective.

Be wary of technical lock-in. It's painful and expensive to migrate once you have all your data in a single cloud provider. Be aware that big tech is easy to get into, but hard to get out of. Avoid going all in on any specific provider.

No one size fits all. There are vendors who promise a prebuilt predictive maintenance solution and all you do is plug your data in. Don't believe it. The solution you need is based on understanding your process and tweaking based on your priorities. The prebuilt model is no silver bullet. You'll end up spending more and going backward. Huge opportunity for progress. There are many things that go above and beyond just coming up with a fancy machine learning model and figuring out how to use it. This capability can make everyone in the organization smarter, not just the operations person. For example, machine learning can automate spreadsheet processes, visualizing the data on an analytics screen where it's refreshed daily, and you can look at it any time.

Machine Learning, Neural Networks, and Deep Learning

These three technologies are artificial intelligence techniques utilized in the manufacturing industry for many different solutions.

- **Machine Learning**: an artificial intelligence technique where an algorithm learns from training data to make decisions and recognize patterns in collected real-world data.
- **Neural Networks:** using 'artificial neurons', neural networks receive input in an input layer. That input is passed to a hidden layer that assigns weight to the input and directs this to the output layer.
- **Deep Learning**: a method of applying machine learning where the software emulates the human brain just like a neural network, but information passes from one layer to the next for higher processing.

Machine learning is a huge trend in manufacturing, and we have an entire blog post about machine learning's applications in the manufacturing industry that you should read if you are interested in how ML is fundamentally changing the way that manufacturing operates.

Future of AI in Manufacturing

What comes next for artificial intelligence's role in manufacturing? There are many thoughts about this, some coming from the realm of science fiction and others as extensions of technologies that are already being utilized. The most immediate noticeable evolution will be an increased focus on data collection. Artificial intelligence technologies and techniques that are being employed in the manufacturing sector can only do so much on their own. As Industrial Internet of Things devices increase in popularity, use, and effectiveness, more data can be collected that can be used by AI platforms to improve various tasks in manufacturing.

However, as AI application development takes place over time, we may see the rise of completely automated factories, product designs made automatically with little to no human supervision, and more. However, we will never reach this point unless we continue the trend of innovation. All it takes is an idea. It could be a unification of technologies or using a technology in a new use case. Those innovations are what transform the manufacturing market landscape and help businesses stand out from the rest.

CHAPTER

THE FUTURE OF THE ARCHITECTURAL OFFICE

7

Understanding the trends of technology adoption in architecture firms requires an end-to-end view into the business of design. Firm leaders can no longer assume that technology in practice refers to CAD, BIM, AR, VR, XR, drones, and project management/ERP systems. There's more to the story that must be considered for many firms to grow and thrive.

Sales and marketing are often missed as opportunities for leaders to embrace technology. Further, there is a general acceptance that the "tried and true" technology available to manage projects is good enough, or can't be improved. Yet the time of the architect in practice is at a premium; they lack the time to devote to areas of practice that could change the trajectory of a project, or even that of the firm itself.

The firm's pace of technology adoption also affects the rest of the design and construction ecosystem. When firms lag in the use of modern, efficient technology resources and tools, information flow suffers; collaboration becomes a struggle; and clients may choose to work with firms that are taking the lead in modernization through technology.

Most, if not all, large firms in the United States have the resources dedicated to ongoing development of technological capability. They also employ a large percentage of architects, so the perception may be that the "have nots" will continue to lag and fail to gain market share over bigger competitors. Technology, though, is the great leveler in terms of making small and mid-sized businesses in any industry take on the giants in their space. Finding a path to adoption of leading technologies that serve all aspects of the firm's business is something all architects should be seriously exploring.

It is this relationship that we believe holds the key to innovation in the built environment. As we work toward a more symbiotic relationship between these two vital communities in the construction ecosystem, AIA looks to these companies for leadership, insight, and support to help our members create a blueprint for a better world.

Fig. 1.

'In the future architects may work in a more consultative, networked manner.'This step is carried on the level of staff in one consultancy, and on the scale of many offices and even firms: Collaboration through networking. On the level of the single consultancy, it could happen among the workers, through the office environment.

Moving away from the office desk as the main place of productivity seems one of the new ideas in office environment design already applied in firms like Apple. It has been realized that "packing employees tightly into spaces will not necessarily result in greater productivity", according to Philip Tidd from the design and architecture firm Gensler.

As for networking happening in the same firm among branches, it is basically a 'strategy of trying to break the traditional work process into smaller 'chunks', for which [architects] could charge a separate fee for, rather than drawing out a long process and receiving only one fee. Some firms created a sister company carrying out pre-design services that often are neglected as architects' contributions.

These include consultation analysis, strategic thinking, and preparatory work prior to the design stage. Other consultancies set up satellite companies with certain specialties like industrial urbanism for example. Clients can still take huge benefits from this where they are having a plan for a definite time and budget.

Globalization and integrated working (BIM) are major urges for networking on an even larger scale than a firm to a global level. In one initiative, this concept allows keeping a small number of core employees, with technical work given to a network of trusted consultants, while they focus on one domain the building process. In another sense, this networking provides a one-stop-shop service through a network of consultants offering a full range of services.

Now we discuss a major term in the development of the future architectural practice: Financial literacy: 'All architects need to ensure their financial and economic skills keep pace with the increasingly sophisticated and complex financial environment of the globalized economy. Developing financial skills is a core value for practice if the firm were to deal with future economic perils. A simply design-led practice cannot reach out to the extent the client's needs anymore. Seeing beyond building a building now is a skill taken for granted by clients.

On an equally important side are the IT systems. Though these invaded the industry a long time ago, they are gaining ground with each new invention, technology, and new method explored.

At this point, we can understand why certain types of architecture firms/ offices can remain stable, grow, or falter in the coming years. Responding to the challenges of interdisciplinarity in architecture practice, networking, branching, financial and commercial literacy, IT development, integration of architecture education with practice, and developing a culture of practice within a firm are the major practices to adopt in order to keep up with the pace of practice in the future.

The firm types that the report suggests to maintain stability in the near future have already incorporated many of these factors in their modes of practice. The ones that will most probably grow are the ones that are efficiently integrating these practices in their systems. Where these practices cannot be applied, the firm is most likely vulnerable to be swept away by the growing architecture industry.

SUPER USERS

Design technology is changing both architectural practice and the role of the architect and related design professionals. With new technologies and work processes appearing every week, how can practitioners be expected to stay on top and thrive? In a word, Superusers.

Superuser is the term given to the user account that has overall control of the Android operating system and is usually achieved by rooting the device or the OS. Rooting means unlocking the OS restrictions to the user so that he/she may be able to make changes that are otherwise restricted by the OS. In other operating systems, this is known as administrator/admin (Windows) and root (Unix/Linux).

Superuser is also the name of an application used in Android that manages what other apps can do to a rooted device. It does this by giving that specific app superuser status as well.

Important Concept: Principle of Least Privilege

The principle of least privilege is an important concept in information security. It is the practice of limiting access rights for users to the bare minimum permissions they need to perform their work. Linux employs this principle by restricting user permission to read, write or execute only the files or resources they need to do their jobs. In other words, users are given the least amount of privilege necessary. So on Linux, if a user needs to be able to read a file, but should not have the ability to write to the file, they are given read permission, but not write permission. If a certain user needs to be able to reset a user password, but that user should not be allowed to add a new user, they are given the proper permission to do only those tasks that are necessary to complete their job.

Why are Administrative Privileges Useful?

Requiring users to have administrative privileges before important system changes are made is useful because it helps to prevent your system from being broken, intentionally or unintentionally.

If you had administrative privileges all of the time, you might accidentally change an important file, or run an application which changes something important by mistake.

Only getting administrative privileges temporarily, when you need them, reduces the risk of these mistakes happening.

Only certain trusted users should be allowed to have administrative privileges. This prevents other users from messing with the computer and doing things like uninstalling applications that you need, installing applications that you don't want, or changing important files. This is useful from a security standpoint.

Superuser Accounts in Windows, Linux, & Unix/Unix-like Systems

In Windows systems, the Administrator account holds superuser privileges. Each Windows computer has at least one administrator account. The Administrator account allows the user to install software, and change local configurations and settings, and more. Standard users have substantially curtailed privileges, while guest user accounts are generally limited even further, to just basic application access and internet browsing. In Linux and Unix-like systems, the superuser account, called 'root', is virtually omnipotent, with unrestricted access to all commands, files, directories, and resources. Root can also grant and remove any permissions for other users. Mac OS X, is Unix-like, but unlike Unix and Linux, is rarely deployed as a server.

As a default, Mac users run with root access, though, as a best security practice, a non-privileged account should be created and used for routine computing to reduce the potential and scope of privileged threats.

Security Implications of Superuser Accounts

If misused, either in error (i.e. inadvertently deleting an important file or mistyping a powerful command), or with malicious intent, superuser accounts can inflict catastrophic damage to a system/organization.

While most security technologies are developed to protect the perimeter, superusers are already on the inside. Superusers may be able to change firewall configurations, create backdoors, and override security settings, all the while erasing traces of their activity.

Inadequate policies and controls around superuser provisioning, segregation, and monitoring further heighten risks. Database administrators, network engineers, and application developers are frequently given full superuser access. Users often share superuser accounts between them, which muddles the audit trail. In the case of Windows PCs, users often log in with administrative account privileges—far broader than what is needed.

In one of the more notorious tales of a rogue insider, Edward Snowden, an IT contract worker for the NSA, abused his superuser privileges to access, copy, and leak over 1 million highly sensitive NSA files. In the wake of this scandal, the NSA targeted 90% of it system administrators for elimination, to better establish a least-privilege security model.

Hackers covet superuser accounts knowing that, once they assume these accounts, he/she essentially becomes a highly privileged insider. Additionally, malware that infects a superuser account, can leverage the same privilege rights of that account to cause damage and steal data.

How to Secure & Monitor Superuser Accounts

Organizations looking to rein in and protect superuser accounts will implement some or all of the following best practices:

- **Enforce least privilege access:** Limit superuser membership to the minimum people. This can mean temporarily elevating privileges temporarily when needed, but without granting full superuser rights to the account. In Unix and Linux systems, the sudo command allows a normal user to temporarily elevate privileges to root-level, but without having direct access to the root account and password.
- **Segment systems and networks:** By partitioning users and processes based on different levels of trust, needs, and privilege sets, you can constrain where and how a superuser can act.
- **Enforce separation of privileges:** This will entail separating superuser functions from standard account requirements, separating auditing/logging

capabilities within the administrative accounts, and separating system functions (read, edit, write, execute, etc.).

- **Enforce superuser password rotation and security:** Passwords should meet rigorous security standards. Passwords should be regularly rotated, including after each use for the most powerful accounts.
- **Monitor and audit all superuser sessions:** Record, log, audit, and control all superuser session activity to provide accountability and meet with compliance demands.

Technologies for Managing/Securing Superusers

Privilege Access Management (PAM), also called Privileged Identity Management (PIM) or just Privilege Management, involves the creation and deployment of solutions and strategies to manage superuser and other types of privileged accounts across an environment. PAM solutions:

- Discover all superuser and privileged accounts
- Enforce least privilege (remove admin rights)
- Superuser privilege management (SUPM) – granular control over privilege elevation
- Enforce password security best practices for superuser accounts
- Audit all superuser session activity

AUTODESK

Architectural design is a discipline that blends technical and creative design to create buildings or structures that are not only safe and durable, but attractive and useful. Architects typically create architectural designs by understanding the space, what it is to be used for, and creating a functional structure for the space. Architectural design encompasses many phases of the design process from schematic design and design development to construction of the structure. Autodesk provides the technology to help with all aspects of the design and collaboration process.

The Architecture toolset gives you all the tools you need to complete your projects faster and scale your project pipeline. Boost architectural design and drafting productivity by up to 61%* with time-saving features and task automation:

- **Access our library** of 8,500+ architectural components, including multi-level blocks
- **Automatically generate** floor plans, elevations, sections and ceiling grids
- **Quickly place** walls, doors and windows with real-world construction

Architecture toolset features

Discover specialised tools for architects

8,500+ architectural components

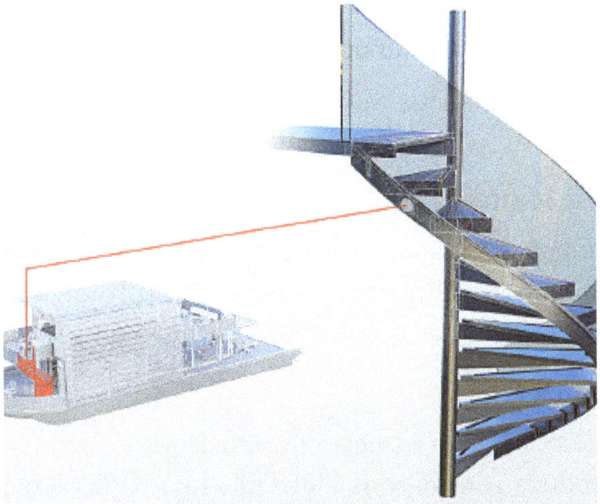

Fig. 2. Stairs model designed with the Architecture toolset

Make use of over 8,500 intelligent architectural components, including multi-level blocks, to support various layer standards. Should one of the pre-existing layer standards not meet the needs of your project, you can create your own by customising an existing one.

Automatic object generation

Save time and increase productivity by automatically generating commonly used architectural objects such as floor plans, elevations, sections and ceiling grids.

Walls, doors and windows

Use elements with real-world behaviour and construction, allowing for quicker placement in the documents and drawings that you create.

Drawing version management

Check out and check in files to maintain versioning, prevent unauthorised modifications and ensure drawing integrity. Easily revert to an earlier version of your drawing with comments history and view the drawing name appended with check-in time.

Support for layer standards

The toolset creates multiple layers according to the current standard, using predefined layer standards and matching layer key styles. This lets you automatically generate layers as needed when you add objects to a drawing.

Display System

With the Display System, you only have to draw an architectural object once. The appearance of that object will change automatically to meet the display requirements of different types of drawings, view directions and levels of detail.

Designing with space and zone objects

Enhance your design options. Organise reports with spaces and use zones to structure spaces into various groups, according to different schemes.

Detail Component Manager

Use the Detail Component Manager dialogue box to seamlessly navigate between different detail component databases. A hierarchical tree view and a filter feature make it easy to locate individual components within a database.

Architectural renovation

Display existing, demolished and new constructions in a single drawing. This lets you design and produce renovations more quickly, while avoiding errors typically caused by editing multiple drawings.

Types of architectural design software

2D architectural design software

Fig. 3. Create, edit and annotate 2D architectural drawings (floor plans, landscaping layouts, etc.) more quickly and with greater precision.

3D architectural design software

Fig. 4. Visualise your architectural design in 3D and create realistic models with materials, textures and automated tools.

Rendering software

Fig. 5. Generate immersive photorealistic renderings to experience how architectural designs will perform in context for project reviews.

BIM software

Fig. 6. Use an intelligent 3D model-based design process to more efficiently plan, design, construct and manage buildings.

DEVELOPER AI

AI seems to be the buzzword on everybodys lips these days. There is little doubt that AI and machine learning has potential to help us develop new services that would be impossible or extremely hard to deliver without this technology. Apple's Siri and Amazon's Alexa are examples of that. If the worst prophecies become reality, we could be implementing the doom of humanity, the Skynet of real life. In the other end of the spectrum, it could turn out to be just a hype, and it will die of natural causes and be replaced by other hypes. AI seems to be the buzzword on everybodys lips these days. There is little doubt that AI and machine learning has potential to help us develop new services that would be impossible or extremely hard to deliver without this technology. Apple's Siri and Amazon's Alexa are examples of that. If the worst prophecies become reality, we could be implementing the doom of humanity, the Skynet of real life. In the other end of the spectrum, it could turn out to be just a hype, and it will die of natural causes and be replaced by other hypes. Personally we think the answer falls somewhere in between. We believe AI and machine learning has great potential, but we're far from a Skynet scenario, at least yet.

Artificial Intelligence Engineers (AI Engineers) or AI Developers work with Artificial Intelligence technology to solve problems. They go over both classic and machine learning software models. The demand for these IT specialists is considerable, thanks to the development of Artificial Intelligence and Machine Learning in several areas of the IT business.

Artificial Intelligence (AI) developers create the software and apps that a company might utilize. They create systems that adapt to the needs of the company based on the information gathered and assessed.

An AI developer's job description is self-explanatory: they create artificial intelligence software and applications that a company might utilize. They create systems that adapt to the needs of the company based on the information gathered and assessed. One example is AI that chooses which movies and TV series to recommend to you from your favorite streaming service or which things to recommend based on previous purchases.

Responsibilities

The definition of an AI developer is pretty self-explanatory: they develop the artificial intelligence software and applications that a particular business might use. They program systems that will change to suit the business's needs based on the data collected and analyzed. One example of this is the AI that decides what movies and TV shows to recommend to you from your favorite streaming site or recommended products based on past purchases.

Because of this, AI developers often work with data engineers, machine learning engineers, and data scientists. They also maintain those systems to make sure that everything is running smoothly. Some of the duties that an AI developer might have include:

- Answer various business challenges using AI software
- Designing, developing, implementing, and monitoring AI systems
- Explain to project managers and stakeholders the potential and limitations of AI systems
- Develop data ingest and data transformation architecture
- Be on the lookout for new AI technologies to implement within the business
- Train teams when it comes to the implementation of AI systems

AI Developer vs. Machine Learning Engineer

AI Developers and Machine Learning Engineers are similar careers, and they do work with each other in order to make the best systems to use for the business. However, there is a distinction between the two. For the most part, that distinction comes down to the difference between AI and machine learning. While there is quite a bit of overlap, **Machine Learning is only one part of AI**, rather than the whole of it.

Machine Learning

Machine learning is the use of software programs and applications that are able to learn from past applications how to **provide a more improved and optimized experience.** It utilizes statistics and operations research in order to help the software to adapt over time as it's used. While this is convenient and helpful, it is not entirely AI.

AI

AI pulls from both Machine Learning and Deep Learning, which **implements larger neural networks** to learn more complex programs and broadens the knowledge of the software program or application. The point of AI is not just to adapt, but to be "smart" as it does so. Think of your smartphone, or home appliances such as a smart fridge or smart trash can. Your GPS is also a good example of AI. A machine learning engineer is responsible for developing the machine learning processes that the business uses, especially when it comes to collecting data or in response to data. AI developers instead work with AI, bringing their businesses into the future.

Top Tools Used by An AI Developer

An AI developer — or any software professional — is only as good as their tools. While one of the duties of an AI developer is to **create AI systems from scratch**, they use tools and languages that just about every programmer uses in order to create those systems and to make them accessible to those who use them. Some of the tools that an AI developer might use include:

- Programming languages like Java, Scala, and Python
- Deep learning platforms such as H20.AI
- Deep learning libraries
- Google assistants to implement within AI systems
- Cloud platforms like Azure or Google Cloud AI
- IBM Watson AI solutions
- APIs like OpenGL or PhysX
- Profiling tools like Perl or Perforce
- Analytic tools like TensorFlow, Torch, and PyTorch

Skills Neededfor AI Developers

So you have the education and the experience. The next question is whether you have the right personality. The skills needed to be an AI developer can be easily learned if you have the time to dedicate to it, as well as the kind of personality that's right for the job. Some of the skills you'll need to be an AI developer include:

Mathematics and Algorithms

AI development, like most programming, is a matter of mathematics. AI developers should be experts at problem solving who love to work through a logic challenge. They should also be familiar with algorithms – how they work, how they're made, and how they can be improved. If you have the kind of mind that's constantly solving math equations, this is a great job for you.

Probability and Statistics

Probability and statistics are the main thing that makes AI work. It's all about searching for patterns and trends so that you can predict what's needed and adapt accordingly. AI developers should be familiar with a variety of statistical methods and probability theories in order to make their AI productions succeed.

Fluency in Programming Languages

Do you sometimes feel that you speak in Java or Python? AI developers are programmers, so it's important to be an expert in common programming languages. That includes Python and R, as well as Java, C++, and Scala. These programming languages will help you to develop more complex and more optimized algorithms.

Multi-Tasking and Proficiency With Multiple Computing Tools

AI developers work with data scientists and data analysts, who collect their data from a wide variety of sources. There's simply too much data in the world to leave it to just one or two sources. Thus AI developers should be handy when it comes to multiple computing tools and data collection methods, as well as skilled at multitasking and having multiple things on their plate.

Flexibility and Quick Learning

As stated above, you'll have to use multiple different sources when it comes to data collection and analysis, as well as multiple tools for the AI development itself. AI developers should be able to be flexible, shifting from project to project. They should also be quick learners who are able to learn a new system when one is introduced.

Advantages of an AI Developer

Artificial intelligence applications have great benefits and have the potential to disrupt any industry. Here's the list:

- **Human Error Reduction**: The term "human error" was used to describe the fact that humans make mistakes from time to time. Computers do not make these errors if they are programmed correctly. Artificial intelligence makes choices based on the previously obtained data and an algorithm set. Hence, errors are decreased, and the prospect of obtaining better precision and accuracy is increased.
- **Takes risks instead of humans**: This is one of artificial intelligence's most significant advantages. By developing an AI Robot that can do challenging tasks, we can transcend many of humanity's risky limitations. It can be utilized effectively in every type of natural or man-made disaster, whether it is going to Mars, defusing a bomb, exploring the deepest regions of the oceans, mining for coal and oil.
- **Available 24 7**: Humans are created in such a way that they need to take time off to replenish themselves and prepare for a new day at work, and they even have weekly off days to keep their professional and home lives separate. But, unlike humans, we can use AI to make machines work 24 hours a day, seven days a week with no breaks, and they don't get bored.
- **Helping with Repetitive Tasks**: We will be doing a lot of repetitive tasks in our day-to-day work, such as writing thank-you emails, double-checking documents for flaws, and so on. We can use artificial intelligence to efficiently automate these monotonous operations and even remove "boring" duties from humans' schedules, allowing them to be more creative.

- **Digital Assistance:** Some of the most advanced companies use digital assistants to communicate with their customers, reducing the need for human resources. Many websites also use digital assistants to supply things that users seek. We can discuss what we're searching for with them. Some chatbots are created in such a way that it's difficult to tell whether we're conversing with a machine or a human.
- **Faster Decisions:** By combining AI with other technologies, we can make computers make decisions and carry out activities faster than humans. While a human will consider numerous aspects, both emotionally and practically, before deciding, an AI-powered machine will focus on what it has been designed to do and will produce results more quickly.
- **Daily Applications:** Apps like Apple's Siri, Microsoft's Cortana, and Google's OK Google are regularly used in our daily lives, whether it's for finding a place, taking a selfie, making a phone call, or responding to an email.
- **New Discoveries:** AI is at the heart of a slew of new inventions in practically every field that will aid humans in solving the most complex issues.

SPACEMAKER AI

It is a Norwegian startup that develops AI tools to help real estate developers and architects. So that they may make better design selections while constructing cities. Furthermore, it promises to empower property development professionals such as real estate developers, urban planners, and architects. As a result, every multi-building residential complex may be evaluated and developed with the best environmental design.

The beginnings of Spacemaker AI

Havard Haukeland and Carl Christensen created Spacemaker AI in late 2016. Havard Haukeland has a background in architecture and technology, having worked as an architect and in urban design. Carl Christensen earned a bachelor's degree in computer engineering and a master's degree in business administration and economics.

The digital solution was developed as part of a four-year scientific research project funded by Aspelin Ramm, AF Eiendom, Stor-Oslo Eiendom, and SINTEF, among others. Spacemaker AI then earned up to 15 million Norwegian kroners ($1.8 million) in funding from The Research Council of Norway, Innovation Norway, and Simula Research Laboratory to further develop their digital solution.

They have evolved from a small firm with 20 workers in one year to a small company with 20 employees in October 2017. They were considering the use of artificial intelligence in city planning and construction sites at the time. A group of investors joined together in September 2017 to invest 22 million Norwegian kroners ($2.65 million) in the startup. In addition, a portion of the Norwegian leadership group in CBRE opted to invest with CBRE, which is one of the leading commercial property consultants registered in New York.

How Spacemaker is Helping to Build Sustainable Urban Cities?

With expanding urban populations, we need cities that are both sustainable and livable. However, using traditional construction procedures, the same structure cannot be built. The available land should be utilised properly to produce a pleasant residency while developing new urban districts. In addition, many additional issues must be considered while developing sustainable metropolitan communities. For example, space optimization, sunlight exposure, noise, wind, and a variety of other factors.

To do this, Spacemaker created AI-based software that allows for a sense-check of their building blueprints. In addition, it demonstrates design optimization taking into account the numerous elements mentioned above.

This programme does so by crunching multiple data sets. Physical facts, legislation, environmental conditions, and other preferences are all included. Following that, it presents at most twenty to thirty possibilities, taking into account all aspects.

XKOOL TECHNOLOGY

XKool Technology is a tech-based startup founded in Shenzhen in 2016, focuses on applying artificial intelligence solution to urban planning and architectural design. It is committed to assisting urban planning, architectural design and development decisions intelligent, and empowering AI to promote the development of the entire architectural industry.

As the leading company to apply artificial intelligence to urban planning and architectural design, XKool has successfully implemented "artificial intelligence design cloud platform" and "artificial intelligence design cloud service" using cutting-edge technologies such as deep learning, machine learning, and big data.

Through simple operation and intelligent services in the cloud, XKool would assist design institutes, real estate developers, planning departments to design and decision-making faster and more accurately.

Using AI technologies to push design innovation, we have indeed created more market and public participation in urban transformation. XKool can efficiently and reliably provide big data analytics results and decision-making support for decision-makers in the early stage of a project. It prevents investors and developers from blindly entering the market but with reasonable judgments in the case of rational cognition. The innovation of the XKool AI Design Cloud Platform is to let the computer address highly repetitive calculation, data analysis and application in the design process and allow the architect to focus more on the work that requires human innovation.

This mode internalizes some of the architect's expertise into the computer's computational intelligence, which to some extent reduces the threshold of architectural design. Consequently, more people could have the opportunity to work on architectural designs with the help of AI products.

Therefore, we invite a larger group of people to participate in urban transformation via big data. In addition, our urban dynamic planning system is an interactive installation which uses a human-machine interactive interface that allows the public to express their vision of a future city visually. It also has the potential to assist city council in urban development decision-making.

XKool's AI Design Cloud Platform is implemented through Software-as-a-Service (SaaS) technology. We put our product on the cloud, and the users access the software and hardware service on the cloud through IDs they purchase. The users, the XKool product and our team form a network.

Some users authorize us to use the data produced during their use of the XKool product. After professional evaluation and cleaning, the data is used to train the models of the XKool product to enhance its quality and intelligence.

By using the feedback data, the tool that we hope to create becomes smarter and closer to our goal. This collective action through controlled data addressing does not damage the establishment of a professional and intelligent tool but contributes to the realization of our business goal.

In contemporary architectural practice, architectural projects are already new and shared belongings even without the use of AI. One architectural project is the result of the collective decision-making and hard work of the architects, engineers, construction workers, project owners, etc.

We tend to no longer think that one primary architect has authorship to a building because different players influence the design decisions.

The involvement of AI has strengthened this trend.

When it comes to a change in the meaning of design in the era of AI, in fact, design is regarded by many people as a proof of human creativity, and it is considered as the creation of unprecedented things in the world. However, we believe that design behaviour is only useful to find the op-timal solution among all possibilities that already exist. AI only helps us complete the search for an optimal solution more efficiently.

We speculate that, even after AI is widely used in the design process, the physically built environment in the city might not seem to differ much from that in the era without AI. However, even if the urban physically built environment is not altered dramatically, some soft and invisible control systems would indeed be added, which will significantly improve the intelligence level of the city.

AI is not a unique technology used in the process of transforming the built environment of a city. It will be used with other technologies, such as the Internet of Things and robotics, to design, build, and manage cities more efficiently and intelligently.

AI can reveal a user's behavioural patterns and preferences using various behaviour data which it produces in a network with machine learning technology. Moreover, based on the similarity of these patterns and preferences, it can predict and connect different groups of people dispersed in the network.

In the future, the AI system may even be able to combine the other network behaviours of a user, to predict that the user at some probability is an architect with the computing result, and finally to recommend him/her to the online or offline architect community.

RE-DESIGNING DESIGN

Much of human progress over the past century has been magnificent. Technology that brings information to the remotest corners of the world and medicine that heals diseases once thought incurable are all signs of what humans can accomplish. Game-changing innovations are what we need more of right now, too. With just 10 years to reduce our global carbon dioxide output by 45 percent (or else), we need unprecedented and far-reaching solutions across industries, policy, and all sectors of society. Luckily, the design community is ahead of the curve.

Digital design tools also have followed an exponential evolution path. Looking backward, softwares used by the designers within the digital fields were the same as those in traditional graphic design. Recently, they have become more specific, with deeper integration into digital workflows and now proposing new, object-oriented capabilities that require an unusual level of rationality from their users. Tools are the best friends and enemies of designers because they influence their work deeply, especially when their promise is to make the work easier and faster.

Digital media creates interesting retroactive loops that influence the perception and overall vision of the people who define it. Marshall McLuhan formulates this effect succinctly: "We shape our tools and thereafter our tools shape us." John Maeda, one of the most visible and influential prophets of the future of work in the AI area draws a prospective design history in three steps: First, "classical design" led by charismatic individuals who define the right way to make things; second, "design thinking," or that ambition to connect organisations with the reality perceived by their users, utilizing empathy and the design of experiences; and finally third, "computational design," where algorithms and computational power-driven by Moore's law are rising the design to an unprecedented level of personalization and scalability. This kind of discourse might be analyzed and discussed sometimes, but never ignored, because one cannot deny they convey a real power of auto-realization.

Academic researches in the field of computer science should send weak signals to designers but they are difficult for most of us to get, even when they are made available to the public. A few exceptional popularizers such as Yann LeCun have the ability to describes in an accessible language how AI works and what it could be used for. However, potential connexions between IA and design practices often stated, mostly in experts and academic publications seem to be overlooked most of the time by design professionals.

Advanced computational approaches have been explored in engineering, architecture, or industrial design fields. They are known under labels such as Generative design (design approach that makes use of algorithms to generate designs), Algorithmic design (generative design approach characterized by an identifiable correlation between the algorithm and its outcome), and Parametric design (an approach based on the use of parameters to describe sets of designs).]

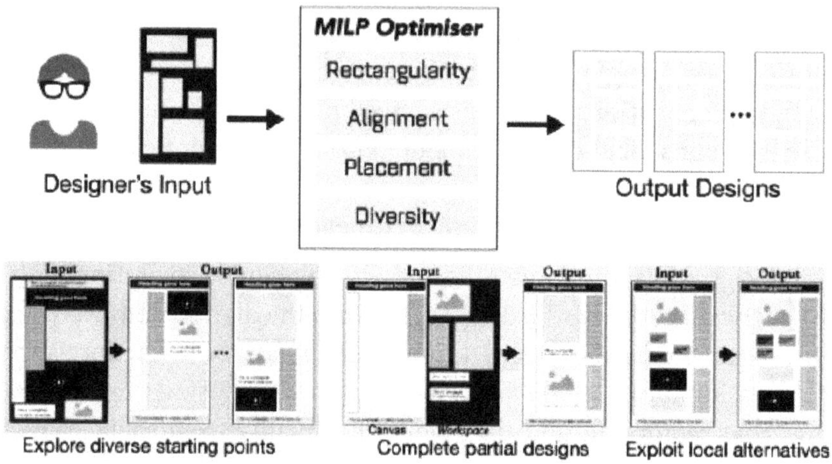

Fig. 7. Interactive Layout Design with Integer Programming

However, machine learning that is at the core of the AI concept will bring these design practices to a much higher level.

A focus on user experience design

Researcher discovered recently a research project recently called GRID, led by a team of researchers from the User Interface Research Group of the Aalto University in Finland. The purpose of this project, funded by the European Research Council under the European Union's Horizon 2020 research and innovation program, is to propose a system that generates coherent layout grid variants that optimise the page space. In addition, they presented the concept of a tool with an interface allowing the user (a designer) to select elements and drag them into a work area. The interface presents several options that can be selected and saved.

Other experiments go beyond this. For example, a team from the Technological Peking University in partnership with Adobe Research, tested a system based on neural networks in order to harmoniously arrange randomly positioned geometric shapes on a surface. This was the first project of its kind using antagonistic neural networks. In practice, a first network decomposes a simple image into geometric forms and then submits proposals for arrangement to a second network, which will try to discriminate the most relevant proposals. The two networks thus adjust their parameters iteratively. One trains itself to generate increasingly correct layouts, the other trains to recognize them.

Google Research described a prediction system for graphical user interfaces. It states explicitly the similarity between the self-completion models of search engines or some advanced text editors. This system would be able to predict user interface elements likely to be used during the design process of an HMI and make suggestions, positioning them appropriately and respecting the hierarchy and structure. By partially automating the design, the researchers aim to make the work of designers and developers simpler. Certainly, this would also have the side effect of strongly standardizing the work. This model could also be used to measure the quality of the user experience. According to the authors of the article, however, the problems posed by autocompletion for graphical interfaces are more complex than for text, because they are non-linear and two-dimensional.

Working with an AI

These examples emphasize the importance for designers to define their practice in regard to AI, as the chances that most of them will be confronted by it in the near future are increasing. In that light, see four directions that will shape our relations with this new tool.

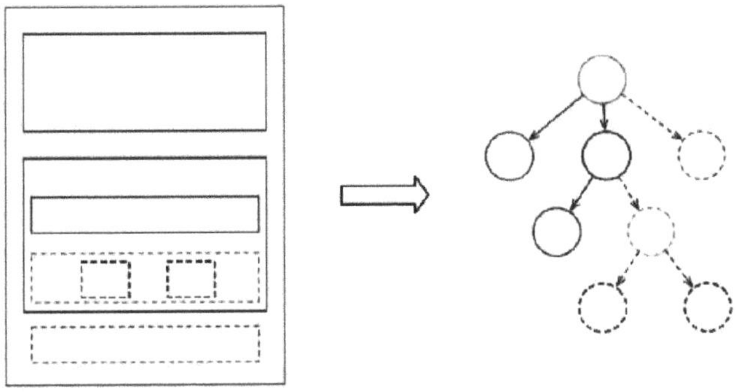

Fig. 8. Generating graphic layouts with wireframe discriminators

Assistant

AI executes repetitive or boring tasks requiring none or very little expertise and lets the designer focus on higher-value activities

Master

AI reviews designer deliverables evaluates their efficiency based on the assumptions and bias of the engineers who designed it and/or a basic set of paradigms.

Coach

AI helps the designer to perform better by challenging him positively. Proposing alternate concepts, and helping to identify the most promising ideas.

Competitor

AI performs better than designers in most of their tasks. Either they are faster in performing design activities, or more accurate because they can deliver tailor-made products at the micro-scale of individuals.

Some are obviously more desirable than others and it seems urgent to define values, and ethics designers will need to acquire and develop in order to master their near future professional environment.

Future designers will have, in particular, to demonstrate an understanding of the bias technology can introduce, and they must demonstrate an ability to use it in a way to benefit humanity. Thus, to reply to the McLuhan quote, they will have to gain the ability to shape their own tools. Aside from this ambition, I believe that design practitioners, with their creativity, empathy, and resilience have a central role to play in the challenges our societies are facing

Closing thoughts

Designers must not merely undergo the revolution of their practice. They must embrace it. The risk for design practitioners would be to find themselves like the British workers of early industrial times, the luddites, who saw no alternative than destroying the machines that were taking work away from them. Or, even worse, maybe, they could become progressively disconnected from how things are made, consequently delegating the design of experiences to others with lower attention to humans.

CHAPTER 8
AI AND THE CITY OF THE FUTURE

Information architecture (IA) is a science of organizing and structuring content of the websites, web and mobile applications, and social media software. An American architect and graphic designer, Richard Saul Wurman, is considered to be a founder of the IA field. Today, there are many specialists working on IA development who have established the Information Architecture Institute. According to the IAI experts, information architecture is the practice of deciding how to arrange the parts of something to be understandable.

Information architecture aims at organizing content so that users would easily adjust to the functionality of the product and could find everything they need without big effort. The content structure depends on various factors. First of all, IA experts consider the specifics of the target audience needs because IA puts user satisfaction as a priority.

Also, the structure depends on the type of the product and the offers companies have. For example, if we compare a retail website and a blog, we'll see two absolutely different structures both efficient for accomplishing certain objectives. Information architecture has become the fundamental study in many spheres including design and software development.

The concept of "smart cities" is no longer confined to the realms of futuristic science fiction—they're quickly becoming part of our everyday reality. Technologies like self-driving buses that communicate with traffic lights and AI-monitored CCTV cameras are being implemented in cities from Singapore to Las Vegas, and the technology behind these smart-city initiatives promises innovative solutions for both municipalities and their citizens—offering safer and more efficient living for an ever-growing population.

The smart-city promise is often delivered without the fine print though: namely, that a single attack waged against just one component of a connected infrastructure could disable an entire smart city in a matter of minutes. The attack could come from a single line of code.

This looming threat is turning the promises of revolutionized living standards into a potential menace to public safety. More than 40 local governments across the U.S. were victimized by ransomware in the first eight months of 2019 alone, halting public services and systems for weeks. And as municipal networks expand to encompass thousands of connected devices, facilities, and even critical infrastructure, cities must ready themselves for the inevitable threats these technologies will incur.

Smart cities are continuing to rapidly harness new technologies to drive efficiencies and improve living standards, but this digital transformation has been far from ubiquitous.

Despite all the new tech, many local governments still rely on outdated, sometimes decades-old IT that is especially vulnerable to attack, in part because updating major public sector systems is an enormous undertaking that can require years of bureaucratic red tape.

A postmortem of the infamous Atlanta ransomware breach in 2018, for instance, found that its information technology was "woefully disorganized and outdated," and by her own admission, the mayor had not prioritized cybersecurity enough.

Meanwhile, the coming 5G rollout will unlock an explosion of IoT devices. This fifth generation of cellular networks will allow cities to integrate smart sensors with self-driving vehicles, maintenance robots, and a host of other innovative technology. Current security tools are programmed to only look for historical threats against conventional technology systems.

As a result, they are blind to novel attacks that target smart cities' bespoke IoT networks. In the context of 5G, future attacks will strike faster than ever before, and be able to break into just one connected device in order to spread an infection across an entire cityscape in seconds. No team of human security professionals can mount a response under that kind of time pressure. Of course, these critical challenges represent lucrative opportunities in the eyes of cybercriminals.

The Path to Future-proof

We don't have to look far to find a solution to defending cities powered by emerging technologies, though. In fact, artificial intelligence (AI) is the most effective and simplest way to protect cities at scale, with dozens of the largest U.S. utilities, transportation systems, counties, and municipalities already making use of "cyber AI immune systems"— which use algorithms to instantly fight back against cyberattacks, and stop emerging threats in their tracks.

Armed with AI that evolves with an organization, governments not only protect themselves against existing threats, but are also prepared to face whatever vulnerabilities new technologies bring.

Perhaps no city better understands the imperative of AI—both to build smart infrastructures and to defend them—than Las Vegas, whose leadership has placed a sizable bet on AI across the board. The city is already hanging sensors from traffic signals that include motion-detecting cameras, LiDAR scanners, infrared monitors, weather probes, and sound detectors. Their sensors even use machine-learning software to look for litter and other problems in street images, all while the first completely autonomous shuttle deployed on a public roadway zips along beneath them.

Las Vegas takes an ingenious approach to cybersecurity by operating under a surprising assumption: Motivated attackers will inevitably infiltrate their targets. Whereas conventional cyber defenses attempt to stop known threats by keeping them outside the network perimeter, there are simply too many potential access points to secure in an expansive smart city.

Fig. 1.

Fig. 2.

Fig. 3.

Fig. 4

Fig. 5

At the same time, sophisticated criminals and nation-state actors are always finding uncharted weaknesses in new IoT devices. Attempting to lock the bad guys out is simply a losing strategy.

The AI x Future Cities project uses Midjourney to imagine what sustainable architecture might look like in a perfect future.

For the green cities they inhabit, Manas Bhatia's AI-generated series envisions tall, futuristic skyscrapers covered in algae that also serve as vertical gardens and biophilic air purification towers; the city of the future that is a green energy utopia with modern structures and no pollution.

While using these text-to-image programs, one needs to be careful of the choice of words. For the desired output one may have to run several iterations, modifying their initial prompt (text which you give to the AI as input) as they go.

INFORMATION ARCHITECTURE BASICS

Information architecture (IA) is the practice of structuring and presenting the parts of something — whether that's a website, mobile app, blog post, book, or brick-and-mortar store — to users so that it's easy to understand.

For the user to be able to make sense of content, structure it with two major factors in mind: the user's context and the user's needs.

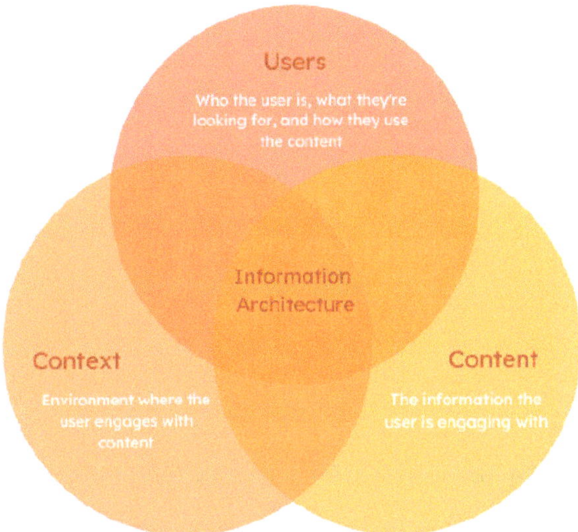

Fig. 6. Information Architecture Basics

Context is the environment in which the user engages with the content. To figure out the context, consider where, when, why, and how the user is seeking out and engaging with your content.

Structure content according to the user's needs, as well as their goals, behaviors, and expectations. To identify these, you must know who the user is (ie. who will be consuming the content), what value the content provides them, and how they actually use the content.

Why Information Architecture is Important

Information architecture is central to user experience online. Information architects add structure and navigation systems to simplify complex information for users.

Well-planned information architecture makes it easy and fun to engage. Whether you're playing a game on your mobile phone or scrolling a B2B website, it helps you find what you need to reach your goals.

To better understand why information architecture is useful, it's a good idea to start with how the human brain works.

UX, IA, and Cognitive Psychology

Cognitive psychology is the study of processes that happen inside the human brain. Cognitive science and psychology look at these human habits:

- Memory
- Attention
- Learning
- Decision-making
- Perception
- Problem-solving
- Creative thinking

Studying cognitive psychology can give you insights that can help improve user experience and design. Let's talk about some of the most common cognitive principles for design.

Mental models

People create mental models to understand and interact with the world. Each mental model is unique and changes constantly, as we collect more information.

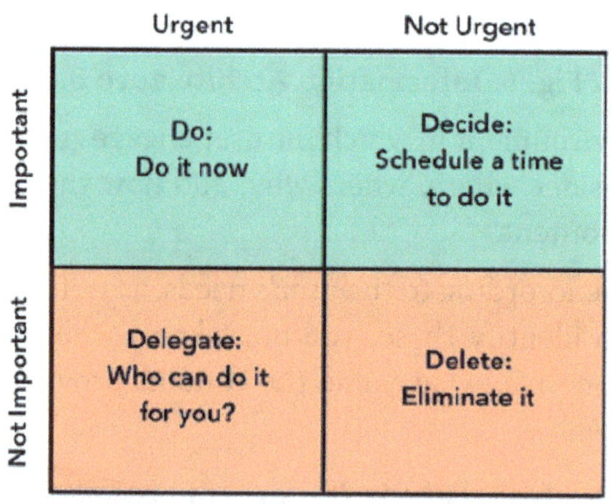

Fig. 7. The Eisenhower Decision Matrix

Mental models are the personal version of the world you have in your head. Applying models to different tasks and situations can help you better solve problems for your users. For example, the Eisenhower Decision Matrix is a mental model of time management. It simplifies the act of prioritizing work tasks.

Gestalt principles

Put roughly, gestalt is the German word for "shape." But like most words that cultures share, there is more to the translation. The term gestalt also talks about the way a shape or object reacts to the space around it and how a collection of things can be greater than the sum of its parts.

Gestalt principles help you design for users with concepts like proximity, similarity, closure, continuity, and figure-ground. You can learn more about this principle in this post about the law of proximity, or by watching the video below:

Cognitive load

Cognitive load is the approximate amount of information a working memory can hold at once. A human mind can only remember a limited amount at any given time. That makes it essential to create instructions that don't overload it.

It's also useful to remember that outside events and situations can also impact your users' cognitive load.

For example, during the 2020 pandemic, many people had a hard time focusing. This "brain fog" often extended to simple and routine tasks due to increased cognitive load.

Recognition Patterns

The human brain records information like events, people, and places. Recognition patterns make it easier to pull up that stored information.

They also create logical comparisons with new data as you take it in. Recalling patterns helps you guess what might happen next, assuming that it will align with what you've seen happen before.

So, when you visit a website you might expect parts of that site to match other websites you visit. Designers use these assumptions to improve the user experience.

How IA Can Impact Your Business

Great information architecture is valuable because it helps users find information quickly. This means that the IA on your site could impact:

- Lead generation
- Employee performance
- Hiring
- Marketing ROI
- Customer service

And information architecture isn't just helpful online. It keeps you from getting lost on the subway, helps you reach your new dentist's office on time, and keeps you from walking into the kitchen at your favorite restaurant.

But IA is a powerful force in digital products because if you get lost on a website, there's no one waiting there to help you find your way. If you get lost on an ecommerce site you're likely to leave and never come back. That means you don't get the product you wanted and that company doesn't get your business.

Information architecture lets you get involved in the decision-making process on your site. It helps you give users what they're looking for with every click. And it establishes a logical framework that builds trust.

So, what do information architects do that make IA so valuable?

Information Architecture Systems

Information architecture involves research, planning, and communication. And information architects' work often starts with a complex mass of information. When they finish, they have an informational structure that is clear and easy to navigate.

To build out this complex structure, an information architect typically performs a range of tasks including user research, card sorting, content inventory, site mapping, and labeling. IAs may repeat some of these steps later in the UX design process with different objectives.

The information architect's goal is always to understand the user. They want to understand their needs and goals and how they look for information. Then they create a structure to meet those needs, goals, and behaviors.

Moving through this process requires expert knowledge of four different systems: organization, labeling, search, and navigation. The goal is to design each system to meet the user's needs.

Organization systems

Organization systems, also called classification systems, categorize information. A system can be:

Hierarchical: Organized by importance, often visually

Sequential: Organized with a logical path, like a step-by-step checkout process

Matrical: Organized by the individual user, like a choose-your-own-adventure of internal links

There are also other ways to organize information. Alphabetical, chronological, topical, or user-segment-based organization systems are all popular online.

Organization systems divide and organize information. Information architects use research, inventories, and analysis to create categories.

Labeling systems

Labels create a relationship between the user and the content. Information architects create labels with headings and subheadings for each category.

Labels are words chosen to represent information that the reader can't see, but that they can guess.

So, labels offer context that helps your users understand where to find more information. Labels need to be easy to understand and feel familiar to your audience. This helps your website communicate efficiently.

For example, say a site visitor lands on a homepage and wants to know about a company's mission, values, history, and leadership team.

Instead of putting all that on the homepage, an information architect might use the label "About" in the top navigation. Because they see "About" labels on other websites, visitors can guess what it means on that website too.

Search systems

An IA's search system covers how users look up information. For digital product information architecture, a search system typically includes a search engine, filters, and other tools. It also includes how search results display. Results might show chronologically by date, alphabetically by title or author, or based on popularity.

Navigation systems

An IA's navigation system refers to how users can move through a site's hierarchy and access the information they're looking for.

A navigation system might include:

- Main navigation interface
- Sub-navigation menus
- Breadcrumbs
- Pagination

Navigation helps users find specific information. It's a collection of different pieces that form patterns that visitors recognize. For example, in hierarchical navigation, users navigate from top to bottom.

During this stage, information architects decide how users will navigate through a site and how pages on the site connect.

Now let's look at some important guidelines to follow when designing information architecture.

The role of information architecture in design

Nowadays, when the user-centered approach in design is a top trend, many designers learn the principles of information architecture science which they believe is a foundation of efficient design. IA forms a skeleton of any design project. Visual elements, functionality, interaction, and navigation are built according to the information architecture principles. The thing is that even compelling content elements and powerful UI design can fail without appropriate IA. Unorganized content makes navigation difficult and inexplicit, so the users can easily get lost and feel annoyed. If the users face first bad interaction, they may not give the second chance to your product.

Many companies don't see the importance of information architecture because they think it's impractical. It's hard to argue that IA takes some time to create it and requires specific skills to do it efficiently. However, powerful IA is a guarantee of the high-quality product since it reduces the possibility of the usability and navigation problems. This way, well-thought information architecture can save both time and money of the company which otherwise they would have spent on fixing and improvement.

IA and UX design

After reading everything written above, many people may have the question: "Isn't IA the same as UX design?". Technically, these terms relate to each other but they are far not the same. IA is a blueprint of the design structure which can be generated into wireframes and sitemaps of the project. UX designers use them as the basic materials so that they could plan navigation system.

UX design means much more than content structuring. In the first place, UX designers aim at making pleasant interaction model, so that users feel comfortable using the product. They encompass various aspects influencing users' behavior and actions such as emotion and psychology when the IA experts stay focused on the user's goals.

Let's get this straight: good information architecture is a foundation of efficient user experience, so the IA skill is essential for the designers. Effective IA makes the product easy to use but only united with design thinking the product has the powerful user experience.

IA system components

If you want to build strong information architecture for the product, you need to understand what it consists of. Pioneers of the IA field, Lou Rosenfeld and Peter Morville in their book "Information Architecture for the World Wide Web" have distinguished four main components: organization systems, labeling systems, navigation systems and searching systems.

Organization systems

These are the groups or the categories in which the information is divided. Such system helps users to predict where they can find certain information easily. There are three main organizational structures: Hierarchical, Sequential, and Matrix.

Hierarchical. In one of our previous articles, we've mentioned a well-known technique of content organization which is called visual hierarchy. It is initially based on Gestalt psychological theory and its main goal is to present content on the carrier, be it a book page or poster, web page or mobile screen, in such a way that users can understand the level of importance for each element. It activates the ability of the brain to distinguish objects on the basis of their physical differences, such as size, color, contrast, alignment etc.

Sequential. This structure creates some kind of a path for the users. They go step-by-step through content to accomplish the task they needed. This type is often used for the retail websites or apps, where people have to go from one task to another to make the purchase.

Matrix. This type is a bit more complicated for the users since they choose the way of navigation on their own. Users are given choices of content organization. For example, they can navigate through content which is ordered according to date, or some may prefer navigation along the topic.

Information Architecture Principles

The eight principles of IA were first proposed by information architect and UX designer Dan Brown issue of the Bulletin of the American Society for Information Science and Technology. His aim was to define a set of "guidelines based in universal truths that provide a sketch of what makes any information architecture good."

These principles have been widely adopted in the IA field and can help guide your designs. Below is a brief description of each principle with some examples.

The Principle of Objects

According to this principle, pieces of content, like objects, are unique and dynamic. They have their own attributes, behaviors, and life cycles.

Information architects should consider these attributes to best use that content. For example, you might want to archive product pages of retired items or simply re-categorize them.

Before you begin thinking about how to organize and structure content, you have to figure out the kinds of content you'll create. Will you be creating blog posts and product pages primarily? What about videos? Do you want to embed videos within blog posts or product pages?

Once you find the content types you'll have and how they relate to each other, then you can begin mapping how to best provide this information to visitors.

The Principle of Choices

The principle of choices is about limiting the number of choices for the user to only the most meaningful and relevant. These choices should relate to a particular task.

For example, if you have an email opt-in form popup, there should only be three choices for the user: opt-in, not opt-in, or close the popup. This reduces the level of cognitive effort required of the user, improving their experience.

The beauty company Alaffia provides a great example of such a popup.

The Principle of Disclosure

According to this principle, only disclose what is necessary for the user to understand what they'll find next and make a decision.

Take the newsletter opt-in form popup from above. Ideally, you'd include a short headline and a sentence of description to try to convince visitors to opt in, and that's it. If they do opt in, you might redirect them to a landing page or send a welcome email with more information, but only at that step.

Or, consider the Google search results page. Besides providing 10 results for your search query, it also includes a "People also ask" box. This box only shows the related search queries. To see the answer, you have to click the arrow to expand the box.

The Principle of Exemplars

According to the principle of exemplars, you should provide examples of content for things that aren't necessarily clear or intuitive upon reading.

Ecommerce sites are a great example of this. Take Jungalow's home page — it shows images for the categories "wallpaper" and "plants + planters." While the category names are clear, the visuals help readers understand the colorful, bohemian products they can expect if they click one of the links.

The Principle of Front Doors

The principle of front doors is the idea that your website or application has multiple access points. Not all visitors will land on your homepage first — they could arrive on a product page, blog post, or landing page, so you have to construct your website accordingly. By placing navigation aids and important information and elements on different pages, you'll ensure that visitors know where they are on your website. It also makes the steps they can take next clear, no matter where they first arrive.

Nude Barre perfectly exemplifies this principle. Besides a navigation header with drop-down menus and a search box, there's a big footer at the bottom of each page.

This footer contains important navigation links as well as a short description of the company. Users can easily understand what the company does, find the information they're looking for, or browse wherever they are on the site.

The Principle of Multiple Classification

According to the principle of multiple classification, users should have many ways to browse the content on your site. This is important because people prefer different methods for finding information.

Some, for example, may prefer to browse your site by category using sub-navigation menus. Others may prefer to search by keyword using a search bar. Others still may scroll down to your footer to find the navigation options, and so on.

Here's a look at the fitness website Ailey Extension. It provides:

- A navigation bar with sub-navigation menus
- A search bar
- Breadcrumbs
- A footer with navigation links

Fig. 8. The fitness website - Ailey Extension

The Principle of Focused Navigation

The principle of focused navigation means that navigation menus and aids should be consistent across your site and only contain relevant content.

If, for example, you use breadcrumbs on your blog, then you should use breadcrumbs everywhere on your site. Or, say you have a primary navigation menu with Products and Services links and each has its own submenu. Then you should only list products under the Products link and services under the Services link. Otherwise, you'll confuse visitors.

Check out HubSpot's homepage (Fig.9). You can see a well-organized sub-navigation menu that clearly outlines which links belong to Education, Services, and so on.

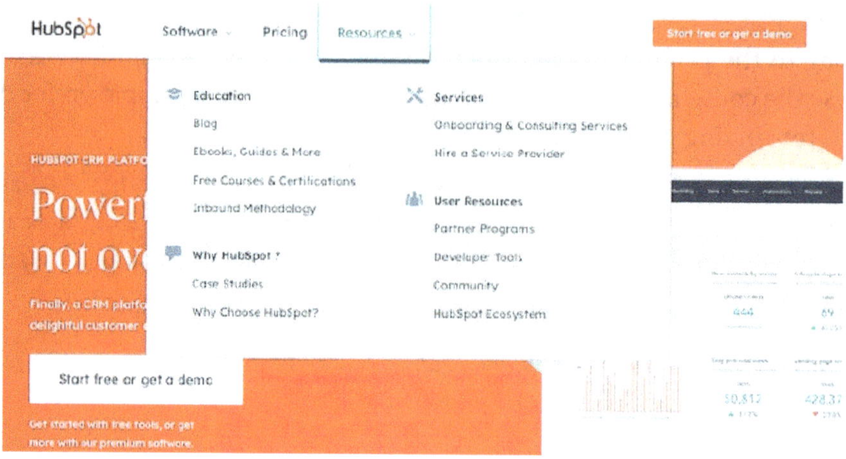

Fig. 9. HubSpot's homepage

The Principle of Growth

The principle of growth says you should construct your IA so it can accommodate your site as it scales.

This means you should be able to add new content within a section as well as add new sections as a whole. Here's a helpful illustration (Fig. 10):

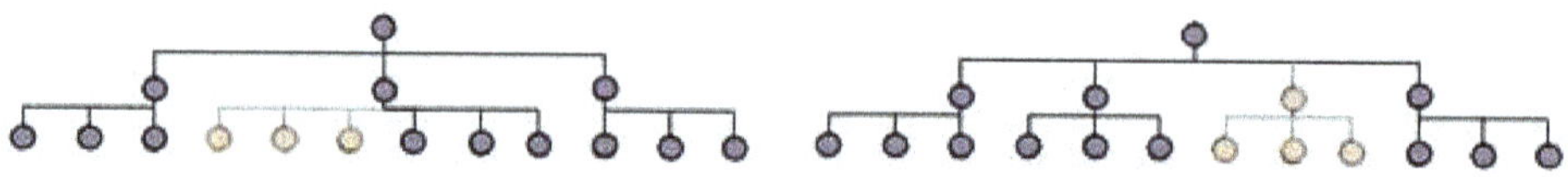

Fig. 10. The Principle of Growth

Say you run an ecommerce store. You might have a category for women's apparel that only contains shirts and pants right now. But, over time you can add more sub-categories like dresses or shoes. Or, you might create a whole new category for accessories where you can list scarves, hats, jewelry, and more.

Remember these principles are to guide your design process — not dictate it. For a more in-depth look at IA principles, check out this excellent video from CareerFoundry that further explains context, structuring content, and cognitive load.

Information Architecture Diagram Examples

Since a website's content structure depends on the specific needs of the user, no structure will look exactly the same. The IA of an ecommerce store can look completely different from a blog and still meet users' needs.

Most websites and apps, no matter their niche, share one similarity: They have three or four levels of hierarchy at most. That way, the content users want will still be accessible in a few clicks, but the website navigation won't be too broad.

You can see this in the IA diagrams — visual sitemaps that outline websites in a skeletal form — below.

Duke Library

As part of its 2013 website redesign, Duke created and published an IA blueprint (Fig. 11).

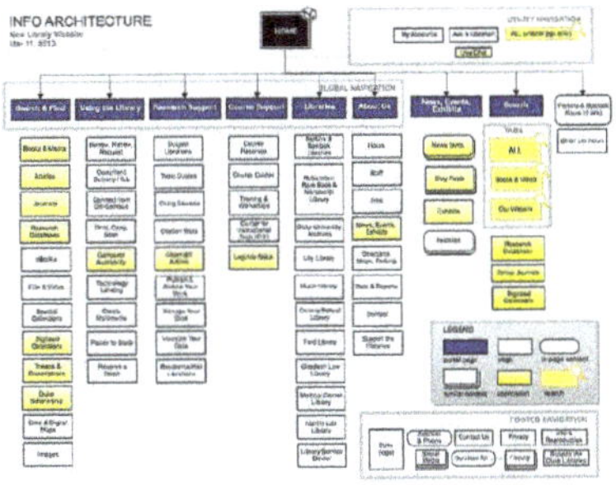

Fig. 11 Duke Library - sub-categories

Its new IA would have six main categories:

- Search & Find
- Using the Library
- Research Support
- Course Support
- Libraries
- About Us

The most important pages fall under these categories. They make up the site's global navigation, and users can access the sub-categories in a drop-down (Fig. 11).

The other parts of the sitemap show what content would appear above the navbar in the header ("utility navigation"), the content area of the page ("news, events, exhibit" and the search box), and the footer.

Charity App

Below is the IA for a mobile app from UX designer Bogomolova Anfisa. Most apps from Pinterest to Goodreads have a similar structure.

According to this IA, a user first sees instructions to help them understand and use the app. Then they see a welcome page and can log in with Facebook credentials or email, or register an account if they haven't already.

From there, they're taken to the main page, which contains options to view their bookmarks, messages, profile, or create a new post.

"The Museum"

Below is the IA for the mobile app of a client that design agency Pixel Fridge worked with (Fig. 12). The six purple boxes represent the major sections of the museum's website — but user research and testing showed that not all six were considered equally important.

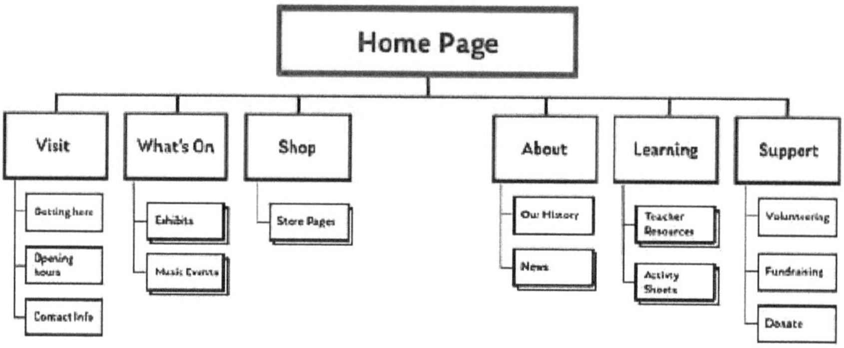

Fig. 12. IA for the mobile app

On the left are the categories and subcategories that they put in the navigation header. On the right are the categories and subcategories placed in the website footer.

Travel Booking Website

Like the Duke Library website and "The Museum," this travel booking website has six major categories. These categories are:

- Account management
- Book a trip
- About
- Destination
- Customer service
- Travel tips

If you think these examples look like something you'd see during the user experience (UX) design progress, you're right. While IA covers disciplines, from technical writing to library science, it's particularly important within the UX field.

Below (Fig. 13), we'll look at the relationship between IA and UX. While both concepts apply to virtual and physical spaces, we'll focus on the former to help you create websites, mobile apps, and other digital products that are easy to use.

What is the difference between Information Architecture and UX?

Information architecture and the user experience are closely connected, but they're not the same thing.

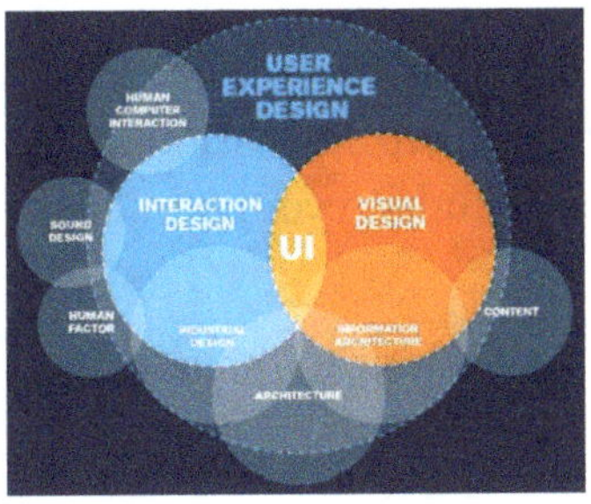

Fig. 13. User Experience Design

Creating a good information architecture is key to a good user experience — you can't have one without the other. Even the most stunning websites won't delight users if the underlying organization is poor.

But UX is a much broader topic than IA. It encompasses everything related to how a user perceives, interacts with, and feels about a product or service.

Building an IA is just one step of the UX design process. Other steps include content inventory, user research and testing, wireframing, and prototyping. Let's talk about how to create information architecture for your website.

How to Create Information Architecture for Your Website

IA is a crucial step in the creation of any digital product. Whether you're designing your first website or building an app for your business, you need a logical structure.

You may choose to work with a professional information architect or tackle IA on your own. Information architecture is often collaborative. Design, development, and engineering teams often work together on the process. But even a small solo project can improve with an understanding of the basics.

Each information architecture project is unique, so the order of the steps might vary. But these steps can help you do the research, analysis, and organization it takes to create a great structure for your next digital project.

Content Inventory and Analysis

Collect all the information in one place to do an inventory of your content. This usually means creating a catalog of all existing digital content. If you're building a new site, pull together your ideas and in-progress content. This gives you a sense of how the current website works, including:

- Important sections and pages

- Main topics and subtopics
- Quality of content
- The current organization of information

It also helps you decide what to keep, what to discard, and what new content you'll need. Start by putting all this information into a spreadsheet so it's easier to manage. The information you include in your spreadsheet will depend on the project you're working on.

In the case of a website, you'll want to include:

- Current URLs
- Page title
- Date of last update
- Page type (such as blog posts or product pages)
- Media (such as photos and video files)
- Author
- Focus keywords

This is a good time to update outdated content and remove content that no longer fits your vision for the site. It can also help you see what information you might be missing and repair broken links.

User Research

Next, you'll focus on learning user habits. This step might include user interviews and creating buyer personas.

If you're working on a solo project, it's important to remember that you are not your user. Because the process of categorizing is somewhat intuitive, it can be easy to default to your personal preferences. Instead, use this step to focus on your unique users and what they want from your website.

First, get a sense of your users' vocabulary. For example, online shopping carts often use the word "item" or "product." If you're in the United States, you probably use the word product more often.

Depending on your target audience, this word choice can have a big impact on the online experience for your shoppers.

Next, try some of the processes that information architects use.

Card sorting can help you understand user behaviors and habits for categorization.

Tree testing can help you see how your users respond to navigation and labels. This process will show you how easily users can find information on your site.

After each round of research, take careful notes on what works and what you need to approach in a different way for future testing.

Create Categories

One of the reasons that categorizing is difficult is that there are many ways to approach it. Another challenge is that many people categorize based on personal habits or existing systems. This is a problem if those approaches don't work well for the user.

For example, say you have a corporate website that's organized around acronyms and internal vocabulary. That website will be tough for new employees and clients to understand.

To create categories that work for the largest audience, start with your full list of content. Next, apply your user research to prioritize and group that content.

Start with categories that apply to the largest groups of similar content. For example, if your marketing website has 15 blogs on Facebook, Instagram, and TikTok, you could simplify that grouping to "Social Media."

Next, organize these groups of content into sections. If you have limited time and resources, you can make educated guesses. But it's best to do frequent user testing and to use that research to inform each section.

You can also use competitor research to inform your categorization efforts. Once you learn their approach to site structure you can decide what ideas you want to borrow and which you want to improve on.

As you review your site content you will probably find some content that doesn't quite fit. Sometimes this is content that fits into many categories and sometimes it doesn't align with any existing group.

User research can help with this. It can also help you decide whether an outlier deserves its own sub-category.

Labeling

Once you have your high-level categories, it's time to give those categories labels.

While it can be tempting to use the same terms for your labels that you used while you created your categories, this may not be the best strategy.

The way that you label each category has a major impact on how well users can use your website. So, what are the qualities of a good label?

THE INFORMATIONAL CITY

The informational city is the spatial expression of a new form of social organization that is made up of the interaction of new information technology, and social and cultural information. It describes major processes of social and economic restructuring in our society, and the role of technology both in shaping these.

It analyses the interaction of socioeconomic and spatial processes. An important social consequences of these spatial developments is the loss of control (and meaning) of place, as networks and spatial flows become dominant.

Two important features that characterize the processes of technological change should be kept in mind as I develop my analysis. First, although it seems obvious, it is important to remark that this technological revolution is based on information, just as the first industrial revolutions were based upon energy. Therefore, these processes of technological change directly affect information processing activities, the activities that are at the core of information and society.

Also, because information has something to do with manipulation of symbols and therefore with intelligence, and therefore with the human mind, and therefore with culture-the importance of this particular revolution is that for the first time productive forces and the cultural society have become directly tied and interdependent.

Although intelligence and information were important in all technological revolutions, this is the first time in history in which the way we think becomes directly connected to the way we produce and the way we develop. The source of our material development and the structure of our way of thinking are intimately related. This is a major change from former technological revolutions such as the industrial revolution which were based more on energy than on information, even if there was always an informational component.

Second, as with all major technological revolutions, the information revolution is process-oriented rather than product-oriented. The difference lies less in the development of new products (there are of course new products but there are always new products) but in the focus of the technology on the process itself. For instance, a chip is not something that one uses directly but is something one uses to introduce into all kinds of processes. It was the same with the energy revolution and with all major technological revolutions throughout history; that is why they are revolutions and not simply technical innovations.

Being process-oriented, revolutionary effects are pervasive. They are not confined to one particular domain of the human experience. They are linked to the way we produce, consume, manage, live and die. The revolutionary change of the technological paradigm is intimately linked to the change in the material basis of our social structure.

The Impact of the Information Revolution on Interpersonal Networks

The same thing has happened in terms of social relations. Some pundits have proposed the idea that telematic systems would push people into their homes: people would stay home, communicating from there, looking at videos, watching television through satellite receiver devices. These pundits warned that this could lead to the development of a massive suburban world through the diffusion of homes throughout large metropolitan areas, and that the density and intensity of urban life would disappear.

We can examine this proposition through the example of Minitel, the French system in which the telephone company gives terminals to homes. It was originally intended to substitute for the Yellow Pages, but it also allows people to send messages and to contact services.

Minitel is a big success; it is used in more than one million French homes for a variety of purposes, generally unintended. For instance, while no one seems to be very interested in being updated minute by minute about weather conditions in the Paris area, the most important use of Minitel is to exchange erotic messages. For one franc per three minutes, this is a national pastime.

It is also interesting to compare the effects of Minitel with some of the ideological statements from the left to the effect that these technocratic devices would kill social movements, since everybody would be playing "earth invader" games at home. Yet the reality is different. In 1986 when Minitel was first introduced, organizers of the first major student demonstrations in Paris forgot about pamphlets and used Minitel instead. They gave rendezvous points and passed on messages through Minitel, showing again, fortunately, the dominance of culture over technology. Although the technology was different, its use was framed, shaped, organized and dominated by culture.

In terms of relationship to spatial forms, consider what happened in Los Angeles, where private enterprise tried to introduce Minitel. Only 10,000 homes in the Los Angeles area were recruited for the experiment, and it was abandoned after about two years because it was not profitable enough. If one compares the success of this telematic technology with the urban form, we see that Los Angeles without Minitel is still an endless suburb while Paris with Minitel is still an intense urban place with lots of street life and cafes and encounters in public places. But the opposite had been predicted in the pseudo-scientific literature.

AMBIENT INTELLIGENCE

Ambient intelligence (AmI) is the element of a pervasive computing environment that enables it to interact with and respond appropriately to the humans in that environment.

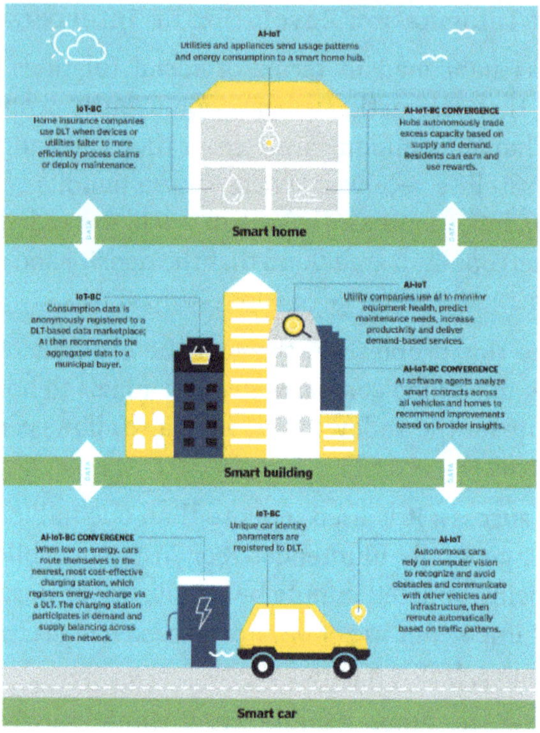

Fig. 14 depicts some of the application areas of AmI; it shows some smart and intelligent systems surrounding the user deploying the AI technologies. In this sense AmI is not a particular technology, but essentially an experience of the user with respect to the service provided by those systems. The cost functions for optimizing the AmI solutions are usually related to improving the subjective human experience, which is only indirectly measurable. Therefore, a successful application of AI and AmI requires us to select the best objective/ cost functions that meet the subjective human experience in AmI.

That capacity is enabled by unobtrusive embedded devices in the environment and natural user interfaces (NUI), providing some services autonomously in response to perceived needs and accepting user input through voice, gesture and other non-interruptive methods.

Popular examples of ambient intelligence include Google Assistant and Amazon Alexa – devices that automatically respond to a person's voice.]

The progress in Artificial Intelligence (AI) and Ambient Intelligence (AmI) follows the rules and laws similar to those in the area of ICT. Many of these principles, such as Moore's law, are exponential. Despite some signs indicating that progress is slowing down, rapid growth is likely to be maintained for AI and AmI in the foreseeable future.

In recent research, AI has already reached and surpassed the level of human intelligence in several tasks, such as games, the so-called superintelligence, whereas AmI is a seemingly less challenging task. On the other hand, through embodiment, embedding and interactions with humans, super-AmI might emerge even faster than superintelligence.

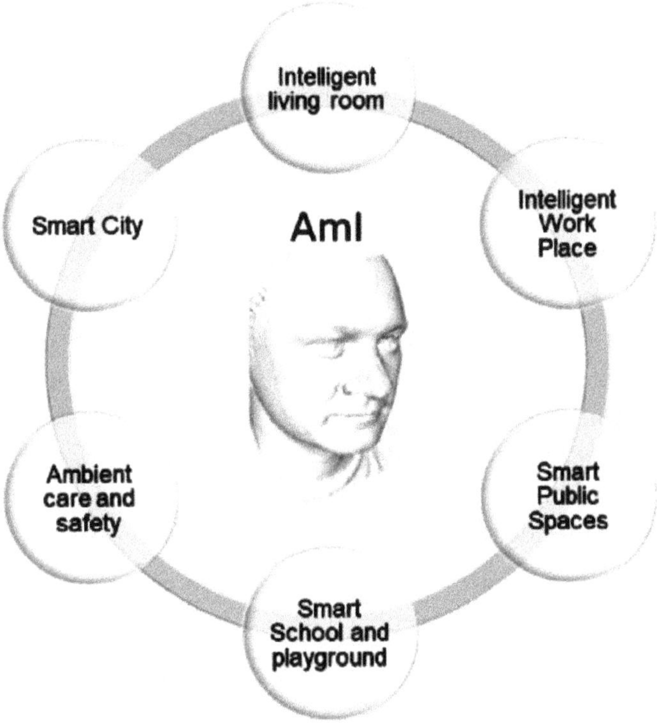

Fig. 15. Application areas of ambient intelligence (own source).

Indeed, some researchers in the field prefer to use the terminology Computational Intelligence (CI) – for instance, in IEEE publications – over artificial intelligence (AI). In this paper we will adopt the terminology "superintelligence" that is related to AI and AmI technologies alike.

The embedding of AI in the natural environment around a user requires the rapid development of advanced technologies in electrical and software engineering. Several advances have been made in the decades after the Handbook of Ambient Intelligence and Smart Environments was published.

The applications of AI in smart environments have encountered different challenges, for example, the task of recognizing the context that surrounds the user. The human centricity of AmI requires that the computational intelligence is closely bound to the needs and goals of the user and that the learning takes place in a rich living environment. The representation of meaning and knowledge of the environment require semantic models of entities, activities and their relations.

Information society fosters AI and AmI

The main hypothesis is that AI and AmI are two closely related disciplines, both heavily dependent on the development of the information society, and both strongly influencing human development. To better understand the driving forces that support and proliferate the future development of AI and AmI, we briefly review the information-society laws, as one of the indicators of the past and the future.

An information society is a society where the creation, distribution, use, integration and manipulation of information is a central economic, political and cultural activity. Its main drivers are digital information and communication technologies (ICTs), which have resulted in an information explosion and are profoundly changing all aspects of our society. The information society has succeeded the industrial society and might lead to the knowledge or intelligent society.

The explosive growth of information can be demonstrated with a variety of data. For example, the world's technological capacity to store information grew during the period from 1986 to 2007 at a sustained annual rate of 25%. The world's capacity to compute information grew from 3.0×10^8 MIPS in 1986 to 6.4×10^{12} MIPS in 2007, experiencing a growth rate of over 60% per year for the past two decades. This progress resulted in a huge boost for human civilization, as demonstrated by the rapid growth in the number of Internet users.

The progress of the information society can also be presented through several information-society laws or computing laws. There are several important laws shared by ICT, AI and AmI, for example, Moore's law, Kryder's law, Keck's law and Makimoto's law, among many others.

Moore's law can be employed for the growth of the capabilities of electronic devices, e.g., chips, which is exponential; the number of transistors in a dense integrated circuit doubles about every 2 years. This has been valid for half a century. Kryder's law can be employed when, for example, disk capacity grows exponentially, even faster than Moore's law. Keck's law (similar to Gilder's law) can be employed when, for example, communication capabilities (actual traffic) grow exponentially. It was successfully used to predict the trends for data rates in optical fibres in the past four decades. Makimoto's law can be used, for example, for a 10-year cycle between research and standardization, meaning that one can predict future commercial capabilities by looking into today's research facilities.

It is worth mentioning that there are many more related laws. They present the core properties of progress in past decades and also provide good indications for the near future. The laws themselves, the number of associated rules and the consequences are fascinating. For example, the total production of semiconductor devices equates to one transistor per one metre of our galaxy's diameter and billions of transistors per one star in our galaxy. The calculation is based on the data that transistor production reached 2.5×10^{20} in 2014, which is 250 billion billion. In comparison, our Milky Way galaxy has a diameter between 100,000 and 180,000 light years, it contains 100–400 billion stars and 100 billion planets. Incidentally, there are also around 100 billion neurons in our heads, according to numerous reports.

In recent years there were several reports stating that the use of exponential laws in the information society, such as Moore's or Keck's law, is slowing down since we are approaching the physical limits. Although there are hard limitations in many processes, in particular for the exponential ones, we do not need to jump to conclusions.

Ambient intelligence powering IoT

AmI communication elements are always on and receptive to human input and other variables.

In addition to home and business settings, ambient intelligence can also be used in a completely automated environment to assess conditions, interact with other devices, perform management functions and transmit data externally.

Some elements of an AmI environment:

- **Embeddedness:** Computers are not typically standalone devices in the environment but many manmade and organic systems have built-in intelligence and computing abilities. The current Internet of Things (IoT) development, which involves outfitting just about any type of object imaginable with computing ability and connectivity, is leading us to embedded computing.
- **Transparency:** Transparency, in the context of transparent computing, essentially means "invisibility." People interact with embedded systems naturally - asking a question rather than, for example, picking up a tablet and typing a search query.
- **Context awareness:** This component is the ability of a system or system component to gather information about its environment at any given time and adapt behaviors accordingly. Contextual or context-aware computing uses software and hardware to automatically collect and analyze data to guide responses. Potential systems for data collection and response include sensors, emotion analytics and Affective computing software.
- **Machine learning:** This capacity makes it possible for devices in the environment to learn from experience, extrapolate from current data and expand on their knowledge and capabilities autonomously.
- AmI, the Internet of Things, artificial intelligence (AI), robotics, Nanotechnology and other developing trends are transforming the world

to such an extent that the current scenario is sometimes called the fourth industrial revolution.

Relations between AI and AmI, super-AI and super-AmI

AI, also called machine intelligence (MI), is the intelligence demonstrated by machines, in contrast to the natural intelligence (NI) displayed by humans and other animals. AI, therefore, implements human cognitive functions such as perceiving, processing input from the environment and learning. Whenever intelligence is demonstrated by machines in the surrounding environment, it is referred to as ambient intelligence. Due to its focus on humans and the environment, AmI represents far more than just a huge number of AI application areas; rather it is a network of different areas.

Under the AmI framework, AI research can be regarded as AmI-oriented from its core since it is often characterized as the study of *intelligent agents*. An intelligent agent therein is a system that perceives its environment and takes actions to improve its chance of success.

The birth year of AI is now generally accepted as 1956, with the Dartmouth conference, where John McCarthy defined the terminology of *Artificial Intelligence*. In Europe, several researchers recognize the paper of Alan Turing, published in 1950, as the start of AI. However, while the concept was the same, the terminology in the 1950 paper was *Machine Intelligence* (MI). Whatever the case, Alan Turing is regarded by many as the founding father of computer science due to his seminal contributions, including the halting problem, the Turing test, the Turing machine, and the decoding of Hitler's Enigma machine that helped to end the war more quickly and thus saved millions of human lives. Whereas AI and AmI have seen their share of over-optimism and corresponding over-criticism, the overall, and the recent, progress corresponds to the exponential growth of the information-society laws. Each year there are scores of new achievements attracting worldwide attention in academia, gaming, industry and real life. For example, autonomous vehicles are constantly improving, and they are being introduced into more and more countries, whereas IoT, smart homes and smart cities are at the centre of current research.

AI and AmI are everywhere, and they are already making a big impact on our everyday lives. Together, they make around 100 trillion decisions a day. Smartphones, cars, banks, houses and cities all use artificial intelligence on a daily basis. We are probably aware of it when we use Siri, Google or Alexa to get directions to the nearest petrol station or to order a pizza. More often though, users are not aware that they are using intelligent services, e.g., when they make a purchase by credit card with a system in the background checking for potential fraud, or when an intelligent agent in a smart home regulates user-specific comfort.

How big and complex the research efforts in AI and AmI have become is even evident from a quick look at a basic teaching book for universities [59]. Each of the chapters in the book is represented in detail in several additional books and courses at top universities.

Amazing progress has been demonstrated, for example, in chess, where humans have been playing the game for 1500 years, and computers' domination was first demonstrated in 1997. In 2018, AlphaZero learned only from the formal rules of the game, and just for 4 hours, and displayed superior performance to Stockfish, which won several championships. AlphaZero played the first 100-game match with 28 wins, 72 draws, and zero losses.

When fed with huge numbers of examples and with fine-tuned parameters, AI methods and in particular deep neural networks (DNNs) regularly beat the best human experts in increasing numbers of artificial and real-life tasks, such as diagnosing tissue in several diseases. There are other everyday tasks, e.g., the recognition of faces from a picture, where DNNs recognize hundreds of faces in seconds, a result no human can match.

Ambient intelligence

The first of several sections of the paper is used to define AI, the AmI background and the dilemmas faced. Indeed, AmI shares its progress with the progress of IC technologies and AI, spurring it on its own from time to time. For example, one is related to a side effect of the information society – an information overload because of computers and electronic devices being faster by a factor of a million to a billion when basic information tasks such as computation or storing information are concerned. As a result, we do not want to deal with electronic devices when everyday tasks are involved, for example, when controlling home appliances. We prefer to set guidelines and let the AmI take care of it – including the control and execution.

Ambient intelligence refers to electronic environments that are sensitive and responsive to the presence of people. The term was originally developed in the late 1990s, and was later extended to the environment without people as well: "In an ambient intelligence world, devices work in concert to support people in carrying out their everyday life activities, tasks and rituals in an easy, natural way using information and intelligence that is hidden in the network connecting these devices (for example The Internet of Things)."

A modern definition was delivered by Juan Carlos Augusto and McCullagh: "Ambient Intelligence is a multi-disciplinary approach which aims to enhance the way environments and people interact with each other. The ultimate goal of the area is to make the places we live and work in more beneficial to us. Smart Homes is one example of such systems, but the idea can also be used about hospitals, public transport, factories, and other environments."

AmI is aligned with the concept of the "disappearing computer". The AmI field is very closely related to pervasive computing and ubiquitous computing, and also to context awareness, and human-centric computer interaction design. Among the most important properties of AmI systems we can find:

- *embedded*: devices are integrated into the environment; they are "invisible".
- *context-aware*: they recognize a user, possibly also the current state of the user and the situational context.
- *personalized*: they are often tailored to the user's needs.
- *adaptive*: AmI systems change their performance in response to changes in the user's physical or mental state.
- *anticipatory*: they can anticipate user's desires without conscious mediation.
- *unobtrusive*: discrete, not providing anything but the necessary information about the user to other devices and humans.
- *non-invasive*: they do not demand any action from the user, rather they act on their own.

In the light of these features, several contributions related to the JAISE journal can be incorporated, for example:

- Ambient intelligence: Technologies, applications, and opportunities.
- Ambient intelligence – the next step for artificial intelligence.
- Handbook of Ambient Intelligence and Smart Environments.

These are seminal works contributing to the field of AmI, accompanied by several others. In the following sections, several areas especially important for AI and AmI are analysed, starting with agents and the Semantic Web.

When multi-agent systems meet the semantic web: Representing agents' knowledge in AmI scenarios

The concept of a software agent is based on representing an autonomous entity in a computer program that is embedded in a specific environment for the intelligent management of complex problems, probably interacting with other agents. This idea has given rise to the definition of multi-agent systems (MAS). These systems aim to coordinate the various actors within them and to integrate their particular goals into a common objective. MAS applications cover different situations: the management of problems whose elements are physically distributed; when the solution to solve a problem consists of using heterogeneous knowledge that is maintained by different agents, etc.

A traditional problem in developing MAS lies in finding a common way to represent the knowledge these agents share. One of the most commonly used alternatives in the past 10 years to solve this problem is the adoption of ontologies to express the domain information the agents are working on.

In a nutshell, an ontology allows us to formally define the terms and relationships that comprise the vocabulary of a domain along with a series of operators to combine both elements. Once defined, the vocabulary is shared by all the agents and used by them to make specific statements about the domain. Thus, an agent using the ontology of that domain can interpret any statement made with that vocabulary.

With the rise of the Semantic Web, technologies to define and manage ontologies such as languages, standards, reasoners, etc. have increased considerably. The original idea of the Semantic Web concentrates on the services available on the Internet being carried out through intelligent agents that are capable of processing information on the Web, reasoning with it and interacting with other agents and services to satisfy the requirements imposed by users.

Currently, the combination of MAS and Semantic Web technologies is presented as an alternative to manage knowledge, not only at the Web layer but at a more general scale where systems and organizations need to understand their domain and reason about it to act intelligently.

Next, let us review some relevant papers published in JAISE that have dealt with the integration of MAS and Semantic Web technologies and the fields of AmI where such proposals have been applied.

They propose augmenting perceptual data gathered from different sensors using ontologies that define concepts such as location, spatial relations, colours, etc. As a result, symbolic and meaningful information is obtained from the environment. Moreover, they use common-sense reasoning to reason about the elements in the environment. This knowledge-representation model is embedded into a smart environment called PEIS-HOME. The top level of this system is presented as an agent that can communicate with other artificial agents and humans on the conceptual level using the symbolic information represented by ontologies.

Another proposal by researchers describes a framework called PlaceComm to collect and share knowledge about the concept "place" as a key abstraction. An ontology named the Place-Based Virtual Community is developed to represent common concepts for any place: context, time, device, activity, service, etc. A MAS is used in this framework to gather different types of data, such as context and user information. The agents use the ontology to exchange information within the system. Several applications are presented as a proof of concept, as applications to guide the user in a place or to pose queries about the people in a place.

Following a similar approach, researchers introduce an adaptive framework to develop smart-environment applications. This work provides generic ontologies to represent context, security and performance management, and therefore it is possible to reuse knowledge by separating these ontologies from domain ontologies. The ontologies are connected to applications through rules. To achieve adaptivity, the authors propose a context-aware micro-architecture based on three agents, i.e., context monitoring, context reasoning, and context-based adaptation agents.

In a more recent work by researchers, a MAS is introduced for managing the development of the Internet of Things (IoT) systems. The authors provide an agent platform called *Sol* to deal with IoT requirements such as the diversity of heterogeneous devices and communication among devices regardless of the technologies and protocols supported by such devices. The agents' knowledge is represented by using an ontology named *SolManagementOntology*, which contains concepts such as service, agent profile, group of agents, etc. This ontology aims to represent the information of the IoT system that is managed and exchanged in the agent platform. As a proof of concept the authors show the performance of the Sol platform in an intelligent-museum scenario.

Finally, it is worth mentioning the survey by researchers on software-engineering practices for the development of applications in AmI. In this survey the authors include relevant works on the representation of knowledge through ontologies in MAS along with their reasoning capabilities. They identify the adoption of these multi-agent systems as a compelling alternative for developing middleware solutions that are necessary in AmI applications.

Shifting now to works devoted to the use of MAS based on semantic technologies for specific AmI applications and services, the fields most frequently related to these works are those of human-centric applications, smart spaces, health, security and reputation.

One of the most productive areas of work has to do with human-centric applications. Researchers propose an agent-based framework to study human behaviour and its dynamics in a variety of domains, from driving activities to the assistance of naval operations. This framework is composed of several levels, ranging from the agent-interaction level to the individual agent-design level. In this work not only are human states (physical and mental) and behaviours represented using ontologies, but also the agents' internal processes (beliefs, facts, actions) are defined in this manner. Another work focused on studying human interactions with the environment is that by researchers.

Here, the authors utilize semantic agents in the form of Web services to compose ad-hoc architectures capable of acting with the environment. The agents are empowered with four abilities: perception, by using input Web services; understanding, by fusing different sources of information; decision, by reasoning on the available information; and action, by using output Web services.

The agents' knowledge (here called the *Agent's memory*) is composed of three ontologies that represent events in the environment and their models, including meta-models to represent the relationships among the events. These ontologies are not only used to store agents' knowledge, but also as part of the content of the agents' communication language. The authors apply their system to daily-activities scenarios for monitoring and assisting elderly and disabled people. More specific work on the modelling of human activity within a smart home is presented by researchers.

This model is composed of three ontologies to represent user information, smart-home context and activity daily living processes. Moreover, the authors adopt an upper-level ontology called DOLCE + DnS Ultralite to achieve the integration with domain-specific ontologies to offer interoperability with other smart-home applications. The concept of the agent is modelled to represent both the human user or the artificial agent's profile and the static information.

The research line on smart spaces has also been studied as a practical field to apply the integration of MAS and Semantic Web technologies. For instance, researchers study the management of semantic conflicts among agents in open environments. Such environments produce unpredictable and unreliable data, which may end by generating contradictory knowledge in the agents. In this work, the authors present an automatic approach to coping with conflicts in the OWL ontologies that represent the agents' knowledge base.

A different work by researchers focuses on monitoring and saving energy in the context of a smart university building. Rule-based agents are integrated into the middleware that monitors the use of energy in the International Hellenic University. These agents are capable of behaving both in a reactive and deliberative manner, based on the knowledge acquired from the middleware and represented using ontologies and rules. Finally, it is worth mentioning the work by researchers where a smart space is simulated to test context-aware services for smartphones.

The authors introduce the UbikMobile architecture that allows the design of simulated environments in a graphical manner. Following an agent-based social simulation approach, software agents are employed as users to perform automatic tests by interacting with the services developed for smartphones.

Health is another field of research where agents and Semantic Web technologies have been applied. As an example, researchers have developed an agent-based system to prevent unipolar depression relapse. Several ontologies have been developed to model the depression process, including the recovery and relapse stages. Agents' observations from sensors, agents' belief base, and agents' actions are all modelled using ontologies. Using this knowledge, a multi-agent system is built to monitor and reason about the depression status of the user. Another example can be found in the work of researchers, which is focused on the management of diabetes through an intelligent-agent platform called COMMODITY.

There are also some works related to security and reputation. Thus, researchers investigate the improvement of user-verification methods through an agent-based system. Firstly, sensor agents observe entry points and store the gathered data in an ontology. Then, a classification agent uses these data together with the users' previous behaviours to detect any possible anomaly and raise the alarm. The ontology shared by these agents allows them to represent concepts such as access points, workers' and non-workers' profiles, different types of sensors (biometric, card reader, video sensors, etc.) as well as events, actions, types of anomaly, etc. Some examples of use, such as stolen-card and forged-fingerprint scenarios are shown as a proof of concept for the system.

On the other hand, researchers have developed a reputation system among intelligent agents, named CALoR (Context-Aware and Location Reputation System), which is mainly based on agents' spatial and temporal interactions. The authors represent through ontologies the concepts related to these features of location and temporality. These ontologies also contain entities to represent information about recommendation protocols, including action fulfilment and recommendations received from other agents. The agents are implemented in the JADE platform to show several tests of their reputation system when distance and temporal information are introduced in intelligent ambient systems.

AMBIENT INTELLIGENCE FOR SMART CITIES

Kevin Aston, cofounder and executive director of the Auto-ID Center at the Massachusetts Institute of Technology (MIT), first mentioned, in a presentation in 1999, the Internet of Things (IoT) to describe the network connecting objects in the physical world to the Internet. Since then, the rapid development of smart sensors like accelerometers, humidity or pressure sensors, and also high-speed wireless networks such as Wi-Fi or Zigbee have worked hand in hand with numerous AmI methods, including fuzzy-logic-based classifiers or machine-learning algorithms, to support many innovative smart-city applications. According to researchers, there are many highly ranked and significant areas of smart-city applications involving various sensors and/or AmI methods, such as those below:

- *Smart Parking* – monitoring the availability of parking spaces in the city;
- *Structural Health* – monitoring the vibrations and material conditions in buildings, bridges and historical monuments;
- *Noise Urban Maps* – monitoring the noises in bar areas and central zones in real time;

- *Smartphone Detection* – detecting an iPhone or Android phone or, in general, any mobile device that works with a Bluetooth or Wi-Fi interface;
- *Electromagnetic Field Levels* – measuring the energy radiated by cell stations and Wi-Fi routers;
- *Traffic Congestion* – monitoring vehicles and pedestrian levels to optimize driving and walking routes;
- *Smart Lighting* – Intelligent and weather-adaptive lighting in street lights;
- *Waste Management* – detecting rubbish levels in containers to optimize rubbish-collection routes;
- *Smart Roads* – Intelligent highways with warning messages and diversions according to climate conditions and unexpected events like accidents or traffic jams.

In addition, there are other aspects of smart-city applications, such as smart water involving portable water monitoring, the detection of water leakages along pipes or monitoring water-level variations in rivers, dams and reservoirs. Other examples of smart-city applications include smart metering that involves energy-consumption monitoring and management in smart grids or the measurement of water flow or pressure in water-transportation systems.

In all these smart-city applications, fuzzy-logic-based classifiers, machine-learning or statistical approaches can be applied to learn the 'regular' patterns of changes in the flow rate, pressure, usage or another measured parameter, obtained from the smart sensors installed in the underlying application during the training phase. This may help to quickly identify any irregular pattern(s) of changes or movements occurring in the testing or deployment environment, possibly due to various causes such as disasters, faulty sensors, leakage, improper system operations, or the unexpected side effects of reactive processes, among others.

In any case, this will help to alert the system administrator about any recovery procedure or pro-active maintenance to avoid any possible damage, risk or shutdown of the overall system.

For instance, deep-learning approaches such as the multi-layer perceptron (MLP) neural network or the long-short-term memory (LSTM) model of the recurrent neural networks are applied for the task of energy forecasting in some real-world applications involving smart meters installed in different smart buildings in a city of South East Asia.

In addition, energy data sets obtained from the Global Energy Forecasting Competition or other online sources are used to compare the performance of the involved AmI approaches for energy prediction. The resulting energy-prediction models can also be used to facilitate the concerned organizations in formulating effective energy-saving strategies to achieve a better energy efficiency for the whole building or enterprise.

The progress of ICT and the information society has been exponential for the past 50 years and will continue at approximately the same pace for several decades to come if the ingenuity of researchers and designers manages to find new solutions to bypass the physical limitations of semiconductor technology.

The progress of AI, in general, and superintelligence, in particular, is even brighter. Even on only reasonably better hardware, new solutions will be created due to more advanced software algorithms and systems. Each year several killer AI applications appear, ones that most researchers doubted would be possible in the near future. The progress just amazes us.

The success of AmI relies heavily on the progress of the information society, ICT and AI. We humans are satisfied if the advanced technologies take care of us and do not want our attention or even additional activities besides giving occasional guidelines and orders. We like the invisible computer with the advanced AI hidden in the environment. Some devices like Google home are still present, but the hardware is just the microphone. What matters is the system connected, embedded and with all the other properties of AmI systems.

AmI is sharing its fate and fame with the field of AI – and the trend towards systems bypassing human capabilities is already here. These systems take care of our needs and desires, enable a better, safer, more comfortable life with a smaller environmental burden. Like superintelligence, super-ambient-intelligence (SAmI) is destined to develop as contemporary of superintelligence or even as the first pioneer, harvesting its physical attachment to the real world and constant interactions with humans.

However, the progress will likely not be straightforward as several challenges indicate in terms of design contexts and societal changes. In addition, the AmI term problem is related to the distribution of the field, in particular the near-synonyms "pervasive computing" and "ubiquitous computing". These terms are currently prevailing at least in the sense of conference attendees. At the same time, the concept, methods and approaches are the same.

Among most relevant AmI areas are the ones described in this paper: semantic web and agents, ambient assisted living, electronic and mobile healthcare, taking care for elderly, medical applications, e-learning, smart home and smart cities.

Hopefully, this special issue on AmI will provoke discussions and awareness, from AmI experts to the general public, and from media to government decision-makers, helping them to understand that the times are changing rapidly, and that new approaches and methods are coming faster than expected, even by the experts.

SWARM INTELLIGENCE

Swarm intelligence is the discipline that deals with natural and artificial systems composed of many individuals that coordinate using decentralized control and self-organization. In particular, the discipline focuses on the collective behaviors that result from the local interactions of the individuals with each other and with their environment.

Examples of systems studied by swarm intelligence are colonies of ants and termites, schools of fish, flocks of birds, herds of land animals. Some human artifacts also fall into the domain of swarm intelligence, notably some multi-robot systems, and also certain computer programs that are written to tackle optimization and data analysis problems.

In the natural world, Swarm Intelligence (SI) enables social organisms to rapidly aggregate their collective insights and reach optimal decisions by forming real-time closed-loop systems that converge in synchrony. Swarm Intelligence has been deeply studied across many social species, from schools of fish and flocks of birds, to swarms of honey bees. In recent years, advances in networking technology and artificial intelligence have enabled human groups to form similar systems online, moderated by AI algorithms.

Often referred to as Artificial Swarm Intelligence (ASI) or simply "human swarming," this novel approach has been shown to significantly increase the accuracy of group decisions across a wide variety of tasks, from handicapping sporting events to forecasting financial markets.

Swarm Intelligence in Architectural Design

Swarm intelligence can be described as the collective behaviours of artificial or natural selforganised and decentralised systems (Aryanpour, 2012). Swarm behaviours of animals inspire swarm intelligence strategies in computer media. Swarm behaviours in nature emerge to enhance food-finding, protection mating and sufficient energy using abilities of limited-skilled animals when they are individual. There are different words used to express the swarm behaviour of other animals.

For instance, for insects, the term 'swarm' is used. For birds 'flocking', for quadrupeds 'herding' and fish 'shoaling' or 'schooling' is preferred. To simulate this behaviour mathematically to implement them to computer media, experts have tried to represent three rules emerging in swarm behaviours. These are separation as moving in the same direction with neighbours, alignment as remaining close to neighbours and cohesion as avoiding collisions with neighbours.

The term swarm intelligence first introduced in 1989 in robotics by Gerardo Beni and Jing Wang to express emergent collective behaviour in the context of cellular robotic systems. Steven Johnson has searched one of the early hypothetical application potentials to the realm of architecture in his book 'Emergence: The Connected Lives of Ants, Brains, Cities and Software', published in 2001. In his novel, he dealt with the idea based on creating a form of living especially for humans benefitting from the emergence logic of swarm behaviour of animals and examined the similarities between the smallest scale ants to the larger-scale cities. In architecture, swarm intelligence investigates the role of agency within the generative design process, and architects can benefit from swarm intelligence for deconstructing modernist tectonic hierarchies. Swarm intelligence is used in architecture in such areas; visualisation, self-organisation of multi-agent system, architecture form design, urbanism.

Today some architectural firms and star architects are benefitting from swarm intelligence for form generation, structure finding and enhancing space quality by translating mathematically modelled animal particle system to architectural tectonics. Today, swarm intelligence is used in architecture by these firms and architectural schools for architectural design; Zaha Hadid Architects, London; Kokkugia, New York and London; Biothing, London; R&Sie(n), Paris; Cecil Balmond, London; Casey Reas, Los Angeles; London and Foster + Partners, London; and schools: Architectural Association; UPenn; Columbia GSAPP; TU Delft; CITA and USC.

THE SELF-REGULATING/INTELLIGENT CITY

The term 'intelligent city' (IC) has been used with various meanings. At least four different descriptions of what an intelligent city is can be found in the literature:

- ICs have been frequently defined as virtual reconstructions of cities, as virtual cities. The term has been used interchangeably as an equivalent of 'digital city', 'information city', 'wired city', 'telecity', 'knowledge-based city', 'electronic communities', 'electronic community spaces', 'flexicity', 'teletopia', 'cyberville', covering a wide range of electronic and digital applications related to digital spaces of communities and cities.
- Another meaning was given by the World Foundation for Smart Communities, which links digital cities with smart growth, a development based on information and commnication technologies. 'A Smart Community is a community that has made a conscious effort to use information technology to transform life and work within its region in significant and fundamental, rather than incremental, ways'.
- ICs are defined as environments with embedded information and communication technologies creating interactive spaces that bring computation into the physical world. From this perspective, intelligent cities (or intelligent spaces more generally) refer to physical environments in which information and communication technologies and sensor systems disappear

as they become embedded into physical objects and the surroundings in which we live, travel, and work.

- Intelligent cities are also defined as territories that bring innovation systems and ICTs within the same locality, combining the creativity of talented individuals that make up the population of the city, institutions that enhance learning and innovation, and virtual innovation spaces facilitating innovation and knowledge management.

The diversity in understanding what intelligent cities are, is due to the multiple scientific and technology disciples and social movements that take part in their creation, namely the movements towards 'cybercities', 'smart growth', 'intelligent communities' and 'intelligent innovation environments'. We should underline, however, that major movements shaping intelligent cities, like Smart Communities and the Intelligent Community Forum, promote under ICs innovation, smart growth, and digital community spaces.

The distinctive characteristic of intelligent cities is their increased performance in the field of innovation, because innovation and solving of new problems are distinctive features of intelligence. In this sense, intelligent cities and regions constitute advanced territorial systems of innovation, in which the institutional mechanisms for knowledge creation and application are facilitated by digital spaces and online tools for communication and knowledge management.

Clusters and systems of innovation

The way for intelligent cities and regions is paved by clusters of innovative organizations forming networks, technology districts, poles, and systems of innovation.

Today, the mainstream view for innovation is that it is systemic. Theories of innovation have radically changed during the past few years. Both the traditional Schumpeterian model, regarding innovation as an internal activity of the firm and the linear innovation model in which new product development follows a step-by-step sequence from discovery, idea generation, business case analysis, to product development, testing, and launce, have been found inadequate. Innovation is increasingly regarded as a collaborative and evolutionary process taking place within environments augmenting discovery and idea generation and selecting the most plausible innovations.

The systemic theory of innovation was initially formulated at national level. Founding publications described and focused on national systems of innovation. Gradually however, there was a shift towards the regional and local levels. A series of publications have shown that innovation processes are embedded in regional conditions shaping regional systems of innovation. Researchers identified five major mechanisms than explain the regional embeddedness of innovation:

- Many of the preconditions of innovation, such as qualifications of the labor force, education, research institutions, knowledge externalities and spillovers, are immobile, giving some regions advantages over others.
- Industrial clusters are localized giving rise to specific innovation patterns within networks and industry sectors.
- A common technical culture may develop through collective learning taking place into a regional productive system.
- University-industry links and knowledge spillovers are region specific.
- Regional policy is playing an active role in innovation providing support through institutions and agencies.

The structure of such regional agglomerations and territorial systems of innovation (technology districts, technopoles, innovative clusters, technology parks, innovating regions) can be described in terms of components, knowledge networks, institutions, and innovation outcomes.

In innovation-led clusters, main actors come from the company, the R&D, the technology transfer, and the funding sectors. Components of the systems are innovative firms; supplier firms; customer firms; universities; research organizations; technology transfer institutions; IPR lawyers; consultants; training institutions; incubators; funding organizations; government agencies; monitoring organizations.

Components are organized in networks because innovation is based on their combined action. What gives value to components is their cooperation. The reason for the networks' existence is to enable innovation, facilitate and augment creativity at the company level, the latter being the ultimate producer and beneficiary of innovation. Various forms of networks appear within innovation systems: clusters, technology districts, small innovation systems, flexible short term alliances. The connecting substance of all networks is knowledge. What flows within innovation networks is mainly knowledge. All kinds of knowledge flow within innovation networks.

Researcher, reviewing the literature on knowledge types argues that knowledge can be divided into three categories: declarative (about facts), procedural (dealing with know-how), and conditional (linking conditions and effects); it can also take two forms, 'explicit knowledge' that is transmittable in formal languages, codified and captured in libraries, archives and databases; and 'tacit ' knowledge which has a personal dimension that makes it hard to formalize and transmit in other ways than personal communication. Researcher has explained that tacit knowledge is spatially sticky, and this quality sustains the trend of innovative activities towards agglomeration.

A critical element for the operation of knowledge networks is institutional action. Institutions for knowledge creation, information dissemination, intellectual property management, knowledge assessment and funding act as switches which turn funding on and off and take 'kill' or 'go' decisions in the innovation process. To do so, institutions are placed upon the knowledge networks linking the company with its external partners. Knowledge networks and institutional regulation change from one innovation round to the other, enabling a constant renewal of technologies and avoiding technology lock-in.

Knowledge networks architecture changes with respect to the innovation processes that take place in the system. Innovation routes, such as cooperative R&D, strategic intelligence, product innovation, process innovation, spin-off creation, opening new markets, attraction of knowledge-intensive organizations, involve fundamentally different knowledge networks. Different forms of innovation demand different partners and alliances. A cooperative R&D project demands quite different network architecture from a cooperative project of strategic intelligence for a cluster.

The entire landscape of knowledge networks within innovative clusters is extremely complex and variable. In the connectivity of components (partners) two conditions predominate:

- The creation of knowledge networks with various architectures, which are separated by science and technology borders; and
- The operation of switches regulating the flow of knowledge between the components, which are administrated by knowledge creation, transfer, and application institutions, namely R&D centers, technology intermediary organizations, and companies.

Major forms of innovation within clusters (product, process, and organizational innovations) stand on different architectures of knowledge networks, focusing on new product development, technology transfer, and the supply chain. Because innovation relies on knowledge and information networks, digital spaces and collaborative IT applications have become an important source of novel product, process, and organizational solutions.

Technology plays a crucial role in smart cities, and creative technological techniques effectively assist cities in becoming smarter. Smart cities use ICT to automate processes and improve the quality of people's lives in urban regions. Moreover, it employs integrated intelligence technologies to improve municipal infrastructure and enable responsive governance to involve inhabitants in city administration. Various modern technologies and approaches allow smart service models to improve efficiency and operations in healthcare, transportation, energy, education, and many other areas. It is well recognized that cities can be classified as "*Smart*" if they meet the criteria outlined in Fig. 16.

Global internet users have gradually increased over the last decades. With the development of internet technology and many other types of networks and communication strategies, the Internet of Things (IoTs) has become one of the most crucial forms of infrastructure in smart cities. Furthermore, IoT technology is considered the most important and critical component of modern smart city initiatives, which generate a large amount of data.

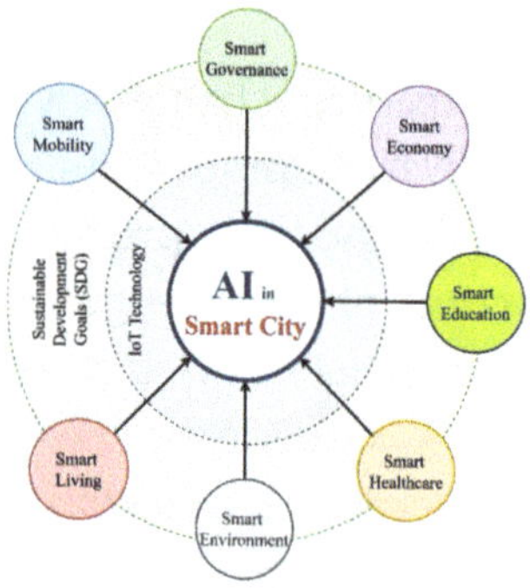

Fig. 16. Major domains of smart city.

The term "*Internet of Things*" can be described as a set of technologies that allow users to access data generated by various devices through wireless and wired internet networks. Over 1.6 billion IoT components and devices were used in smart cities in 2017, increasing 39% from 2015. In 2018, around 3.3 billion IoT devices and components were estimably used. Furthermore, IoT components and devices were expanded by 42% and 43% in 2017 and 2018, respectively. The growth of smart devices and components in smart cities has aided the expansion of IoT-based solutions. For example, in a smart home setting, data created by electronic household equipment, such as refrigerators, are exchanged and saved to provide user-customized services. It might be difficult to pinpoint the most precise and efficient actions when dealing with enormous amounts of complex data. AI, DRL, and ML are examples of sophisticated methodologies that may be utilized to analyse massive data to get the best possible conclusion.

Smart city initiatives in major countries are now focusing on AI-based smart applications. According to statistics, the AI industry will be worth $190 billion by 2025. By 2021, global investment in cognitive and AI systems will total $57.6 billion, with AI being deployed in 75% of enterprise apps. China owns the largest number of smart cities in the world, which manage its cities and public spaces using metering devices, cameras, embedded sensors, and other monitoring technologies, as well as data mining, processing, and AI-based analysis techniques. China is said to have about 800 smart city pilot programs active or planned, accounting for more than half of all smart city pilot programs worldwide. China's AI has progressed swiftly since 2015, and the Chinese government has taken several steps to stimulate AI research, catapulting Chinese AI into a new era. In recent years, AI has been used in smart city studies and practices, with academics observing how it is becoming an increasingly significant aspect of smart urbanism. AI may promote efficiency and improve the quality of life for the smart cities of the future by drawing on vast resource pools and combining contemporary machine vision, NLP, ML, robotics and other technologies. Successful AI algorithms rely on large amounts of data to perform useful tasks. This information may be obtained through the use of digital and mechanical technologies that transfer and store essential data and process it to give a satisfying solution to a problem.

Smart city AI technologies can be categorized into machine learning (ML), natural language processing (NLP), speech, vision, expert systems, and robotics. Machine learning (ML) is a subset of AI that enables software programs to grow increasingly effective at predicting outcomes without explicitly programming them to do so. Machine learning algorithms estimate new output values by using past data as input. Natural-language processing (NLP) is a branch of AI that studies how computers interact with human languages. The objective is to create a computer program or algorithm that can understand the contents of papers, including the nuances of language in context. Speech recognition is an interdisciplinary topic of computer science and computational linguistics that uses AI to generate results. Speech recognition, voice recognition, speech to text, and text to speech are some of the other names. NLP and automated speech recognition are two AI areas that are related yet distinct. Computer vision is a branch of AI that allows computers and systems to extract useful information from digital photos, videos, and other visual inputs and then act or make suggestions based on that data. An expert system is a computer program that employs artificial intelligence approaches to handle issues in a specific subject that would normally need human skill. Robotics is the production of robots that can-do tasks without human involvement, whereas AI is the process of systems imitating the human mind in terms of decision-making and learning.

DIGITAL CITIES

The digital city is the dominant form of community space corresponding to a territory. Digital cities cover a very wide range of digital networks and software applications facilitating multiple aspects of the social and economic life of cities: commerce, transactions, security, health, education, work, leisure, transport, and others.

This understanding is based on an assumption of strong similarity between the physical city and its digital counterpart; a similarity that goes beyond the image of physical space and includes structural and functional characteristics as well. The 'digital city is a metaphor called to denote a complex digital product with properties structurally similar to the ones of physical cities'.

We won't agree with this description. It is common knowledge that a digital city is structurally different from the physical city of reference. Not all elements of the physical city have their equivalent digital representation.

Imaginary elements may also take part in the digital construction. Proximity in terms of distance and time is warped. Even in simulations, 2D in the case of urban transport agents and 3D in the case of reconstruction of historical spaces and city buildings, similarity does not go beyond the form of the city. The functional aspects of the city are poorly represented through extreme simplification; social and economic relations are not represented at all.

For us, a digital city is a community digital space, which is used to facilitate and augment the activities and functions taking place within the physical space of the city. The community space is built as network of distorted representations of the city. The representation is distorted for two reasons. First, it represents a city partially and not accurately; and second, it may include virtual elements non-existent in the physical space. The community space is network-based because each element of the digital city is linked to an element of the physical city, and to other digital elements of the community space; and limitless relationships and dynamic combinations between its constituting digital elements are possible.

The distorted digital representations reflect both the space and the functions of the physical city. The informational part of the digital city represents the activities of the city; the site-seeing part represents the physical space of the city; e-market applications represent commerce and stores of the city; e-health applications represent health services, and so forth. Through these representations and their links to physical city infrastructure and services, a digital city may inform and mediate in transactions and provision of real services of commerce, health, education, government.

Understanding the digital city more as a distorted representation than a metaphor or simulation of the physical city implies that the architecture of digital cities is not homologous to physical ones; it doesn't derive from the physical city and its functions, but from the qualities of the digital elements and the scope of their existence. The digital dimension has its own rationality; it is not merely a derivative of physical space. Researcher gives a good account of the diversity of digital cities' architecture. He compares four different types of cities on the web, and looks at their architecture of data, form, and functions:

- A commercial digital city, which concentrates on commercial information with principal scope of making money for its owners. Digital cities created by

America Online (AOL) follow this model and are structured as portals similar to 'yellow pages'. They provide local information, relevant news, community resources, entertainment, and commerce, together with advertising local markets such as auto, real estate, employment, and health.

- A policy-driven or governmental digital city, the digital city of Amsterdam, which was created to facilitate communication between the municipal council and the citizens.
- A virtual city, the virtual Helsinki, which represents the city using 3D models of buildings and public spaces, offering virtual tours and broadband communication between the citizens and various service providers located in the city.
- A multi-purpose digital city, the digital city of Kyoto, in which people can get information on traffic, weather, parking, shopping, take a view of the physical environment and sightseeing thought 3D models and panoramic pictures, and have opportunities for interaction with other residents and visitors.

The architecture of the four cases varies enormously. In the most advanced multi-purpose and multi-functional digital city of Kyoto, the construction of the city is based on three layers. The first, which Ishida calls 'information layer', contains data; it is a repository of raw material, html archives, real-time sensory data, media, text, and other data organized in geographical databases. The second layer is the 'interface layer', which contains maps of the city, 3D representations, city furniture, cars, buses, trains, avatars that simulate the human presence and all the graphic design and objects that visualize the city. The third layer is the 'interaction layer' where people interact with each other, exchange information and communicate.

In the other cases (commercial city-portal, communication platform, and virtual city) architectures are simpler. The city is reduced to just a directory of urban information organized as a portal of logical and meaningful categories; to a platform for communication, a forum giving access to the municipal discussion and debate; to an aggregate of visual data.

Through this comparative study, it becomes clear that the architecture of digital cities is not uniform, but it is objective-driven, designed to fulfil scopes of information, communication, and service delivery. However, it seems possible to devise a universal model of digital cities from which all combinations and alternative designs may derive. Looking at a large number of digital cities on the web, we found that their architecture may be described by a four level structure. The first is the information storehouse, a database including all digital content, in any form, texts, images, diagrams, sounds, video, and multimedia. The digital content is usually organized according to the logical patterns, the districts, and the hierarchy of the city. The second is the applications level, which structure the digital content and provide online services. A digital city that offers information services, e-market, and e-government, includes at least three applications, which assume the tasks of delivering information, commercial, and governmental services.

The third and upper level is user interface, which includes all the web pages that users visit in order to get the services provided by the digital city. Driving a user in the different areas of the digital city, the user interface may utilize maps, 3D images, texts, and diagrams. Then, a fourth level is administration, a tool crossing the database and the applications, which enables managing the user rights to the applications and the digital content of the database.

This universal architecture of digital cities is composed of three vertical levels (content, applications, and interface) and multiple horizontal applications (functions), depending on the breadth of the digital city services (representation, information, work, leisure, commerce, transactions, etc.) (Fig. 17). The model is generic and by customization may serve any concept of digital city, specialized in site-seeing, e-government or e-work. The structure is independent of the medium on which the city runs. The latter may be the Internet, a municipal network or a metropolitan network made of fiber optic lines or wireless links.

This conception, which is common to many digital city developers, suffers from overplanning. The digital city is conceived as a fully controlled digital construction created by a central agency, which has absolute control over all its elements and functions. This would never happen in a real city. Cities emerge from multiple actions of their people rather than being created by a central planning agency of absolute power. They materialize the effect of countless simultaneous preferences, choices, and actions, rather than the will of a central planning authority.

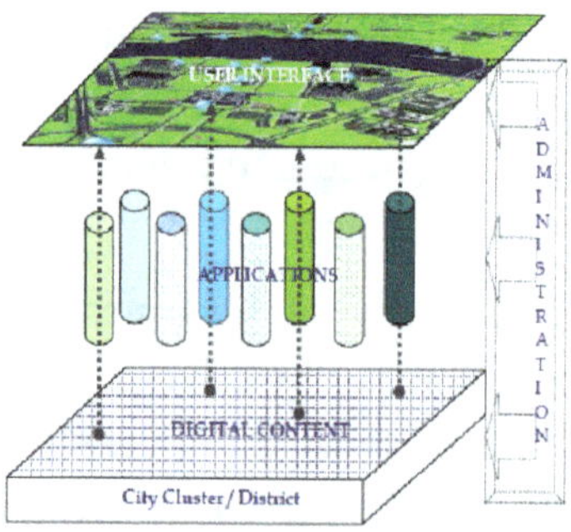

Fig. 17: Digital Cities Structure

Transferring the organization principles of physical cities on the level of digital ones implies avoiding the characterizations of individual websites as digital cities. On the contrary, the sum of websites referring to the form, activities, and functions of a city should be considered a digital city, regardless of the number of these websites and their hosting in various cities and regions of the globe.

Architecture of Intelligent Cities

Intelligent cities are created by the fusion of innovative clusters and digital cities, with the purpose to enhance knowledge and innovation. The fusion is based on two objective conditions: (1) innovation and digital cities are both community-based processes, and (2) innovation and digital cities are both knowledge-based processes. The fusion stands on collaborative knowledge networks and online regulation of knowledge and innovation processes.

Integration of innovation and broadband is quite obvious in the criteria of the Intelligent Community Forum (ICF) for the selection of Top Intelligent Communities. 'ICF has developed a list of Intelligent Community Indicators that provide the first global framework for understanding how communities and regions can gain a competitive edge in today's Broadband Economy. The Indicators demonstrate that being an Intelligent Community takes more than "being wired." It takes a combination of:

- Significant deployment of broadband communications to businesses, government facilities and residences, with government providing a catalyst through regulation, incentives and even network construction when necessary.
- Effective education, training and workforce development that builds a labor force able to perform "knowledge work."
- Government and private-sector programs that promote digital democracy by bridging the Digital Divide to ensure that all sectors of society benefit from the broadband revolution and by expanding citizen participation in government decision-making.
- Innovation in the public and private sectors, ranging from egovernment initiatives and efforts to create economic "clusters" to the formation of risk capital to fund the development of new businesses, which are the engine of economic growth.
- Effective economic development marketing that leverages the community's broadband, labor and other assets to attract new employers.

Intelligent cities and regions are not lifeless spaces, complexes of buildings, physical infrastructures, and electronic components and digital applications. On the contrary, they correspond to vivid human communities, which creatively deploy the skills of the population, their collective institutions for learning and innovation, and physico-digital infrastructures for communication and online cooperation.

From this point of view, an intelligent city is a multiplayer territorial innovation system. It combines knowledge-intensive activities, institutions for cooperation and distributed problem solving, and digital communication infrastructure and tools to maximize this problem-solving capability. As fusion of innovative clusters and digital community spaces, it is structured in three levels.

L1: The basic level of an intelligent city is the city's productive clusters, in manufacturing and services. This level gathers the creative class of the city made by knowledgeable and talented people, scientists, artists, entrepreneurs, venture capitalists and other creative people, determining how the workplace is organized and how the city is developing. Proximity in physical space is an important factor that facilitates knowledge cooperation and exchange among producers, suppliers, service providers, and knowledge workers.

L2: A second level is made of institutional mechanisms regulating knowledge flows and co-operation in learning and innovation. This level gathers institutions enhancing innovation: R&D, venture capital funds, technology transfer and training centers, intellectual property, spinoff incubators, technology and marketing consultants. Institutions manage intangible mechanisms of social capital and collective intelligence that guide the matching of individual capabilities and skills, and actualize the complex processes of innovation within the clusters of the city.

L3: The third level is made up by information technology and communication infrastructures, digital tools and spaces for learning and innovation. These technologies create a virtual innovation environment, based on multimedia tools, expert systems, and interactive technologies, which facilitate market and technology intelligence, technology transfer, spin-off creation, collaborative new product development, and process innovation. This is a working environment operating in close connection with innovative organizations and institutions regulating knowledge and innovation.

The three levels are integrated and work complementary to each other. Within innovative clusters, digital city applications complement knowledge networks and institutional switches regulating innovations. Four functions, which are characteristic of intelligent cities, emerge out of this integration.

F1: Collective strategic intelligence

A field of innovation which has enormously profited on the information society is strategic intelligence. Digital cities may promote a particular form of strategic intelligence, 'collective strategic intelligence', in which information collection, assessment, and dissemination rely on the combined action of a group of people, a community, or a business cluster.

Collective strategic intelligence differs substantially from business intelligence, the most known form of intelligence. The latter concerns the exploitation of company information gathered from suppliers and customers; it uses data from enterprise resource planning (ERP) and customer relationship management (CRM), and applying data mining and data compilation techniques produces reports elucidating hidden aspects of the business environment and activity. Collective strategic intelligence, on the contrary, is cooperative.

Data comes from a group of organizations or other actors, which disclose and share internal information. Information assessment is also collective and combines individual views and evaluations from the group members. Outcomes are more robust and provide information about wider trends and landscapes. Cooperative digital platforms for collective strategic intelligence combine two types of applications: technology/market watch, and benchmarking.

Technology watch is a systematic form of collection, analysis, understanding and diffusion of information concerning new product announcement, technologies, industrial statistics, performance indicators, market shares, price trends, etc. Data are stored into databases, portals, blogs and other digital repositories according to predefined templates. Data may focus on an industry sector or a territorial entity. Benchmarking is a form of analysis, which compares performances and drawn lessons from the best.

It has proven a powerful tool of intelligence and the techniques of comparative analysis have spread out in many fields of management and policy development. Benchmarking started from companies, and has spread out to clusters, territories, and policies as well. It provides insights to any type of organization or institution, company, R&D lab, education institution, hospital, financing institution, etc. or collective subject, such as the industry sector, cluster, region, policy and strategy as well. The methodology seeks to define the range of performance variation in any field of activity, the best performance, the distance from the best, and the practices that sustain performances. Identification of best performance and the underlying best practice are the essential pillars of any form of benchmarking (see for instance.

F2: Technology transfer

Technology transfer process usually involves moving know-how from an R&D organization to a receptor organization (20). Major forms of technology transfer involve licensing, cooperative R&D, and spin-offs. Licensing agreements concern the transfer of intellectual property rights in order to make, use, and sell a certain product, design, or service by a party that has the right to give this permission. Cooperative R&D or contract R&D agreements are comprehensive legal agreements to share research personnel, equipment, and intellectual property in a common research objective /project. Spin-off creation offers a mechanism to commercialize technologies originated from a university lab, a government R&D centre or private R&D organization.

It involves the creation of a new company from the parent organization, which undertakes the commercial exploitation of a technology. Types of technology transfer closer to the market also include consultancy and technical services provision, purchase of equipment, and training.

Digital platforms facilitating technology transfer are based on data bases of technologies and R&D results. Technologies are stored into the databases and online marketplaces of technology for license are created. Organizations offering technologies introduce their offers and the conditions of exploitation. Users may seek solutions to their technology needs, and then contact the provider. There is a fundamental difference from patent data bases, which store patent abstracts designed to protect an idea from violation. In most cases patent databases obscure the technology, making it difficult to foresee relevant applications. On the contrary technology transfer platforms seek to elucidate possible uses and application of technology in different industry sectors and activities.

Technology marketplaces are coupled with other online services related to technology transfer: consultative services assessing a portfolio of intellectual property; evaluation of better solutions to a given problem or need; legal assistance through the deal-making process.

F3: Collaborative innovation

This newest form of innovation recognizes the critical role of communities and networks as fundamental conditions of innovation. Interactions within scientific communities bridging separate knowledge fields, complementary roles and skills along the innovation chain, information flows among suppliers, producers, and customers, are all ingredients of participatory creative processes leading to new products. Innovation is less of an individual achievement than the joint effort of a group of people working together, interacting, and sharing the same values and goals.

The leading role of communities and systems in the field of innovation is acknowledged by most contemporary explanations of how innovation is produced: brokering theories, systemic theories, and tacit knowledge explanations of the innovation process.

The supply of innovation communities with digital platforms and cooperative work environments enables the formation of virtual clusters equipped with online innovation management tools, such as creativity tools, virtual customers, collaborative product design tools, market research, and marketing tools.

These platforms offer collaborative environments for product development; may lead the user to problem resolution step-by-step, for instance through the stages of new product development; include advanced methodologies and tools; and learning and experimentation through simulation. The result is a substantial improvement of human innovation skills, because of collaboration and offering of advanced technologies and product development tools to even the most remote knowledge worker.

F4: Promotion of clusters and localities

Promotion and electronic commerce is a mainstream function of digital cities. It may take multiple forms: direct marketing, attraction of people and investments, procurement and purchasing, auctions, travel, community and e-government services.

The focus is the supply chain of products and services produced by a cluster or locality. Information and knowledge networks are necessary for the functioning and optimization of the supply chain. The partners are connected by information channels and the flow of information between two partners has to be monitored to ensure the optimization of the system.

Within the supply and trade channels, digital cities have multiple added-values. Virtual spaces may facilitate, enhance, and reduce costs in all forms of transactions: logistics in the supply chain; marketing and advertising; information on policies, regulations, technical standards, and incentives; finding partners, buyers, sellers, and services.

The difference from individual promotion and ecommerce is that collective applications promote a cluster or locality together with its products and services. For small producers and global markets, this is an advantage. For new products in niche markets, a global market is necessary, which cannot be reached without digital tools. Apart from the intra-functional integration among knowledge networks operating within clusters, institutions regulating learning and innovation, and digital spaces, which takes place within each of the above mentioned functions (F1, F2, F3, and F4), intelligent cities are environments for inter-functional integration also. Collective strategic intelligence is truly important for technology transfer, product innovation, and marketing. In many cases technology transfer is a precondition for product innovation. The latter depends on promotion and opening of new markets. Knowledge networks traverse innovation forms and processes, and digital spaces do the same as well.

Intelligent cities are still in their early days. To date, most applications are being developed with respect to innovative clusters and technology parks, as intelligent clusters, technology districts, and technology parks. In these islands of innovation, the innovation system is being enriched with communication infrastructure, expert systems, and knowledge management tools, creating an integrated physico-virtual innovation system.

Its architecture, as described, includes three levels (physical, institutional, digital) and four functions (intelligence, technology transfer, innovation, and promotion). Within the physico-digital innovation environment, human and institutional factors predominate. Digital spaces and the online expert tools act as facilitators of human and collective intelligence.

GLOSSARY

Algorithm: A set of rules that a machine can follow to learn how to do a task.

Artificial intelligence: This refers to the general concept of machines acting in a way that simulates or mimics human intelligence. AI can have a variety of features, such as human-like communication or decision making.

Autonomous: A machine is described as autonomous if it can perform its task or tasks without needing human intervention.

Backward chaining: A method where the model starts with the desired output and works in reverse to find data that might support it.

Bias: Assumptions made by a model that simplify the process of learning to do its assigned task. Most supervised machine learning models perform better with low bias, as these assumptions can negatively affect results.

Big data: Datasets that are too large or complex to be used by traditional data processing applications.

Bounding box: Commonly used in image or video tagging, this is an imaginary box drawn on visual information. The contents of the box are labeled to help a model recognize it as a distinct type of object.

Chatbot: A chatbot is program that is designed to communicate with people through text or voice commands in a way that mimics human-to-human conversation.

Cognitive computing: This is effectively another way to say artificial intelligence. It's used by marketing teams at some companies to avoid the science fiction aura that sometimes surrounds AI.

Computational learning theory: A field within artificial intelligence that is primarily concerned with creating and analyzing machine learning algorithms.

Corpus: A large dataset of written or spoken material that can be used to train a machine to perform linguistic tasks.

Data mining: The process of analyzing datasets in order to discover new patterns that might improve the model.

Data science: Drawing from statistics, computer science and information science, this interdisciplinary field aims to use a variety of scientific methods, processes and systems to solve problems involving data.

Dataset: A collection of related data points, usually with a uniform order and tags.

Deep learning: A function of artificial intelligence that imitates the human brain by learning from the way data is structured, rather than from an algorithm that's programmed to do one specific thing.

Entity annotation: The process of labeling unstructured sentences with information so that a machine can read them. This could involve labeling all people, organizations and locations in a document, for example.

Entity extraction: An umbrella term referring to the process of adding structure to data so that a machine can read it. Entity extraction may be done by humans or by a machine learning model.

Forward chaining: A method in which a machine must work from a problem to find a potential solution. By analyzing a range of hypotheses, the AI must determine those that are relevant to the problem.

General AI: AI that could successfully do any intellectual task that can be done by any human being. This is sometimes referred to as *strong AI*, although they aren't entirely equivalent terms.

Hyperparameter: Occasionally used interchangeably with *parameter*, although the terms have some subtle differences. Hyperparameters are values that affect the way your model learns. They are usually set manually outside the model.

Intent: Commonly used in training data for chatbots and other natural language processing tasks, this is a type of label that defines the purpose or goal of what is said. For example, the intent for the phrase "turn the volume down" could be "decrease volume".

Label: A part of training data that identifies the desired output for that particular piece of data.

Linguistic annotation: Tagging a dataset of sentences with the subject of each sentence, ready for some form of analysis or assessment. Common uses for linguistically annotated data include sentiment analysis and natural language processing.

Machine intelligence: An umbrella term for various types of learning algorithms, including machine learning and deep learning.

Machine learning: This subset of AI is particularly focused on developing algorithms that will help machines to learn and change in response to new data, without the help of a human being.

Machine translation: The translation of text by an algorithm, independent of any human involvement.

Model: A broad term referring to the product of AI training, created by running a machine learning algorithm on training data.

Neural network: Also called a *neural net*, a neural network is a computer system designed to function like the human brain. Although researchers are still working on creating a machine model of the human brain, existing neural networks can perform many tasks involving speech, vision and board game strategy.

Natural language generation (NLG): This refers to the process by which a machine turns structured data into text or speech that humans can understand. Essentially, NLG is concerned with what a machine writes or says as the end part of the communication process.

Natural language processing (NLP): The umbrella term for any machine's ability to perform conversational tasks, such as recognizing what is said to it, understanding the intended meaning and responding intelligibly.

Natural language understanding (NLU): As a subset of natural language processing, natural language understanding deals with helping machines to recognize the intended meaning of language — taking into account its subtle nuances and any grammatical errors.

Overfitting: An important AI term, overfitting is a symptom of machine learning training in which an algorithm is only able to work on or identify specific examples present in the training data. A working model should be able to use the general trends behind the data to work on new examples.

Parameter: A variable inside the model that helps it to make predictions. A parameter's value can be estimated using data and they are usually not set by the person running the model.

Pattern recognition: The distinction between pattern recognition and machine learning is often blurry, but this field is basically concerned with finding trends and patterns in data.

Predictive analytics: By combining data mining and machine learning, this type of analytics is built to forecast what will happen within a given timeframe based on historical data and trends.

Python: A popular programming language used for general programming.

Reinforcement learning: A method of teaching AI that sets a goal without specific metrics, encouraging the model to test different scenarios rather than find a single answer. Based on human feedback, the model can then manipulate the next scenario to get better results.

Semantic annotation: Tagging different search queries or products with the goal of improving the relevance of a search engine.

Sentiment analysis: The process of identifying and categorizing opinions in a piece of text, often with the goal of determining the writer's attitude towards something.

Strong AI: This field of research is focused on developing AI that is equal to the human mind when it comes to ability. *General AI* is a similar term often used interchangeably.

Supervised learning: This is a type of machine learning where structured datasets, with inputs and labels, are used to train and develop an algorithm.

Test data: The unlabeled data used to check that a machine learning model is able to perform its assigned task.

Training data: This refers to all of the data used during the process of training a machine learning algorithm, as well as the specific dataset used for training rather than testing.

Transfer learning: This method of learning involves spending time teaching a machine to do a related task, then allowing it to return to its original work with improved accuracy. One potential example of this is taking a model that analyzes sentiment in product reviews and asking it to analyze tweets for a week.

Turing test: Named after Alan Turing, famed mathematician, computer scientist and logician, this tests a machine's ability to pass for a human, particularly in the fields of language and behavior. After being graded by a human, the machine passes if its output is indistinguishable from that of human participant's.

Unsupervised learning: This is a form of training where the algorithm is asked to make inferences from datasets that don't contain labels. These inferences are what help it to learn.

Validation data: Structured like training data with an input and labels, this data is used to test a recently trained model against new data and to analyze performance, with a particular focus on checking for overfitting.

Variance: The amount that the intended function of a machine learning model changes while it's being trained. Despite being flexible, models with high variance are prone to overfitting and low predictive accuracy because they are reliant on their training data.

Variation: Also called *queries* or *utterances*, these work in tandem with intents for natural language processing. The variation is what a person might say to achieve a certain purpose or goal. For example, if the intent is "pay by credit card," the variation might be "I'd like to pay by card, please."

Weak AI: Also called *narrow AI*, this is a model that has a set range of skills and focuses on one particular set of tasks. Most AI currently in use is weak AI, unable to learn or perform tasks outside of its specialist skill set.

BIBLIOGRAPHY

Aarup, M., Arentoft, M. M., Parrod, Y., Stader, J., and Stokes, I. (1994). OPTIMUM-AIV: A knowledge-based planning and scheduling system for spacecraft AIV. In Fox, M. and Zweben, M., editors, Knowledge Based Scheduling. Morgan Kaufmann, San Mateo, California.

Abu-Mostafa, Y. S. and Psaltis, D. (1987). Optical neural computers. Scientific American, 256: 88-95.

Acharya, A., Tambe, M., and Gupta, A. (1992). Implementation of production systems on message-passing computers. IEEE Transactions on Parallel and Distributed Systems, 3(4): 477-487.

Adelson-Velsky, G. M., Arlazarov, V. L., Bitman, A. R., Zhivotovsky, A. A., and Uskov, A. V. (1970). Programming a computer to play chess. Russian Mathematical Surveys, 25: 221-262.

Adelson-Velsky, G. M., Arlazarov, V. L., and Donskoy, M. V. (1975). Some methods of controlling the tree search in chess programs. Artificial Intelligence, 6(4): 361-371.

Agmon, S. (1954). The relaxation method for linear inequalities. Canadian Journal of Mathematics, 6(3): 382-392.

Agre, P. E. and Chapman, D. (1987). Pengi: an implementation of a theory of activity. In Proceedings of the Tenth International Joint Conference on Artificial Intelligence (IJCAI-87), pages 268-272, Milan, Italy. Morgan Kaufmann.

Aho, A. V., Hopcroft, J. E., and Ullman, J. D. (1974). The Design and Analysis of Computer Algorithms. Addison-Wesley, Reading, Massachusetts.

Ait-Kaci, H. (1991). Warren's Abstract Machine: A Tutorial Reconstruction. MIT Press, Cambridge, Massachusetts.

Ait-Kaci, H. and Nasr, R. (1986). LOGIN: a logic programming language with built-in inheritance. Journal of Logic Programming, 3(3): 185-215.

Ait-Kaci, H. and Podelski, A. (1993). Towards a meaning of LIFE. Journal of Logic Programming, 16(3-4): 195-234.

Allais, M. (1953). Le comportment de l'homme rationnel devant la risque: critique des postulats et axiomes de l'école Américaine. Econometrica, 21: 503-546.

Allen, J. (1995). Natural Language Understanding. Benjamin/Cummings, Redwood City, California.

Asimov, I. (1950). I, Robot. Doubleday, Garden City, New York.

Astrom, K. J. (1965). Optimal control of Markov decision processes with incomplete state estimation. J. Math. Anal. Applic., 10: 174-205. .

Austin, J. L. (1962). How To Do Things with Words. Harvard University Press, Cambridge, Massachusetts.

Bacchus, F. (1990). Representing and Reasoning with Probabilistic Knowledge. MIT Press, Cambridge, Massachusetts.

Bacchus, F., Grove, A., Halpern, J. Y., and Koller, D. (1992). From statistics to beliefs. In Proceedings of the Tenth National Conference on Artificial Intelligence (AAAI-92), pages 602-608, San Jose, California. AAAI Press.

Bach, E. (1986). The algebra of events. Linguistics and Philosophy, 9: 5-16.

Bachmann, P. G. H. (1894). Die analytische Zahlentheorie. B. G. Teubner, Leipzig.

Bain, M. and Muggleton, S. H. (1991). Non-monotonic learning. In Hayes, J. E., Michie, D., and Tyugu, E., editors, Machine Intelligence 12, pages 105-119. Oxford University Press, Oxford.

Bajcsy, R. (1988). Active perception. Proceedings of the IEEE, 76(8): 996-1005.

Bajcsy, R. and Lieberman, L. (1976). Texture gradient as a depth cue. Computer Graphics and Image Processing, 5(1): 52-67.

Baker, C. L. (1989). English Syntax. MIT Press, Cambridge, Massachusetts.

Baker, J. (1975). The Dragon system-an overview. IEEE Transactions on Acoustics, Speech, and Signal Processing, 23.

Ballard, B. W. (1983). The *-minimax search procedure for trees containing chance nodes. Artificial Intelligence, 21(3): 327-350.

Bar-Hillel, Y. (1954). Indexical expressions. Mind, 63: 359-379.

Brooks, R. A. (1989). Engineering approach to building complete, intelligent beings. Proceedings of the SPIE-The International Society for Optical Engineering, 1002: 618-625.

Brown, J. S. and Burton, R. (1975). Multiple representations of knowledge for tutorial reasoning. In Bobrow, D. G. and Collins, A., editors, Representation and Understanding: Studies in Cognitive Science. Academic Press, New York.

Brudno, A. L. (1963). Bounds and valuations for shortening the scanning of variations. Problems of Cybernetics, 10: 225-241.

Bryson, A. E. and Ho, Y.-C. (1969). Applied Optimal Control. Blaisdell, New York.

Buchanan, B. G. and Mitchell, T. M. (1978). Model-directed learning of production rules. In Waterman, D. A. and Hayes-Roth, F., editors, Pattern-Directed Inference Systems, pages 297-312. Academic Press, New York.

Buchanan, B. G., Mitchell, T. M., Smith, R. G., and Johnson, C. R. (1978). Models of learning systems. In Encyclopedia of Computer Science and Technology, volume 11. Dekker.

Buchanan, B. G. and Shortliffe, E. H., editors (1984). Rule-Based Expert Systems: The MYCIN Experiments of the Stanford Heuristic Programming Project. Addison-Wesley, Reading, Massachusetts.

Buchanan, B. G., Sutherland, G. L., and Feigenbaum, E. A. (1969). Heuristic DENDRAL: a program for generating explanatory hypotheses in organic chemistry. In Meltzer, B., Michie, D., and Swann, M., editors, Machine Intelligence 4, pages 209-254. Edinburgh University Press, Edinburgh, Scotland.

Buchler, J., editor (1955). Philosophical Writings of Peirce. Dover, New York. .

Bundy, A. (1983). The Computer Modelling of Mathematical Reasoning. Academic Press, New York.

Cox, R. T. (1946). Probability, frequency, and reasonable expectation. American Journal of Physics, 14(1): 1-13.

Cragg, B. G. and Temperley, H. N. V. (1954). The organization of neurones: A cooperative analogy. EEG and Clinical Neurophysiology, 6: 85-92.

Cragg, B. G. and Temperley, H. N. V. (1955). Memory: The analogy with ferromagnetic hysteresis. Brain, 78(II): 304-316.

Craik, K. J. W. (1943). The Nature of Explanation. Cambridge University Press, Cambridge.

Crevier, D. (1993). AI: The Tumultuous History of the Search for Artificial Intelligence. Basic Books, New York.

Crockett, L. (1994). The Turing Test and the Frame Problem: AI's Mistaken Understanding of Intelligence. Ablex, Norwood, New Jersey.

Cullingford, R. E. (1981). Integrating knowledge sources for computer 'understanding' tasks. IEEE Transactions on Systems, Man and Cybernetics, SMC-11.

Currie, K. W. and Tate, A. (1991). O-Plan: the Open Planning Architecture. Artificial Intelligence, 52(1): 49-86.

Curry, H. B. and Feys, R. (1958). Combinatory Logic, volume 1. Elsevier/North-Holland, Amsterdam, London, New York.

Cybenko, G. (1988). Continuous valued neural networks with two hidden layers are sufficient. Technical report, Department of Computer Science, Tufts University, Medford, Massachusetts.

Cybenko, G. (1989). Approximation by superpositions of a sigmoidal function. Mathematics of Controls, Signals, and Systems, 2: 303-314.

Doyle, J. and Patil, R. S. (1991). Two theses of knowledge representation: language restrictions, taxonomic classification, and the utility of representation services. Artificial Intelligence, 48(3): 261-297.

Drabble, B. (1990). Mission scheduling for spacecraft: Diaries of T- SCHED. In Expert Planning Systems, pages 76-81. Institute of Electrical Engineers.

Draper, D., Hanks, S., and Weld, D. (1994). Probabilistic planning with information gathering and contingent execution. In Proceedings 2nd AIPS.

Dreyfus, H. L. (1972). What Computers Can't Do: A Critique of Artificial Reason. Harper and Row, New York, first edition.

Dreyfus, H. L. (1979). What Computers Can't Do: The Limits of Artificial Intelligence. Harper and Row, New York, revised edition.

Dreyfus, H. L. (1992). What Computers Still Can't Do: A Critique of Artificial Reason. MIT Press, Cambridge, Massachusetts.

Dreyfus, H. L. and Dreyfus, S. E. (1986). Mind over Machine: The Power of Human Intuition and Expertise in the Era of the Computer. Blackwell, Oxford. With Tom Athanasiou.

Dreyfus, S. E. (1969). An appraisal of some shortest-paths algorithms. Operations Research, 17: 395-412.

Dubois, D. and Prade, H. (1994). A survey of belief revision and updating rules in various uncertainty models. International Journal of Intelligent Systems, 9(1): 61-100.

Duda, R., Gaschnig, J., and Hart, P. (1979). Model design in the Prospector consultant system for mineral exploration. In Michie, D., editor, Expert Systems in the Microelectronic Age, pages 153-167. Edinburgh University Press, Edinburgh, Scotland.

Dyer, M. (1983). In-Depth Understanding. MIT Press. .

Dzeroski, S., Muggleton, S., and Russell, S. J. (1992). PAC-learnability of determinate logic programs. In Proceedings of the Fifth Annual ACM Workshop on Computational Learning Theory (COLT-92), Pittsburgh, Pennsylvania. ACM Press.

Ernst, H. A. (1961). MH-1, a computer-operated mechanical hand. PhD thesis, Massachusetts Institute of Technology, Cambridge, Massachusetts.

Erol, K., Hendler, J., and Nau, D. S. (1994). HTN planning: complexity and expressivity. In Proceedings of the Twelfth National Conference on Artificial Intelligence (AAAI-94), Seattle, Washington. AAAI Press.

Etzioni, O. (1989). Tractable decision-analytic control. In Proc. of 1st International Conference on Knowledge Representation and Reasoning, pages 114-125, Toronto, Ontario.

Etzioni, O., Hanks, S., Weld, D., Draper, D., Lesh, N., and Williamson, M. (1992). An approach to planning with incomplete information. In Proceedings of the 3rd International Conference on Principles of Knowledge Representation and Reasoning.

Evans, T. G. (1968). A program for the solution of a class of geometric-analogy intelligence-test questions. In Minsky, M. L., editor, Semantic Information Processing, pages 271-353. MIT Press, Cambridge, Massachusetts.

Fox, M. S. (1990). Constraint-guided scheduling: a short history of research at CMU. Computers in Industry, 14(1-3): 79-88.

Fox, M. S., Allen, B., and Strohm, G. (1981). Job shop scheduling: an investigation in constraint-based reasoning. In Proceedings of the Seventh International Joint Conference on Artificial Intelligence (IJCAI-81), Vancouver, British Columbia. Morgan Kaufmann.

Fox, M. S. and Smith, S. F. (1984). Isis: a knowledge-based system for factory scheduling. Expert Systems, 1(1): 25-49.

Frean, M. (1990). The upstart algorithm: A method for constructing and training feedforward neural networks. Neural Computation, 2: 198-209.

Frege, G. (1879). Begriffschrift, eine der arithmetischen nachgebildete Formelsprache des reinen Denkens. Halle, Berlin. Reprinted in English translation in [van Heijenoort, 1967].

Friedberg, R., Dunham, B., and North, T. (1959). A learning machine: Part II. IBM Journal of Research and Development, 3(3): 282-287.

Friedberg, R. M. (1958). A learning machine: Part I. IBM Journal, 2: 2-13.

Fu, K.-S. and Booth, T. L. (1986a). Grammatical inference: Introduction and survey-part I. IEEE Transactions on Pattern Analysis and Machine Intelligence, PAMI-8(3): 343-359. Reprinted from IEEE Trans. on Systems, Man, and Cybernetics, Vol. SMC-5, No. 1, January 1975.

Fu, K.-S. and Booth, T. L. (1986b). Grammatical inference: Introduction and survey-part ii. IEEE Transactions on Pattern Analysis and Machine Intelligence, PAMI-8(3): 360-375. Reprinted from IEEE Trans. on Systems, Man, and Cybernetics, Vol. SMC-5, No. 4, January 1975.

Fuchs, J. J., Gasquet, A., Olalainty, B., and Currie, K. W. (1990). PlanERS-1: An expert planning system for generating spacecraft mission plans. In First International Conference on Expert Planning Systems, pages 70-75, Brighton, United Kingdom. Institute of Electrical Engineers.

Fung, R. and Chang, K. C. (1989). Weighting and integrating evidence for stochastic simulation in ayesian networks. In Proceedings UAI-89.

Furukawa, K. (1992). Summary of basic research activities of the FGCS project. In Fifth Generation Computer Systems 1992, volume 1, pages 20-32, Tokyo. IOS Press.

Furuta, K., Ochiai, T., and Ono, N. (1984). Attitude control of a triple inverted pendulum. International Journal of Control, 39(6): 1351-1365.

Grosz, B., Appelt, D., Martin, P., and Pereira, F. (1987). Team: An experiment in the design of transportable natural-language interfaces. Artificial Intelligence, 32(2): 173-244.

Grosz, B. J. and Sidner, C. L. (1986). Attention, intentions, and the structure of discourse. Computational Linguistics, 12(3): 175-204.

Grosz, B. J., Sparck Jones, K., and Webber, B. L., editors (1986). Readings in Natural Language Processing. Morgan Kaufmann, San Mateo, California.

Gu, J. (1989). Parallel algorithms and architectures for very fast AI search. PhD thesis, University of Utah.

Guard, J., Oglesby, F., Bennett, J., and Settle, L. (1969). Semi-automated mathematics. Journal of the Association for Computing Machinery, 16: 49-62.

Hubel, D. H. (1988). Eye, Brain, and Vision. W. H. Freeman, New York.

Huddleston, R. D. (1988). English Grammar: An Outline. Cambridge University Press, Cambridge.

Huffman, D. A. (1971). Impossible objects as nonsense sentences. In Meltzer, B. and Michie, D., editors, Machine Intelligence 6, pages 295-324. Edinburgh University Press, Edinburgh, Scotland.

Hughes, G. E. and Cresswell, M. J. (1968). An Introduction to Modal Logic. Methuen, London.

Hughes, G. E. and Cresswell, M. J. (1984). A Companion to Modal Logic. Methuen, London.

Hume, D. (1978). A Treatise of Human Nature. Oxford University Press, Oxford, second edition. Edited by L. A. Selby-Bigge and P. H. Nidditch.

Hunt, E. B., Marin, J., and Stone, P. T. (1966). Experiments in Induction. Academic Press, New York.

Hunter, G. (1971). Metalogic: An Introduction to the Metatheory of Standard First-Order Logic. University of California Press, Berkeley and Los Angeles.

Hunter, L. and States, D. J. (1992). Bayesian classification of protein structure. IEEE Expert, 7(4): 67-75.

Huttenlocher, D. P. and Ullman, S. (1990). Recognizing solid objects by alignment with an image. International Journal of Computer Vision, 5(2): 195-212.

Huygens, C. (1657). Ratiociniis in ludo aleae. In van Schooten, F., editor, Exercitionum Mathematicorum. Elsevirii, Amsterdam.

Hwang, C. H. and Schubert, L. K. (1993). EL: a formal, yet natural, comprehensive knowledge representation. In Proceedings of the Eleventh National Conference on Artificial Intelligence (AAAI-93), pages 676-682, Washington, D.C. AAAI Press.

Hyatt, R. M., Gower, A. E., and Nelson, H. L. (1986). Cray Blitz. In Beal, D. F., editor, Advances in Computer Chess 4, pages 8-18. Pergamon, New York.

Kowalski, R. and Sergot, M. (1986). A logic-based calculus of events. New Generation Computing, 4(1): 67-95.

Koza, J. R. (1992). Genetic Programming: On the Programming of Computers by Means of Natural Selection. MIT Press, Cambridge, Massachusetts.

Kripke, S. A. (1963). Semantical considerations on modal logic. Acta Philosophica Fennica, 16: 83-94.

Kruppa, E. (1913). Zur Ermittlung eines Objecktes aus zwei Perspektiven mit innerer Orientierung. Sitz.-Ber. Akad. Wiss., Wien, Math. Naturw., Kl. Abt. IIa, 122: 1939-1948.

Kuehner, D. (1971). A note on the relation between resolution and Maslov's inverse method. DCL Memo 36, University of Edinburgh.

Kukich, K. (1992). Techniques for automatically correcting words in text. ACM Computing Surveys, 24(4): 377-439.

Kumar, V. (1991). A general heuristic bottom-up procedure for searching AND/OR graphs. Information Sciences, 56(1-3): 39-57.

Kumar, V. and Kanal, L. N. (1983). A general branch and bound formulation for understanding and synthesizing and/or tree search procedures. Artificial Intelligence, 21: 179-198.

Kumar, V. and Kanal, L. N. (1988). The CDP: A unifying formulation for heuristic search, dynamic programming, and branch-and-bound. In Kanal, L. N. and Kumar, V., editors, Search in Artificial Intelligence, chapter 1, pages 1-27. Springer-Verlag, Berlin.

Kumar, V., Nau, D. S., and Kanal, L. N. (1988). A general branch-and-bound formulation for AND/OR graph and game tree search. In Kanal, L. N. and Kumar, V., editors, Search in Artificial Intelligence, chapter 3, pages 91-130. Springer-Verlag, Berlin.

Kurzweil, R. (1990). The Age of Intelligent Machines. MIT Press, Cambridge, Massachusetts.

Kyburg, H. E. (1977). Randomness and the right reference class. The Journal of Philosophy, 74(9): 501-521.

Kyburg, H. E. (1983). The reference class. Philosophy of Science, 50: 374-397.

Löwenheim, L. (1915). Über möglichkeiten im Relativkalkül. Mathematische Annalen, 76: 447-470. Reprinted in English translation in [van Heijenoort, 1967].

Lowerre, B. T. and Reddy, R. (1980). The HARPY speech recognition system. In Lea, W. A., editor, Trends in Speech Recognition, chapter 15. Prentice-Hall, Englewood Cliffs, New Jersey.

Lowry, M. R. and McCartney, R. D. (1991). Automating Software Design. MIT Press, Cambridge, Massachusetts.

Loyd, S. (1959). Mathematical Puzzles of Sam Loyd: Selected and Edited by Martin Gardner. Dover, New York.

Lozano-Pérez, T., Mason, M., and Taylor, R. (1984). Automatic synthesis of fine-motion strategies for robots. Interl J of Robotics Research, 3(1): 3-24.

Lucas, J. R. (1961). Minds, machines, and Gödel. Philosophy, 36.

Moussouris, J., Holloway, J., and Greenblatt, R. (1979). CHEOPS: A chess-oriented processing system. In Hayes, J. E., Michie, D., and Mikulich, L. I., editors, Machine Intelligence 9, pages 351-360. Ellis Horwood, Chichester, England.

Muggleton, S. (1991). Inductive logic programming. New Generation Computing, 8: 295-318.

Muggleton, S. (1992). Inductive Logic Programming. Academic Press, New York.

Muggleton, S. and Buntine, W. (1988). Machine invention of first-order predicates by inverting resolution. In MLC-88.

Muggleton, S. and Cao, F. (1990). Efficient induction of logic programs. In Proc. Workshop on Algorithmic Learning Theory, Tokyo.

Muggleton, S., King, R. D., and Sternberg, M. J. E. (1992). Protein secondary structure prediction using logic-based machine learning. Protein Engineering, 5(7): 647-657.

Mundy, J. and Zisserman, A., editors (1992). Geometric Invariance in Computer Vision. MIT Press, Cambridge, Massachusetts.

Noyes, J. L. (1992). Artificial Intelligence with Common Lisp: Fundamentals of Symbolic and Numeric Processing. D. C. Heath, Lexington, Massachusetts.

Nunberg, G. (1979). The non-uniqueness of semantic solutions: Polysemy. Language and Philosophy, 3(2): 143-184.

Nussbaum, M. C. (1978). Aristotle's De Motu Animalium. Princeton University Press, Princeton, New Jersey.

O'Keefe, R. (1990). The Craft of Prolog. MIT Press, Cambridge, Massachusetts.

Olawsky, D. and Gini, M. (1990). Deferred planning and sensor use. In Proceedings, DARPA Workshop on Innovative Approaches to Planning, Scheduling, and Control. Morgan Kaufmann.

Olesen, K. G. (1993). Causal probabilistic networks with both discrete and continuous variables. IEEE Transactions on Pattern Analysis and Machine Intelligence (PAMI), 15(3): 275-279.

Oliver, R. M. and Smith, J. Q., editors (1990). Influence Diagrams, Belief Nets and Decision Analysis. Wiley, New York.

Olson, C. F. (1994). Time and space efficient pose clustering. In Proceedings of the IEEE Conference on Computer Vision and Pattern Recognition, pages 251-258, Seattle, Washington.

Ortony, A., editor (1979). Metaphor and Thought. Cambridge University Press, Cambridge.

Osherson, D. N., Stob, M., and Weinstein, S. (1986). Systems That Learn: An Introduction to Learning Theory for Cognitive and Computer Scientists. MIT Press, Cambridge, Massachusetts.

Pullum, G. K. (1991). The Great Eskimo Vocabulary Hoax (and Other Irreverent Essays on the Study of Language). University of Chicago Press, Chicago, Illinois.

Purdom, P. (1983). Search rearrangement backtracking and polynomial average time. Artificial Intelligence, 21: 117-133.

Putnam, H. (1960). Minds and machines. In Hook, S., editor, Dimensions of Mind, pages 138-164. Macmillan, London.

Putnam, H. (1963). 'Degree of confirmation' and inductive logic. In Schilpp, P. A., editor, The Philosophy of Rudolf Carnap. Open Court, La Salle, Illinois.

Putnam, H. (1967). The nature of mental states. In Capitan, W. H. and Merrill, D. D., editors, Art, Mind, and Religion, pages 37-48. University of Pittsburgh Press, Pittsburgh, Pennsylvania. Original title was "Psychological predicates"; title changed in later reprints at the request of the author.

Pylyshyn, Z. W. (1974). Minds, machines and phenomenology: Some reflections on Dreyfus' "What Computers Can't Do". International Journal of Cognitive Psychology, 3(1): 57-77.

Pylyshyn, Z. W. (1984). Computation and Cognition: Toward a Foundation for Cognitive Science. MIT Press, Cambridge, Massachusetts.

Quinlan, J. R. (1986). Induction of decision trees. Machine Learning, 1: 81-106.

Quinlan, J. R. (1990). Learning logical definitions from relations. Machine Learning, 5(3): 239-266.

Quinlan, J. R. (1993). Combining instance-based and model-based learning. In Proceedings of the Tenth International Conference on Machine Learning, pages 236-243, Amherst, MA. Morgan Kaufmann.

Quinlan, J. R. and Cameron-Jones, R. M. (1993). FOIL: a midterm report. In Brazdil, P. B., editor, European Conference on Machine Learning Proceedings (ECML-93), pages 3-20, Vienna. Springer-Verlag.

Quirk, R., Greenbaum, S., Leech, G., and Svartvik, J. (1985). A Comprehensive Grammar of the English Language. Longman, New York.

Russell, S. J. (1986b). A quantitative analysis of analogy by similarity. In Proceedings of the Fifth National Conference on Artificial Intelligence (AAAI-86), Philadelphia, Pennsylvania. Morgan Kaufmann.

Russell, S. J. (1988). Tree-structured bias. In Proceedings of the Seventh National Conference on Artificial Intelligence (AAAI-88), volume 2, pages 641-645, St. Paul, Minnesota. Morgan Kaufmann.

Russell, S. J. (1992). Efficient memory-bounded search methods. In ECAI 92: 10th European Conference on Artificial Intelligence Proceedings, pages 1-5, Vienna, Austria. Wiley.

Russell, S. J., Binder, J., and Koller, D. (1994). Adaptive probabilistic networks. Technical Report UCB/CSD-94-824, Computer Science Division, University of California at Berkeley.

Russell, S. J. and Subramanian, D. (1993). Provably bounded optimal agents. In Proceedings of the Thirteenth International Joint Conference on Artificial Intelligence (IJCAI-93), Chambery, France. Morgan Kaufmann.

Russell, S. J. and Wefald, E. (1991). Do the Right Thing: Studies in Limited Rationality. MIT Press, Cambridge, Massachusetts.

Russell, S. J. and Wefald, E. H. (1989). On optimal game-tree search using rational meta-reasoning. In Proceedings of the Eleventh International Joint Conference on Artificial Intelligence (IJCAI-89), pages 334-340, Detroit, Michigan. Morgan Kaufmann.

Ryder, J. L. (1971). Heuristic analysis of large trees as generated in the game of Go. Memo AIM-155, Stanford Artificial Intelligence Project, Computer Science Department, Stanford University, Stanford, California.

Stonebraker, M. (1992). The integration of rule systems and database systems. IEEE Transactions on Knowledge and Data Engineering, 4(5): 415-423.

Strachey, C. S. (1952). Logical or non-mathematical programmes. In Proceedings of the Association for Computing Machinery (ACM), pages 46-49, Ontario, Canada.

Subramanian, D. (1993). Artificial intelligence and conceptual design. In Proceedings of the Thirteenth International Joint Conference on Artificial Intelligence (IJCAI-93), pages 800-809, Chambery, France. Morgan Kaufmann.

Subramanian, D. and Feldman, R. (1990). The utility of EBL in recursive domain theories. In Proceedings of the Eighth National Conference on Artificial Intelligence (AAAI-90), volume 2, pages 942-949, Boston, Massachusetts. MIT Press.

Subramanian, D. and Wang, E. (1994). Constraint-based kinematic synthesis. In Proceedings of the International Conference on Qualitative Reasoning. AAAI Press.

Sugihara, K. (1984). A necessary and sufficient condition for a picture to represent a polyhedral scene. IEEE Transactions on Pattern Analysis and Machine Intelligence (PAMI), 6(5): 578-586.

Sussman, G. J. (1975). A Computer Model of Skill Acquisition. Elsevier/North-Holland, Amsterdam, London, New York.

Sussman, G. J. and McDermott, D. V. (1972). From PLANNER to CONNIVER-a genetic approach. In Proceedings of the 1972 AFIPS Joint Computer Conference, pages 1171-1179.

Sussman, G. J. and Winograd, T. (1970). MICRO-PLANNER Reference Manual. AI Memo 203, MIT AI Lab, Cambridge, Massachusetts.

Sutton, R. S. (1988). Learning to predict by the methods of temporal differences. Machine Learning, 3: 9-44.

Swade, D. D. (1993). Redeeming Charles Babbage's mechanical computer. Scientific American, 268(2): 86-91.

Turing, A. M. (1936). On computable numbers, with an application to the ntscheidungsproblem. Proceedings of the London Mathematical Society, 2nd series, 42: 230-265. Correction published in Vol. 43, pages 544-546.

Turing, A. M. (1950). Computing machinery and intelligence. Mind, 59: 433-460.

Turing, A. M., Strachey, C., Bates, M. A., and Bowden, B. V. (1953). Digital computers applied to games. In Bowden, B. V., editor, Faster Than Thought, pages 286-310. Pitman, London. Turing is believed to be sole author of the section of this paper that deals with chess.

Tversky, A. and Kahneman, D. (1982). Causal schemata in judgements under uncertainty. In Judgement Under Uncertainty: Heuristics and Biases. Cambridge University Press.

von Mises, R. (1928). Wahrscheinlichkeit, Statistik und Wahrheit. J. Springer, Berlin. Translated into English as [von Mises, 1957].

von Mises, R. (1957). Probability, Statistics, and Truth. Allen and Unwin, London.

Von Neumann, J. (1958). The Computer and the Brain. Yale University Press, New Haven, Connecticut.

Von Neumann, J. and Morgenstern, O. (1944). Theory of games and economic behavior. Princeton University Press, Princeton, New Jersey, first edition.

von Winterfeldt, D. and Edwards, W. (1986). Decision Analysis and Behavioral Research. Cambridge University Press, Cambridge. .

Voorhees, E. M. (1993). Using WordNet to disambiguate word senses for text retrieval. In Sixteenth Annual International ACM SIGIR Conference on Research and Development in Information Retrieval, pages 171-80, Pittsburgh, Pennsylvania. Association for Computing Machinery.

Wos, L., Carson, D., and Robinson, G. (1964). The unit preference strategy in theorem proving. In Proceedings of the Fall Joint Computer Conference, pages 615-621.

Wos, L., Carson, D., and Robinson, G. (1965). Efficiency and completeness of the set-of-support strategy in theorem proving. Journal of the Association for Computing Machinery, 12: 536-541.

Wos, L., Overbeek, R., Lusk, E., and Boyle, J. (1992). Automated Reasoning: Introduction and Applications. McGraw-Hill, New York, second edition.

Wos, L., Robinson, G., Carson, D., and Shalla, L. (1967). The concept of demodulation in theorem proving. Journal of the Association for Computing Machinery, 14: 698-704.

Wos, L. and Robinson, G. A. (1968). Paramodulation and set of support. In Proceedings of the IRIA Symposium on Automatic Demonstration, pages 276-310. Springer-Verlag.

Wos, L. and Winker, S. (1983). Open questions solved with the assistance of AURA. In Bledsoe, W. W. and Loveland, D. W., editors, Automated Theorem Proving: After 25 Years: Proceedings of the Special Session of the 89th Annual Meeting of the American Mathematical Society, pages 71-88, Denver, Colorado. American Mathematical Society.

Wright, S. (1921). Correlation and causation. Journal of Agricultural Research, 20: 557-585.

Wright, S. (1934). The method of path coefficients. Annals of Mathematical Statistics, 5: 161-215.

Wu, D. (1993). Estimating probability distributions over hypotheses with variable unification. In Proceedings of the Thirteenth International Joint Conference on Artificial Intelligence (IJCAI-93), pages 790-795, Chambery, France. Morgan Kaufmann.

Yang, Q. (1990). Formalizing planning knowledge for hierarchical planning. Computational Intelligence, 6: 12-24.

Yarowsky, D. (1992). Word-sense disambiguation using statistical models of Roget's categories trained on large corpora. In Proceedings of COLING-92, pages 454-460, Nantes, France.

Yip, K. M.-K. (1991). KAM: A System for Intelligently Guiding Numerical Experimentation by Computer. MIT Press, Cambridge, Massachusetts.

Yoshikawa, T. (1990). Foundations of Robotics: Analysis and Control. MIT Press, Cambridge, Massachusetts.

Younger, D. H. (1967). Recognition and parsing of context-free languages in time n3. Information and Control, 10(2): 189-208.

Zilberstein, S. (1993). Operational rationality through compilation of anytime algorithms. PhD thesis, University of California, Berkeley, California.

Zimmermann, H.-J. (1991). Fuzzy Set Theory-And Its Applications. Kluwer, Dordrecht, The Netherlands, second revised edition.

Zobrist, A. L. (1970). Feature extraction and representation for pattern recognition and the game of Go. PhD thesis, University of Wisconsin.

Zue, V., Seneff, S., Polifroni, J., Phillips, M., Pao, C., Goddeau, D., Glass, J., and Brill, E. (1994). Pegasus: A spoken language interface for on-line air travel planning. In ARPA Workshop on Human Language Technology.

Zuse, K. (1945). The plankalkül. Report 175, Gesellschaft für Mathematik und Datenverarbeitung, Bonn. Technical report version republished in 1989.

INDEX

www.ingramcontent.com/pod-product-compliance
Lightning Source LLC
LaVergne TN
LVHW062221200926
848484LV00006B/1450
9781787151161